The Defense of Community in Peru's Central Highlands

FLORENCIA E. MALLON

The Defense of Community in Peru's Central Highlands: Peasant Struggle and Capitalist Transition, 1860–1940

Princeton University Press

Published by Princeton University Press, 41 William Street,
Princeton, New Jersey 08540
In the United Kingdom: Princeton University Press, Oxford

Library of Congress Cataloging in Publication Data will be found on the
last printed page of this book

ISBN 0-691-07647-2
ISBN 0-691-10140-X pbk.

Publication of this book has been aided by a grant from the Paul Mellon
Fund of Princeton University Press

This book has been composed in Linotron Caledonia

Princeton University Press books are printed on acid-free paper,
and meet the guidelines for permanence and durability
of the Committee on Production Guidelines for Book Longevity
of the Council on Library Resources

Printed in the United States of America

9 8 7 6 5 4

Dedicated to don Moisés Ortega,

teacher, poet, and historian of his beloved valley.

Contents

List of Maps and Appendixes

Maps

Appendixes

List of Abbreviations

AFA	Archivo del Fuero Agrario (Lima)
AGN	Archivo General de la Nación (Lima)
AHM	Archivo Histórico Militar (Lima)
AMA	Archivo Municipal de Acolla (Yanamarca Valley)
AMM	Archivo Municipal de Marco (Yanamarca Valley)
ANF	Archivo Notarial Flores (Jauja)
APJ	Archivo Prefectural de Junín (Huancayo)
BCIM	Boletines del Cuerpo de Ingenieros de Minas, Ministerio de Fomento
BNP	Biblioteca Nacional del Perú, Sala de Investigaciones (Lima)
RPI	Registro de la Propiedad Inmueble de Junín (Huancayo)
SINAMOS	Archivo de Comunidades, Oficina Regional de SINAMOS (Huancayo)
UNI	Universidad Nacional de Ingeniería, Archivo (Lima)
YC	Latin American Collection, Manuscripts, Yale University

Map 1. The Central Region in Peru as a Whole.

Preface

Rather than follow the path customary for many research projects, in which one begins with a fairly broad topic and then slowly, painstakingly narrows it down in the process of research and writing, this study has gone in exactly the opposite direction. It began as a neatly conceived community study which proposed to reconstruct and analyze the migration patterns of peasants from four villages in the central highlands of Peru to the mines in the same region of the country. Inexorably, it has expanded until it sits somewhere between remaining a study of four communities in the Yanamarca Valley, and becoming a regional analysis of the development of capitalism in Peru's central sierra. A partial explanation for this lies in the fact that, as students of the peasantry constantly remind us, it is impossible to study peasants in isolation. As the project proceeded, therefore, I found myself asking questions that could not be answered by remaining at the community level.

Equally important, however (and perhaps easier to see ex post facto), this intermediate level of research and generalization seems particularly well suited to my subject. Because it is possible to examine the Yanamarca Valley in the context of the development of capitalism in the central region as a whole, and connect it to historical processes at the national level, events within the village take on broader, richer meaning. At the same time, because I examine the local process in the Yanamarca Valley using concrete empirical data, it is possible to put flesh on the bones of that skeleton historians call "the development of capitalism." It is in this methodological "no person's land," then, somewhere between the regional and the community study, that this book must be located. No doubt anthropologists and historians will shudder at my unorthodox mixing of conceptual levels and methodologies. Yet this approach allows me to do most justice to both the people and the history of Peru's Yanamarca Valley.

Another aspect of the study which has tended to expand is the chronological focus. Though the book's title still reflects the initial definition of the period I made while in the field, and indeed those are the years for which my archival research is most complete, the complex history of the region and the Yanamarca Valley defies neat categories or periodization. I have thus found myself moving backward and forward in time, so that overall the book deals with the years from 1780 to the present. Nonetheless, the main focus continues to be the years from 1860 to 1940 because, after all, the development of capitalism picked up speed in the late nineteenth century and was well under way by 1940. Earlier and later materials are less exhaustive, and are meant to pursue events or facets related to the core period, or to draw out the ultimate implications of the themes explored in the book.

No study, particularly one as wide-ranging as this one, can be completed without immense and varied debts to many people. In Peru, I developed separate networks of friendship and indebtedness in the various regions where I did research. In Lima, I owe thanks to the staffs of the Archivo del Fuero Agrario, the Archivo General de la Nación, the Sala de Investigaciones in the Biblioteca Nacional del Perú, the archival collection at the library of the Universidad Nacional de Ingeniería, and especially to Humberto Rodríguez Pastor, Graciela Sánchez Cerro, Guillermo Durand Flores, Mario Cárdenas, Elia Lazarte, and María Mendo Muñoz. For sharing research ideas and data, and providing support (moral and intellectual) and generous criticism: Víctor Caballero, Alberto Flores Galindo, José Ignacio López Soria, Nelson Manrique, Gerardo Rénique, Guillermo Rochabrún, Humberto Rodríguez Pastor, Cristina Rossel, the students of the Taller de Estudios Andinos at the Universidad Nacional Agraria La Molina, and Ernesto Yepes. For enriching my experience and providing assistance and friendship: Gian Franco Brero, Olinda Celestino, Marisol de la Cadena, Wilma Derpich, Marcia Koth de Paredes and the Comisión Fulbright del Perú, Yolanda Kronberger, Kenneth Langton, Helen O'Brien, and Juan O'Brien.

At the provincial level I wish to thank the staffs of the Prefectura de Junín, the Registro de la Propiedad Inmueble de Junín, and the Oficina Regional de SINAMOS, all in Huancayo, for graciously giving me access to the documentary collections housed in their offices. In Jauja, I owe a special debt to Jesús Violeta Flores Pinto, notary public, who patiently gave me access to her archive of notarial documents, allowing me to occupy a corner of her office daily for many months. This experience was not only academically fruitful, but also personally rewarding. For extremely valuable research assistance, support, and orientation of many kinds, and sharing the joy of discovery: Manuel Baquerizo, Victoria Bravo Soto, Olinda Celestino, Efraín Franco, Nelson Manrique, María Angélica Salas, Rodrigo Sánchez,

Hermann Tillmann, and, most especially, Ludy Ugarte. And for generosity in talking with me about themselves and the history of their region: Felipe Artica, Ricardo Tello Devotto, and Hernán Valladares.

It is, of course, in the Yanamarca Valley itself that I owe the greatest debts. Many thanks to all those connected with the municipal archives in the districts of Acolla and Marco for putting up with the constant questions and interruptions of a nosy *gringa*. For taking the time to explain things to me, both about themselves and about the valley: Oscar Teófilo Camarena, Mauricio Huamán, Germán Maita, Víctor Maita, Atanacia Misari Camacachi, Moisés Ortega, Fortunato Solís, Francisco Solís Camarena, Lydia Solís de Maita, and Elías Valenzuela. For friendship, caring, and support, the kind that can never be repaid and will certainly never be forgotten: Moisés Ortega, Emiliana Contreras de Ortega, Juan Mateo, América Ortega de Mateo, Claudia Mateo Ortega, Paula Mateo Ortega, Lydia Solís de Maita, Eliana Maita de Esteban, and Pilajia de Esteban. And even though I have mentioned him several times, an added thanks must go to Moisés Ortega, without whose guidance, patience, and selfless desire to share I would have written a much poorer and less humanistic study. It is only right that this book be dedicated to him.

In the United States, I am thankful to many people for their guidance, help, and stimulation. My parents, Ignacia Bernales Mallon and Richard D. Mallon, taught me to love Latin America and provided examples of dedication to their work and fellow human beings. I owe much, personally and intellectually, to the friendship and discussions I have shared with Virginia Domínguez, Steven Hahn, Gilbert Joseph, Rachel Klein, Julia Preston, and, most especially, Barbara Weinstein. I have also been fortunate to benefit from the guidance and teaching of many excellent professors and scholars. Ironically it was only once I began to write my book that I understood the true importance of the contribution made to my training by my undergraduate teacher, John Womack. In graduate school, Richard Morse and Alfred Stepan offered valuable suggestions, criticisms, and much-needed humor all along the way. Karen Spalding's knowledge of Peru, generous praise and criticism, and courageous intellect have been a source of inspiration, and her enthusiastic involvement in my work has helped to cement a warm and authentic friendship. My dissertation director, Emília Viotti da Costa, has contributed more to my intellectual development than I can possibly repay. Her keen, incisive mind, constant questioning and challenge, and selfless dedication to teaching have inspired in me both admiration and affection. And finally, I am grateful to my husband, Steve J. Stern. His patient and loving support, as well as his direct and sometimes hard-hitting criticism, have left me no alternative but to keep on growing, both intellectually and personally. We have also begun to share the experience of parenting Ramón Joseph, who more than anyone else has helped to put this book in perspective.

It would have been difficult for me to embark on a graduate career without the financial assistance of Yale University through their University Fellowships program. The Social Science Research Council/ American Council of Learned Societies and the Fulbright-Hays Training Fellowship Program both made different contributions to financing the dissertation that is the basis of this book and part of the writing. Betty Jo Newton, Katy Spohn, and Dianne Covington typed versions of the manuscript. Héctor Pérez transcribed the tape of the interview upon which a good part of Chapter IX is based. Sanford G. Thatcher, assistant director at Princeton University Press, and Yoma Ullman, my copyeditor, each made very different but crucial contributions to the transformation of the manuscript into a book. And Carmen Diana Deere and Peter F. Klarén made thoughtful and valuable comments on the text.

I would like to close this lengthy list of acknowledgments with an anecdote. In the last month of my research, in hopes of obtaining information on popular movements in the 1930s, I visited an old peasant leader in Jauja. Although he refused to give me any empirical or personal information, he did provide me with a valuable piece of advice. The study of history, he said, is only useful and worthwhile if, in addition to telling us about the past, it provides us with the tools to change our future. It is in this spirit that this book is offered. I hope that whatever limited insights it may yield can be as collectively utilized as they were collectively arrived upon.

The Defense of Community in Peru's Central Highlands

Introduction

When Mariano Castillo traveled to Jauja from the Yanamarca Valley to dictate his last will and testament in 1914, he was one hundred and twenty years old.[1] Born in 1794, he was a mature young man during the Wars of Independence, sixty years old when Ramón Castilla abolished Indian tribute and freed the slaves, and eighty-seven when the Chilean army invaded Peruvian territory during the War of the Pacific. And yet Mariano Castillo lived on, witnessing the first attempts at national industrialization, the spread of *enganche*[2] and labor migrations, the beginning of U.S. investment in mining, and the arrival of the railroad. Had we been able to talk to him in 1914, as he so lucidly completed the notarizing of his will, he would have had much to tell us. For Mariano Castillo—who had seen his homeland transformed from a Spanish colony into an independent republic, watched and perhaps even fought as caudillos battled each other for control of the state, suffered the pauperization of his village at the hands of a foreign invader, and experienced the arrival of the railroad and a foreign mining company—had also witnessed several stages of an even more dramatic transformation: the transition to capitalism in Peru's central highlands.

One purpose of this book is to analyze the development of capitalism from Mariano Castillo's point of view; that is, at the empirical and personal level, and with careful attention to the peasantry's role in the process. Aside from the obvious humanistic importance of such an endeavor, there are significant methodological and theoretical reasons for this type of focus. Historically, transitions and transformations do not occur in a linear fashion. Because they are affected by the actions of human beings, these processes take a contradictory, dialectical path, the ultimate character of which is defined by the struggles of people as individuals and as classes. In order to understand the

[1] ANF, Protocolos Notariales, Luis Salazar, Book 26: July 24, 1914, 936–37.

[2] Literally, "the hook." *Enganche* was a form of labor acquisition in which owners of haciendas or mines would advance money to merchants with connections in the area's peasant villages. These merchants would then advance cash to peasants in exchange for the obligation to work off the debt, at a set daily "wage," at the hacienda or mine whose owner had provided the money.

development of capitalism, then, it is necessary to get down to the level where class conflict and the contradictory reproduction of power relations determine the form that transition will take. It is precisely this type of analysis that I propose to undertake here.

Yet, as any historian will tell us, the larger context within which a set of relationships or beliefs exists will often alter their function or meaning. Thus while it is possible to identify, at the local level, the series of relationships, struggles, and beliefs that make up village life, these take on larger significance only when placed in a regional and national context and tied to a particular mode of surplus extraction and set of power relationships. In other words, it is necessary to define the mode of production within which the village exists and reproduces itself.[3]

Of course, to define the mode of production, and especially the peasantry's position in it, is easier said than done. Much theoretical ink has been spilled over the last fifteen years in an attempt to do precisely this. Is Latin America completely capitalist? Is there an articulation of capitalist and noncapitalist modes of production? Do certain noncapitalist *forms* of production survive within a predominantly capitalist *mode* of production? How do peasants fit into these larger constructs? The theoretical literature has provided many, varied, and at best partial answers to these questions.[4]

---

[3] By mode of production, I mean the particular way material life is produced and reproduced in a given society or civilization. This includes two analytically separable but interrelated dimensions. First, the relations of production, understood as a specific set of relationships between human beings in the process of economic production—the way that surplus labor is appropriated, the way that the social product is distributed among the agents of production, and the way that ownership of the means of production (land, tools, animals, and raw materials) is distributed at a social level. And secondly, the forces of production, understood as a given state of technology, technique, and productivity of labor that is defined by the nature and organization of the labor process—the way that labor power, the object of labor (raw materials, land), and the instruments or means of labor are combined to yield a particular product. In class terms, a mode of production involves a dominated (surplus producing) class and a dominant (surplus appropriating) class. The reproduction of their class relation involves economic, political, and ideological elements.

[4] For a good summary of this debate and a good bibliography, see Richard L. Harris, "Marxism and the Agrarian Question in Latin America," *Latin American Perspectives*, V: 4 (Fall 1978), 2–26; and Colin Henfrey, "Dependency, Modes of Production, and the Class Analysis of Latin America," *Latin American Perspectives*, VIII: 3–4 (Summer and Fall 1981), 17–54. For some implications of this debate for Peru, see Barbara Bradby, "The Destruction of Natural Economy," *Economy and Society*, IV: 2 (May 1975), 127–61; Rodrigo Montoya, *A propósito del carácter predominantemente capitalista de la economía actual*, 2d ed. enl. (Lima: Mosca Azul Editores, 1978), and *Capitalismo y no-capitalismo en el Perú: Un estudio histórico de su articulación en un eje regional* (Lima: Mosca Azul Editores, 1980); Guillermo Rochabrún, "Apuntes para la

One of the most promising lines of enquiry into the nature of Latin American reality has been born of a reaction against the limits of dependency theory. Many social scientists welcomed dependency theory's main contribution to the literature, which was to see Latin American societies as integrated wholes where traditional and modern sectors, rather than being separate spheres of a dual society, were intimately related as a result of their common historical ties to the world market. But these scholars were nevertheless interested in going beyond an analysis of the circulation of commodities in a market system: they sought in addition to understand the nature of production and the social and cultural relationships associated with it. Some, therefore, turned to the theory of articulation of modes of production, which had its origin among the French structuralists.[5]

As originally conceived, articulation of modes of production made it easy to apply the highly abstract concept of mode of production to the complex empirical reality of a given society. According to this line of reasoning, any particular territory or society was a historically constituted social formation containing such a broad variety of relations and forms of production that it simply could not be explained by referring to a single mode of production. Thus the need arose to view a social formation as the sum of two or more articulated modes of production, in which one was usually dominant. The articulation could, of course, take different forms: the other modes or relations could be in the process of being destroyed by the dominant mode; they could be the first signs of the dominant mode's erosion and ultimate destruction; or they could be reproduced because they fulfilled a particular function for the dominant mode as a whole. But in all cases, articulation as a concept facilitated the historical and empirical analysis of specific social realities.

This certainly seemed to be the case in dealing with the historical periodization of transition from one set of relations and forms of pro-

comprensión del capitalismo en el Perú," *Análisis*, No. 1 (January–March 1977), pp. 3–24; and Vol. IV, No. 3 of *Latin American Perspectives*, "Peru: Bourgeois Revolution and Class Struggle," especially William Bollinger, "The Bourgeois Revolution in Peru: A Conception of Peruvian History," 18–56.

[5] Among the authors who have contributed crucial work to the articulation of modes of production theory are: Etienne Balibar, "The Basic Concepts of Historical Materialism," in Louis Althusser and Etienne Balibar (eds.), *Reading Capital* (London: New Left Books, 1970), pp. 199–308; Claude Meillassoux, "From Reproduction to Production," *Economy and Society*, I: 1 (February 1972); and Pierre-Philippe Rey, *Les alliances des classes* (Paris: Maspero, 1973). For a useful summary and critique, see Aidan Foster-Carter, "The Modes of Production Controversy," *New Left Review*, No. 107 (January–February 1978), pp. 47–78.

duction to another. By avoiding long and ultimately sterile debates over when a society was "really" feudal and when it was "really" capitalist, articulation permitted a much more intricate analysis that took into consideration the slow, contradictory, and often nonlinear patterns of historical change. It permitted scholars to appreciate the rich complexity of transitional societies, and of the many and varied relations present within them, and still be able to place them in a theoretical framework.[6]

But perhaps most important for Latin America, articulation of modes of production facilitated the analysis of Third World social formations. In areas where capitalism did not emerge organically from the internal relations of a society, but was instead brought in through colonial or neocolonial contact, one would expect the complexity of social and economic relations to be even greater. Articulation could therefore provide a context within which it was possible to explain the penetration of capitalism, while at the same time understanding the multiple, long-lasting, and stubborn resistance of noncapitalist cultural, economic, political, and social forms to its dominance.[7]

Until now, however, articulation theory has not delivered on its rich analytical promise. One major problem has been that some scholars, in their eagerness to categorize the intricacy of Latin American social formations, have tended to multiply modes of production until the concept threatens to lose all theoretical value.[8] In this context any relation of production, no matter what role it plays in the larger social formation, can be seen as a mode of production. The tendency is to lose sight of the broader complexity of the concept of mode of production, which describes not only a particular type of economic relation, but also the cultural, political, and ideological constructs that are necessary to reproduce it. In order to preserve the theoretical richness of the concept, therefore, it seems important to establish some form of hierarchy among those relations that are, and those that are

[6] Balibar, "Basic Concepts," especially pp. 293–308.

[7] Henfrey, "Dependency," pp. 37 and 40; Foster-Carter, "Modes of Production," pp. 50–51, 56–64; and Norma Stoltz Chinchilla and James Lowel Dietz, "Toward a New Understanding of Development and Underdevelopment," *Latin American Perspectives*, VIII: 3–4 (Summer and Fall 1981), 138–47.

[8] See especially Montoya, *A propósito*, and Norman Long, "Structural dependency, modes of production and economic brokerage in rural Peru," in Ivar Oxaal, Tony Barnett, and David Booth (eds.), *Beyond the Sociology of Development: Economy and Society in Latin America and Africa* (London: Routledge and Kegan Paul, 1975), pp. 253–82. For an extremely sophisticated presentation of the same tendency, see Roger Bartra, "Sobre la articulación de modos de producción en América Latina," in *Modos de producción en América Latina* (Lima: Delva Editores, 1976), pp. 5–19.

not, part of a separate mode of production. Historically, it becomes important to analyze when and how a particular mode of production becomes dominant in a social formation, and when subordinate modes of production are transformed into mere surviving forms or relations of production utilized and reproduced by the dominant mode.

In addition to being criticized for not being theoretically clear, articulation theory has been castigated for being too structuralist and abstract. According to these critics, theorists have seen reality as derived from theory, rather than being made up of people, events, and concrete relationships. Thus an articulation of modes of production approach has tended to substitute a history of structures and modes of production for a history of human beings, social classes, and their struggles.[9]

Clearly, neither of these problems can be solved at a theoretical level. Theory has value insofar as it explains reality and helps make sense of events. We start to clarify the validity and coherence of theoretical constructs when we try them out in relation to a particular, concrete reality. And it is in the context of these concerns that this book hopes to make a theoretical as well as historical contribution.

On one level, the book examines a region, or subcategory of the Peruvian social formation, during a period of historical transition. It begins when a noncapitalist mode of production was dominant, though with some emerging capitalist tendencies in the sphere of exchange. It follows the region through a long period of articulation between modes, during which capitalism slowly became dominant. Finally, it examines the years during which noncapitalist forms of production coexisted in ever-shrinking proportions within the capitalist mode.[10]

[9] See in particular Pierre Beaucage, "¿Modos de producción articulados o lucha de clases?" in *Modos de producción en América Latina*, pp. 37–58. Foster-Carter also brings up a similar point, "Modes of Production," pp. 51–52, 68–69.

[10] There are many aspects associated with a capitalist mode of production, including the generalization of commodity circulation, the continual reinvestment of profits for further expansion of profit-making activity, and repeated innovation and expansion of technology. But in the end the crucial factor is that surplus labor is appropriated from a class of "free" wage laborers who, because they have been stripped of their means of production, must sell their labor power in the marketplace. Because labor power becomes a commodity just like anything else, the appropriation of surplus labor is realized in the sphere of circulation, appearing as a free contract rather than as an extraction of surplus by the capitalist. This is distinct from a noncapitalist mode of production, where laborers control means of production and surplus labor must therefore be appropriated through means other than economic—"tradition," established relations of dependence, direct compulsion, violence itself. Until labor is "freed" from access to the means of production, then, capitalism as a mode of production cannot become dominant, despite the existence of commodity circulation, profit-making activity, or even some limited technical innovation.

The dates of the study, 1860 to 1940, delimit the crucial decades during which the region underwent the major—though not the only—stages in the overall process of transformation.

Yet, on another level, theoretical terms and concepts play no more than a background or auxiliary role in the book. Rather than hitting the reader between the eyes from every paragraph, theory is present in how the questions are asked and in what material is emphasized. As a historian, I have dealt with the tension between telling a story and contributing to a theoretical debate by providing empirical, historical, and analytical material in such a way as to illuminate broader questions and concerns. But the theoretical framework, while crucial to the effective organization of data, does not eclipse the richness of the experiences, conflicts, triumphs, and defeats of the people themselves.

In essence, then, this book examines the transition to capitalism in the central sierra of Peru from the perspective of the region's peasantry. It tells the story of how villagers and hacienda peons attempted to limit the transition's effects on the quality of their daily lives, and how in the process they helped define the form that transformation took. In order to accomplish this, I ask three basic questions in historical perspective. First, what was the specific character of capitalist penetration in the countryside? Second, did the penetration go far enough to transform the agrarian class structure, and if so, what was the role of the peasantry in this transformation? And finally, what implications does the penetration of capitalism have for the existence of the peasantry as a class, both in terms of structure and consciousness?

My study shows that it was ultimately the peasants, in their efforts to use traditional relationships as weapons to resist hurtful change, who ended up changing both their relationships and themselves. It makes clear that the penetration of capitalism by itself did not automatically lead to the spread of capitalist relations, but instead encountered major resistance from the peasant household economy. Only after peasant self-sufficiency had been subjected to decades upon decades of erosion through indebtedness and other forms of conflict did it become possible for capitalist relations to begin to dominate at the village level; even then the process was strongly resisted from within. In the end, what made the transition successful was the rise of an agrarian bourgeoisie from wealthy peasant origins that, after taking control of community politics, was able to convert its accumulated wealth into capital by developing agricultural enterprises based on the exploitation of wage labor. Yet for the majority of the village population, the transition to capitalism did not mean increased prosperity or development, but rather decreasing access to resources and greater insecurity in a market society: in short, increasing poverty and pauperization.

The organization of the book exhibits some underlying assumptions about the periodization of capitalist transition in Peru, and about the relationship of the central highlands to the overall process. Part One, which covers the period from 1780 to 1900, analyzes the way in which a particular sector of the Peruvian elite (including a sector in the central region) attempted to tie into, and profit from, the new world market system developing around England. For the central highlands, this meant that the penetration of commercial capital obeyed new laws: the laws of circulation of British industrial capital. This change, of course, had important effects on both the landowning elite and the peasantry. But at neither the national nor the regional level did it lead to a complete transition to capitalism.

For a complete transition to capitalism to have occurred, a major change in the sphere of production as well as the sphere of circulation would have been necessary. In other words, in addition to producing goods for a new market, the actual way in which the goods were produced would have had to change. While this might not have meant a substantial modification in the technology or forces of production, at least not initially, it certainly would have meant a major change in the relations of production, the key to which was the separation from the means of production, or proletarianization, of a socially significant portion of the peasant population. For a variety of reasons, some of which will be explored in this study, this did not occur in Peru during the nineteenth century.

Part Two of the book (1895–1930) focuses on the period in which capitalism, while admittedly not penetrating all areas of Peru, became the dominant mode of production in the Peruvian social formation as a whole. After the failure of several national attempts at industrialization and modernization, the Peruvian elite—an amalgamation of emerging bourgeois elements and traditional landowners—finally opted to attempt successful development through an unequal alliance with foreign capital. The growth of the Cerro de Pasco Corporation, a U.S. company, represented this alliance in the central highlands. For the peasants, it meant a substantial modification in their relationships to the larger regional economy, but without capitalist relations becoming dominant within village production.

Part Three (the 1930s and beyond) examines the effect of the world depression on Peru, focusing most directly on the local level to trace the process through which capitalist relations became dominant in the central highland villages. At the very moment when the state recognized the juridical and economic existence of the Indian community, providing an institutional structure within which communal relations and land tenure could be legitimized, the wealthier peasants began to establish the political and economic preconditions for the generalization of capitalist relations in village agriculture, including the control of community institutions and the accumulation and further commodification of land. Finally, as the 1940s and 1950s witnessed the development of the capitalist farmer and entrepreneur from peasant origins, the new class contradictions emerging within the village community are considered.

One final caveat. It seems fairly clear that, by the beginning of the nineteenth century, the villages in the central highlands were neither "Indian" in the classic sense, nor closed corporate communities.[11] Economically speaking, immediately after independence the central sierra villages were already internally differentiated in terms of income, access to land and credit, and type and amount of outside activity on the part of their inhabitants. While there certainly were community lands, which were owned in common by the village and to which members of the community had overlapping rights of usufruct, a good percentage of the land was already privatized and intensely subdivided. Throughout the century, peasants took part in outside commercial and labor relations, outsiders settled in the community and bought land, and merchants developed credit networks and purchased land even if they did not themselves live in the villages.

In terms of race, both the economic openness of the villages and the relatively high levels of commercial activity in the region as a whole militated against the establishment of fixed or rigid racial categories. As people from the outside moved into the communities and intermarried with their inhabitants, the racial composition of the population became increasingly diverse and categories of economic and

[11] For the classic formulation of the closed corporate community, see Eric Wolf's article "Closed Corporate Communities in Mesoamerica and Central Java," *Southwestern Journal of Anthropology*, 13 (1957), 1–18. For recent critiques and reformulations, see A. Terry Rambo, "Closed Corporate and Open Peasant Communities: Re-opening a Hastily Shut Case," *Comparative Studies in Society and History*, 19 (1977), 179–88; and Steve J. Stern, "The Struggle for Solidarity: Class, Culture, and Community in Highland Indian America," forthcoming, *Radical History Review*.

racial status tended to overlap. Already by the 1780s, the central sierra had been calculated as having one of the highest percentages of *mestizaje*[12] in the Peruvian Viceroyalty (see Chapter One), and the upward trend of this percentage continued through the nineteenth and into the twentieth centuries. As a result, the image of the closed Indian community facing a hostile white outside world simply did not obtain for the Mantaro region. Instead, the central sierra village is better described as a dynamic and differentiated peasant community, whose inhabitants thought of themselves as much in economic as in racial terms.

Ultimately, therefore, the penetration of capitalism did not open up the community for the first time to market relations, labor migrations, social and economic differentiation, or *mestizaje*. Indeed, by the beginning of the twentieth century, all these trends were well advanced in local society. Rather than initiating them, capitalist transition changed the conditions and extent of their development and, perhaps most importantly, their meaning for the village population. The social, economic, and ideological dimensions of these changes form the central theme of this study.

[12] *Mestizaje* is the process of miscegenation through which the Indian and white races blend to produce the *mestizo*.

PART I

The Peasants Confront Commerce, 1860–1900

Here, even though you see us / As owners of the land, /
In order not to die of poverty / We live our lives at war.

—Patricio Manns, "Ya no somos nosotros."

CHAPTER ONE

The Human Geography

This valley of Jauja is surrounded by snow-covered mountains;
spread throughout it are small settlements where the Huancas have
their fields. (1553)

This province and valley of Xauxa is very fertile and of
great abundance . . . it produces excellent bacon and ham, among
the best in the land. (1629)

It is a very beautiful valley, with a temperate climate. . . .
It provides Lima with bacon, ham, quinoa, and chick peas. . . .
It provides the neighboring provinces with lard, bacon, grains,
flour, clothes, frieze, and tallow for the mines. (1785)[1]

From the colonial period on, the central highlands were considered an especially prosperous and well-endowed region of Peru. Certainly nature had been generous with the area. In the Mantaro Valley, at the center of the region, flat, fertile lands extended out from the river in both directions, and even in dry season, the fields were shaded by luxuriant vegetation. North from Jauja, one of the valley's important commercial centers, one passed through the more jagged, yet still productive, Yanamarca Valley and then descended into Tarma, another area of agricultural abundance. Further east was the *ceja de selva*, literally "eyebrow of the jungle," where in the eighteenth century explorers were already wresting control of rich subtropical lands

---

[1] The first quote is from Pedro Cieza de León, *La crónica del Perú* (Lima: Ediciones Peisa, 1973), p. 203. The second is from Antonio Vásquez de Espinoza, *Compendio y descripción de las Indias* (1629), as cited by Clodoaldo Alberto Espinosa Bravo, *Jauja Antigua* (Lima: Talleres Gráficos Villanueva, 1964), pp. 71–72. The third is from "Indice y Descripción del Partido de Santa Feé [sic] de Atun Jauxa, realizado por orden de Don Juan María de Galvez y Montes de Oca, primer Gobernador Intendente del Departamento de Jauja," 1785, as cited by Olinda Celestino, "La economía pastoral de las cofradías y el rol de la nobleza india: El valle del Mantaro en el siglo XVIII," Documentos de Trabajo, Centro de Investigaciones sobre América Latina, Bielefeld University (West Germany), November 1981, pp. 5–6. Frieze is a rough, coarse woolen cloth or material. Quinoa is a South American plant with an edible, cereal-like seed.

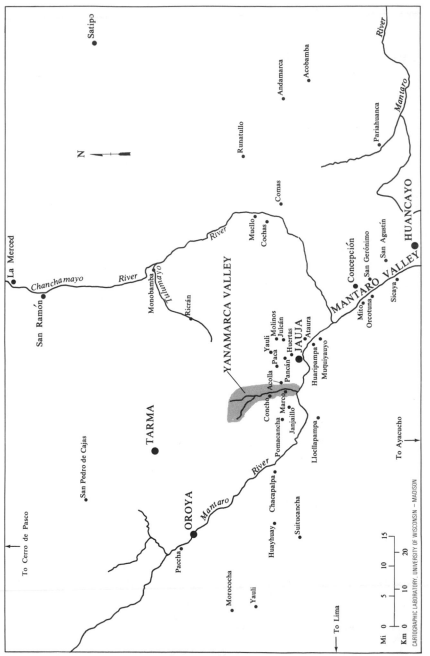

Map 2. The Central Region: Mantaro and Yanamarca Valleys.

from local Indian tribes and setting up the first sugar haciendas.[2] And to the west of Jauja, following the Mantaro River into higher and more forbidding landscapes, was located one of the richest mining areas of Peru—Oroya, Cerro de Pasco, Morococha, Yauli, and, even further west, the province of Huarochirí (see Map 2).

The productive potential of the central sierra was surpassed only by its commercial prosperity. Located strategically on most of the routes which connected the south of Peru with Cerro de Pasco and Lima, the Mantaro Valley was a major center of *arrieraje*, or mule driving. Indeed the town of Huancayo, at the valley's southern tip, was a gateway to the north and south, and had originated as a resting place for muleteers traveling in both directions.[3] And Huancayo was no exception. Throughout the valley, in towns and peasant villages, commercial activity was a familiar sight, as *arrieros* wound their way along mountainous paths, driving their heavily laden mule trains before them.

This chapter presents an overview of how these abundant resources and potentialities were exploited in the late eighteenth and early nineteenth centuries. On a general level, it presents the cast of characters in the local society and economy and follows them through their adaptations to the region's ecology and to each other. It introduces both the regional oligarchy—composed of landowners, merchants, and mineowners—and the peasantry, analyzing them separately and in interaction with each other. The purpose here is not to engage in historical narration, but rather to build a backdrop against which the narration will make more sense. For it is ultimately in the context of a careful understanding of the central highlands—its people, resources, and general layout—that the events of the nineteenth and twentieth centuries will take on their fullest meaning.

Mineowners, Merchants, and Landowners

By the second half of the eighteenth century, economic opportunities in the central sierra were concentrated in three sectors: mining, agriculture and livestock raising, and commerce. The three were often interrelated. Merchants in the mining area could use the resources

---

[2] Stéfano Varese, *La sal de los cerros* (Lima: Ediciones Retablo de Papel, 1973), pp. 169–73.

[3] Nelson Manrique, *El desarrollo del mercado interior en la sierra central, 1830–1910 (Informe de Investigación)*, Taller de Estudios Andinos, Serie: Andes Centrales No. 6 (La Molina, Universidad Nacional Agraria, 1978), pp. 22–23.

acquired in trade to buy mines.[4] Or a mineowner might own or rent an hacienda, a large agricultural or livestock property from which he or she could stock the mines with produce or labor.[5] Despite the overlap, however, each sector had its own internal logic and dynamic that differentiated it from the rest, and tended to define the types of people most likely to take a leading role within it.

In mining, the dominant form of enterprise was small, privately owned, and technologically primitive. Ore extraction was casual and unplanned, using only the simplest tools. The ore was then transported on muleback to the mineral haciendas, located at a distance in the river valleys surrounding the mining towns. There the silver was separated from the ore through the patio process, a method of cold chemical amalgamation invented in the sixteenth century that used mercury to extract silver from low-grade ores.[6] The labor force, though it included some "free" workers specializing in mining, was composed mainly of peasants recruited forcibly from their villages. Until the second half of the eighteenth century, the majority were acquired through the mita, a state-sponsored labor draft; but after the 1780s arrangements between entrepreneurs and state officials were increasingly handled on a case-by-case, informal basis. Despite occasional roundups of "vagrants" who were then forced to work in mining, the end result was that most mineowners faced an endemic labor shortage.[7]

While these mining methods could at times yield extremely high profits, especially in the case of a new mine or a particularly rich vein, in general the low level of technology and the instability of the labor force resulted in substantial insecurity of production and financing. At any given moment, it was common to find a large number of mines out of production entirely.[8] For those that remained in operation, the local aviadores, or merchants who provided credit, charged exorbitant interest rates and forced many mineowners to accept part of their

[4] John Fisher, Minas y mineros en el Perú colonial, 1776–1824 (Lima: Instituto de Estudios Peruanos, 1977), pp. 208–209.

[5] AGN, Protocolos Notariales, Juan Cosío, Book 155, June 1820; Ignacio Ayllón Salazar, Book 37, August 25, 1821, 715–15v; José de Felles, Book 239, July 4, 1848, 117.

[6] Fisher, Minas y mineros, pp. 77–79; Estevan Delsol, Informe sobre las minas de Salpo, Quiruvilca y Huamachuco, en el Departamento de La Libertad (Lima, 1880), pp. 30–75. In contrast to an agricultural or livestock hacienda, where the land or pasture was directly exploited, a mineral hacienda was simply the location at which the metal was separated from the ore through the patio process, i.e., through cold chemical amalgamation using salt and mercury.

[7] Fisher, Minas y mineros, pp. 181–84, 188–97.

[8] Ibid., p. 77.

loans in overpriced commodities.[9] Ultimately, therefore, mining was a risky business. On one side stood the lucky entrepreneurs, who had found an especially profitable claim, developed good connections with merchants, or owned sufficiently large and diversified enterprises to enable them to weather the inevitable ups and downs. On the other side were the majority of mineowners, small proprietors of one or two claims, who essentially held their breath and plunged into an industry where gains and losses could be equally dramatic. There were enough success stories to prop up the hopes of most, but abandoned mines and rapid turnover of ownership were silent testimonies to the all-too-frequent cases of disastrous investment.

Agriculture, both more secure and less spectacularly profitable than mining, consisted of large and small property sectors. In the fertile and well-watered valley floors, small properties predominated and most land belonged to peasant communities. Those plots that did belong to white or *mestizo* landowners were generally *chacras*, small- to medium-sized holdings producing limited quantities of commercial crops such as wheat, alfalfa, or vegetables.[10] Since this limited production could easily be sold on local or regional markets, the *chacra* was a fairly safe investment for its owner. The labor demands were also slight, and could be met easily with family labor or, in the case of more prominent owners, with small amounts of seasonal hired labor.

It was on the arid uplands above the valleys, *puna* suited only for livestock or hardy Andean crops such as potatoes or quinoa, that haciendas had multiplied. Their formal boundaries were usually quite extensive, but only a small proportion of the land was actually used at any given time for growing crops or pasturing animals. Hacienda owners, or *hacendados*, used labor from resident peasant families, supplemented by occasional levies from neighboring villages, to tend flocks or fields. Resident households, or *colonos*, received a subsistence plot, the right to pasture their own animals (*huacchas*) on hacienda lands, and a limited number of subsistence items such as clothes, coca, and so on. In exchange, they were obliged to work a certain amount of time per week as agricultural laborers or shepherds on the *hacendado*'s fields, transport the hacienda's produce to market, and provide personal service (*pongaje*) in the landowner's house.[11]

[9] Ibid., pp. 206–207.

[10] This pattern was particularly developed in some of the Mantaro Valley communities around Jauja, such as Huerta, Molinos, and Pancán. See ANF, Protocolos Notariales, Manuel Víctor Morales, passim.

[11] This picture of labor relations on haciendas is a composite of several sources. See especially AGN, Protocolos Notariales, Francisco Palacios, Book 570, July 20, 1867,

From the point of view of the *hacendado*, the large estate was a safe investment because it was able to combine market and subsistence activities in a flexible fashion, depending on local economic conditions. In times of economic expansion, the landowner could either increase the production of marketable agricultural or livestock products, or rent the land out to a merchant, miner, or other entrepreneur interested in taking advantage of commercial opportunities. In times of economic decline, it was possible to retire from the market, producing for subsistence or making more land available for use by additional peasant families. But, equally important, the large estate was a source of prestige and influence. It provided a strong and secure base for the acquisition of credit. The use of peasant labor, both from *colonos* and from neighboring villages, allowed landlords to build a solid patronage network upon which they could call in times of labor scarcity or social or political disorder.

Commerce constituted the third important sector of the regional economy. In addition to the region's strategic location on many routes which connected the center and south of Peru, the local mining industry itself generated an active trade in a variety of commercial products: mules, hides, mercury, salt, wool, meat, textiles, and many other goods. Merchants and *arrieros* of many different backgrounds were able to make substantial profits. While some limited their activities to local or regional routes, others took on the greater risks of interprovincial or interregional trade. In several cases, merchants settled in the central highlands became involved in supplying mules for trade with the mines, breeding them as far south as Salta, in Argentina.[12] And commercial activity was not limited to trading alone. In both the mining and agrarian sectors, merchants were key providers of credit and made good use of their money by charging high interest rates. In more than a few instances, moreover, merchant creditors ended up owners of property when debtors were no longer able to meet their payments.

788–97v; José Ramón Valdivia, Book 992, November 3, 1882, 220–22v; APJ, "Solicitud de los colonos de la hacienda Yanamarca contra el arrendatario Landa," Huancayo, 1908; "Copia de las partes pertinentes del fallo en el caso de los colonos de la hacienda Yanamarca contra el arrendatario Isaías Grandes," Huancayo, December 15, 1923; and Rodrigo Sánchez, "El cambio social en dos comunidades del Valle de Yanamarca: Un modelo empírico," B.A. Thesis in Anthropology, Universidad Nacional del Centro del Perú, Huancayo, 1968.

[12] For references to the Salta mule trade, see Alberto Flores Galindo, "Túpac Amaru y la sublevación de 1780," in Alberto Flores Galindo (ed.), *Túpac Amaru II: 1780* (Lima: Ediciones Retablo de Papel, 1976), pp. 286–88, especially p. 288; and AGN, Protocolos Notariales, Juan Cosío, Book 155, June 1820.

To a certain extent, every wise entrepreneur was in part a merchant. With market conditions changeable and uncertain, it made sense to develop the kinds of networks that could help in making investment decisions. Besides, it was often in commerce or moneylending that the largest and quickest profits could be made with the least personal risk. Businesspeople interested in remaining solvent or expanding their portfolio could not afford to ignore this fact.

On the other hand, merchants also diversified their economic activities through a variety of strategies, including debt foreclosure, outright purchase, and renting. A typical medium-sized trader, for example, would include within his or her assets not only a sizable pack of mules and a storeful of marketable goods, but also a series of *chacras* dedicated to the production of commercial crops, such as alfalfa, corn, wheat, and wood.[13] Larger, more prestigious merchants often rented haciendas, using the properties to pasture flocks of sheep whose wool and meat were in high demand in the mining centers.[14]

Yet the existence of diversification should not blind us to each sector's distinct character. Mining, as a high-risk, high-turnover industry, was composed mainly of small- to medium-sized entrepreneurs who, at least during the colonial period, did not have important connections with the higher echelons of the bureaucracy or the elite close to the viceregal court. Of all the miners registered in 1790, for example, only two had titles of nobility, and both of these had been acquired during the eighteenth century.[15] In general, then, while there might be an occasional aristocratic or influential mineowner, the industry as a whole was less than stable, serving instead as a source of accumulation—and of ruin—for new fortunes.

Commerce was also, in some ways, a mercurial sector. Engaged in it were individuals on a spectrum from the prestigious member of a Lima commercial house, all the way to the somewhat ragged petty trader who plied the dusty trails between villages. At times, the merchant of humble origins could profit from a lucrative trade to the point of becoming wealthy and notable. But the vagaries of commerce and the ever-changing nature of markets could easily bring the same person down again as the result of one or two ill-advised business decisions. What differentiated commerce from mining, however, was the

---

[13] ANF, Protocolos Notariales, Manuel Víctor Morales, Book 5: October 3, 1872, between 112v and 113, and passim.

[14] AGN, Protocolos Notariales, Baltazar Núñez del Prado, Book 454, August 1833, 153–56; Juan Cosío, Book 155, November 1819, 161v–63.

[15] Fisher, *Minas y mineros*, pp. 78–79.

availability of a broader variety of alternatives. While the adventurous entrepreneur could make or break a fortune in both sectors, in commerce it was easier for the cautious to reproduce or slightly increase their fortunes through a judicious combination of moneylending, muledriving, small-scale commercial agriculture, and actual trading.

Stability was greatest in agriculture. Especially on the larger holdings, whose value was calculated both in market terms and in prestige and security, there was a higher incidence of entrenched aristocratic landowners. Eighteenth-century *hacendados*, in contrast to mineowners, were often titled nobility or prestigious colonial bureaucrats; and in at least some cases the properties were held in entailment, a practice designed to impede their free circulation.[16] Thus while there certainly was a market in land, and haciendas were often rented, turnover in actual ownership tended to occur more regularly on smaller holdings. Large estates changed hands permanently most often as a result of economic or personal disaster rather than market conditions.

Thus the regional economy operated on two tiers. On one was the large agricultural estate, limited to the frigid *punas*, more constant in ownership, adapting successfully to the booms and busts of the economic cycle. On the other were the more animated and fluctuating activities of mining, commerce, and small-scale commercial agriculture, where opportunities were present for accumulation and anyone with some luck and business sense could make money. Particularly during periods of economic boom or expansion, this second tier could generate impressive wealth. But as we shall see (Chapter Two), there were important limits to how far fortunes made in commerce or mining could advance into the more exclusive circles of the colonial elite.

The distance between the two tiers was due in part to the nature of production relations in the region. Despite the existence of much commercial and entrepreneurial activity, with few exceptions labor was not free but bound up in a viable subsistence economy. Markets, while they existed, tended to be shallow, and both the exchange of goods and the acquisition of labor for production necessitated extra-economic compulsion. Making and maintaining a fortune was as much a function of social and political influence as it was the result of economic skill. Commerce and production operated through the estab-

---

[16] Fisher, *Minas y mineros*, p. 78; AGN, Protocolos Notariales, Baltazar Núñez del Prado, Book 454, August 1833, 153–56; José de Felles, Book 239, July 4, 1848, 109v–37; Juan Antonio Meléndez, December 1839, 968v–85v; Francisco de Paula Casós, Book 144, October 2, 1837, 55–75; and José María de la Rosa, Book 638, December 17, 1821, 496v–502v.

lishment of monopolies and spheres of influence, and all transactions, from the acquisition of sufficient mercury to amalgamate silver ores to the maintenance of sufficient credit for the mule trade, depended on how successfully a mineowner, merchant, or businessperson developed and maintained the right networks.[17] As a result it was the *hacendados*, more often members of influential aristocratic families, who were most successful in maintaining patron-client networks and extracting surplus from a dependent labor force. Not only were they able to tie peasant labor to their estates through nonmonetary and nonmarket agreements, but they could enforce these arrangements because they had access to private and public forms of violence. Mineowners and merchants, on the other hand, more often faced labor or credit shortages. No matter how adept, they were handicapped unless they could develop the right connections.

In the eighteenth and early nineteenth centuries, then, it was ultimately power, both state and private, that underwrote the extraction of surplus and the acquisition of labor in the central highlands. While local markets for goods and land did exist, much trade with the peasant communities was carried out through the *repartimiento de mercancías*, a forced distribution of goods sponsored by state officials.[18] For access to labor, most entrepreneurs again depended on political networks, whether directly through state institutions of labor acquisition, or indirectly through various forms of public or private compulsion.[19] In the final analysis, the expansion of commerce and commercial production was limited by the mode of production. Mineowners, merchants, and *hacendados* all depended on extra-economic means to maintain or expand their enterprises. Beyond a certain point, the precapitalist nature of the regional economy blocked further growth or

[17] An excellent example of this was the system for distributing mercury. Although in theory all miners should have had equal access to this essential mineral, access varied quite dramatically in practice. According to Fisher (*Minas y mineros*, pp. 167–69), the establishment of distribution centers in only a few locations discriminated both against those miners who were further away, and against the smaller miners who had less possibility of making the trip to pick up the mineral. In addition, there were always merchants who, despite the existence of a law against selling mercury to anyone other than miners, managed to buy it up anyway and resell it to miners in exchange for a promise to sell them silver at a discount, or simply for higher prices. Thus, it was always those with the right connections who came out ahead.

[18] While the *repartimiento* system was technically abolished in 1780 after the Túpac Amaru rebellion, it persisted in various forms until the nineteenth century. See John Fisher, *Government and Society in Colonial Peru: The Intendant System, 1784–1814* (London: The Athlone Press, 1970), especially pp. 21–23, 26–28, 79, 87–88, 90–99.

[19] Fisher, *Minas y mineros*, pp. 181–91.

transformation. And at the very center of this economy was the peasant village.

The Peasant Community

When Jacoba Arias dictated her last will and testament from her bed in Acolla, a village in the Yanamarca Valley, she owned nearly fourteen hectares of land divided up into fairly small units and dispersed through various *parajes*, or regions, of the community where she lived. This allowed her to utilize the many climatic differences that altitude, angle of the slope, and direction of the sun created on the jagged and irregular Andean landscape, and to diversify the crops she planted. In addition, she possessed forty head of sheep, three teams of oxen, six bulls, one cow, and three mules. She was therefore able to supplement her family's vegetable and grain diet with meat, milk, cheese, and lard; plow and fertilize her fields, and spin the woolen thread for her family's clothes, all without depending on the market. The fact that she owned three mules, however, meant that she also occasionally engaged in petty commerce, whether to sell an agricultural surplus, supplement family earnings, or acquire a few luxury items. Yet despite the impressive size and variety of her holdings, Jacoba Arias was neither Spanish nor *mestiza*. In fact, she dictated her will through an interpreter because she spoke only Quechua.[20]

While it is doubtful that all peasant families in Acolla possessed as much land as she did, Jacoba Arias was typical in a very important way. She was part of a diversified family economy which, through a combination of agricultural and livestock activities, provided for the majority of its own subsistence needs. As in other parts of the central highlands, the goal of the peasant family economy in the Yanamarca Valley was to strive for the closest possible approximation to self-sufficiency. To do so, each family needed access to lands in three basic zones: the humid lowlands in the center of the valley, the sloping agricultural lands that rose to meet the mountaintops to the east and west, and the extensive, relatively flat lands on the other side of the mountain ranges.

The lowlands bordered the Yanamarca River on both sides and, because they would often flood during the rainy season, were ill-suited for agriculture. This was particularly true in the southern and lowest part of the valley, where between November and May the waters of

[20] ANF, Protocolos Notariales, Manuel Víctor Morales, Book 5: February 8, 1873, 153–54v.

the river that did not go underground formed a temporal lagoon. Throughout this area, lands were used for pasturing sheep and cattle and were communally owned by the individual peasant villages. The lagoon, however, was shared communal property to which all the villages in the valley had a common right.[21]

It was on the long slopes rising from the lowlands toward the mountains that peasant families grew their crops. While the rains irrigated the fields between November and May, the slant of the land prevented the accumulation of water, protecting the young seedlings from mildew and rot. Yet the rocky soil and intricate variations in slope created a series of tiny microenvironments, where actual fertility, humidity, and access to sunlight could change radically from one part of the hill to another, or even within a single agricultural plot. Cultivation was thus a complex task, requiring extensive and specialized knowledge of both crop and land. Peasants adapted to these conditions by spreading their holdings, in small units, throughout the available surface, taking advantage of even the slightest change in angle or quality of the soil. Within each *chacra*, they often planted alternating rows of different seeds, fitting the needs of the crop to the characteristics of the land at even the most minute scale.[22]

Beyond the mountains to the east and west, the Yanamarca Valley communities had access to lands in a higher ecological zone. To the east, the community of Acolla had extensive pasturelands which, given their higher altitude and greater propensity for frost, were better adapted to livestock than to crops. In the family division of labor, someone less capable of heavy agricultural work—either a young child or an elderly person—made the three-hour daily trip on foot, perhaps

[21] Data on communal pasturelands was obtained from: AMA, Libros de Actas, 1928–1934, Sesión extraordinaria, September 29, 1930, pp. 121–22; Sesión de junta general, October 15, 1931, pp. 172–75; Asamblea de junta general, October 12, 1932, pp. 260–65; 1934–1939, Sesión, March 27, 1934, pp. 6–8; Asamblea extraordinaria, January 2, 1938, pp. 319–23; and passim. AMM, Libros de Actas, 1922–1929, Sesión, July 10, 1928, pp. 233–34; 1929–1943, Sesión ordinaria, October 23, 1929, pp. 9–13; Sesión ordinaria, November 3, 1930; and passim. Archivo SINAMOS, cc 205 (Marco), "Copia, Acta de amparo en posesión de la Laguna de Marco, entre las comunidades de Acolla, Chocón, Marco y Pachascucho," December 11, 1889, included in Dirección de Asuntos Indígenas, Expediente 13382, "Relativo a las diferencias suscitadas entre las comunidades de Marco y Tragadero sobre establecimiento de servidumbre por el paso de ganado," 41. Also from William B. Hutchinson, "Sociocultural Change in the Mantaro Valley Region of Peru: Acolla, A Case Study," Ph.D. Dissertation, Indiana University, 1973, pp. 59–62; and through informal conversations and observations in the Yanamarca Valley, particularly talks with Moisés Ortega.

[22] Direct observations and informal conversations in the Yanamarca Valley, and Hutchinson, "Sociocultural Change," pp. 137–38.

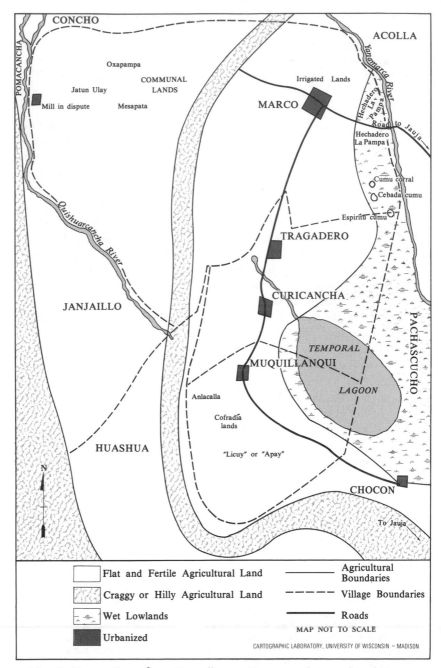

CONCHO

ACOLLA

POMACANCHA

Oxapampa

COMMUNAL
LANDS

Irrigated Lands

Jatun Ulay

Mill in dispute

Mesapata

MARCO

Yanamarca River

Hechadero La Pampa

Road to Jauja

Hechadero
La Pampa i

Cumu corral

Cebada cumu

Espíritu cumu

Quishuarcancha River

TRAGADERO

CURICANCHA

JANJAILLO

PACHASCUCHO

TEMPORAL

MUQUILLANQUI

LAGOON

Anlacalla

Cofradía
lands

HUASHUA

"Licuy" or "Apay"

CHOCON

N

To Jauja

	Flat and Fertile Agricultural Land	————	Agricultural Boundaries
	Craggy or Hilly Agricultural Land	– – – –	Village Boundaries
	Wet Lowlands	▬▬▬	Roads
	Urbanized		

MAP NOT TO SCALE

CARTOGRAPHIC LABORATORY, UNIVERSITY OF WISCONSIN – MADISON

Map 3. Marco, Tragadero, Muquillanqui: Parajes *and Agricultural Zones.*

spinning woolen thread while caring for the flock. To the west, the direction of the winds mitigated the frigidity of the climate, allowing the various villages that made up the community of Marco to alternate agricultural and livestock activities.

As in other peasant societies, a balanced household economy in the Yanamarca Valley depended on maintaining an equilibrium between access to resources and available family labor.[23] Given the seasonal nature of agricultural work, a yearly balance depended on the utilization of each member's full potential in various activities. During harvest or planting, for example, every available hand, whether young or old, male or female, worked in agriculture. At other points in the crop cycle, however, an adult and several older children sufficed to cultivate the fields, leaving others to tend the flocks, spin the wool, weave the clothes, and care for the household. In dry season, most hands were available for secondary activities. Some men, particularly the younger, single ones, worked in the mines or subtropical regions, or plied commercial routes as small *arrieros*.[24] Other people in the household specialized in handicraft or artisanry for barter or sale, weaving or embroidering special cloth, making *mantas* (carrying cloths or shawls), hats, ponchos, and blankets, carving wood, and so on. The overall balance of activities meant that, in a good agricultural year, a family was able to meet its subsistence needs, market a crop surplus and a few extra commodities in the community or in Jauja, buy a few necessities, especially coca and alcohol, and even indulge in a few novelties offered by itinerant peddlers. In a bad year, the proportion of nonagricultural activities increased, both outside and inside the household. The men migrated in larger numbers, the women produced more handicraft and, if necessary, the family sold some sheep or cattle. Because it was flexible, a diversified family economy could survive both good and bad years. But the balance was more fragile than it seemed at first glance.

[23] See A. V. Chayanov, *The Theory of Peasant Economy*, ed. Daniel Thorner, Basile Verblay, and R.E.F. Smith. Published for the American Economic Association (Homewood, Ill.: R. D. Irwin, 1966), especially pp. 109, 148–49. For an application of some of Chayanov's concepts to the Peruvian central highlands, see Juan Martínez Alier, *Los huacchilleros del Perú* (Paris and Lima: Ruedo Ibérico-Instituto de Estudios Peruanos, 1973).

[24] For examples of labor migrations, see ANF, Expedientes y Libros Judiciales, Libro de Juicios Verbales, Acolla, 1875–1876, Maita vs. Rosales, 3–3v; Libro de Juicios Verbales, Marco, 1876, Arrieta vs. Arias, 17–17v, and Franco vs. Camarena, 43–43v; Libro de Juicios Verbales, Acolla, 1876, September 16, 1876, Remusgo vs. Villar; Libro de Conciliaciones, Marco, 1877, Capcha vs. Rosales, 26–26v, and Fernanda Tabraj vs. several others, 27v–28.

The peasant economy faced a series of internal contradictions. Household self-sufficiency was based on maintaining an equilibrium between family labor and available means of production, yet no family could successfully regulate its own size or sex composition. Since much agricultural land was private property, the system of partible inheritance also militated against preserving a balance from one generation to the next. Even after a household had inherited lands from both the male and female lines, it was often necessary to buy more *chacras* to efficiently employ and reproduce family labor.[25] Because *chacras* were small to begin with, subdivision through inheritance combined with the buying and selling of plots to create an extremely fragmented pattern of land tenure, where boundary conflicts among and within families were a daily occurrence.[26]

Even if a family retained access to sufficient resources, meteorological changes and differential fertility made agriculture a risky occupation. A night of frost, an hour of hail, too much or too little rain at the wrong time—no one knew when or where disaster could strike. The need to insure subsistence under such conditions increased competition even more, as families fought with each other to maintain access to lands in many different microenvironments. Yet the same circumstances heightened the urgency of cooperation, since few households, no matter how much they treasured the ideal of self-sufficiency, could regularly make ends meet without the aid of neighbors.

Ideally, reciprocal exchanges of labor and goods served both to sustain household equilibrium and encourage cooperation. Through extended-family networks and ritual kinship ties, households gave labor in exchange for agricultural and livestock products, strengthening their webs of mutual obligation. Most exchanges of labor or goods within the community were verbal and nonmonetary. An agreement often

[25] Information on land tenure, land sales, and inheritance abounds in the ANF. On land tenure and inheritance see, for example, Protocolos Notariales, Manuel Víctor Morales, Book 7: January 20, 1877, 153–55v, and March 17, 1877, 189v–91; Book 8: December 13, 1878, 175 and inserts; and Expedientes y Libros Judiciales, Libro de Juicios Verbales, Marco, 1876: "División y partición de bienes de Nicolás Fabián," September 4, 1876. On land sales, see Protocolos Notariales, especially Luis Salazar, Book 6: September 5, 1895, 139v and inserts; Manuel Víctor Morales, Book 7: April 21, 1876, 44v and inserts; Book 9: November 30, 1880, 75–75v and inserts, and passim.

[26] For land conflict between peasants, see the Juicios Verbales at the ANF; for example, Libro de Resoluciones, Marco, 1864: 1, 2–4v, 10v–11, 15v–16, 27v–28, 29–29v; Libro de Juicios Verbales, Acolla, 1875–1876: 1, 2v–3, 5–5v; Libro de Juicios Verbales, Marco, 1876: 5, 22–22v; and Libro de Conciliaciones, Marco, 1877: 1–1v, 2v–3v, 5v–6v.

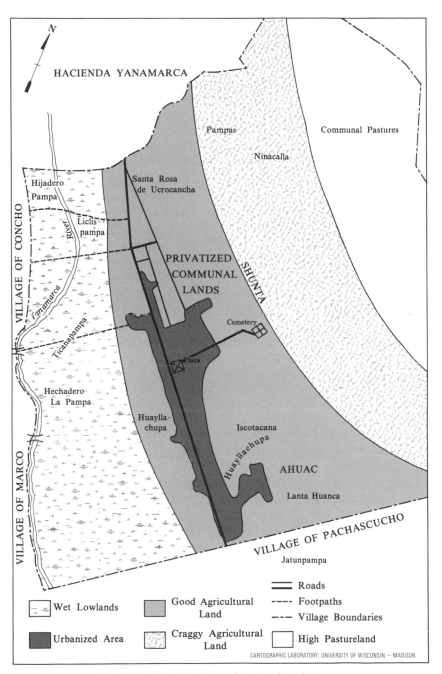

Map 4. Acolla: Parajes *and Agricultural Zones*.

used in agriculture was the planting of a field *al partir*, by which the owner of the plot provided the land and seed, the other party provided the labor, and the harvest was split two ways.[27] In livestock breeding, a common method of labor exchange was for the owner of a group of animals to hand them over to another who was already caring for his or her own flock. The latter would then add the former's animals to the flock in exchange for half the issue.[28]

But perhaps the most interesting custom was *ishapa*, which brought together a household owning land and a household owning sheep. The agreement began with the herd of sheep being fenced in on the agricultural plot, seven nights in each section of the field, in order to fertilize it. Then each household would plant half the plot with potato, using their own seed, and be responsible for their own harvest. In the second year of the contract, households traded the rows they planted in order to compensate for possible ecological variation and cultivated *ollucos*, a local root crop. Quinoa was planted in the third and final year, and again the rows were traded. Then the agreement would end unless specifically renewed.[29]

Even if a family did not engage in formal labor contracts, it often needed assistance during the heaviest points in the agricultural cycle. Following a ritual custom, the household head would *suplicar* (beg) neighbors and relatives for help to carry out a particular task. In return, the host family provided food, coca, and alcohol for the workers. In most cases, the host was expected to reciprocate with a comparable labor contribution in the future.[30]

Through the various ceremonies that punctuated the life cycle, from the first cutting of a child's hair and baptism to marriage and the construction of a new family house, households of different economic means sought to tie themselves to each other in a more general and lasting way. In each of the life-cycle ceremonies, it was customary to choose a set of godparents, preferably from wealthier households. In addition to providing a gift for their godchild, the godparents were expected to give a large fiesta, providing food, liquor, coca, and music

[27] I have confirmed the use of *al partir* through conversations in Acolla; in ANF, Protocolos Notariales, Manuel Víctor Morales, Book 8: June 10, 1878, 79–81; and ANF, Expedientes y Libros Judiciales, Libro de Juicios Verbales, Marco, 1876, 5.

[28] ANF, Expedientes y Libros Judiciales, Libro de Juicios Verbales, Acolla, 1875–76, Taipe vs. Pizarro, May 8, 1876; "Expediente sobre robo de ganados, Blancas vs. Espinoza," 1918, especially 42v–43, 50–50v.

[29] Hutchinson, "Sociocultural Change," pp. 26–27.

[30] Conversations and direct observation in Acolla, and Giorgio Alberti and Enrique Mayer, *Reciprocidad e intercambio en los Andes peruanos* (Lima: Instituto de Estudios Peruanos, 1974).

for all those who attended. If the ties of godparenthood remained strong, each couple that formed a household could depend, once they had settled down, on the aid of six different sets of godparents: two from the cutting of hair, two from baptism, one from the marriage ceremony, and one from the *zafacasa*, or roofing of the new house. The ties also applied to the godparent's and the godchild's extended families, and everyone called each other *compadre*.

Ideally, the relationship of *compadrazgo* was filled with mutual affection and respect. Each *compadre* was entitled to a special place in the other's household, and was the first to be called upon or to call on the other in times of need. Of course, some relationships (especially baptism and marriage) were more important than others, and many did not work smoothly. But overall, the system provided important advantages to both wealthy and poor households. For the wealthy, it meant that they broadened their network of patronage, and could call on their godchildren and *compadres* in the future to fill various labor needs. For the poor, it meant they could expect their godparents or *compadres* to intercede for them and help them in a variety of circumstances, such as debt, land conflicts, or bad harvests.

At times, the maze of household reciprocity, cooperation, and kinship extended beyond the boundaries of the village. Through intermarriage, *compadrazgo*, inheritance, or even purchase, peasants gained access to labor and means of production in nearby communities and towns.[31] Given the intricate variety of Andean microenvironments, this access often allowed families to plant additional crops that were not adapted to the land within their village. Yet in the end, it was to their own community, and to the richly textured fabric of community life, that peasants owed their prime allegiance.

Through a combined system of religious and political offices, village organizations used existing patterns of household cooperation to cement community solidarity. At the political level, the village was divided into two or more administrative subdivisions, each with its own officials. The households belonging to one unit worked together on community projects, whether it meant cleaning the irrigation ditches, providing a set number of adobe bricks for the construction of a building, or planting community fields. At the religious level, a number of *cofradías*, or religious lay brotherhoods, were responsible for organ-

[31] ANF, Protocolos Notariales, Manuel Víctor Morales, Book 4: December 1, 1869, inserts between 150 and 151; Book 7: September 2, 1876, 96v–97v; Book 8: January 30, 1879, inserts between 204v and 205; Book 8: September 1, 1879, 315–16, and passim.

izing the annual fiestas, rituals, and masses through which the village honored its saints. Each year, the membership of each *cofradía* chose a *mayordomo* who was responsible for all the administrative tasks connected with the celebration. This official organized *cofradía* work parties to plant the church lands they owned, arranged for the necessary masses, processions, meals, and drink, and paid for any excess expense out of his own pocket.[32]

By investing time, labor, or even money in community projects and religious fiestas, households integrated themselves into a village network of overlapping responsibilities and obligations. Fulfilling their duty to the community took time and resources away from the household economy, a fact that was often resented, particularly by the poorer families. In most cases, however, the peasants complied, for in return they received access to important rights, whether in protection, water, pastures, or agricultural land.

Although the system of communal organization provided many benefits to participating households, it could not erase the conflict built into all levels of the peasant society and economy. Instead, existing conflict was redirected through communal organizations, with the survival of the many taking precedence over the squabbles of the few. Although households continued to fight with their neighbors and relatives over lands, they were willing to call a truce if their communal subdivision needed to make adobe bricks for a community building. If two subdivisions were fighting over labor obligations to the village, they were willing to stop long enough to solve a land or water conflict with a neighboring community. And even if two communities were struggling over pastures, they would forget their differences if an hacienda invaded the lands of any one of their neighbors.

Channeling conflict through community structures was a double-edged sword, however, for it could often transform individual problems between *comuneros* (villagers) into community issues. Thus the inevitable disagreements between villages—land boundaries, overlapping rights to common pastures, access to water, the trampling of one community's fields by another's animals—fed into the innumerable petty rivalries between individuals, creating violent, endemic com-

---

[32] For the system of religious and political offices, see Archivo SINAMOS, cc 205 (Marco), Inventory of church *cofradía* property and its uses, 1893, included in "Expediente sobre la reivindicación del molino de propiedad comunal," 1938; Archivo SINAMOS, cc 205 (Marco), Copy of the *expediente* of the founding of the Parish of Marco (ca. 1875), included in Dirección de Asuntos Indígenas, Expediente 4366, "Marco vs. Francisco Carlé and Víctor Colca," 1942, 10–12; Richard Adams, *A Community in the Andes: Problems and Progress in Muquiyauyo* (Seattle: University of Washington Press, 1959), pp. 24–81; Hutchinson, "Sociocultural Change," pp. 24–25.

petition. And the tales of struggle between neighboring communities were a common thread woven into the very fabric of village history and oral tradition.[33]

The complex texture of community life, then, was composed of both competition and cooperation, solidarity and conflict. Despite the delicate balance between opposing tendencies, villages were able to distribute communal resources, advance community projects, and confront incursions by outsiders. Unifying themselves through relations of reciprocity and ritual kinship, households managed to overcome or circumvent the tendency toward rivalry, reestablishing a balance between resources and available family labor by cooperating with each other. Even though alliances were fragile at all levels, in the end they worked well enough to maintain and reproduce the community and family economy through the generations. Yet the continuing viability of village and household self-sufficiency was not the result of total insularity.

Indeed, the peasants of the central highlands were no strangers to the ebb and flow of commercial capital. Since the beginning of the colonial period, they had provided money, goods, and labor to the commercial economy. Through a process that lasted centuries, advancing in periods of economic boom and stagnating in periods of economic depression, peasants were indebted, their lands privatized, and their labor used on haciendas, in *obrajes* (textile workshops), and in mines.[34] For hundreds of years, however, commercial capital did not destroy the basic core of peasant self-sufficiency. Instead, com-

[33] ANF, Protocolos Notariales, Manuel Víctor Morales, Book 4: July 16, 1869, 94v–95v; March 15, 1871, 350v; September 30, 1871, 436v–37v; Book 7: February 21, 1876, 23v–24; May 19, 1877, 216–16v; June 23, 1877, 235v–36v; Luis Salazar, Book 1: September 10, 1880, 148–48v; ANF, Expedientes y Libros Judiciales, Libro de Conciliaciones, Marco, 1877, 18–20; and informal conversations, Yanamarca Valley.

[34] For data on the activities of commercial capital in the colonial period, see Karen Spalding, "Kurakas and Commerce: A Chapter in the Evolution of Andean Society," *Hispanic American Historical Review*, 53:4 (November 1973), 581–99; "Tratos mercantiles del Corregidor de Indios y la formación de la hacienda en el Perú," *América Indígena*, XXX:3 (July 1970), 595–608; "Hacienda-Village Relations in Andean Society to 1830," *Latin American Perspectives*, II: 1 (Spring 1975), 107–21; Carlos Sempat Assadourian, "Integración y desintegración regional en el espacio colonial. Un enfoque histórico," *Revista EURE*, No. 4 (March 1972), pp. 11–24; Steve J. Stern, "Nuevos aspectos sobre la mano de obra indígena: El caso de los 'asientos' de Huamanga, 1570–1640," *Revista del Archivo Departamental de Ayacucho*, No. 1 (1977), pp. 26–37; "Las luchas sociales y la evolución de la explotación de la mano de obra indígena en Huamanga colonial," *Ideología* (Ayacucho, Peru), 1977, pp. 47–52; Steve J. Stern, *Peru's Indian Peoples and the Challenge of Spanish Conquest: Huamanga to 1640* (Madison: University of Wisconsin Press, 1982); and Brooke Larson, "Rural Colonial Society and Economic Change: The Cochabamba Region in the Late Colonial Period," Ph.D. Dissertation, Columbia University, 1977.

mercial penetration occurred through channels which were also central to the reproduction of village life: the diversified activities and market relations of the peasant household economy, and the institutions of the Catholic church.

In most of the region's villages, local *cofradías* financed the community fiesta complex by exploiting lands and other properties granted to them over their several centuries of existence. Reflecting the economic status of their members, village brotherhoods were usually quite poor when compared to the more powerful "Spanish" *cofradías* in the area's towns. In the Yanamarca Valley, for example, the nine *cofradías* in Acolla held barely sixteen small to medium *chacras*, an amount of land equivalent to the holdings of two relatively poor families. In Marco, nine brotherhoods held thirteen *chacras*, though several of them were large. Yet, like their wealthier "Spanish" counterparts, village *cofradías* held a large proportion of local commercial property. In addition to agricultural lands the Acolla brotherhoods owned ten stores, eight of them in the village's main plaza and two on the main street, which was also the principal commercial route between the towns of Jauja and Tarma. And the Santísimo Sacramento, Marco's most prestigious organization, controlled one of the valley's two grain mills.[35]

Thus despite their comparative poverty, village *cofradías* were an important commercial force in community life. To cover the fiesta or ritual expenses for the saint honored by his *cofradía*, a *mayordomo* had to convert the resources owned by his brotherhood into money.[36] In the case of agricultural lands, the *mayordomo* would organize collective work parties composed of *cofradía* members to plant, cultivate, and harvest the fields, and then sell the produce on the market.[37] In the case of other properties, or if the brotherhood could not levy sufficient laborers to manage an agricultural field, the assets were rented out to merchants or wealthier peasants. While the renting out of properties created a particularly auspicious opportunity for merchants wishing to involve themselves in the village economy, the exploitation of *cofradía* property in general increased the number of monetary and commercial transactions in the community.

It was during the actual *cofradía* celebrations that commercial ac-

---

[35] See Archivo SINAMOS, "Expediente sobre la reivindicación del molino," 134–36v, for material on Acolla; and Archivo SINAMOS, Expediente 4366, 10–12, for material on Marco.

[36] Archivo SINAMOS, "Expediente sobre la reivindicación del molino," 134–36v.

[37] Hutchinson, "Sociocultural Change," p. 24.

tivity increased most dramatically. Merchants flocked to the community, bringing a varied stock of merchandise to increase the joy and solemnity of the occasion. Any peasant participating in the fiesta found it difficult to refuse what was offered, whether it was some coca or *aguardiente* (cane liquor) to share with his or her friends, or some candles to honor the saint. But the hardest hit was always the *mayordomo*. Given the poverty of local brotherhoods, the rent or products from *cofradía* properties were never enough to cover expenses, which included not only the religious aspects of the fiesta (processions, masses, wine, incense, candles, ornaments and clothes for the saint's image, and oil for ceremonial lamps), but also food, drink, and music for the entire community.[38] Even with careful planning, the *mayordomo*, and usually his relatives, *compadres*, and friends, ended the fiesta with a large debt. More often than not, the largest sums were owed to outsiders, especially to the priests and merchants. And the new *mayordomo*, elected a year in advance to help him plan for next year's celebration, returned home with the discomforting knowledge that, no matter how much he and his family managed to save, the coming year would bring economic hardship.[39]

While the local *cofradías* indebted peasants directly through their participation in a complex ritual calendar, the *cofradía* system as a whole affected them indirectly by promoting commercial agriculture in the villages and shrinking the overall pool of resources available to the peasant community. The larger, more prestigious town brotherhoods were powerful agricultural and commercial landlords, owning properties in the most fertile sections of the region's villages. Several of the *cofradías* in Jauja, in addition to owning the best stores in the town's central plaza, owned large, fertile fields and profitable grain mills in the neighboring Mantaro Valley communities of Huertas, Molinos, and Pancán.[40] The same organizations monopolized exten-

[38] For information on fiesta expenses and *cofradías*, see Archivo SINAMOS, Expediente 4366, 10–12; Hutchinson, "Sociocultural Change," pp. 24–25; Adams, *Community in the Andes*, pp. 54–57. For a comparison with Mexico, see Charles Gibson, *The Aztecs under Spanish Rule* (Stanford: Stanford University Press, 1964), pp. 127–35; and William B. Taylor, *Landlord and Peasant in Colonial Oaxaca* (Stanford: Stanford University Press, 1972), pp. 169–70.

[39] Hutchinson, "Sociocultural Change," p. 25.

[40] ANF, Protocolos Notariales, Manuel Víctor Morales, Book 1: July 20, 1864, 111v–12v; Book 3: July 14, 1868, 190–90v; Book 4: January 12, 1870, 140–41; Book 5: July 8, 1873, 217v–18; Book 6: April 6, 1875, 215–16; and ANF, Expedientes y Libros Judiciales, "Luis Y. Ibarra contra la Obra Pía del Carmen, sobre propiedad de los terrenos 'Putaj,' " began June 23, 1906.

sive tracts of land in the western part of the Yanamarca Valley,[41] where
the benign climate, the fertility of the soil, and the proximity of the
main commercial route to Oroya all combined to yield high rents. If
the lands were not rented out to Jauja merchants,[42] they were offered
to wealthier members of the area's communities, widening the gap
between rich and poor. And even if the *cofradías'* ownership of these
lands did not immediately affect the peasant's individual household
economy, it put important limits on a community's access to a diversified resource base and could, in the long run, help to upset the
balance between land and population.

The role of the parish priest in the community was also central to
the penetration of commercial capital. From the moment of birth to
the moment of death, it seemed, peasants were always handing money
to the priest, whether for baptism, marriages, funerals, or masses. If
a peasant did not have the money for these parochial services, the
priest was more than willing to officiate on credit, and charge later.
The level of peasant indebtedness to the priest often allowed the latter to accumulate lands in the parishes to which he was assigned.
Moreover, the prestige of being connected with the church facilitated
the priest's commercial and moneylending activities, both in the community and the regional economy as a whole.[43]

Beginning with the colonial period, therefore, the Catholic church
was an important spearhead of commercial capital in the peasant community. Through the *cofradía* system and the priests, the church indebted peasants, promoted commercial agriculture and market relations, and monopolized some of the best lands in the villages. But
church activities did not, by themselves, set into motion a process of
social and economic differentiation within the village. In the final
analysis, it was the very nature of the peasant household economy,
adapting and resisting through centuries of bad harvests and oscillat-
ing market conditions, that opened up the village to the incursions of
commercial capital.

[41] ANF, Protocolos Notariales, Luis Salazar, Book 19: January 13, 1909, 15–17v; Book
56: September 23, 1926, 1978v–1981v; Book 57: September 29, 1926, 2003v–2007;
Book 60: January 2, 1928, 1239–42; and Archivo SINAMOS, cc 239 (Tragadero), "Plano
de Conjunto levantado por Luis M. Gamio, 1937," in Expediente 10530, "Levantamiento del plano de la comunidad de Tragadero," began 1936.

[42] See, for example, ANF, Protocolos Notariales, Manuel Víctor Morales, Book 13:
February 1, 1888, 51–52; and March 19, 1888, 58v–60.

[43] For the priest's commercial activities, see ANF, Protocolos Notariales, Manuel
Víctor Morales, Book 9: April 21, 1881, 104v–105v; May 16, 1881, 109v–110v; May 26,
1881, 111v and inserts after 159; Book 10: October 7, 1882, 35v–37v; December 6,
1882, 66v–67v; March 18, 1883, 91v–92.

Over their several centuries of colonial experience, the peasants of the central highlands had developed a flexible family economy. This household economy was diversified enough to satisfy the majority of its subsistence needs, and also to sell a large enough surplus on the market to pay the merchants for fiestas and a few essential commodities, the priest for religious services, and government officials for tribute and taxes. But the system was also vulnerable, for every family sooner or later faced a financial emergency: a disastrous harvest, a death in the family, the obligation to become a *mayordomo* or godparent. Whatever the particulars of the individual case, the household had to find additional access to cash. And while these emergencies did not always result in the commercial penetration of the peasant community, there were many periods of economic expansion when merchants were eager to use peasant indebtedness to gain access to land and labor in the villages.

The eighteenth century was precisely that kind of period. Particularly in the second half of the century, when the regional economic revival was most pronounced, the participation of village peasants in the commercial economy seems to have increased markedly. The availability of work outside the community structure, particularly in mining and *arrieraje*, tended to break down the traditional patterns of village life. By 1791, for example, close to 40 percent of the central highland population was *mestizo*—one of the highest percentages in Peru, and almost twice the national average.[44]

There were also important changes in the internal structure of community politics. All during the century, the authority and prestige of the traditional leaders—the *kurakas* and *caciques*—declined steadily as the parallel system of *alcaldes* (mayors), which had its origins in the Spanish reforms of the sixteenth century, gradually increased in importance.[45] Since the *alcaldes* were more formally and intimately tied to the colonial bureaucracy, their growing power at the local level was a new potential wedge that colonial officials and their allies could use in their efforts to acquire labor and distribute goods within the

[44] Francisco Gil de Taboada y Lemos, *Memorias de los Virreyes* (Lima, 1859), Appendix, pp. 6–9.

[45] Adams, *Community in the Andes*, p. 47. Also, in a document of land conflicts between the communities of the Yanamarca Valley and the hacienda Yanamarca, the *ayllu* Allauca (later the community of Acolla) is represented by its *cacique*, don Melchor Julian Canchaya, in 1710. Yet, by 1791, the community of Acolla is represented by Ilario Ingaroca, *alcalde ordinario*. See "Hacienda Yanamarca vs. las comunidades Concho y Acolla, 1840–1842," Notarial copy of the original *expediente*, Moisés Ortega, personal archive, Acolla, 604v and 582v–83, respectively.

villages. And the decreasing influence of the *kurakas*, who despite the changes brought on by the colonial experience were still the only notables who could claim a part of their legitimacy directly through reference to Andean traditions, could not help but have a strong effect on village culture and solidarity.[46]

Changes in the social, economic, and cultural fabric of community life were mirrored by changes in the system of land tenure. Although evidence is sketchy, it seems that, between 1750 and 1820, both the percentage of privately owned lands, and the percentage of lands owned by *mestizos* or outsiders, increased dramatically in many villages. In Muquiyauyo, for example, a village on the Mantaro's western bank, the percentage of land owned by outsiders and *mestizos*, including *cofradía* lands, rose from 35 percent in 1742 to 66.5 percent in 1819.[47] The decline of the *kuraka* elite was also evident on the land. In 1774 Josefa Astocuri y Limaylla, descendant of two of the most important *kuraka* families in the central highlands, had her possessions auctioned off by the *corregidor* (local Spanish official). Among them was the hacienda Concepción de Layve, one of the largest and richest properties in the Mantaro Valley.[48]

The combined effects of commercial penetration and pressure on community lands cut deeply into the resources available within the peasant sector. There were also cases of hacienda expansion at the expense of neighboring communities.[49] Not surprisingly, the general result was a sharpening of both racial and class tensions in the region.[50] Yet despite these tendencies, the end result was not a decreasing viability of the peasant sector as a whole. As it turned out, the dramatic resilience of the central highland peasantry was due at least in part to the unique balance of power which obtained between the region's communities and haciendas.

[46] For the effect of colonization and colonialism on the *kurakas*, see Spalding, "Kurakas and Commerce," and Stern, *Peru's Indian Peoples*, pp. 30–44, 133–34, 174–75, and passim.

[47] Adams, *Community in the Andes*, pp. 19–22.

[48] AGN, Protocolos Notariales, Juan de Cubillas, Book 198, February 8, 1848, 601v–21v; and José de Felles, July 4, 1848, 109v–37.

[49] See, for example, "Hacienda Yanamarca vs. las comunidades Concho y Acolla," 568–83.

[50] Ibid., 575–76, includes an incident in 1790–1791 in which a meeting between representatives of the community of Acolla and the hacienda Yanamarca, set up to attempt to settle the boundary between the two, resulted in open conflict. The peasants attacked the government officials and took away the land titles belonging to the hacienda, and the officials were forced to beat a hasty and disorganized retreat. Although the dispute with the hacienda went on intermittently for over two centuries, this is the only case in which peasant reaction was so militant.

The Balance of Forces

In large portions of the central sierra, the hacienda developed much less of a territorial presence than it did in other parts of Peru. The reasons for this are still unclear. Some historians have pointed to the anti-Inca alliance the region's inhabitants (Huancas) developed with the Spanish during the conquest, arguing that afterwards this gave local *kurakas* the influence they needed to get a royal decree forbidding the formation of large estates out of communal lands.[51] Certainly it does seem true that the area's *kurakas* were particularly successful at getting what they wanted. In fact, some of the richest and most productive haciendas formed during the colonial period belonged to *kurakas* rather than Spaniards.[52] But as other scholars have pointed out, the notorious tendency among colonials to disregard decrees they found oppressive suggests that a simple law would not have been enough to safeguard Indian communities from incursion.[53] There must have been other explanations as well.

Another possibility is simply the ecology of the area, and the fact that valley lands were not easily adaptable to the extensive agricultural methods of the great estate. Given the high yields of land on the valley floors, it was sufficiently profitable to engage in intensive commercial agriculture on a relatively small scale. Rather than take on the labor and management problems of a large production unit, therefore, many Spaniards probably preferred to use valley lands as *chacras*, interspersing them with plots owned by peasants or Indian villages.[54] It was in the high *punas*, where the frigid, dry climate and easy adaptability to sheep raising made extensive methods of exploitation necessary, that the large estate could most easily flourish. And this argument seems to make sense if we survey landholding patterns in the central region as a whole. Cerro de Pasco and Tarma, provinces with larger areas of *puna*, also contained the largest number of haciendas.[55] In the Mantaro and Yanamarca Valleys, on the other hand,

[51] Waldemar Espinoza Soriano, *Enciclopedia Departamental de Junín* (Huancayo: Editorial San Fernando, 1974), I:169–73.

[52] See, for example, the inventory of properties belonging to the families Astocuri and Limaylla, in AGN, Protocolos Notariales, Juan de Cubillas, Book 198, February 8, 1848, 601v–21v; and José de Felles, July 4, 1848, 109v–37.

[53] Manrique, *El desarrollo del mercado interior*, pp. 71–73, especially p. 73.

[54] Espinoza Soriano, *Enciclopedia Departamental*, I:218–19, 223–24; ANF, Expedientes y Libros Judiciales, "Luis I. Ibarra contra la Obra Pía del Carmen, sobre propiedad de los terrenos 'Putaj,'" began June 23, 1906; and Adams, *Community in the Andes*, pp. 14–21.

[55] Manrique, *El desarrollo del mercado interior*, p. 3.

the concentration of haciendas was much weaker and those that did exist were also in the *puna*.[56]

But perhaps most crucial was the historical development of the balance of forces in the area. In the first century and a half after conquest it was the larger mining centers, such as Potosí and Huancavelica, and the important cities such as Lima and Cuzco, that attracted the richest and most powerful Spaniards. In the central highlands, even the mines of Cerro de Pasco did not develop until later.[57] Thus in the earlier years the Spanish settlers who arrived in the area tended to be smaller merchants, notaries, petty colonial officials, small-time officers in the military. With a few exceptions, they were generally content to share a smallholding pattern with Indian communities in the valleys, carving their *chacras* out of available public lands, buying plots from villages or *kurakas* in need of money, taking advantage of periodic redistribution of village lands carried out by the Crown.[58] The Huancas, moreover, a unified ethnic group with strong leaders, had an easy time containing such a weak challenge. Once conditions changed and other Spaniards became interested in the region, the strength of the peasant community in the Mantaro Valley had already been consolidated.

But whatever the specific causes, the end result was that a uniquely wealthy and viable peasant sector developed in the Mantaro and Yanamarca Valleys. Villages generally did not close themselves off from the rest of the world, but participated in the commercial economy from a position of strength. In addition to trading with others, communities also traded among themselves, and some artisanal specialities grew and flourished during the colonial era.[59] Ultimately, a dynamic and open economic style was a defense rather than a liability for the central sierra peasantry. Even as late as the 1870s, there were only forty haciendas in the Jauja and Huancayo regions combined, while less than a quarter of the area's population lived on the large estates.[60]

It is hardly surprising, then, that attempts by regional entrepreneurs to extract labor from the peasant sector in the eighteenth and early nineteenth centuries should have met with such strong resist-

[56] Ibid., pp. 3–4.
[57] Cerro de Pasco began to be exploited only after 1630. See Fisher, *Minas y mineros*, p. 32.
[58] Espinoza Soriano, *Enciclopedia Departamental*, I:207; Adams, *Community in the Andes*, pp. 14–20.
[59] Espinoza Soriano, *Enciclopedia Departamental*, I:204–207.
[60] Manrique, *El desarrollo del mercado interior*, pp. 3 and 6.

ance. Deeply embedded in a healthy subsistence economy and part of a strong community life, few peasants had the need or the desire to sell their labor voluntarily. The most successful forms of labor acquisition were those that relied on state violence, or used already existing market networks to indebt peasants and then force them to work off their debts in mines or on haciendas. Yet as the events of the next century would show, these methods were agonizingly slow and only partially effective. Unless it was possible truly to cut off the peasantry's subsistence base, the central sierra community would continue to be a thorn in the side of commercial production and economic transformation.

CHAPTER TWO

The Background of Change and Conflict, 1780–1879

And whither this process of dissolution will lead, in other words, what new mode of production will replace the old, does not depend on commerce, but on the character of the old mode of production itself.[1]

In the second half of the eighteenth century, a new group of mine-owners and merchants began to profit from the commercial and mining boom in the central highlands and rose to challenge the dominance of the colonial landowning class. Chafing under the limitations of the colonial system of privilege and monopolies, they supported the move toward independence. Once the wars were over, this new group's ambitions were realized when it became possible to buy up haciendas, at a fraction of their original cost, from a colonial elite facing economic ruin. Yet during the first half of the nineteenth century, the new elite's efforts at revitalizing production proved fruitless.

The main problem was that the new regional elite, though eager to break the monopoly of the colonial landowners, had not been interested in modifying the social relations under which goods were produced. Their principal goal had been to facilitate the circulation of land, particularly the coveted great estates of the *puna*. Rather than setting labor free along with land, however, the new *hacendados* simply inherited a precapitalist regional economy in which access to labor was still predicated on extra-economic compulsion. And in the post-independence period of political and economic stagnation, neither old nor new forms of compulsion seemed to work very well.

Only when the guano boom ushered in a new period of economic prosperity and political consolidation at the national level did the trend toward stagnation in the central region reverse itself. From the 1860s, a boom in commercial livestock and *aguardiente* production began to change the face of the central sierra economy. Merchants and landowners developed an intricate system of patron-client relations in or-

---

[1] Karl Marx, *Capital* (New York: International Publishers, 1967), III: 332.

der to gain access to labor markets in the area's villages. Through various methods, commercial capital made inroads into the peasant economy.

But no amount of prosperity changed the fact that social relations remained precapitalist. Because labor was still bound up in a viable subsistence economy, peasant resistance to commercial penetration and labor acquisition remained strong. Beyond a certain point, efforts at commercial expansion came up against a recalcitrant and autonomous village sector. Through the 1870s, therefore, and despite important advances, elite hegemony in the region remained relatively weak and circumscribed.

The Emergence of a New Elite, 1780–1830

With the loss of Potosí to the Viceroyalty of the Río de la Plata in 1776, the mines in the central highlands, particularly those in Cerro de Pasco and Huarochirí, became the most important in the Peruvian Viceroyalty.[2] Between 1777 and 1824, registered silver production at Pasco accounted for an average of 40 percent of Peruvian production.[3] Registered output in the Pasco mines rose from 100,000 to 250,000 *marcos* (approximately eight ounces each) between 1770 and 1790, and did not fall again until 1812 when technical problems forced a number of mines to close down.[4] And while production in Pasco would never rival output in Potosí or New Spain, the relative prosperity of mining in the central highlands had several important effects on the regional society and economy.

Within the mining sector itself, this prosperity was in part generated by the creation of the Tribunal de Minería in 1786. Associated with the Bourbon Reforms, the Tribunal was a mining association that, in return for a registration fee, provided mineowners throughout the Viceroyalty with access to credit and new technological information. Its purpose was to revive the mining industry and tie it more closely to the colonial state. But for mineowners in the central highlands, the Tribunal was most important because it opened up new possibilities for investment.[5]

Since the beginning of the eighteenth century, the exhaustion of

---

[2] John Fisher, "Silver Production in the Viceroyalty of Peru, 1776–1824," *Hispanic American Historical Review*, 55: 1 (February 1975), 25–44, and *Minas y mineros en el Perú colonial, 1776–1824* (Lima: Instituto de Estudios Peruanos, 1977).

[3] Fisher, *Minas y mineros*, p. 217.

[4] Ibid., pp. 215–16.

[5] For a background on the colonial reforms leading up to the creation of the Tribunal, as well as some of the rationale behind it, see ibid., pp. 51–69.

the rich, superficial ore deposits in the Pasco area had led to deeper and deeper excavations, and many of the mines had begun to flood. Although several mineowners in the area had attempted their own primitive solutions, such as bailing or manual pumps, the only effective method was to dig a drainage tunnel below the level of the mine shafts. But the minimum investment needed to construct such a tunnel was too high for most mineowners. Indeed, only two short drainage systems had been completed: the first in 1760 by José Maíz, who had acquired several mines in Yauricocha only a few years before; and the second in 1786 by a group of fifty local miners.[6] Thus, when in 1797 the Tribunal de Minería took over the financing for an extension of the second drainage tunnel to service a number of different mines, the benefits which accrued to the industry were quite substantial. In fact, it was the building of this tunnel, known as the Socavón de Yanacancha, that allowed silver production in Pasco to maintain such a high level through 1810, when excavations once again began to reach the water table.[7]

But even more important than financing the Socavón were the credit possibilities that the Tribunal offered individual mineowners. As we have seen, the majority of owners in the central sierra ran small to medium-sized operations and, because they did not have good connections with the mercantile elite in Lima, encountered substantial difficulties in financing their enterprises.[8] Having to rely on high-interest, short-term loans from local merchants, they faced a constant struggle against indebtedness.[9] The loans available from the Tribunal, therefore, allowed the smaller entrepreneurs to keep their businesses solvent and facilitated new investments. Miguel de Iriarte, for example, owner of three mineral haciendas in Huarochirí, borrowed 12,000 pesos at 4 percent interest for three years in order to exploit the mercury deposits he had recently discovered in that area.[10] And although Iriarte's initial venture was unsuccessful, his sons were subsequently able to pay off the debt with revenue from the three mineral haciendas they inherited from their father, and even invest further profits in the purchase of land.[11]

The mining boom also contributed to an increase in commerce and

[6] For a description of the relationship between drainage and production, see ibid., pp. 223–24.
[7] For a short history of the Socavón de Yanacancha, see ibid., pp. 224–27.
[8] Ibid., pp. 77–79.
[9] Ibid., pp. 46–47.
[10] Ibid., pp. 97, 164.
[11] AGN, Protocolos Notariales, Ignacio Ayllón Salazar, Book 37, August 25, 1821, 712v–18v.

commercial activity. As demand for numerous products expanded in the mining centers, many merchants and *arrieros*, large and small, Spanish, creole and *mestizo*, were able to make substantial profits. Thus commerce, like mining, became a source of accumulation for new entrepreneurs in this period.

One of the most successful merchants was Francisco de Paula Otero. Born in what is today the Argentine province of Jujuy, Otero became involved in the commercial traffic around Potosí and later moved into the central highlands, both as a merchant and an *arriero*. By 1817, he had settled in Tarma and married Petronila Abeleyra, daughter of a mining family. Well integrated into both the commercial and mining sectors, Otero was, by the time of independence, an affluent citizen.[12] Yet by no stretch of the imagination was he a member of the colonial elite. Like others who had followed a similar path, Otero was an upstart who, through a combination of shrewd investments and careful marriage, was able to establish a position for himself within the regional economy.

Between 1780 and 1820, then, the mining and commercial boom in the central highlands resulted in the emergence of a newly prosperous intermediate stratum of mineowners and merchants. Some of them, such as Otero, were migrants from other parts of Spanish America. Some were part of the increasing stream of relatively humble immigrants from Northern Spain.[13] Others were fairly modest *mestizos* or creoles from the area's towns and villages.[14] No matter what their origin, these entrepreneurs had one main thing in common: they had started with very little, whether in money or influence, and had built up their fortunes on the basis of skill and technical experience. As Pedro Iriarte explained in 1821, "When I married the said doña Paula de Odría, I did not take to the marriage more wealth than my knowledge of Mineralogy."[15] But by the time he dictated his last will and

---

[12] For information on Otero, see Raúl Rivera Serna, *Los guerrilleros del centro en la emancipación peruana* (Lima: Edición Talleres Gráficos Villanueva, S.A., 1958), pp. 139–41. On the Abeleyra family's mining connections, see AGN, Protocolos Notariales, Baltazar Núñez del Prado, Book 461, November 14, 1843, 504v–507v; José Benito Ylláñez, Book 284, July 23, 1852, 149v–50v; and Francisco Palacios, Book 570, July 20, 1867, 788–97v, and Book 572, February 24, 1869, 199v–202.

[13] John Lynch, *The Spanish-American Revolutions, 1808–1826* (New York: W. W. Norton and Co., 1973), p. 17; AGN, Protocolos Notariales, Juan Cosío, Book 155, June 1820; Juan Antonio Menéndez, Book 416, September 19, 1834, 281–82.

[14] AGN, Protocolos Notariales, Ignacio Ayllón Salazar, Book 37, August 25, 1821, 712v–18v; Ignacio Ayllón Salazar, Book 5, August 1804, "Venta Tierras Apaguay"; Juan Cosío, Book 155, November 1819, 161v–63.

[15] AGN, Protocolos Notariales, Ignacio Ayllón Salazar, Book 37, August 25, 1821, 714.

testament, Iriarte owned several important mining properties and two haciendas.[16]

Precisely because the new entrepreneurs were not members of the established colonial elite, there were definite limits to how far their accumulation could go within the existing system. Since colonial commerce and production operated through the establishment of monopolies and spheres of influence, the recently emerging provincial stratum, neither titled nobility nor members of the bureaucratic and commercial elite close to the viceregal court, had difficulty in gaining admittance to the inner circles of the colonial economy.[17] Thus, although the prosperity of mining and commerce made possible the rise of a new intermediate elite in the late eighteenth century, the system of colonial privilege prevented them from cementing their position. As their acquisition of wealth in an expanding economy brought the new entrepreneurs into increasingly direct conflict with powerful elite patrons, the new group's standing in society remained uncertain.

Nowhere was this uncertainty more apparent than in agriculture. Given the importance of the great estate as a source of prestige and economic security, few landowners were willing to sell. With a few notable exceptions, therefore, the intermediate provincial elite was unable to gain a significant foothold in the hacienda sector.[18] Instead, some provincials managed to rent haciendas on a short-term basis.[19] Yet renting a property was a poor substitute for outright ownership. Most haciendas, while extremely large, were often poorly maintained, with low quality livestock and little in the way of irrigation or other improvements. If an entrepreneur wanted to expand production for the market, he or she usually had to make a substantial initial invest-

---

[16] Ibid., 714v–16.

[17] Fisher, *Minas y mineros*, pp. 78–79. According to Fisher, of all the mineowners registered in 1790, only two had titles of nobility. One, the Marquesa de Villa Rica, had acquired her title through her father-in-law who, despite his status as an illegitimate son, had bought the title from the Crown in 1703. The other miner, José Maíz, had inherited the title of Marqués de la Real Confianza from his father, who had been granted it in 1771 because he paid for his mercury on time.

[18] The two exceptions I have been able to find are Manuel del Rivero, a Spanish colonel who owned the haciendas Punto and Aychama, and Pedro de Iriarte, who bought the haciendas Cónsac and Lovatón. Yet in the first case, the properties were auctioned off to cover debts from the mule trade (AGN, Protocolos Notariales, Juan Cosío, Book 155, June 1820), and in the second case, Iriarte bought the properties in conjunction with his mother-in-law, Manuela Granados (AGN, Protocolos Notariales, Ignacio Ayllón Salazar, Book 37, August 25, 1821, 715–15v).

[19] AGN, Protocolos Notariales, Baltazar Núñez del Prado, Book 454, August 1833, 153–56; José de Felles, Book 239, July 4, 1848, 117; Juan Cosío, Book 155, November 1819, 161v–63.

ment. Given the format of most contracts, however, it was difficult to demand reimbursement for improvements.[20] Thus tenants risked the loss of their investment if they decided to expand their profits on rented properties.

By the first two decades of the nineteenth century, the new commercial and mining group in the central highlands had begun to test the limits of what was permissible within the existing colonial system. Faced with a traditional elite whose interests were better served by maintaining the existing distribution of land and power than by opening the door to innovation, these miners and merchants chafed under a colonial system that prevented them from realizing the profits they felt were rightly theirs, and from investing freely in all sectors of the economy. Like their counterparts in other regions of Latin America, they were ready for change. Their willingness to work actively for that change depended, however, on whether or not they considered themselves capable of successfully mobilizing and controlling the lower classes.[21]

In Peru as a whole, the central sierra was not the only region where a combined boom in mining and commerce had generated a new group of entrepreneurs who, eager to increase their profits further, wished to break the colonial monopoly. Between 1780 and 1820, these new merchants, arrieros, and mineowners participated actively in a series of uprisings against the colonial administration in Arequipa, Cuzco, and Huánuco. But in every case, what allowed the conservative colonial elite to prevail over this group was their common fear of the lower classes.[22] Throughout the eighteenth century, and culminating in the rebellion of Túpac Amaru in 1780, the Peruvian Viceroyalty had witnessed a number of Indian rebellions against increased exploitation through taxes, commercial penetration, and the repartimientos de

---

[20] In 1837, for example, Pablo Guerra, tenant on the hacienda Tucle, protested at its being up for auction without his investment in improvements being taken into account. AGN, Protocolos Notariales, Francisco de Paula Casós, Book 144, October 2, 1837, 72–72v.

[21] For one of the first formulations of this point for Peru, see Heraclio Bonilla and Karen Spalding (eds.), La independencia en el Perú (Lima: Instituto de Estudios Peruanos, 1972). For an overview of how lower-class reactions affected the strategy of the elite in other independence struggles, see Lynch, The Spanish-American Revolutions, passim. For the specific case of Haiti, see C.L.R. James, The Black Jacobins: Toussaint L'Ouverture and the San Domingo Revolution (New York: Vintage Books, 1963).

[22] Heraclio Bonilla and Karen Spalding, "La independencia en el Perú: las palabras y los hechos," in Bonilla and Spalding (eds.), La independencia en el Perú, pp. 15–64; Alberto Flores Galindo, "Túpac Amaru y la sublevación de 1780," in Alberto Flores Galindo (ed.), Túpac Amaru II: 1780 (Lima: Ediciones Retablo de Papel, 1976), pp. 305–10.

mercancías.[23] Twice during the century, first with the rebellion of Juan Santos Atahualpa in the central highlands in 1742 and again with Túpac Amaru in 1780, the rebellions were widespread and threatened to become social revolutions. And while the fear of social revolution was a common one across the Latin American continent, which was still in the shadow of the Haitian experience, Peru was one of the places where actual events had given the "great fear" a special immediacy. Again and again, the enthusiastic participation of poor Indians and *mestizos* in the provincial uprisings called forth images of social upheaval, and pushed the new entrepreneurial elites back into the conservative camp.[24]

The central sierra was different because, in contrast to other parts of the Viceroyalty, elite control was firm in the last decades of the eighteenth century due to the impressive network of strategic military forts built in response to the uprising of Juan Santos Atahualpa.[25] The rebellion of Juan Santos, which strongly challenged the colonial state's control over the central jungle region, had begun as a messianic movement in the 1740s. Initially an anticolonial movement that united jungle Indians of the Campa tribe against the recent encroachments of European and creole colonizers, the Juan Santos rebellion soon found allies in the highlands. By 1743, several contemporary sources agreed that a substantial number of highland people had migrated to the jungle to take part in the uprising. Then, in 1750, three separate conspiracies broke out in Canta, Huarochirí, and Lambayeque. Although these rebellions were rapidly put down, the colonial government stationed five companies of soldiers in the central highlands, particularly around Jauja and Tarma. When the rebels attempted to take Andamarca in 1752, Spanish soldiers converged on the town from San Gerónimo, Palca, Matahuasi, Comas, Jauja, Huancayo, Ocopa, and Tarma.[26]

In addition to driving missionaries and merchants out of Campa

[23] Scarlett O'Phelan, "Túpac Amaru y las sublevaciones del siglo XVIII," in Flores Galindo (ed.), *Túpac Amaru II*, pp. 68–81.

[24] Bonilla and Spalding, "La independencia," especially pp. 45–46 and 49–51; Pierre Vilar, "La participación de las clases populares en los movimientos de independencia de América Latina," in Bonilla and Spalding (eds.), *La independencia*, pp. 155–74.

[25] Until recently, it was thought that no rebellions had occurred in the central highlands during the 1780s. Steve J. Stern, however, has recently discovered documentation in the Archivo General de la Nación which points to two conspiracies or rebellions in the Mantaro Valley, one in 1780 and another in 1781. Though a detailed analysis of these events must await his forthcoming work on the subject, it seems fair to say that both conspiracies were repressed rather quickly, at least in part due to the network of forts built in the area during the rebellion of Juan Santos Atahualpa.

[26] This account of the Juan Santos Atahualpa rebellion is drawn from Stéfano Varese, *La sal de los cerros* (Lima: Ediciones Retablo de Papel, 1973), pp. 170–203.

territory, therefore, the Atahualpa rebellion succeeded in turning the central highlands into an armed camp. Only in 1788, close to fifty years after the movement began, did the first tentative exploration penetrate into Chanchamayo. For eighty years after that, all jungle outposts would be heavily fortified and militarized.[27] Yet ironically enough, this militarization would also allow the emerging commercial and mining elite to act on their dissatisfactions with the colonial system. Secure in their ability to control the lower classes, the new entrepreneurs in the central highlands organized a series of guerrilla bands, providing the only substantial pocket of Peruvian support for independence.

When General Juan Antonio Alvarez de Arenales, one of the commanding officers of San Martín's Army of the South, created an insurgent government in Tarma in 1820, he named Francisco de Paula Otero, one of the most prominent members of the new entrepreneurial group, governor of the recently "liberated" area. As one of the earliest and most prestigious defenders of independence, Otero held this post throughout San Martín's stay in Peru, and became general commander of the central region's guerrilla forces under Bolívar. At the end of the war, he was named governor of Arequipa, where he helped consolidate the Republic. When he finally retired, Otero returned to Tarma where, in the company of his wife and children, he enjoyed the new properties and wealth that independence had allowed him to acquire.[28]

Although Otero was uniquely successful in his bid for political power, there were numerous local entrepreneurs who distinguished themselves in the Wars of Independence. Custodio Alvarez, a Spanish mineowner and merchant in Yauricocha, organized guerrilla bands in Cerro de Pasco and Huánuco.[29] Antonio Aliaga, Rafael and Manuel de Cevallos, and Juan Evangelista Vivas, all creoles from the area, participated actively in the guerrilla campaign.[30] Inocencio Artica, prosperous *mestizo* and renter of one of the area's haciendas, organized a guerrilla band in his home village of Chacapalpa.[31] And no matter how varied their cultural, national, and racial backgrounds, all

[27] Ibid., p. 207.
[28] Rivera Serna, *Los guerrilleros del centro*, pp. 139–41: Comisión Nacional del Sesquicentenario de la Independencia del Perú, *Colección documental de la independencia del Perú* (hereafter CDIP), Tomo 5, Vol. 1 (Lima, 1971): 86–87, and Vol. 3 (Lima, 1972): 105, 111, and passim.
[29] Rivera Serna, *Los guerrilleros del centro*, pp. 48 and 54.
[30] Ibid., pp. 57, 60–61.
[31] CDIP, Tomo 5, 3: 24–25; AGN, Protocolos Notariales, Juan Cosío, Book 155, November 1819, 161v–63.

these participants had one thing in common. They were part of an upwardly mobile, innovative group of entrepreneurs who, unable to break into the traditional elite, wished to break down the system of colonial monopolies.

Throughout the Wars of Independence in Peru, from San Martín's first landing in September 1820 to the final battle at Ayacucho in December of 1824, the central sierra was one of the main centers of operations for both the Royalist and *patriota* (rebel) armies. An important reason for this was, of course, the existence of a comparatively strong *patriota* movement in the area. But the central sierra was also an ideal headquarters for an army, both strategically and economically. The existence of a strong and solvent agricultural economy, within both the Indian villages and the haciendas, could provide soldiers with food, mules, and horses. The commercial and mining sectors constituted a wide base for revenue, at least initially. The large number of *arrieros* could easily transport military goods and serve as spies. And perhaps most important, the nature of the terrain and the limited number of mountain passes facilitated the defense of the area and allowed guerrilla bands to make incursions almost to the very doors of Lima without being discovered.

But the constant presence and exactions of both armies tended to erode the already fragile alliance between local *patriotas* and the region's lower classes. Almost from the beginning of the conflict, the leaders of the independence movement had been aware of how important this alliance was. Among the first things that Arenales did on his initial visit to the sierra, for example, was to abolish Indian tribute.[32] Yet the *patriota* leaders clearly understood that the success or failure of their bid for support did not lie in decrees, but in the actual quality of the relationship that the guerrilla bands established with the local population. In this sense, the presence of a prosperous *mestizo* sector among those supporting independence undoubtedly helped to mediate relations with the peasant community.[33] No amount of mediation, however, could change the fact that, despite their calls for support and their repeated assurances that they were fighting for the freedom of all people, the *patriotas* were scarcely more committed to the fate of the lower classes than were the Royalists.

[32] CDIP, Tomo 5, 1: 86–87.

[33] The most notable case of this was Inocencio Artica. In his community of Chacapalpa, patriotic sentiment existed to the point that, when the town was burned by the Royalists in February 1822, three villagers—Miguel Artica, Paula Huamán, and Eufrasia Ramos—were executed as *patriotas* after their tongues had been cut out. Rivera Serna, *Los guerrilleros del centro*, p. 128.

Although they were deeply dissatisfied with the colonial system, in class terms the insurgents had a great deal more in common with the colonial elite than with the peasants, Indians, and poor *mestizos* that made up the overwhelming majority of the central highland population. Interested in eliminating the restrictions placed on their accumulation of property and profit by the system of colonial monopolies, the *patriota* leaders did not need or want to promote profound social change. Insofar as they needed the support of the lower classes for soldiers, horses, supplies, and revenues, or as long as they saw the reforms as part of their effort to open up the economy, they were willing to abolish tribute and forced labor. But these piecemeal efforts did not change the fact that the War of Independence was an elite battle fought by taxing and conscripting Indians, peasants, and poor *mestizos*.[34]

It is therefore not surprising that many central highland peasants saw little difference between *patriotas* and Royalists. Some took advantage of the confusion produced by battle to invade haciendas and take the cattle for their own use, whether or not the property was under *patriota* control.[35] Others were happy to serve either side, as long as their customary patterns of work were not greatly disturbed.[36] Most communities, forced to face raid after raid, exaction after exaction, found it ever more difficult to survive. And the insurgent leaders, unable to resist the pressure of the Royalist army, abandoned many towns to be burned.[37]

Throughout the confusion, the peasants continued to serve as the base for a struggle from which they derived no benefit. Only in 1824 was Simón Bolívar finally able to take definitive political and military control of Peruvian territory[38] and, on December 8th of that year, two peasant armies consummated Peruvian independence in a relatively bloodless battle on the plains of Ayacucho.[39] As a reward for their sacrifices, the peasants of Peru would have the dubious distinction of being taxed by the Republic. The successful elite guerrillas, on the other hand, would realize their ambitions for additional wealth and

---

[34] A variant of this argument was first advanced in Bonilla and Spalding (eds.), *La independencia*, especially Bonilla and Spalding, "La independencia," pp. 15–64, and Vilar, "La participación," pp. 155–74.

[35] See, for example, CDIP, Tomo 5, 1: 203, 231.

[36] CDIP, Tomo 5, 1: 243–45; 282–83.

[37] See, for example, the case of Ramón Morales and the village of Comas, CDIP, Tomo 5, 1: 451–55.

[38] Lynch, *The Spanish-American Revolutions*, p. 269.

[39] Ibid., pp. 271–72.

power by buying out the traditional elite whose properties had been ravaged by the war.

After Independence: New Conditions for Accumulation and Resistance

Throughout the first decades after independence, *patriota* leaders and soldiers took advantage of the low prices and economic devastation brought on by the war to buy up properties. In August 1833, for example, Francisco de Paula Otero bought the hacienda Cachicachi, originally valued at 30,000 pesos, for 12,500. As a merchant who had previously rented the estate explained, since it was located on the commercial route between Jauja and Tarma,

> not only did both armies take whatever livestock was pasturing there, but even the rooms and chapel were left completely destroyed, and thus the property has no other production than its natural pastures, and to make it productive it is necessary to replace the stolen livestock with some capital.[40]

To make it productive was exactly what Otero proposed to do, and in the years after the purchase he made a series of investments precisely toward that end.[41] Unable to enter the circle of the colonial elite before independence, he was more than eager to make up for lost time.

As is borne out by the example of Otero, political influence on the *patriota* side during the war tended to facilitate the consolidation of a fortune in the years immediately afterward. In December 1830, Custodio Alvarez, Otero's *compadre* and leader of several guerrilla bands, bought the livestock hacienda Cacaracra and Huamancaca, located in Tarma, from another owner ruined by the wars.[42] In 1837 Manuel de Cevallos and Miguel Ugarte, both active in the guerrilla effort, bid against each other at the auction of the haciendas Tucle and Huancatana, located on the west bank of the Mantaro River and

---

[40] AGN, Protocolos Notariales, Baltazar Núñez del Prado, August 1833, 153–56.

[41] The results of these investments can be seen clearly in the rental contract on the same property carried out by Otero's descendants three decades later. See AGN, Protocolos Notariales, Francisco Palacios, Book 570, July 20, 1867, 788–97v.

[42] The fact that Otero and Alvarez were *compadres* is borne out by Rivera Serna, *Los guerrilleros del centro*, p. 109; and CDIP, Tomo 5, 3: 29, 32, and passim. The contract on the hacienda can be found in AGN, Protocolos Notariales, José Simeón Ayllón Salazar, Book 60, December 1830.

belonging to the will of the late Countess of San Antonio.[43] Yet social and political influence were no longer the sole criteria in the purchase of landed property, for it was two relatively unknown figures, Juan de Dios and Manuel Valladares, who carried out the most impressive accumulation of all.

The Valladares brothers began as residents of Cerro de Pasco.[44] Although Manuel apparently served as a *granadero* in the insurgent army during the Wars of Independence,[45] neither brother occupied a prominent position within the *patriota* forces. Nevertheless, in 1848 Juan de Dios bought the hacienda San Agustín de Quiracan, on the plains of Bombón to the south of Cerro de Pasco.[46] Four years later, Manuel bought the hacienda Laive from Manuel Salazar y Baquíjano, descendant of the Countess of Vista Florida.[47] While the connection between the sales and the economic ruin caused by the war was clear in both cases, it was particularly dramatic in the case of Laive. As Salazar y Baquíjano explained in the contract,

> The property has suffered almost complete ruin due to the wars of Independence . . . in its capital composed of livestock, tools and other assets, and has been reduced to nothing, or its mere shell, to the extreme that before it could be rented for two to three thousand pesos a year, whereas after the war of Independence aforesaid, I can only manage to rent it to Juan de Dios Valladares, brother of the buyer, for the contemptible sum of five hundred pesos per year, and having to pay for improvements.[48]

Manuel Valladares was therefore able to buy the hacienda for a mere 20,000 pesos, which was only the price of the land itself. In return, he received a huge property which, it was rumored, would support up to forty thousand head of sheep after some investment.[49]

But Manuel Valladares did not stop there. In the next twenty years he bought, among other properties, the haciendas Cónoc, Chamise-

---

[43] The fact that Manuel de Cevallos was active in the guerrillas is mentioned in Rivera Serna, *Los guerrilleros del centro*, pp. 60–61, and CDIP, Tomo 5, 3: 259, 285. Miguel Ugarte is mentioned in CDIP, Tomo 5, 3: 238, as being on the insurgent side. The contract is in AGN, Protocolos Notariales, Francisco de Paula Casós, Book 144, October 2, 1837, 55–73.

[44] AGN, Protocolos Notariales, José de Selaya, Book 703, March 4, 1844, 199–99v.

[45] CDIP, Tomo 5, 4: 431. A *granadero* is a soldier belonging to a special unit, or elite company, of the army.

[46] AGN, Protocolos Notariales, José de Selaya, Book 703, March 3, 1844, 109–97v.

[47] AGN, Protocolos Notariales, José de Felles, Book 239, July 4, 1848, 109v–37.

[48] Ibid., 111v.

[49] Ibid.

rías, Jajarma, and Runatullo (some of the largest and best known in the area), and stocked them with large herds of livestock. When he died in 1867, he left to his successors one of the largest fortunes in the central highlands.[50] As his wife Josefa Ramos, a barely literate, self-made woman from the peasant village of Mito, was to comment in her will several decades later, it was during the time of their marriage that "we acquired all the assets included in the inventories that were done at the time of my husband's death."[51]

At least in the central highlands, then, independence from Spain allowed a new elite to take control of the regional economy. Despite dramatic advances, however, the new entrepreneurs were unable fully to cement their position in the first half of the nineteenth century. Politically, events on the coast and the generally chaotic situation throughout Peruvian territory did not allow the recently formed *hacendado* class in the central sierra to establish complete control. Against the backdrop of a ruined economy, elite factions from several regions struggled to gain control of the state apparatus in Lima, and no single group was able to secure a lasting position of authority.[52] Thus Peru witnessed a series of battles between caudillos, each of whom found it necessary to search out a base of support in the highlands before descending on the presidential palace.[53] In the final analysis, without the backing of a centralized and effective state, the regional elite could not establish the political institutions it needed to consolidate its hold over the local population.

For there were related economic problems. Within the villages, the depression brought on by the war encouraged peasants to revert to subsistence. Thus, although in the late 1820s the Bolivarian decrees transformed individually distributed community lands into private property and helped to consolidate the gains made by *mestizos* and outsiders in the decades immediately before independence, the depression tended to reverse the advances made by commercial capital within the peasant economy itself. As a result, the central sierra elite faced both a shortage of labor and a lack of infrastructure to support the revival of trade and commercial production.

[50] AGN, Protocolos Notariales, José Ramón Valdivia, Book 994, June 11, 1886, 100–102.

[51] Ibid., 100v.

[52] Lynch, *The Spanish-American Revolutions*, pp. 272–74; Frederick B. Pike, *The Modern History of Peru* (New York: Frederick A. Praeger Publishers, 1967), pp. 64–71; Flora Tristán, *Peregrinaciones de una paria* (Lima: Moncloa-Campodónico Editores, 1971), especially pp. 291–368.

[53] Pike, *Modern History*, pp. 64–90.

In the case of the labor supply, since peasants had access to land, animals, and other means of production, the elite had difficulty in making them work outside their communities. Aside from direct compulsion, which became increasingly ineffective from the end of the eighteenth century, the only other way to force peasants to work outside their villages was by creating in them a need for money or products that could not be fulfilled within the confines of the community. Certainly this was one of the purposes of the Indian head tax, or tribute, which, although it had been abolished by San Martín in 1821 and again by Bolívar in 1824, was reinstated in 1826 under the name of *contribución de indígenas*.[54] Yet even if we make no allowance for the level of economic depression or the ineffectiveness of the collection system, the *contribución* alone could hardly have created a large enough need for money among peasants to supply the regional elite with the quantity of labor necessary to revive the regional economy. The entrepreneurs were therefore left with three choices: take away the land, leaving the peasants no alternative but to sell their labor "voluntarily"; increase commodity circulation within the village to the point where peasants not only developed a need for certain commodities they could not produce, but also owed money to merchants and had to seek part-time employment elsewhere to pay off their debts; or bring in laborers from outside the area. Given the economic strength and internal solidarity of the central highland village, the first alternative was clearly impossible in the short run; the second was only viable under conditions of economic revival; and the third, as is clear from the case of Carlos Renardo Pflücker, proved to be more trouble than it was worth.

In the 1840s Carlos Pflücker, mineowner in Morococha, attempted to put together a copper mining company. Unable to attract sufficient workers in the central highlands, he decided to import labor from Germany. As it turned out, the German workers mutinied, causing a considerable scandal in Lima.[55] But labor in the mines was only the first of Pflücker's problems.

Once the minerals were extracted, Pflücker found the local peasantry unwilling to provide even the most minimal infrastructural support for the transportation of the ores. Though he advanced money to

[54] For San Martín's abolition of tribute, see ibid. For Bolívar's abolition of tribute and its subsequent reinstatement, see ibid., p. 277.

[55] For the entire story of Pflücker's experiment with German labor, see *Exposición que presenta Carlos Renardo Pflücker al Supremo Gobierno con motivo de las últimas ocurrencias acaecidas en la hacienda mineral de Morococha* (Lima: Imprenta del Correo Peruano, 1846), pp. 6–9, 15–16, and passim.

peasant *arrieros* in an effort to assure the movement of mineral, he apparently lost much of it because village muledrivers were undependable, or because they ended up being victims of the innumerable requisitions of animals carried out during the many civil wars of the period.[56] Not only did local *arrieros* often refuse to make the trip to Lima, but peasants also resisted growing the commercial crops necessary for the mule trade. "Even he who passes through this valley exclusively for pleasure," Pflücker complained,

> cannot help but feel amazed and aghast when he sees the huge tracts of land without cultivation, while from one town to the next the only voice he hears is—"there is no pasture"—and it is necessary to be in charge of a pack of mules to understand the horror invoked by that voice.[57]

It was only through concerted and protracted efforts, which included the distribution of seed to the villages with promises, threats, and cajoling, that some alfalfa was planted in fields near Morococha.[58] But this was an expensive, frustrating, and, most importantly, piecemeal way to overcome peasant resistance. Even if other entrepreneurs also used it, this method could not lead to a general revival of the regional economy.

In the final analysis, we can only explain the regional elite's inability to break through the barrier of peasant resistance by pointing to major contradictions within the independence movement itself. Though the emerging provincial elite that spearheaded the Peruvian *patriota* movement was certainly dynamic, innovative, and at odds with the colonial system, it had neither the political power nor the social motivation to carry out major economic or social transformations. Increasingly motivated by the expanding industrial market in England to intensify production of raw materials, particularly minerals and wool, the new miner-*hacendados* did not change the social relations through which these commodities were produced. Instead they attempted to intensify the extraction of surplus from peasants with access to the means of production, and found that they could not coax the small producers out of the subsistence economy into which they had retired after independence. Only in the 1860s would a series of factors external to the region create the conditions necessary for a new commercial boom in the central highlands. Even then it was clear that, as long as

[56] Ibid., p. 9.
[57] Ibid., p. 11.
[58] Ibid.

peasants had significant access to land and other means of production in their communities, their resistance would continue to keep the elite from fully realizing its goal in production and commerce.[59]

Economic and Political Consolidation, 1860–1879

When the elite in the central sierra attempted a new revival of the regional economy in the 1860s and 1870s, it did so in response to tendencies at the national level. As the guano boom generated new revenues and higher levels of economic activity, prices began to rise on the Lima market. In response to this, *hacendados* in the central sierra initiated an expansion and rationalization of production, sending increasing quantities of wool, meat, and butter to the capital. On the heels of military expeditions that reconquered the region's eastern subtropical lands from the rebellious Campa Indians, colonists hastened to carve out new haciendas and supply local markets with *aguardiente*. Though the mining sector as a whole continued to stagnate, every now and then the discovery of a rich vein of silver would bring windfall profits, and an entire city would be transformed by an influx of people eager to take advantage of the new opportunities. By diversifying their holdings among the three productive sectors—mining, livestock, and subtropical agriculture—the regional elite succeeded in developing an investment structure that was reasonably impervious to the inevitable fluctuations in profitability.

Diversification, then, was a form of insurance. Despite the impressive accumulations of property that had occurred in the nineteenth century, the regional economy was beset with recurring crises. Because of Junín's strategic geographical location, the destruction and exactions brought on by the Wars of Independence were only the first in a long line of military incursions that lasted throughout the nine-

[59] There have been many debates on the role of peasant resistance and class conflict in the transition to capitalism. Although the theoretical literature dealing with these particular issues is less developed for Latin America, many of the same issues inform the literature on the transition in Europe. For the most recent example of these debates, see Robert Brenner, "Agrarian Class Structure and Economic Development in Pre-Industrial Europe," *Past and Present* No. 70 (February 1976), pp. 30–75, and the subsequent debate in later issues of the journal; also Robert Brenner, "The Origins of Capitalist Development: A Critique of Neo-Smithian Marxism," *New Left Review* No. 104 (July–August 1977), pp. 25–92. A similar debate was also carried out in the pages of *Science and Society* in the early 1950s. For the most recent compilation of the original materials, plus some added articles, see Rodney Hilton (ed.), *The Transition from Feudalism to Capitalism* (London: New Left Books, 1976). For the best and most convincing example of the "class struggle position," see Maurice Dobb, *Studies in the Development of Capitalism*, rev. ed. (New York: International Publishers, 1963).

teenth century, as warring elite factions often decided who controlled the presidential palace by battling it out on the plains and plateaus of the central highlands.[60] Within the productive sector, the lack of irrigation made crop failure an ever-present danger, the low quality of livestock limited the yield per animal for marketable wool and dairy products, and the low level of technology in the mines made constant profits impossible without heavy capital outlays. It is not surprising, therefore, that elite families took out insurance against a crisis in any one sector by throwing their net widely.

This diversification was also motivated by market conditions. Though demand was expanding both regionally and nationally, the lack of a developed internal market made it neither constant nor predictable. By investing across the board in the various branches of agriculture and mining, therefore, entrepreneurs were in a good position to take advantage of a sudden rise in demand or price for a particular product. Of course, the widespread nature of investment meant that owners tended to keep expenditures at a minimum within each productive unit, favoring extensive, as opposed to intensive, exploitation of resources. While this pattern had its speculative aspects, it was also the most rational adaptation to the high-risk situation the local elite had to face.

The mining sector was a prominent example of the multiple problems facing investors. Although the industry had managed to recover partially from the almost total destruction it faced during the Wars of Independence, by 1870 the miners were facing a new and equally serious crisis. The main reason for this was that technology had changed little from the colonial period. Until the 1820s the patio process, a method of cold chemical amalgamation used since the sixteenth century, had provided extremely high profits for local mineowners. After independence, however, the skyrocketing costs of transportation and the raw materials necessary for amalgamation reduced profits to a minimum on low-grade ores.[61]

In an 1870 petition to Congress requesting national protection for the mining industry, a prominent mineowner complained that both salt and mercury, essential elements in the amalgamation process, had

[60] The central highlands and the Arequipa region in the south were the two areas most often involved in elite revolts. See Pike, *Modern History*, pp. 56–180. Also, "Antenor Rizo Patrón al Congreso pidiendo protección para la industria minera," Lima, 1870, pp. 6–7.

[61] For a description of mining and mining technology, see Estevan Delsol, *Informe sobre las minas de Salpo, Quiruvilca y Huamachuco, en el Departamento de La Libertad* (Lima, 1880), pp. 30–75.

risen dramatically in price. According to his figures, mercury had risen by 66 percent and salt by 40 percent, reducing the profit per *marco* of silver (approximately eight ounces) from 8 *reales* to 1.5 *reales*.[62] An informed observer who visited Cerro de Pasco in the late 1870s agreed with this analysis, although his calculations were a bit different.[63] Yet with either calculation, the problem was the same. Until it was possible to invest capital in new technology, the older mines in the Cerro de Pasco area would not be profitable.

Most miners did not have the necessary capital. Thus they engaged in speculation, extracting as much ore as they could from their mines and stockpiling it, or filing as many *denuncios* (claims) on new mines as they could, in preparation for a change in conditions or technology that would raise the price of their properties. In few cases were the mines actually worked: in 1879, only 20 percent were in operation.[64]

As mineowners entrenched themselves to weather the industry's latest crisis, new investment possibilities opened up in subtropical agriculture. Though the *ceja de selva* had been colonized in the colonial period, the massive rebellion of Juan Santos Atahualpa had made the area unsafe for whites from about the middle of the eighteenth century.[65] Only a hundred years later, when the central government showed new interest, was the area slowly reconquered. With the founding of La Merced in 1869, the Chanchamayo Valley was reopened to commercial agriculture.[66] The Monobamba and Uchubamba Valleys, further to the south, more densely populated, and less susceptible to Campa attacks, had opened up a few years earlier.[67]

All along the *ceja de selva*, new haciendas and smaller properties began to supply the regional market with coca, coffee, and *aguardiente*. Since coca and *aguardiente* were consumed on a regular basis in the area's peasant communities, both for ceremonial and work purposes, demand was high and relatively constant. The fact that production was consumed within the region cut down on the cost and risk of transportation. But most important, the fertility and humidity

---

[62] "Antenor Rizo Patrón al Congreso," 1870, p. 6.

[63] Delsol, *Informe sobre las minas*, pp. 75–82.

[64] Ibid., p. 35.

[65] For an excellent treatment of the eighteenth-century rebellion and its aftermath, see Varese, *La sal de los cerros*.

[66] See Concejo Municipal de la Merced, *Los pioneros de Chanchamayo*, 1969, pp. 39–40.

[67] Varese, *La sal de los cerros*, p. 207, and map of areas of Campa influence, inserted before Bibliography.

of the virgin subtropical lands kept initial levels of investment relatively low.[68]

Through the 1870s, local production demonstrated its comparative advantage in competition with *aguardientes* imported from other regions of the country. The local *aguardiente* rapidly dominated the markets in Tarma, Yauli, Jauja, and Huancayo. By the early 1880s, it was also displacing the liquors from Lima, Ica, Huánuco, and Huancabamba on the Cerro de Pasco market.[69] Many landowners, mineowners, and merchants, quick to see the strong market possibilities, invested in subtropical agriculture throughout the decade.

There were several ways to obtain land in the *ceja de selva*. In the recently opened Chanchamayo Valley, the cheapest way was to follow the practice of mineowners with new mines and present a *denuncio* to the government. This assured possession of the land with only a symbolic payment. Several mineowners and other members of the regional elite made use of this method.[70] Others bought lands from owners unwilling or unable to make good use of them. In the Monobamba and Uchubamba Valleys, however, a denser peasant population forced the elite to buy up lands in small lots in the area's peasant communities.

Pedro Teodoro Reyes, also the parish priest in Jauja, was particularly successful at convincing peasants to sell. Between 1869 and 1876, he bought over fifty individual plots of land from peasant owners, and a few lots from other merchants, and formed a sugar hacienda in Monobamba. Whenever Reyes was confronted with a recalcitrant owner, he would merely buy all the property around that lot and put pressure on the peasant until he or she finally agreed to sell.[71]

Whatever the inconveniences of this method it was similar to the *denuncio* in one respect: it was cheap. If little money was spent on obtaining the land, it was possible to use scarce resources to improve it. Pedro José Bravo, for example, made fifteen purchases of land in the Monobamba Valley between 1866 and 1868 that averaged ten

[68] BNP, Document No. D7942, "Expediente iniciado por la Junta constructora del camino de Chanchamayo," Lima, June–July 1886, pp. 31ff., Report on Initial Petition, July 6, 1886.

[69] Ibid.

[70] BNP, Document No. F–739, "Razón de personas que han recibido terrenos en Chanchamayo," n.d. (probably early 1870s).

[71] ANF, Protocolos Notariales, Manuel Víctor Morales, numerous documents between 1869 and 1879, especially Book 4: February 20, 1871, 343–43v; Book 6: April 21, 1874, 51v–53; Book 7: March 1, 1876, 26v–27v; and a legalization of fifty-two informal sale contracts, in Book 7: August 12, 1876, inserted between 100v and 101.

pesos each. In an 1871 petition to legalize his purchases, the Jauja merchant explained:

> These lands that were virgin lands, are today converted into only one property, or better said an hacienda called "Vista Alegre;" and in order to have it in its present state, with rooms, a machine to distill *aguardiente*, tools, canefields, coffee groves, etc., I have made heavy and, to a certain extent, incalculable expenditures, which now force me to perfect the sales in order to preserve my rights. The amount I have invested in acquiring the lands is almost insignificant; but I should point out that the indicated lands were not productive for those who sold them.[72]

Thus the attraction of subtropical agriculture lay in the fact that entrepreneurs could make a large profit with almost no initial investment in land, and comparatively low fixed costs. This almost ideal combination made the *ceja de selva* one of the most dynamic sectors of the regional economy.

Livestock breeding was the third important productive activity in the central highlands. Neither as prosperous as subtropical agriculture nor as stagnant as mining, the livestock hacienda nevertheless seemed the most solid and constant investment in the region. By the 1870s, properties that had been mere shells after the Wars of Independence maintained between twenty-five and thirty thousand head of sheep.[73] *Hacendados* marketed their animal products in Cerro de Pasco, Lima, and Europe. Some even managed to import high-quality livestock in an attempt to improve their holdings.

The majority of *hacendados* knew perfectly well that it was important to invest in high-quality livestock, not only because it produced greater quantities of wool or milk, but also because the products could be sold at a higher price. In the long run, therefore, an improved flock could help offset the risk and cost of the long and tortuous trip from the hacienda to the Lima market. Several of the largest *hacendados*, including Valladares, Olavegoya, and Del Valle, carried out experiments with imported livestock.[74] At first these experiments were

---

[72] ANF, Protocolos Notariales, Manuel Víctor Morales, legalization of fifteen informal rent contracts, in Book 4: February 14, 1871, inserted between 362v and 363.

[73] See, for example, AGN, José de Felles, Protocolo 239, July 8, 1848, 111v, in comparison with Francisco Palacios, Protocolo 590, August 8, 1878, 346–46v; or AGN, Baltazar Núñez del Prado, Protocolo 454, August 1833, 153–56 in comparison with Francisco Palacios, Protocolo 570, July 20, 1867, 788–97v.

[74] Interview with Hernán Valladares, Huancayo, June 3, 1977; AGN, José de Selaya, 1874, 851v–52 and attached inventory; ANF, Protocolos Notariales, Manuel Víctor Mo-

limited to sheep, since the English market was requiring progressively better qualities of wool for the textile industry. But the importation of sheep did not result in a substantial improvement of the flock as a whole. In any serious attempt at improvement, it was necessary to take the low-quality sheep out of the reproductive process. Not only did the *hacendados* lack the necessary resources to withstand the initial decline in production implied by such a measure, but it also would have meant forcing the resident shepherds to give up their right to pasture their own flocks (*huacchas*) on hacienda lands, something the shepherds would have been unwilling to do. Thus it was both the lack of funds and the very nature of social relations on the haciendas that limited the progress of the livestock industry.

Notwithstanding their various rates of profit and dynamism, all productive sectors had two problems in common: the lack of capital and the scarcity of labor. In a country with an extremely limited internal market, and where elite groups did not have the economic power necessary to permanently separate peasants from their access to means of production, both problems existed at the national level. On the coast, landowners had managed to mitigate their difficulties by importing Chinese coolies and using the funds from both this trade and guano to set up the country's first mortgage bank.[75] In the central highlands, however, miners and *hacendados* were forced to rely on personal relationships with the region's merchants.

Not surprisingly, the expansion of agricultural production for the market had also generated a boom in commerce. *Arrieros* from peasant villages wound their way through narrow mountain passes and across the valleys, bringing *aguardiente* and coca leaf from newly colonized lands to the regional markets in Jauja and Cerro de Pasco, taking butter, wool, and silver down to Lima, and returning with European luxury items and cheaper manufactured goods. Attracted by Cerro de Pasco's position as political and mining center of the department of Junín, European and North American commercial houses

rales, Book 6: June 16, 1874, 96–99v; Luis Esteves, *Apuntes para la historia económica del Perú* (1st ed., Lima, 1882; 2d ed., Lima: Centro de Estudios de Población y Desarrollo, 1971), p. 37.

[75] Heraclio Bonilla, *Guano y burguesía en el Perú* (Lima: Instituto de Estudios Peruanos, 1974); Humberto Rodríguez P., "Los trabajadores chinos culíes en el Perú," mimeographed (Lima, 1977); Watt Stewart, *Chinese Bondage in Peru: A History of the Chinese Coolie in Peru, 1849–1874* (Durham, N.C.: Duke University Press, 1951); Ernesto Yepes del Castillo, *Perú 1820–1920: Un siglo de desarrollo capitalista* (Lima: Instituto de Estudios Peruanos-Campodónico Ediciones, 1972), especially pp. 65–71; and Juan O'Brien, personal communication about the role of the coolie trade in the initial accumulations carried out by the Pardo family, Lima, 1977.

set up offices there. By serving as intermediaries for the larger merchants and commercial houses in Lima and Cerro de Pasco, numerous local traders and retailers also prospered greatly in this period.

But because markets were shallow, money and labor scarce, and production risky, a successful merchant could not limit him or herself to buying in the cheapest market in order to sell in the dearest. To make a profit from the circulation of goods, he or she also had to become involved in the circulation of other commodities whose price was more difficult to determine, such as credit, power, and prestige. Since money was tight, the only way to insure a rapid and extended circulation of goods was to sell on credit. But merchants did not stay in business unless they could collect on their credit obligations, whether by themselves or with the help of a powerful and prestigious patron. Thus the buying and selling of merchandise was but the tip of the iceberg. Underneath was an extended market for social and political influence, without which no other commercial or productive activity would have functioned smoothly.

It was on this social and political market that mineowners and *hacendados* negotiated their access to capital and labor. Through both commercial and productive activities, they joined with merchants to forge mutually beneficial relationships. The largest merchants used their connections with commercial houses in Lima and Cerro de Pasco to provide loans to the local elite. In return, they often received preference in renting commercial properties or marketing regional products in Lima. The middle-sized merchants were the regional elite's intermediaries. As *apoderados*, they did the legal paperwork for the more powerful elite families, collecting on debts, finalizing property contracts, fighting battles over inheritances, boundary disputes, and labor problems. As merchants in their own right, they provided a link to the petty commodity traders and political authorities in the peasant communities, making it possible for mineowners and *hacendados* to obtain a labor force through debt or patron-client relations. In payment for their many services, the intermediate merchants received loans at lower interest rates and the support of powerful families in commercial and political transactions.[76]

The Valladares family, owners of the largest and richest livestock haciendas in the Mantaro area, were at the center of one of the most extensive webs of patronage and clientele in the region. Like many *hacendado* families, they had settled in Concepción, a town midway

[76] The nature of local commercial life becomes clear from even a cursory glance at ANF, Protocolos Notariales, Manuel Víctor Morales, 1863–1882.

along the Mantaro River's eastern bank, around the middle of the nineteenth century. Several well-connected merchants, attracted by the concentration of powerful landowners, also settled in Concepción. The Valladares financed the expansion of their family enterprise by taking out loans with these merchants, using the funds to improve their existing properties, acquire new ones, and embark on various commercial ventures. In return, the larger merchants handled the Valladares' extensive trade in livestock and livestock products.[77]

Guillermo Kirchner, a German merchant who settled in Concepción and married into a local family, developed a particularly profitable relationship with the Valladares clan. In addition to providing loans to the *hacendados*, Kirchner formed commercial partnerships with other merchants in order to market the region's products in Lima. In 1874, for example, he joined with Juan B. Rossi, a Lima-based Italian merchant, to market both highland and subtropical products, including butter, coffee, flour, and wool. The partnership opened offices in Lima, Concepción, and Huanta, in the neighboring department of Ayacucho.[78] In 1877, several members of the Valladares family signed contracts with Rossi to place the butter from their haciendas on the Lima market.[79]

Although their relations with merchants such as Kirchner provided elite families with essential capital and markets, the maintenance of power and prestige at the regional level depended on how successfully they could tie themselves into the large local network of smaller merchants and landowners. This network provided a channel for the penetration of elite influence into local life; but it also articulated, in an independent way, the entire intermediate level of productive and commercial activities. As owners of smaller commercial properties, mules, cattle, and sheep, small- and middle-sized entrepreneurs kept the local economy going. They grew the alfalfa that fed the mule trade, milled the flour for local food supplies, stocked the local stores, and financed the petty traders. They were, in short, the service sector of the regional economy.

Nicolás Manrique, a Jauja merchant, provides an excellent example of this multifaceted activity. Throughout the 1860s and early 1870s,

[77] ANF, Protocolos Notariales, Manuel Víctor Morales and Luis Salazar, various documents, 1870–1882, especially Morales, Book 8: April 1, 1879, 237v–38v, and September 19, 1879, 325v–26.

[78] ANF, Protocolos Notariales, Manuel Víctor Morales, Book 6: September 6, 1874, 129v–31v.

[79] ANF, Protocolos Notariales, Manuel Víctor Morales, Book 7: March 13 and 14, 1877, 182v–83v, 185–85v.

Manrique maintained a diversified business in the Jauja area. He owned seven small properties, spread through several of the area's villages, on which he grew alfalfa and wheat. In Monobamba, he was the owner of a small hacienda where he grew cane and distilled *aguardiente*. He ran two commercial establishments in Jauja, stocked in part with merchandise obtained directly, and often on credit, from commercial houses in Lima. He owned fourteen mules, financed other merchants and petty traders, and was *apoderado* for the Valladares family over a period of seven years, receiving loans from them at extremely low interest rates.[80]

Through local government, landowners and merchants further strengthened their personal, social, and economic ties. According to municipal law all *anexos*, or towns and villages within a district, were politically dependent on the council operating in the district capital.[81] Since judicial and administrative officials in each *anexo* were accountable to the district council, the merchants and landowners who dominated politics at the district level often incorporated local posts into their networks of patronage, using them for personal as well as municipal business. An excellent example of this was the system of labor drafts for municipal projects. Officials in the peasant villages were required to provide occasional quotas of laborers for construction and maintenance activities in the district capital.[82] Though council members rarely used municipal labor drafts for their own purposes while in office, the contacts they established with village officials through

[80] ANF, Protocolos Notariales, Manuel Víctor Morales, "Last Will and Testament of Nicolás Manrique," Book 5: October 3, 1872, inserted between 112v and 113.

[81] Peru: "La Constitución y leyes orgánicas del Perú dadas por el Congreso de 1860" (Lima: Imprenta del Estado, 1869), "Ley orgánica de municipalidades," Capítulo I, Artículos 7–9, 150.

[82] The legal basis of this requirement is obscure. According to Augusto E. Bedoya, subprefect of Tarma in 1890, peasant communities had always been dependent on the political, not the municipal, authorities. This meant that the prefects and subprefects, whose power came directly from the central government, were charged with making decisions on the use of peasant labor from the villages. Apparently, however, a number of prefects gave municipalities the right to use peasant labor on municipal projects. See the report of Bedoya to the prefect of Junín, APJ, "Solicitud del Alcalde de Tarma Francisco L. Alvariño al Prefecto," June 13, 1890, inserted in 2v–5.

It is clear, moreover, that the use of peasant labor on municipal projects was an established custom, whether legal or not. The mere fact that, according to Bedoya, the central government had passed decrees on the subject in 1850, 1869, and 1870 points to the persistence of the problem. See also Rodrigo Sánchez, Research Notes: Alcaldía de Jauja, Oficios varios, 1891–1893; APJ, "Solicitud de Ataura al Prefecto contra la Municipalidad de Jauja," August 10, 1892; and APJ, "Solicitud de Indígenas Tarmeños," April 26, 1892.

the administration of the public works program facilitated their access to labor in the future.

The municipal government's endemic shortage of funds opened up additional opportunities for local merchants. The municipality could not pay regular personnel to carry out essential municipal services, especially lighting the capital's streets, collecting taxes for the use of market facilities, and charging tolls on the district's bridges. Thus the council opened up these *ramos* to public auction on a yearly basis. Using the previous year's auction price as an initial base figure, merchants bid against each other for the exclusive right to administer each service.[83] The fact that merchants were willing to pay for such a right meant that they were sure they could fulfill their obligation and still make a profit. By supervising the collection of taxes on commercial traffic and market activities, moreover, they could increase their store of favors with other merchants, whether patrons or clients.

Even if a merchant or landowner did not participate directly in municipal government, he or she could expand his or her network of dependency by financing a man's bid for local office. According to established custom, any person entering a legal contract had to provide proof of his or her intention to fulfill its terms. The usual procedure was to bring a friend or patron to act as *fiador*. This second person would accept liability for the contract in case the first did not comply. While this custom was a general one for all contracts, it was particularly binding in cases where a man was assuming political office.[84] By acting as *fiador* in such cases, a merchant could either curry favor with a superior, or bind more tightly an inferior.

Thus municipal office constituted another branch of the regional and local market for influence and power. As in the case of credit, local government provided channels through which merchants and landowners of all sizes could weave extensive webs of patronage and clientele, connecting upwards and downwards to other sets of dependent relations, forming a huge tapestry that touched all levels of local life. In the commercialized, precapitalist economy of the central highlands, this tapestry functioned as a substitute for an internal market, funneling and articulating the flow of credit, commodities, and labor from one sector of the economy to another. As economic dynamism increased, the concentric and overlapping circles of patron-client

---

[83] Examples of these auctions, called *remates de ramos*, can be found throughout ANF, Protocolos Notariales, Manuel Víctor Morales, 1863–1879.

[84] For examples of various types of *fianzas*, see ANF, Protocolos Notariales, Manuel Víctor Morales, 1863–1879 and passim.

relations made increasingly deep incursions into the peasant society and economy.

The Peasant Village and the Limits of Power

While the decade of the 1870s was not the first time that peasants in the central highlands had felt the pressures of commercialization, this period differed from its predecessors in the intensity of the confrontation between the individual peasant holding and the small- to medium-sized commercial enterprise. Many merchants, for example, found commercial agriculture in the villages extremely profitable. While not bearing the risk and expense of a large commercial property, they could provide needed goods and services to a dynamic economy. Taking advantage of a peasant family's occasional need for cash, some bought up lands in the communities, planting alfalfa, wheat, and other crops that would bring a good price on the regional market.[85] Others reorganized the petty commercial activities of local peasants, developing transport businesses that utilized small peasant *arrieros* to ply the local commercial routes.[86] Some also used peasant indebtedness to funnel labor to the area's mines and subtropical haciendas.[87] But in all cases, the traditional market activities of the village household economy were redirected to meet the needs of the commercial sector.

The process of penetration was not a homogeneous one, but varied according to local conditions and opportunities. Some villages, because of their position on commercial routes and the fertility of their lands, suffered a sustained incursion of commercial capital on the land itself. It was in these communities that the prestigious *cofradías*, the

[85] ANF, Protocolos Notariales, Manuel Víctor Morales, Book 2: August 29, 1865, 108v–17v; October 26, 1866, 261v–62; Book 3: January 25, 1867, 6v–9; Book 4: December 31, 1871, 496v–98v; Book 5: October 3, 1872, insert between 112v and 113.

[86] APJ, "Contrato entre Eulalio Martínez y José Echegoyen," November 10, 1887; and Interview with Felipe Artica, Huancayo, June 1977. Of course, written contracts of this nature are difficult to obtain; many agreements in this period were verbal, and evidence of their existence is indirect. See, for example, ANF, Expedientes y Libros Judiciales, Libro de Juicios Verbales, Marco, 1876, Arrieta vs. Arias, May 19, 1876, 17–17v; Franco vs. Camarena, September 19, 1876, 43–43v.

[87] For information on the role of merchants in obtaining labor for mines and haciendas, see Pflücker, *Exposición que presenta Carlos Renardo Pflücker al Supremo Gobierno*, pp. 11–12; Universidad Nacional de Ingeniería (UNI), Tesis No. 14: Ismael Bueno, "Informe sobre Yauli," 1887, 27; ANF, Expedientes y Libros Judiciales, Libro de Juicios Verbales, Acolla, 1876, Remusgo vs. Villar, September 16, 1876; Protocolos Notariales, Luis Salazar, Book 5: August 25, 1893; and APJ, "Carta del subprefecto de Jauja B.S. Leiva al prefecto del departamento de Junín," April 2, 1888, in which Leiva informs the prefect that he is setting up a special service to keep track of labor contracts, since there are so many in the region of Jauja that confusion reigns.

larger merchants, and even some *hacendados*, held *chacras*. Social and economic differentiation was pronounced, and labor migrations frequent.[88] Other villages, while still close to commercial routes, underwent a less direct penetration. The few merchants and other outsiders who owned land usually planted *al partir* with a local peasant family, preserving local cycles and rhythms of agriculture. Most households maintained a higher degree of self-sufficiency, migrating in a more occasional way. The distance between rich and poor was less pronounced, and indebtedness less acute.[89]

Given the intricacy of Andean ecology, communities only a few miles apart could exhibit completely different patterns of penetration. This was the case in the Yanamarca Valley. On the western side, the villages of Chocón, Muquillanqui, Tragadero, and Marco combined a strategic location on two important commercial routes with an abundance of flat, fertile lands. To the south, the main route between Jauja and Oroya cut through the lands bordering the communities of Chocón and Muquillanqui, wound upward across the mountains through a pass at Anlacalla, and into the upper Mantaro Valley. There the

[88] Evidence of direct penetration can be found in ANF, Protocolos Notariales, Manuel Víctor Morales, 1862–1879, passim. For direct penetration in Muquiyauyo, see Richard N. Adams, *A Community in the Andes: Problems and Progress in Muquiyauyo* (Seattle: University of Washington Press, 1959), pp. 11–23. For the Yanamarca Valley, see especially ANF, Protocolos Notariales, Manuel Víctor Morales, Book 10: March 25, 1883, 92v–93v; April 24, 1883, 106–107; Book 11: July 3, 1884, 23v–25; December 20, 1885, 87v–89; Luis Salazar, Book 2: October 24, 1883, 67v–68v (all documents dealing with the western side of the valley). For evidence on the relationship between direct penetration and migration, see especially APJ, "Censo del Valle de Yanamarca, 1899," Community of Tragadero. Although the census is for a later period, both the quantity and age composition of the miners suggests that migration had been going on for a number of years. In Tragadero, 27 percent of the male population were engaged in mining in 1889. Of the mining population, 33 percent were under the age of thirty; 40 percent were between thirty and forty-nine years of age; and 26 percent were fifty or older. Moreover, social and economic differentiation in Tragadero was quite acute by 1899, denoting a process that had been in motion for quite some time. With relation to sheep, 23 percent of the households held under 50 head; an additional 22 percent held between 50 and 100 head; 18 percent held between 101 and 200 head; 15 percent held between 201 and 499 head; and 22 percent held over 500 head of sheep. Thus 45 percent of the households were in a category defined as "poor"; 33 percent were "middle"; and 22 percent were "wealthy."

[89] Information on merchants planting *al partir* was found in ANF, Luis Salazar, Book 7: July 26, 1897, 169–72v; Manuel Víctor Morales, Book 8: June 10, 1878, 79–81, and in informal conversations with Moisés Ortega in Acolla. It is clear, from the 1899 Yanamarca Valley census, that migration from Acolla was much less pronounced, and had been going on for a much shorter time, than in Tragadero. Only 3 percent of the male population migrated to the mines, and all of them were unmarried and under thirty years of age. Social differentiation was also less pronounced in Acolla. Using substantially the same criteria as for Tragadero, we find that 85 percent of the households were "poor"; 6 percent "middle"; and 0.8 percent "wealthy."

road continued west along the river, hugging the cliffs until it reached Oroya, where it connected to Lima and the mining centers. To the north of Marco, a branch of the commercial traffic to Lima and Oroya came across the mountains and wound further north, servicing the large haciendas that sent livestock products to Lima, particularly the hacienda Cachicachi. The path continued northward, then eastward, becoming part of the main road that articulated the Jauja-Tarma-Chanchamayo Valley trade.[90]

Throughout the southwestern part of the Yanamarca Valley, the abundance and fertility of agricultural land complemented the proximity of commercial routes. In the southernmost part, where the road from Jauja and Oroya crossed the valley, red, smooth soils extended all the way from Oxapampa, a *paraje* directly behind the village of Chocón, to the Anlacalla pass. Beyond the mountains, the plains of Hualis and Huashua offered additional opportunities for commercial agriculture. Toward the north, both along the valley itself and behind the mountains, the fertility of the land continued. Because the direction of the winds and the position of the mountains protected the area from frost, it was possible to plant a wider variety of crops, including the more delicate vegetables. And a series of small mule paths crisscrossed the region, connecting the fields to the villages, the villages to each other, and the entire area to the main commercial routes at its southern and northern boundaries.[91]

Jauja merchants were aware of the area's potential from early on. Since the colonial period, important Jauja *cofradías* had owned extensive tracts of land near Chocón. Prestigious merchant families possessed large *chacras* in *parajes* such as Oxapampa, Llamacancha, Anlacalla, Huashua, and, further to the north, in Curicancha, Espíritu Cumu, and Tragadero.[92] Several petty merchants settled in the vil-

---

[90] Information on commercial routes in the area was obtained from interviews with Felipe Artica, Huancayo, June 1977, Elías Valenzuela, Tragadero, October 22, 1977, and Francisco Solís, Tragadero, November 29, 1977; and also from informal conversations held throughout 1977 with Moisés Ortega. Evidence that the hacienda Cachicachi sent livestock products to Lima can be found in AGN, Francisco Palacios, Protocolo 570, July 20, 1867, 788–97v; and ANF, Expedientes y Libros Judiciales, Libro de Juicios Verbales, Marco, 1876, 52–53.

[91] Between September 1977 and January 1978, Moisés Ortega and I took several walks in different parts of the Yanamarca Valley, discussing the quality of the land and the different *parajes*. In February 1978, we summarized our information and discussions on a series of three rough *paraje* maps, one for each of the communities of Acolla, Marco, and Tragadero.

[92] For the existence of Jauja *cofradía* properties in the western part of the valley, see ANF, Protocolos Notariales, Luis Salazar, Book 56: September 23, 1926, 1978v–1981v; and Book 60: January 2, 1928, 1239–1242; Anselmo Flores Espinoza, Book 13: Decem-

lages, particularly in Marco, buying up the better *chacras* and involving themselves in commercial agriculture.[93] From 1870 on, with the increased dynamism of the regional economy, the penetration deepened. Additional outsiders came to settle in the villages.[94] As the distance between rich and poor increased, wealthier peasant families bought back commercial *chacras* from outsiders.[95] Both rich and poor stepped up their labor migrations, the former to accumulate more money, the latter to compensate for the shrinkage of their subsistence base.[96]

Despite their physical proximity, a substantially different pattern obtained in the valley's eastern villages. Although both Acolla and Pachascucho were on the principal commercial route between Jauja and Tarma, and peasants from both communities were active in the mule trade, few merchants owned lands within the village.[97] This difference was due largely to the quality of the land, for although there were large, fertile *parajes* in both communities—especially in the southern sections of Acolla and along the slopes behind the village of Pachascucho—the soil was generally more rocky, and the area more

ber 19, 1938, 1728–1729v; and Archivo SINAMOS, cc 239 (Tragadero), Expediente 10530: "Levantamiento de plano de la Comunidad de Tragadero," 107—"Croquis de la zona en litis entre Tragadero y la parroquia de Jauja." For the accumulation of land in the same area by prestigious outside families, see ANF, Protocolos Notariales, Manuel Víctor Morales, Book 2: December 17, 1866, 297v–99; Book 4: May 13, 1869, 49v–50, December 17, 1870, 325–26; Book 6: November 1, 1874, 166v–68, December 17, 1875, 234–35; Book 7: August 20, 1877, 261v–63; Book 8: January 9, 1878, 3v–5; and passim.

[93] It is unclear exactly when the families who settled in Marco and Tragadero earlier arrived. But from scattered documents on the Hurtado and Onofre families, it would seem that they arrived in the first half of the nineteenth century and married women in the community. See especially ANF, Protocolos Notariales, Manuel Víctor Morales, Book 11: December 29, 1884, inserted at the end of the book; and Expedientes y Libros Judiciales, "Expediente de declaratoria de herederos de Antonio Onofre, iniciado por su madre Rosa Rivera," 1937. The data from Muquiyauyo would seem to corroborate this pattern, although there it occurred a few decades earlier. See Adams, *Community in the Andes*, pp. 20–21.

[94] APJ, "Inscripción Militar, 1898, Valle de Yanamarca," lists several merchants about thirty-five to fifty-five years old who were born outside the district.

[95] See, for example, ANF, Protocolos Notariales, Manuel Víctor Morales, Book 5: August 30, 1872, 72v–73v; September 2, 1872, 75–76; and Book 7: July 20, 1876, 81–82.

[96] In the 1899 census for Tragadero, 49 percent of those who migrated to the mines fall in the "poor" category; 37 percent in the "middle" category; and 14 percent in the "wealthy" category. Given the level of resources controlled by the different groups, it seems reasonable to assume that the upper half of the "middle" category, and the entire "wealthy" category, did not migrate to fill their immediate needs.

[97] A comparison of a total of 174 contracts for the Yanamarca Valley during the nineteenth century, from both Manuel Víctor Morales and Luis Salazar, shows that of 80 contracts for Acolla and Pachascucho, 43.5 percent were with outsiders. By contrast, of 94 contracts for Marco-Tragadero, 76.3 percent were with outsiders.

susceptible to frost and hail. Thus outside merchants did not carry out a sustained incursion on the land itself, but controlled local stores and commerce, engaging in petty money-lending activities through which, at times, they gained access to *chacras* from peasants unable to pay.[98]

These differences in type and degree of commercial penetration were reflected in local government. The petty merchants who settled in Marco had both business and personal relations with the Jauja elite, and used their connections to dominate the local offices of municipal government. By marrying mainly among themselves and with selected wealthier peasant families, and incorporating others into their patronage networks through ritual kinship ties, these merchant families developed a tightly knit circle that attempted to control all aspects of local life. The quality of social relations was generally hierarchical, and few peasants were willing to challenge the authority of the governing clique independently.[99]

Social relations in Acolla and Pachascucho were, by contrast, more egalitarian. While certain families of *mestizo* origin also had an important role in local government, they differentiated themselves much less from the general population. A partial explanation lay, no doubt, in the fact that these families had lived in the community for a longer time, and had incorporated themselves more fully into village society. Yet the very nature of life in Acolla and Pachascucho, with the greater viability of the household economy and the less dramatic quality of social and economic differentiation, militated against the development or success of an authoritarian style.[100]

[98] ANF, Protocolos Notariales, Manuel Víctor Morales, Book 8: June 10, 1878, 79–81; Luis Salazar, Book 7: July 26, 1897, 169–72v; Expedientes y Libros Judiciales, Libro de Juicios Verbales, Acolla, 1875–1876, Rivero vs. Soriano, February 12, 1876, and Rivero vs. Mayta and Inga, May 9, 1876.

[99] Information on the quality of social relationships in the Marco-Tragadero part of the valley came from interviews with Elías Valenzuela, Tragadero, October 22, 1977; Francisco Solís, Tragadero, November 29, 1977; Oscar Teófilo Camarena, Tragadero, November 29, 1977; and conversations with Moisés Ortega throughout 1977, especially on September 15, 1977. See also William B. Hutchinson, "Sociocultural Change in the Mantaro Valley Region of Peru: Acolla, A Case Study," Ph.D. Dissertation, Indiana University, 1973, pp. 29–30; ANF, Protocolos Notariales, Manuel Víctor Morales, Book 11: December 29, 1884, inserted at the end of the book; Expedientes y Libros Judiciales, "José C. Hurtado contra los hermanos Onofre, Agustín Rafael y otros por la muerte de Florián Hurtado," 1918–1923; and "Declaratoria de herederos de Antonio Onofre;" and, finally, AMM, Libros de Actas, 1907–1940, various *sesiones*.

[100] According to village oral tradition, when in the 1880s José de la Rosa Ortega, a prestigious Acolla *mestizo*, led the village's bid for district status, he spent his wife's entire dowry on petitions and trips to Lima. Moreover, in Archivo SINAMOS, cc 205 (Marco), in an 1893 inventory of church *cofradía* property, the priest taking the inven-

The character of social and economic relations also affected the way in which peasants related to the commercial economy. While the needs of the household economy forced most to seek nonagricultural employment at some point during the year, the work most commonly sought varied from one part of the valley to another. Just as the peasants of Acolla and Pachascucho were more successful at preserving household self-sufficiency, so they also tended to work in those outside activities in which they could maintain a greater independence. Almost without exception, the peasants from Acolla were *arrieros*. Owning an average of two mules,[101] they hired their services to a merchant. Most merchants paid a small portion of the money in advance, indebting the peasants and forcing them to carry out the contract.[102] Each *arriero* was responsible for his animals during the trip and for any accident that might happen to the cargo.[103] Since the routes were long, risky, and tiring, it was often difficult to finish a journey with the mules and the cargo completely intact, and a peasant could find himself more indebted at the end of a trip than he was at the beginning. Yet in an important sense, the work rhythms, schedule, and organization still belonged to the peasant. No foreman or overseer told him when to start, how long to travel, or where to rest.

Although peasants from the western sections of the Yanamarca Valley also engaged in petty commerce and *arrieraje*, a much higher proportion of them migrated to the mines.[104] In addition to the higher intensity of social and economic differentiation in this area, the presence of outside merchants with connections to the Jauja elite facili-

---

tory stated that many of the church properties in Acolla were mortgaged by the village authorities during the bid for district status. Since that time, the priest continued, all the letters addressed to the authorities in that village, inquiring about the incident, had gone unanswered. See Archivo SINAMOS, cc 205, "Expediente sobre la reivindicación del molino," 134–36v. In both cases, the more notable families in Acolla showed a willingness to go to great lengths—in the second case, even jeopardizing their standing with powerful church authorities—to act in the village's behalf. While the gestures were by no means wholly unselfish, they show a commitment to village life far greater than that of the Marco families who, despite their greater wealth and better connections, were unsuccessful in the contest with Acolla over which village would be given the status of district capital. See also Hutchinson, "Sociocultural Change," pp. 29–30.

[101] APJ, "Censo del Valle de Yanamarca, 1899." At this time in Acolla, 47 percent of the male population were *arrieros*, with an average of two animals each. As in the case of miners in Tragadero, both the number of *arrieros* and their age structure suggests that this was a long-standing trend.

[102] See footnote 86.

[103] ANF, Expedientes y Libros Judiciales, Libro de Juicios Verbales, Acolla, 1875–1876, Maita vs. Rosales, April 13, 1875, 3–3v; Protocolos Notariales, Manuel Víctor Morales, Book 2: September 21, 1866, 242v; Book 4: November 10, 1871, 451–52.

[104] See footnotes 87 and 88.

tated the recruitment of labor from the communities. As in the case of other nonagricultural activities, migration to the mines occurred mainly during the dry season, or in the lightest parts of the agricultural cycle. The seasonal quality of migration was also beneficial for the mineowners, since the depressed state of the industry made it difficult to keep a mine working all year round. Yet given the hardships of mine labor, the only way to retain a labor force was through coercion. By advancing sums of money to merchants and political authorities in the region's towns and villages, mineowners contracted for seasonal laborers from the peasant communities. In exchange for a cash advance, peasants were required to work off their debt in the mines at a set daily "wage." Until the 1880s, this method of obtaining labor was called *contrata*.[105] Later, when the mining industry expanded once again and the same method was used more widely, it became known as *enganche*.

When a peasant reached the mines, he often found that he was entering a vicious circle of indebtedness. In addition to his initial debt, he received advances of clothing, food, coca, and candles, which were called *acomodanas*, from the merchant's or the mineowner's store.[106] As his debt increased, he was forced to work longer and longer periods before he could pay it all off and return home. If he had started off with a one-month contract, it could be two or three times that long before he finally returned to his community.

The worst part of mine labor was not the debt, however, but the work itself.[107] The mines were damp, dark, and poorly ventilated. The haphazard nature of the shafts made cave-ins a constant danger. The primitive division of labor recognized only two types of workers: the *barreteros*, who extracted the ore from the walls by candlelight with the simplest tools; and the *apiris*, in effect human beasts of burden, who carried the sacks of ore to the surface, winding their way in the darkness through dank, treacherous tunnels. Whether *barreteros* or *apiris*, peasants worked an average of ten hours a day, and kept themselves going by chewing coca.[108] Most would also work several *gua-*

---

[105] Pflücker, *Exposición que presenta Carlos Renardo Pflücker al Supremo Gobierno*, pp. 11–12.

[106] UNI, Tesis No. 10–12, Federico Villareal, "Memoria sobre Yauli," 1885, 13v; and Tesis No. 50, Francisco R. del Castillo, "Informe sobre Huarochirí y Yauli," 1891, 9.

[107] For information on the labor system, see Delsol, *Informe sobre las minas*, pp. 30–33; UNI, Tesis 10–12, Villareal, 13v; Tesis 13, Germán Remy, "Informe sobre Yauli," 1885, 5v–6v; Tesis 14, Ismael Bueno, "Informe sobre Yauli," 1887, 27; Tesis 16, Rafael Muñoz, "Informe sobre Cerro de Pasco," 1887, 2–3.

[108] UNI, Tesis 16, Muñoz, 2–3.

raches, or night shifts, during which they stayed on the job for thirty-six hours straight and rested for twelve.[109] Although many mine owners allowed the workers to extract metal for their own benefit after working hours,[110] it is difficult to imagine that many peasants had the energy to take advantage of this offer. And given the combination of mounting debts and poor working conditions, it is not surprising that most owners complained of a high runaway rate among their workers.[111]

Migration to the mines sped up a process of social and economic differentiation that already existed in the peasant community. Predictably, it was the poorer peasants, migrating because of a basic and immediate need for money, who fell into the deepest debt. The wealthier peasants who migrated, on the other hand, often were able to accumulate money while in the mines.[112] The key difference was the resources they could take with them. A wealthier peasant could plan his migration with greater care, taking several animals from his abundant flock, and depending less on the merchant's advances of food and clothes than did his poorer counterparts. Since his debt did not increase as rapidly, he could afford to work fewer *guaraches*, thus having more time and energy to mine on his own account. He might even develop a special relationship with the merchant or mineowner and work by contract instead of *tarea*. In contrast to the latter, in which a peasant worked by the day to pay off his debt, under a contract the peasant in charge was paid by the meter or ton of mineral, allowing him to organize the production process and hire the laborers himself.[113] Not only was the contract system more independent, it was a great deal more profitable.

In the complex struggle and interplay between household and commercial economy, then, the 1870s was a decade in which the increasing dynamism of commerce strongly challenged peasant self-suffi-

[109] Delsol, *Informe sobre las minas*, p. 32; UNI, Tesis 10–12, Villareal, 13v; Tesis 14, Bueno, 27; Tesis 16, Muñoz, 2–3.

[110] Delsol, *Informe sobre las minas*, p. 32; UNI, Tesis 13, Remy, 6v; Tesis 14, Bueno, 28.

[111] Pflücker, *Exposición que presenta Carlos Renardo Pflücker, al Supremo Gobierno*, pp. 11–12; UNI, Tesis 14, Bueno, 38.

[112] In APJ, "Censo del Valle de Yanamarca, 1899," Tragadero, it is clear that a number of peasants were able to accumulate while in the mines, and had probably been doing so for several decades. Among them: Luis Camarena, 51 years old, 500 head of sheep; Pedro Gamarra, 46, 800 head of sheep; Vicente Onofre, 42, 400 head of sheep and with his older son Antonio, 17, also working in the mines; and José Curi, 68 years old, 800 head of sheep.

[113] For contract mining, see UNI, Tesis 13, Remy, 6v; and Tesis 14, Bueno, 28.

ciency. While some villages or individuals fared better than others, the process of commercial penetration spared no one. Yet the peasants grappled with the commercial economy head on, struggling against indebtedness and the shrinkage of subsistence. The battles were fought over many issues: land, livestock, labor, debt. At times the peasants confronted the elite directly, instituting court proceedings, and trying, whenever possible, to set one elite member against another.[114] When direct confrontation was impossible, peasants engaged in a number of passive resistance strategies, running away from debts or labor obligations or, as we shall see, forging alliances with hacienda peons that allowed them to use hacienda resources for community purposes. And whether or not they succeeded, these peasant strategies cut deeply into the elite's resources.

In livestock, mining, and agriculture, the endemic problems with obtaining and retaining a labor force diverted scarce capital from more productive uses. In the mines, for example, the initial investment in *contrata* was only the first step in a long sequence of capital outlays for labor. Given the high runaway rate in the mines, the owner would often have to employ an agent to chase the fugitive workers, at greater expense to him or herself. According to one prominent owner,

> In [mineral] haciendas that need to employ a large number of workers, one needs a special agent whose only function is to chase after the fugitives, pick them up, and bring them back to the hacienda to fulfill their *contratas*, there being cases in which they run away a second and third time.[115]

Needless to say, the owner's losses from runaways who were never found were quite high, for although every *contrata* had a *fiador*, usually a local petty merchant or small landowner who guaranteed the fulfillment of the work contract with his or her own resources, any mineowner wishing to collect from a *fiador* had to institute court proceedings.[116]

On livestock or agricultural haciendas, the owners used a system of

[114] ANF, Protocolos Notariales, Manuel Víctor Morales, Book 1: November 30, 1864, 155–57, 157–60v; Book 2: February 17–20, 1865, 23v–30; Book 3: October 5, 1868, 212–13.

[115] Pflücker, *Exposición que presenta Carlos Renardo Pflücker al Supremo Gobierno*, p. 11.

[116] See, for example, ANF, Expedientes y Libros Judiciales, Libro de Juicios Verbales, Acolla, 1876, September 16, 1876; "Queja de Pedro Ramos contra el Juez de Paz de Masma," Jauja, May 15, 1903; and "Revisorio referente á la demanda verbal seguida ante el Juez de Paz de Segunda Nominación de esta Ciudad por Don Manuel Núñez Salinas, apoderado de Don Nicanor Galarza," Jauja, 1904–1906.

debt peonage to retain a labor force. In many cases, the total debt owed by the hacienda's labor force reached such enormous sums that the owner considered it as part of the property's value, including it in the inventory, transferring it as part of rent contracts, and listing it separately in his or her will.[117] In 1867, for example, the total debt of the shepherds on the hacienda Cachicachi, as calculated in the will of its owner, was nearly 5 percent of the total value of the property, including lands, livestock, and houses.[118] Yet such a debt could never be a productive investment, since its only purpose was to give legal legitimation to chasing runaways. As an 1882 rent contract for the hacienda Laive explained:

> They [the renters] will receive the hacienda without the debts of the laborers, and will give it back the same way. But in order to chase the fugitive workers or shepherds, they will use each one's debt, of which a current account is kept in the Administration [office], this [debt] will not be charged to them, but will serve only as a compulsion to bring them back to the hacienda.[119]

Both in mines and on haciendas, therefore, the system of debt labor was used to provide a legal basis for either retaining the worker on the property, or for collecting from him or her some form of retribution for the losses in production or time that his or her flight had caused. In practice, however, the system proved far less effective than the mineowners and *hacendados* hoped. In September 1876, for example, Andrés Remusgo, agent for the hacienda Tutumayo, instituted court proceedings against Silvestre Villar, owner of the hacienda Sacas, a small property located in the northern part of the Yanamarca Valley. In his statement to the judge, Remusgo argued that, since April 1873, Villar had owed him thirty-eight pesos from a debt that Doroteo Aquino and Miguel Ilario had contracted while working for the hacienda that Remusgo represented. Apparently, in 1873 Ilario had already been in jail for debt to this hacienda. Villar had rescued him by acting as *fiador*, and had then employed him on his own hacienda Sacas. Three years later, Villar refused to make good on the debt, arguing that since Ilario was still alive he must himself pay it back. Villar then instituted his own court case against Ilario for pay-

[117] AGN, José de Selaya, "Inventario de la Hacienda Cónsac," January 1, 1875, inserted after 852; Felipe Orellana, Protocolo 526, April 10, 1877, 921–23; Francisco Palacios, Protocolo 570, "Testimonio del testamento de Petronila Abeleyra," Tarma, May 23, 1867, 795v–97v.

[118] "Testamento de Petronila Abeleyra," 795v–97v.

[119] AGN, José Ramón Valdivia, Protocolo 992, 1882, 221v.

ment of the thirty-eight pesos. Meanwhile, Remusgo and the hacienda Tutumayo had been waiting for over three years for a satisfactory conclusion to their conflict with Ilario.[120]

In many ways, the Remusgo-Villar-Ilario dispute is typical of labor conflicts in this period. Because of the shortage of labor, *hacendados* were more than willing to compete with one another for workers, even if those workers were fugitives from another hacienda. As the Remusgo case shows, peasants were adept at using divisions and fissures in the elite alliance to either stop or postpone their day of reckoning in land and labor squabbles. Even if litigation was usually decided in the *hacendado* or mineowner's favor, the peasants could make them pay, in both time and money, for their victories.

In addition to the many conflicts over land and labor that haciendas faced with village peasants, the *hacendados* were also forced to confront what to them must have seemed an unholy alliance: that between their *colonos* or peons and peasants living in communities. Not only were many resident peons on haciendas originally members of neighboring communities,[121] but relations with the villages also remained close and were sometimes strengthened by marriage. Thus through inheritance, marriage, or purchase, peons could gain access to land or other properties in the villages, supplementing their income from the lands they received on the haciendas.[122] They also exchanged reciprocal labor obligations with village peasants. The most

[120] ANF, Expedientes y Libros Judiciales, Libro de Juicios Verbales, Acolla, 1876, Remusgo vs. Villar, September 16, 1876, and Villar vs. Ilario, September 16, 1876.

[121] Unfortunately, direct evidence on this point is difficult to obtain. Only one document, Archivo SINAMOS, cc 205 (Marco), Dirección de Asuntos Indígenas, Expediente 13390, "Relativo a la reclamación formulada por el Círculo Cultural Deportivo Marco contra don Francisco Cajigao y hermanos sobre abusos," 1948, 1, states specifically that the peons on the hacienda Cachicachi are originally from the neighboring communities of Janjaillo, Marco, and Tragadero. Nevertheless, from several lists of peons available for the haciendas in the area, particularly for the hacienda Cachicachi (AGN, Francisco Palacios, Protocolo 570, July 20, 1867, 792v–93v) and the hacienda Yanamarca (APJ, "Solicitud de los colonos de la hacienda Yanamarca contra el arrendatario Don Grimaldo Landa," 1909; and APJ, "Varias solicitudes de los operarios de la hacienda Yanamarca pidiendo exoneración de la contribución rústica," 1921), it becomes clear that the last names of the peons are, in the majority of the cases, the same as those of the neighboring villagers. Since over a year of research experience in the area has convinced me that last names are extremely region-specific, varying significantly even from one community to the next, this would seem to be fairly powerful indirect evidence.

[122] I found evidence on the relationship between hacienda and community peasants in: ANF, Protocolos Notariales, Manuel Víctor Morales, Book 8: January 30, 1879; inserts between 204v and 205; September 1, 1879, 315–16; Expedientes y Libros Judiciales, "Declaratoria de herederos de Antonio Onofre"; and Interview with Felipe Artica, Huancayo, II, June 1977.

common favor that an hacienda peon performed for his or her village relations, for example, was to pasture their sheep on the hacienda, passing them off as part of his or her flock and thus entitled to free grazing in exchange for fertilizing hacienda lands with their manure. While most *hacendados* were perfectly aware of what was going on, they had no easy way to prevent this use of hacienda lands to expand community resources.[123]

Despite the increasingly harsh incursions of the commercial sector upon the peasant community, therefore, both village peasants and hacienda peons were usually successful at making the elite pay a high price for their access to labor. Not only were *hacendados* and mine-owners forced to tie up scarce resources in the retention and persecution of a recalcitrant labor force, but the conflicts that arose from this process cut deeply into the elite alliance. There were important differences, for example, between commercial and productive interests. Because merchants acted as agents in the provision of labor, they often found themselves embroiled in costly and frustrating court cases involving fugitive workers.[124] Since labor problems were central to the high risks and costs of production, they also affected merchants indirectly by increasing the possibility of default on the loans they had made to *hacendados* and miners. Thus while the merchants, mine-owners, and *hacendados* ultimately shared an interest in maintaining the overall dynamism of the regional economy, most traders must have occasionally allowed themselves a resentful reflection on why the miners and *hacendados* could not make their control over labor more efficient. As was clear from the Remusgo-Villar case, moreover, labor conflicts also bared the latent contradictions between large and small commercial property. The smaller *hacendados*, with fewer connec-

---

[123] The fact that hacienda peasants increased their flocks with animals belonging to the community has been discussed fairly extensively in the literature. See, for example, Juan Martínez Alier, *Los huacchilleros del Perú* (Paris and Lima: Ruedo Ibérico-Instituto de Estudios Peruanos, 1973); Gerardo Rénique, *Sociedad Ganadera del Centro: Pastores y Sindicalización en una hacienda Alto andina. Documentos 1945–1948*, Taller de Estudios Andinos, Serie: Andes Centrales, No. 3 (La Molina: Universidad Nacional Agraria, 1977); and Florencia E. Mallon, "Microeconomía y campesinado: Hacienda, comunidad y coyunturas económicas en el Valle de Yanamarca," *Análisis*, No. 4 (January–April 1978), pp. 39–51. I discussed this practice and the problems it created with Felipe Artica in our second interview (Huancayo, 1977). Don Felipe was, for several decades, part of the administrative personnel on the hacienda Tucle in the Mantaro Valley region. Finally, Martínez Alier, *Los huacchilleros*, also presents a theory on the connection between this practice and community-hacienda land conflicts (see especially pp. 2–7).

[124] See footnote 116; also, ANF, Expedientes y Libros Judiciales, Libro de Juicios Verbales, Acolla, 1891–1892, Bravo Vial vs. Alvarez, May 18, 1891, 3v–4v.

tions and a more limited access to capital, did not hesitate to seize upon workers fleeing from larger estates and put them to work on their own properties. Thus small proprietors could become allies of the peasants in their battle against the large estates, creating further complications for the regional elite.

In the final analysis, both peasant resistance and divisions within their own ranks made elite control over the regional economy a tenuous and uncertain proposition. While there is no doubt that the commercial boom of the 1860s and 1870s resulted in an increasing penetration of the peasant economy and society, this same expansion generated conflicts and contradictions that impeded the establishment of elite hegemony. It is hardly surprising, therefore, that when the battlefield of the War of the Pacific shifted from the coast to the central highlands in 1881, the strain of the Chilean occupation exacerbated class tensions generated by the earlier commercialization. In a struggle that combined elements of nationalist resistance and class conflict, the peasants not only expelled the Chileans, but also struck back at the increasing pressure on their subsistence base. The battles unleashed by this confrontation would not be terminated for over fifteen years.

CHAPTER THREE

The War of the Pacific and the Problem
of Internal Pacification

We will make rifles from wood, bullets from hard stone.[1]

On the morning of April 15, 1881, Andrés Cáceres, colonel in the defeated Peruvian army, surreptitiously boarded the train at Viterbo, near Lima, and headed for the central highlands.[2] He left behind him an occupied city, and the memory of a two-year military campaign during which the Peruvian forces had been slowly, almost inexorably, pushed back from the sandy wastes of the Atacama Desert to the very doors of Lima. Fought over the huge nitrate deposits discovered in this desert in the mid-nineteenth century,[3] the War of the Pacific had

---

[1] From a *huayno*, or popular folk song, quoted in Adolfo Bravo Guzmán, *La segunda enseñanza en Jauja*, 2d ed. (Jauja, 1971), p. 286.

[2] Andrés A. Cáceres, *La guerra del 79. Sus campañas (Memorias)* (Lima: Carlos Milla Batres, 1973), p. 95.

[3] For some of the most interesting and thoughtful accounts of the War of the Pacific, see Jorge Basadre, *Chile, Perú y Bolivia independientes* (Barcelona-Buenos Aires: Salvat Editores, S.A., 1948), pp. 453–98, and *Historia de la República del Perú*, 6th ed., 17 Vols. (Lima: Editorial Universitaria, 1969), Vols. 6–8; Charles Victor Grosnier de Varigny, *La Guerra del Pacífico* (Santiago: Editorial del Pacífico, 1972); Cáceres, *La guerra del 79*; Antonia Moreno de Cáceres, *Recuerdos de la campaña de la Breña (Memorias)* (Lima: Editorial Milla Batres, 1974); Patricio Lynch, *Memoria que el contra-almirante D. Patricio Lynch presenta al Supremo Gobierno de Chile* (Lima: Imprenta La Merced, 1883–1884); Pascual Ahumada Moreno, *Guerra del Pacífico (Documentos)*, 8 Vols. (Valparaíso: Imprenta de la Librería del Mercurio, 1891); and Guillermo Thorndike, *1879* (Lima: Libre 1, 1977), *El viaje de Prado* (Lima: Libre 1, 1978), and *Vienen los chilenos* (Lima: Promoinvest Compañía de Inversiones, 1978). These last three works, ostensibly novels, are in fact part of a long and carefully researched project on the War of the Pacific. For the most recent analyses of the period of the war, and some of the deeper issues of nationalism and mobilization, see Heraclio Bonilla, "The War of the Pacific and the National and Colonial Problem in Peru," *Past and Present*, No. 81 (November 1978), pp. 92–118. See also Henri Favre, "Remarques sur la lutte des classes au Pérou pendant la guerre du Pacifique," in Association Française pour l'Etude et la Récherche sur les Pays Andins, *Littérature et Societé au Pérou du XIXème Siècle à Nos Jours* (Grenoble: Université de Langues et Lettres, 1975), pp. 54–81; Nelson Manrique, *Campesinado y nación. Las guerrillas indígenas en la Guerra con Chile* (Lima: Centro de Investigación y Capacitación and Ital Perú S.A., 1981), "Los movimientos campesinos en la Guerra del Pacífico," *Allpanchis*, No. 11–12 (1978), pp. 71–101, and "La Guerra del Pacífico y los conflictos de clase: Los terratenientes en la sierra del Perú," *Análisis*, No. 6 (September–December 1978), pp. 56–71.

ended in complete disaster for Bolivia and Peru. Unable to obtain credit in Europe, Peru had not acquired sufficient armaments. In order to raise funds internally, the Congress—made up of the most powerful *hacendados*, mineowners, bankers, and guano consignees— would have had to tax itself. This the members refused to do, even in the face of an imminent Chilean invasion, indulging instead in a long series of debates on free trade, censuring ministers and rejecting all economic plans that attempted to tap their personal fortunes. Council upon council of ministers had been forced to resign, unable or un- willing to take the necessary measures. And as the treasury emptied out, the Peruvian army had begun to lack not only small arms, artil- lery, and ammunition, but also salaries, clothes, shoes, and food.[4]

As many of his compatriots had done during the past two years, Cáceres was about to make one more sacrifice for his *patria*: a nation that existed in barely more than name, and whose defeat was due much more to this fact than to problems of military strategy. After the final battle at Miraflores on January 15, the wounded Cáceres had hidden himself, with the help of friends, in various hospitals and pri- vate homes, frustrating a concerted Chilean search. When the occu- pation forces had required that officers of the defeated army give their addresses, Cáceres had not complied.[5] While his wound healed, he had nursed a plan to retire to the highlands and organize a new army:

> As a result of the disaster at Miraflores, there arose in me the idea of escaping to the highlands and continuing the resistance against the invader, since I thought that, taking advantage of the defensive possibilities the region offered, it would be feasible to mount an obstinate resistance that would force the enemy to waste his ener- gies and moderate his ambitions, limiting him to the area of the coast that he already occupied.[6]

Between 1881 and 1883, Cáceres organized three different armies in the central highlands, each composed mainly of merchants, smaller *hacendados*, and peasants from the region. He and his representatives toured the provinces of Jauja and Huancayo, speaking in Spanish and in Quechua, requesting money, men, and arms.[7] They spoke to the merchants and wealthier peasants from the area's villages, encourag-

---

[4] There is general agreement in the literature, whether pro-Peruvian or pro-Chilean, on the financial and political difficulties existing in Peru during the war. For an espe- cially compelling account, see Thorndike, *1879* and *El viaje de Prado*.

[5] Cáceres, *La guerra del 79*, pp. 86–88.

[6] Ibid., p. 95.

[7] Ibid., p. 99.

ing the formation of guerrilla forces in the peasant communities. With
the aid of peasant guerrillas, Cáceres' army then managed to foil two
separate Chilean expeditions, earning a considerable reputation among
the area's inhabitants.

Yet no measure of heroic exploits or symbols could compensate for
the lack of unity and national purpose of the Peruvian elite. Unable
to unite effectively around either negotiation or resistance, various
elite factions fought against each other, seeming to forget that Peru
was an occupied country. And this confusion was mirrored in the
central highlands. Although Cáceres received support from most groups
in the early months of his campaign, the realities of protracted resistance and the actual presence of the Chilean army soon eroded his
base among the larger mineowners, *hacendados*, and merchants. With
their properties suffering the brunt of wartime exactions, this group
was soon eager to seek peace at any price. Some collaborated actively
with the Chileans, hoping to accelerate negotiations or even profit
from speculation. All looked with trepidation at the mobilization of
peasant guerrillas, wondering if the peasants might not turn on them
after repelling the invaders.

For the peasants, the Chilean invasion of the central highlands
marked their sudden and brutal initiation into the intricacies of international politics. Threatened in their homes by a foreign invader, encouraged by their political authorities, priests, and merchants to fight
against him, they carried out a bold and tenacious rearguard campaign
against the Chilean army, both alone and in alliance with the Cacerista regular troops. They developed an elementary sense of nationalism which was grounded, above all else, in their love for the land
and in a fierce sense of territoriality. And in the heat of battle, they
discovered in themselves a unity and strength that was to take them
far beyond the initial purpose that Cáceres had envisioned for them.

The Resistance of La Breña

When the Chilean occupation army entered Lima on January 17,
1881, they did not find a government able to negotiate the Peruvian
surrender. Nicolás de Piérola, who as dictator had organized the defense of Lima, had fled to the highlands with a small entourage. In
the next two years, Peru would once again be embroiled in a struggle
among caudillos, as various leaders attempted to establish a sufficiently wide territorial base to be recognized as the legitimate Peruvian government. The Chileans, for their part, would throw their sup-

port behind one faction and then another, attempting to find one with which they could successfully negotiate a peace treaty.

When Cáceres retired to the highlands, the Civilista party, composed mainly of progressive *hacendados*, bankers, and guano consignees, received initial recognition from the Chileans and attempted negotiation until the prospect of territorial losses caused an impasse in the discussions. On the other side, a loose coalition of military officers initially gathered around Piérola, refusing to negotiate and preaching continued resistance. By retreating to the sierra, where Piérola had his camp, Cáceres placed himself squarely in the latter faction. Only a few days after Cáceres' arrival on April 26, Piérola named him political and military leader of the central highlands resistance.[8]

Cáceres' choice of the central sierra also exhibited a shrewd understanding of military strategy and local politics. As previous nineteenth-century conflicts had shown, the central highland area was an ideal location for a resistance campaign. Access to the region depended upon a few easily guarded mountain passes. The abundant agricultural and livestock production could maintain an army for long periods of time. But most important for Cáceres, the central highlands provided him with a strong political base. As the descendant of a prestigious *encomendero* family from Ayacucho, Cáceres was related by blood or marriage to some of the more prominent elite families in the central sierra.[9] Thus he could expect help and personal friendship from a number of the region's powerful patrons, and hoped to have at his disposal their clientele networks.

Cáceres also knew that the central sierra elite had participated actively in defending Lima from the Chileans. The Concepción Battalion of the National Guard, composed of Juan Enrique Valladares, his brother Manuel Fernando, his brother-in-law Luis Milón Duarte, and many more prestigious merchants and *hacendados*, had distinguished

[8] On the political divisions and initial alliances in Peru during the occupation, see particularly Basadre, *Chile, Peru y Bolivia*, pp. 453–98; Manrique, *Campesinado y nación*, "La guerra del Pacífico," pp. 64–66, and "La ocupación y la resistencia," in Jorge Basadre et al., *Reflecciones en torno a la Guerra de 1879* (Lima: Francisco Campodónico-Centro de Investigación y Capacitación, 1979).

[9] Moreno de Cáceres, *Recuerdos*, pp. 45, 78; Cáceres, *La guerra del 79*, pp. 18, 126; Bravo Guzmán, *La segunda enseñanza*, p. 308; William B. Hutchinson, "Sociocultural Change in the Mantaro Valley Region of Peru: Acolla, A Case Study," Ph.D. Dissertation, Indiana University, 1973, p. 29. As a member or heir of the first generation of Spanish colonizers, an *encomendero* received access to the labor and tribute of a specific group of Indians, given to him or her in *encomienda* in exchange for his or her promise to Christianize and protect them. *Encomenderos* were included within the class of local notables in all the areas of Peru where they settled.

itself in battle at Miraflores.[10] The Jauja Battalion, led by an important merchant and including within its ranks a number of smaller *hacendados* from the Jauja region, had fought beside it.[11] Together with the forces under Cáceres' command, these two battalions had beaten back the Chileans in a brave counterattack,[12] and Cáceres hoped that they would continue to fight as tenaciously once the battle shifted closer to home.

In contrast to the elite, the central sierra peasants had not participated actively in the war's coastal campaigns. Some of the merchants who lived in or traded with the villages had volunteered for the National Guard battalions, and so had several smaller *hacendados* and owners of medium-sized commercial properties. Don Pedro Remusgo and don Carlos Villanes, for example, owners of small haciendas in the northern part of the Yanamarca Valley, were officers in the National Guard's Jauja Battalion. Among the region's wealthier peasant families, a few had sent their sons to fight at Miraflores. Thus Fidel Crespo, related by marriage to the Ortega family of Acolla, was a sublieutenant. In other cases, villagers had been victims of forced conscription for the makeshift forces organized to defend Lima.[13] But for most peasants, the war was far away, and they had other, more immediate, concerns.

The resistance of La Breña, as Cáceres' campaign in the central highlands came to be called, radically changed this situation. No longer were the battles fought on a distant battlefield. Even in the central sierra, where peasants were accustomed to seeing caudillos pass through with their troops on their way to and from the presidential palace, no one could remember having seen anything like it. In the nine months between May 1881 and February 1882, the region's inhabitants withstood two separate Chilean invasions. They were forced to support both the Peruvian and Chilean armies, a task that decimated supplies very quickly. For an army that numbered fifteen hundred men at its highest level, Cáceres decreed that each province of the department of Junín should provide a monthly quota of twenty-six head of cattle, 3,790 head of sheep, 663 *quintales* (66,300 pounds) of potatoes, twenty-

[10] Interview with Hernán Valladares, Huancayo, June 3, 1977; AHM, "Memorias sobre la Resistencia de la Breña del Teniente Coronel Ambrosio Salazar y Márquez (Escrita por su hermano Juan P. Salazar)," Huancayo, 1918.

[11] Bravo Guzmán, *La segunda enseñanza*, pp. 654–58, has a list of the officers composing the Jauja Battalion of the National Guard.

[12] Cáceres, *La guerra del 79*, pp. 83–84.

[13] Bravo Guzmán, *La segunda enseñanza*, pp. 655–56. For an account of the nature of forced conscription, see Manrique, *Campesinado y nación*, pp. 59–64.

four *quintales* of wheat, and forty-eight *quintales* of corn.[14] And this was the most reasonable exaction. The much more numerous Chilean troops took whatever they could find, wherever and however they could find it. It is not surprising, therefore, that when Cáceres' representatives came to the villages to tell the peasants about their "patriotic duty to combat the Chilean invader,"[15] they usually found a receptive audience.

The village of Comas, to the east of Jauja, was a case in point. Especially after a Chilean detachment passed through the community on February 24, 1882, demanding food for immediate consumption and ordering additional supplies for their return within several days, municipal officials decided that it was time to resist. They wrote to Ambrosio Salazar y Márquez, a wealthy peasant who had passed through their community on February 8 urging the immediate organization of guerrilla bands, and asked for his help in organizing a *montonera*. As they explained, they had been particularly irritated by a letter from Jauja's parish priest, who had demanded provisions for the Chilean garrison in that city and threatened reprisals if the orders were not obeyed.[16]

As peasant enthusiasm for the resistance effort increased, however, so did elite ambivalence. When Cáceres first arrived in the central highlands, most *hacendados* welcomed him warmly as one of their own. During the first Chilean invasion in May 1881, the Valladares gave Cáceres and his wife a place to stay on their retreat from Jauja to Concepción, presenting them with some of the famous butter made on the haciendas Laive and Runatullo.[17] The Peñalosas, a prestigious *hacendado* family in Huancayo, also opened their doors.[18] But the realities of a protracted Chilean occupation tended to change elite attitudes. Even during the first invasion, when the leader of the Chilean expedition sent a message to Huancayo threatening to burn the city unless a heavy exaction was met within forty-eight hours, a fraction of the area's merchants and *hacendados* quietly decided to meet Chilean demands. They raised 60,000 soles—the price of a medium-sized hacienda—and thirty horses, commissioning Manuel Zevallos, a prominent *hacendado*, to take the goods to the Chileans under cover

[14] Ricardo Tello Devotto, *Historia de la provincia de Huancayo* (Huancayo: Casa de la Cultura de Junín, 1971), p. 71; and Cáceres, *La guerra del 79*, pp. 141, 173, and 203.

[15] Cáceres, *La guerra del 79*, p. 99.

[16] AHM, "Memorias sobre la Resistencia de la Breña," Anexo No. 1, 53.

[17] Moreno de Cáceres, *Recuerdos*, p. 45.

[18] Ibid., p. 46.

of night. Cáceres discovered the plan, however, and arrested the mayor of the city, confiscating the goods to use them for his own army.[19] And although the Chilean forces were soon ordered to retreat toward Lima, leaving Huancayo intact, the elite's alternatives were already clear. Either they gave in to Chilean demands, hoping to limit the destruction of their property and investments; or they took a patriotic stand, knowing that Cáceres' minute force could not effectively defend them from Chilean reprisals. No matter how bravely they had fought at Miraflores, many *hacendados* were increasingly ambivalent about continuing the battle in their own backyard.

In January 1882, the arrival of a second Chilean expedition, commanded by Colonel Estanislao del Canto, marked an important watershed in the campaign of La Breña. In contrast to its predecessor, the del Canto expedition was not only an invading force: it was a true army of occupation. Having forced Cáceres to retreat to Ayacucho, del Canto established headquarters in the southern part of the Mantaro Valley. The houses of several prominent citizens in Huancayo were requisitioned to serve as lodgings for the officers of the various Chilean battalions. In both Huancayo and Concepción, del Canto put pressure on local officials and demanded contributions from merchants and *hacendados*. Troop detachments combed the area's villages and haciendas, looking for supplies to maintain the three thousand enemy soldiers.[20]

Faced with a prolonged occupation and unable to rely on immediate help from Cáceres' regular army, the region's inhabitants were forced to take matters into their own hands. Throughout the early months of 1882, the peasants of the area's villages met in community assemblies to organize guerrilla bands and fight the Chileans. They elected merchants, parish priests, and noncommissioned officers— usually from outside the community—as leaders of the *montoneras*.[21]

[19] Cáceres, *La guerra del 79*, pp. 100–101.

[20] For descriptions of the del Canto expedition, see Cáceres, *La guerra del 79*, pp. 134–46; Tello Devotto, *Historia de Huancayo*, pp. 63–66; AHM, "Memorias sobre la Resistencia de la Breña," 5–20; and Manrique, *Campesinado y nación*, pp. 131–80.

[21] *Montoneras* refers generally to bands of armed men organized informally in the countryside to support a particular political cause. This term was already used to refer to armed bands in the central highlands during the Wars of Independence. See Comisión Nacional del Sesquicentenario de la Independencia del Perú, *Colección documental: La actividad patriótica del pueblo en la Emancipación. Guerrillas y montoneras* (Lima: Editorial Lumen, S.A., 1971–1973), Tomo V (4 Vols.). For the general way in which the guerrillas were organized for the La Breña campaign, see AHM, "Memorias sobre la Resistencia de la Breña," 5–20; APJ, "Acta del pueblo de Sincos ofreciendo tomar armas en defensa de la honra Nacional," April 11, 1882; and Cáceres, *La guerra del 79*, pp. 99 and 104.

In the village of Comas, as we have already seen, Ambrosio Salazar y Márquez, a prestigious *vecino* from San Gerónimo de Tunan who owned property in the village of Quichuay and was a graduate of the prestigious Colegio de Santa Isabel in Huancayo, answered the peasants' request for aid by organizing and financing a guerrilla force.[22] On the west bank of the Mantaro River, the parish priest of Huaripampa, Father Mendoza, organized a guerrilla band composed of peasants from the villages of Huaripampa, Muquiyauyo, Llocllapampa, Ullusca, and others.[23] José María Béjar, from an important Jauja family, organized peasant resistance in the village of Sincos, slightly to the south of Muquiyauyo.[24] And at the southwestern limit of the Mantaro area, Corporal Tomás Laimes, a veteran of Miraflores and originally from Huanta, Ayacucho, fomented and centralized guerrilla activity in the villages of Chongos Alto and Huasichancha.[25]

While Cáceres' army, decimated by battles and forced marches, was recuperating in Ayacucho, the peasant guerrillas executed a number of successful rearguard actions against the Chileans. The first of these was the ambush of a Chilean detachment in Comas. On February 24, 1882, a patrol of approximately forty soldiers, under the command of Captain Fernando Germain, passed through Comas on their way to pillage the hacienda Runatullo. The Comas *montonera*, led by Ambrosio Salazar, decided to ambush the patrol upon its return. Organized in a double line, with thirty rifles and fifty *galgueros*,[26] the *Comasinos* attacked the Chileans at Sierra Lumi on March 2. When the battle was over, thirty-five of the forty Chileans lay dead on the field, and the peasants had captured 800 head of cattle and 100 horses from the hacienda Runatullo, as well as 35 horses and as many Winchester rifles belonging to the Chileans.[27]

The *montoneras* continued their resistance in April and May. Along the west bank of the Mantaro River, a Chilean patrol met stiff opposition in Chupaca on April 19, but was finally able to beat back the

[22] Bravo Guzmán, *La segunda enseñanza*, pp. 291, 671; and AHM, "Memorias sobre la Resistencia de la Breña."

[23] Bravo Guzmán, *La segunda enseñanza*, pp. 287–91.

[24] APJ, "Acta del pueblo de Sincos," and AGN, Protocolos Notariales, Claudio José Suárez, Book 890, November 30, 1864, 774–78.

[25] Tello Devotto, *Historia de Huancayo*, pp. 75–76; Nelson Manrique, "Tomás Laimes, un general indio," *Quehacer*, No. 11 (July 1981), pp. 128–35.

[26] *Galgueros* refers to peasants in charge of pushing *galgas*, or large boulders, down on the enemy from the top of the surrounding hills.

[27] Although there are several accounts of the Sierra Lumi action, I have preferred to use the one given in AHM, "Memorias sobre la Resistencia de la Breña," 6–14.

guerrillas and burn the village.[28] Three days later, the *montonera* in Huaripampa, under the leadership of Father Mendoza, engaged another Chilean patrol in fierce combat. Fighting with ten shotguns, five rifles, and numerous sticks, lances, and slingshots, the guerrillas held off the Chileans to the last man.[29] And on the eastern side of the river, the *montoneras* from Tongos, Pazos, and Acostambo fought the Chileans on the 21st and 22nd of May. In the latter village, two peasants were surprised by a Chilean soldier while they attempted to push a boulder down the hill onto an enemy column. The Chilean charged one of the peasants, plunging his bayonet into the guerrilla's chest. The Peruvian, in turn, plunged his knife into the Chilean. The second peasant then used his machete to cut off the Chilean's head. When Cáceres arrived in Acostambo two months later, he found the Chilean soldier's head impaled on a lance and exhibited in a public place.[30]

In addition to inflicting notable casualties, loss of weapons, and loss of morale on the Chilean army, the peasant *montoneras* greatly worried the regional elite. Although the guerrillas had been organized by wealthy or prestigious outsiders in touch with Cáceres' general guerrilla command, the need to rely on an armed and mobilized peasantry had imbued the La Breña campaign with a democratic flavor that most elite members found distasteful.[31] It was one thing to resist the invader, but to create an armed, mobilized, and relatively autonomous peasantry and, even worse, to respect them as citizens—that was an entirely different story. The most dangerous part of it, moreover, was that the peasants were beginning to believe in their equality as soldiers. Not only did they keep the booty and ammunition they obtained from the Chileans, but they also entered haciendas asking for provisions.

For an elite whose regional dominance had been shaky in time of peace, the threat of an armed peasantry in time of war seemed more dangerous than the presence of a foreign army. Some elite members succumbed to pressure from the Chilean high command and collaborated openly. Juan Enrique Valladares, for example, mayor of Concepción and previously the organizer of the Concepción Battalion, wrote a letter to the guerrilla leader Ambrosio Salazar in Comas, asking him to put down his weapons, return the body of the Chilean

[28] Cáceres, *La guerra del 79*, pp. 174–75.

[29] Bravo Guzmán, *La segunda enseñanza*, pp. 287–88.

[30] Cáceres, *La guerra del 79*, p. 175.

[31] Moreno de Cáceres, for example, tells of the distaste that Bernarda Piélago, *hacendada* in Huancayo and Cáceres' aunt, felt when Cáceres insisted on receiving visits from peasants in her house (*Recuerdos*, p. 78).

captain, and give back the horses and rifles captured in the Sierra Lumi ambush.[32] Others were unable to accept that they and the guerrillas were fighting on the same side. Thus Jacinto Cevallos, a prominent *hacendado* from Huancayo, sent a note to the administrator of his hacienda Punto after a *montonera* from the village of Acobamba had stopped there and asked for provisions. The letter called the peasants barbarians, and promised revenge.[33] Of course, some of the area's citizens collaborated with the Chileans out of simpler motives. Guillermo Kirchner, for example, was able to make a neat profit by helping to market the booty obtained from many of the Mantaro Valley communities and haciendas.[34] But whether they were motivated by fear or by profit, an important fraction of the regional elite began to look increasingly like traitors to the peasant guerrillas.

The peasants were extremely angered by elite collaboration. When Ambrosio Salazar wrote back to Valladares, he violently refused to come to terms, even if the Chileans returned to Comas and burned the village to the ground.[35] But perhaps the most indicative reaction came from the Acobamba guerrillas. Having intercepted the note Cevallos sent to his administrator, they decided to send a letter to Cevallos on April 16, 1882. "To Mr. Civilista Don Jacinto Cevallos," they wrote,

> You would think that under the Sun and the earth they would not know that you were a traitor to the homeland where you were born, well they do know, and we know that you with all your friends traitors to our amiable [sic] homeland are in this province communicating and giving explanations on how they can ruin the Peruvians, to those treacherous Chilean bandits invaders [and] like you traitors to their homeland. Also you would think that we couldn't grab the communication that you were passing to your Administrator, well we have it in our hands informed of its contents we must tell you: that all the Guirrillas [sic] that are in the valleys of these hills led by the Commander Gonzales Dilgado [sic] are with the express orders of the General Don Andres Abilino [sic] Caseres [sic] and we have orders to punish the deceitful actions of the traitors of the homeland: and you don't put us in the group of the

[32] AHM, "Memorias sobre la Resistencia de la Breña," Anexo No. 10, 84.
[33] APJ, "Oficio de los guerrilleros de Acobamba a Jacinto Cevallos," April 16, 1882.
[34] "Carta del Coronel Estanislao del Canto, Santiago, Enero 27 de 1885, al Sr. Dn. Guillermo Kirchner, Concepción," included in AHM, "Memorias sobre la Resistencia de la Breña."
[35] Ibid., Anexo No. 11, 86.

barbarians like you told your Administrator because we with reason and justice unanimously rose up to defend our homeland we are true lovers of our homeland where we were born. I [*sic*] don't know what people you call miserable and want to revenge yourself over the course of time: don't you think that we until the present coccasion [*sic*] even though you call us barbarians we still don't walk around committing revenge and other barbarous things, instead we proceed with all loyalty all the Guirrillas even though we know that you are one of the closest associates of the infamous Dr. Giraldez. It's true that the other day since we passed through your Hacienda after having made an advance across these places to fight those Chilean bandits while we were passing through we asked your administrator to give us about eight cattle for our food to give their rations to two thousand men that are at our command: this is all we have done in relation to your hacienda and you think we have committed barbarous acts, but any *hacendado* should be able to tolerate us as patriotic soldiers.

God keep you—[signed] Mariano Mayta, Lieutenant Governor— Faustino Camargo, Captain—Martin Vera, Captain, Lieutenant Governor—Mariano Campos, Lieutenant Governor—Domingo Mercado.[36]

This letter, written in uneducated, shaky, almost illegible handwriting, bears witness to the intense process of ideological growth undergone by the peasants of the central highlands during the La Breña campaign. After suffering a year of Chilean occupation and seeing their homes and fields looted by a foreign invader, the peasants of the region were forced to confront a very basic fact: that the intricacies of national and international politics had an important effect on their daily lives. Out of this confrontation, they developed both an under-

---

[36] APJ, "Oficio de los guerrilleros de Acobamba." The handwriting and grammar on the original note identify its author as a literate, though not particularly schooled, peasant. The simple fact that the author was literate, of course, means that he did not belong to the poorest strata of the community. But the shakiness of the writing points to the fact that he was not rich, either. If one were to generalize from this as to the position of the guerrilla leaders, one would have to conclude that most of them came from the middle peasantry, and did not have the time during the guerrilla campaigns to get the note written by someone specializing in that type of work.

Dr. Giráldez is a reference to the *hacendado* whom Cáceres left in charge of informing him as to the Chilean advance during the invasion of the Letelier expedition in 1881–1882. Although Cáceres left Giráldez a horse on which to reach him, Giráldez never complied. Cáceres, *La guerra del 79*, p. 142. As to the translation of the letter, I have tried my best to preserve a flavor of the original, with equivalent mistakes in spelling and grammar.

standing of national politics and a strong sense of nationalism, though neither would be recognized as such by modern or upper-class standards. Their nationalism, for example, was not a general or symbolic sense of nationhood, but a feeling founded very concretely on their love for their homeland—for the place where they were born, "under the Sun and the earth"—for the land they planted. Thus the Chileans were not enemies because they were Chileans, but because they invaded and destroyed the homeland, the peasants' most precious resource, their source of subsistence and life. In a similar vein, the guerrillas' understanding of national politics was not an abstract analysis of political parties, but a clear grasp of the implications of political debates for developments in their own villages. When they addressed Cevallos as Civilista, therefore, they did not mean that he belonged to that party, but that he was acting as they had heard a Civilista acted: talking to the Chileans, collaborating with them, prolonging their occupation of the Peruvian homeland.[37]

Yet what is most important about this letter, and what must have frightened Cevallos even more than the idea of two thousand peasants passing through his hacienda, is the way in which peasant nationalism and class consciousness fed into one another. Throughout the letter, the guerrillas return to the same theme—how angry they are that Cevallos should consider them barbarians. They knew full well that if a group of regular soldiers under the command of a prestigious officer had entered his hacienda asking for provisions, Cevallos would not have considered them in the same light. It was only because the guerrillas were peasants that the *hacendado* could not see them as his allies. He would rather collaborate with the Chileans, with the invaders, than with Peruvian peasants. And this was the ultimate treachery; for, as the guerrillas stated, "any *hacendado* should be able to tolerate us as patriotic soldiers."

[37] Clearly, the role of the Civilista party in the process of negotiations was a great deal more complex than this. It was initially the Civilistas who set up a government willing to negotiate with the Chileans under the presidency of Francisco García Calderón. However, once it became clear in the negotiations that there could not be a settlement without substantial territorial losses, in particular those territories rich in nitrates, negotiations broke down. Not only did the Civilistas find it difficult to handle the national embarrassment of territorial fragmentation, but some members of the party had substantial investments in nitrates. In fact, the group that finally accepted peace with territorial fragmentation was a sector of the *hacendados*, under the leadership of Miguel Iglesias, rather than the Civilistas. See Manrique, "La Guerra del Pacífico," p. 65 and footnote 22. For the peasants, however, the niceties of these changing political alliances were irrelevant. The word "civilistas" maintained its initial meaning: those who negotiated rather than fought, those against whom Cáceres had organized the La Breña campaign.

Thus the letter from the Acobamba guerrillas was both a statement of outrage and a warning. As they saw it, while the *hacendados* and merchants had stood idly by, paying the Chilean exactions, lodging the Chileans in their houses, it was the peasants who had risen up to fight the invader, even if they only possessed boulders and slingshots. Yet the elite had the audacity, the nerve, to treat the peasants as barbarians and common criminals. But they would pay in the end: as soldiers of Cáceres, the peasants not only had orders to punish "the deceitful traitors of the homeland," they also had the legitimate right to decide who the traitors were.

When Cáceres renewed his efforts against the Chilean forces in July 1882, it was the peasant guerrillas, not the regular army, who formed the vanguard of the struggle. On July 8, for example, the Comas guerrillas, under the command of Ambrosio Salazar, led an attack on Concepción. In a nocturnal battle lasting seventeen hours, these guerrillas, with the help of a small detachment of Cáceres' regular army and scarcely eleven inhabitants of Concepción, exterminated the seventy-nine men that made up the Chilean garrison and appropriated all remaining rifles and ammunition.[38] And the *Comasinos* were not alone. All along the Mantaro Valley, from Marcavalle in the south, through Jauja and on to Tarma, the peasant *montoneras* proved decisive in defeating the occupying army.

Cáceres was extremely impressed by the enthusiasm of the peasant guerrillas. After confirming the enemy's retreat from the department of Junín, he sent an official report of the campaign to the Peruvian authorities in Lima in which he praised the actions of the region's peasants. "The Supreme Government's attention should be especially directed to the spontaneous mass uprising of all the Indians in the Departments of Junín and Huancavelica," he wrote, "with which they have given a most valuable service. This event foreshadows a unanimous movement that will soon transform the nature of the present war."[39] And to ensure the continued support of the peasants, Cáceres issued a decree exonerating all guerrillas from the payment of the Indian head tax.[40]

Cáceres' prediction that peasant participation would change the nature of the war proved a great deal better founded than he realized.

---

[38] "Informe de Ambrosio Salazar a Juan Gastó sobre el combate en Concepción," Ingenio, July 10, 1882, in Bravo Guzmán, *La segunda enseñanza,* pp. 658–63.

[39] "Parte oficial del General Cáceres sobre los combates de Marcavalle, Pucará, Concepción, San Juan Cruz," Tarma, July 31, 1882, in Bravo Guzmán, *La segunda enseñanza,* p. 667.

[40] Tello Devotto, *Historia de Huancayo,* pp. 69–70.

Although by September 1882 the central sierra was once again free of the foreign invader, it was also on the threshold of a class war that, hidden among the folds of national resistance, could explode at any moment. Yet the underlying struggle was not simply one of the peasants against the regional elite. While the increasing penetration of commercial capital into the peasant community had created a particularly high level of class tension before the war, it was in the context of the La Breña campaign that the tension worked itself out. Nationalism, class conflict, and class alliances were thus articulated in a complex pattern, having a great deal to do with the way the guerrillas had been organized in the first place, and with the way that different fragments of the elite had reacted to the Chilean invasion.

In organizing the guerrillas, the Caceristas had relied on smaller merchants, priests, and noncommissioned officers who, through local networks of patronage and clientele, had forged alliances with the wealthier peasants and political authorities in the villages. In this way, the leaders could arm, mobilize, and incorporate the poorer peasants while still controlling the *montoneras* from the top down. The merchants and wealthy peasants, moreover, served as intermediaries between the regional elite and the peasant community, helping to bind the two classes together for a common nationalist cause. But the intermediaries could only be successful if both the peasants and the regional elite continued to support the resistance effort. While this support was still strong in the northern part of the Mantaro Valley, it was eroding rapidly in the south.

The Chilean occupation had polarized the elite along both regional and economic lines. The southern part of the valley had been the main center of Chilean operations, and the central highlands' wealthiest and most prestigious *hacendados*, who lived and had their properties between Huancayo and Concepción, had been forced to bear the brunt of the invasion. Their haciendas suffered the repeated incursions of Chilean patrols. The peasant guerrillas in this area, particularly from Acobamba, Acostambo, Canchapalca, and Comas, fought fiercely and also took supplies from the haciendas. Because the southern merchants and landowners, wanting to protect what was left of their investments and extremely wary of the mobilized peasants, took an increasingly accommodating attitude toward the Chileans, they forced the guerrilla leaders and intermediaries to choose between a collaborationist upper class and a peasantry willing to push forward with the national resistance. Rather than give in to the enemy, the leaders continued the resistance and relied more completely on peasant support, giving the struggle a more popular base and a stronger class dynamic.

In the north, on the other hand, the Chilean presence was more sporadic. Elite fortunes, smaller and more concentrated in commerce, suffered less directly from Chilean exactions. The guerrillas, faced with a more intermittent Chilean threat, were not as independent and militant as they were in the south. The northern elite, therefore, at the margin of the Chilean occupation and less threatened by peasant mobilization, could more easily give Cáceres their continued support. As a result, the northern *montoneras* remained within the confines of the patron-client and multiclass alliances initially forged by the Caceristas.[41]

The north-south dichotomy in the Mantaro Valley illustrates two possible ways in which class tensions and incipient nationalism could interact. Though peasants developed nationalist feeling in both cases, in the south they experienced nationalism in opposition to the collaborationist elite. This deepened hostility between the classes and pushed them toward open confrontation. National unity was therefore undermined at the same time as nationalist feeling began to emerge. In the north, on the other hand, peasants discovered nationalism in the context of a common struggle with the elite against the Chileans, and this common front did not break down in the heat of battle. Thus a more genuine nationalist front, which successfully subsumed class interests, could grow.

What the two cases have in common is the importance of the elite's actions in defining the strength or weakness of national cohesion. Nationalist feeling would have exercised a broader appeal for the lower classes if the elite itself had taken a united nationalist stand, actively defining and controlling nationalism from above. Evidence from the coast, however, as well as from most areas of the highlands, indicates that the majority of the elite was more concerned with the dual threat of lower class mobilization and loss of property than with the invasion of the Chilean army.[42] In this context the northern Mantaro Valley,

[41] The strength of the Cacerista ties in the Jauja region is borne out by the fact that, even after Piérola defeated Cáceres in a bid for national power in 1895, the area around Jauja was considered to be *the* Cacerista stronghold. See especially APJ, "Carta del Subprefecto de Huancayo al Prefecto del Departamento de Junín," Huancayo, February 17, 1897; and BNP, "Carta de Domingo F. Parra a Nicolás de Piérola," Archivo. Piérola, Caja (Antigua) No. 53, Correspondencia Oficial y Particular.

[42] For the coast, see Bonilla, "The War of the Pacific," pp. 101–105. For Cerro de Pasco, see YC, Notes from the Peruvian Legation in the United States to the Department of State, clipping from *New York World* (microfilm), September 2, 1881; also, clipping from the *New York Daily Tribune*, Callao, September 10, 1881. Further ex-

especially the area around Jauja where landowners, merchants, and peasants remained united in their support for Cáceres, seems to have been the exception rather than the southern Mantaro area.

The elite's inability to unite around nationalism was borne out once again on August 31, 1882, when Miguel Iglesias, an *hacendado* from Cajamarca and previously a follower of Piérola, issued the "Cry of Montán." In this proclamation, Iglesias indicated his willingness to negotiate with the Chileans.[43] By offering a viable alternative to the resistance campaign, he drew to his side a number of disaffected officers, politicians, and *hacendados* who were tired of the war, and he thereby posed a direct threat to Cáceres. In the first months of 1883, a number of towns began to declare their support for the "Cry of Montán," and the ideological war between Iglesistas and Caceristas extended into the central sierra.[44] Cáceres met Iglesias' challenge head on, issuing proclamations to his army and to the towns of the central highlands and, at the end of January, marching against Canta, the first town in the region to declare itself in favor of Iglesias.[45]

At different points during the month of April three Chilean divisions, with a total of 6,500 men, marched into the highlands with orders to defeat Cáceres and wipe out all guerrilla resistance. After fighting the Chileans courageously in several limited engagements, Cáceres was finally forced to regroup at Chicla, leaving Canta to the enemy.[46] Knowing that his retreat facilitated the renewed occupation of the Mantaro Valley, he sent a letter to the subprefect of Jauja on April 30, urging the independent organization of guerrilla forces in each of the area's towns and villages and warning the inhabitants against Peruvian "traitors." "Since despite the sanctity of the cause that we defend," he explained,

> there is no lack of perverted Peruvians who, allying with the Chileans, offer their services as spies or guides, or give them cattle, grain, money or other resources to help them with their wicked work of devastation, and others who with false news and other methods dishearten the citizens and oppose the taking up of arms

amples of elite behavior can be found in: YC, U.S. Consulate, Callao, Despatches, "Report by Consul J. H. Moore on Chilean actions in the sierra," June 7, 1882; YC, U.S. Consulate, Callao, Records, Miscellaneous Correspondence Received, "McNulty to Moore," Cerro de Pasco, November 25, 1882 and May 15, 1883; Bonilla, "The War of the Pacific," p. 103; and Manrique, "Los movimientos campesinos," pp. 89–92.

[43] Basadre, *Chile, Perú y Bolivia*, pp. 495–96.
[44] Cáceres, *La guerra del 79*, p. 183.
[45] Ibid., pp. 183–84.
[46] Ibid., pp. 184–94.

in defense of our country, it is necessary that you persecute and denounce these traitors and impose upon them the punishment that their infamous conduct deserves. Advising the inhabitants of this province that those who not only as private citizens, but also as political or municipal authorities, provide any help whatsoever to the enemy, shall suffer the penalties that a traitor deserves.—You shall inform the villages of this idea through their governors, who should read to the communities the content of this letter. Telling them also that they should never, for any reason, obey authorities who in any way collaborate with the enemy.[47]

Cáceres was right to warn against Peruvian "collaborators," for Iglesias' position appealed to several of the *hacendados* in the Mantaro Valley. Luis Milón Duarte, related to the Valladares brothers by marriage and owner, with his wife Beatriz Valladares, of some of the richest haciendas in the central sierra, became Iglesias' political and military governor for the central highland provinces.[48] In a statement he issued from his camp at Chocas on May 6, he summarized the feelings of many elite members when he said that the conditions for peace accepted by Iglesias were the best that could be expected, and that the most important thing was to end the destruction and work hard to reconstruct the country. "Fellow citizens," he began,

> Inspired by patriotism, I did my duty during the war, both in the administration of General La Puerta and the dictatorship of Mr. Piérola, and after our disasters, having acquired the conviction that we were unable to continue the struggle to a successful conclusion, I employed my energies in searching, through peace, for the end to our national troubles, something which is desired by all.
>
> I have been one of the few who has had faith and has persevered in the supreme attempt to redeem our country, and thus the arrows of injustice, calumny and factionalist passions have wounded me. My modest person has suffered all kinds of hostilities; my properties have been sacked and burned, as much by the external enemy as by the internal enemies of peace.[49]

Duarte continued his campaign against the "internal enemies of peace," combining threats and bribes in an effort to render ineffectual Cáceres' guerrilla support. In two further proclamations from Chocas,

[47] "Carta del Subprefecto de Jauja al Gobernador de Huaripampa," Jauja, May 4, 1883, in Bravo Guzmán, *La segunda enseñanza*, p. 673.
[48] Ahumada Moreno, *Guerra del Pacífico*, VIII: 161–62.
[49] Ibid. Chocas is an hacienda located about twenty-five miles east of Lima.

he ordered the disarmament of all private citizens within three days, and the declaration of loyalty to Iglesias by all military and political personnel within eight days. Those not complying with the orders would be judged in civil and criminal court, but those who complied would receive amnesty. And, perhaps most interesting, all the guerrillas who left the *montoneras* would be rewarded and declared exempt from further military service.[50]

Duarte's campaign did not have the desired effect. Although the Chilean division under the command of León García forced Cáceres to retreat to Tarma, they encountered fierce guerrilla resistance all along the road.[51] Then on May 21, protected from the Chileans by the Tarmatambo guerrillas, the Cacerista army began its retreat to the north.[52] Guided by Duarte, two of the three Chilean divisions gave chase.[53] The third division, under the command of Colonel Urriola, was ordered to remain in the Mantaro Valley and, having occupied Huancayo, to clean up the remaining pockets of guerrilla activity.[54]

Urriola's invasion of Huancayo brought class tensions to the boiling point. Many among the city's elite, seconding Duarte's desire that the war be rapidly ended, received Urriola well.[55] But the peasants, veterans of previous occupations, loyal to Cáceres, and still heavily mobilized, did not take kindly to Iglesista "treachery." From this point on, guerrilla activity took on a particularly violent and menacing tone, with the murders of several collaborationist Peruvians in the area being attributed to the *montoneros*.[56] And on July 4, after Urriola had been ordered to march north to Jauja, the guerrillas from Huari took advantage of the Chilean army's absence to invade the city of Huancayo, killing a prominent citizen who attempted to calm them down.[57]

From the point of view of the peasants, the Urriola expedition provided the final proof that local *hacendados* were traitors to the nation.

---

[50] Ibid., VIII: 161.

[51] Lynch, *Memoria*, II: 123–25; Cáceres, *La guerra del 79*, p. 194.

[52] Cáceres, *La guerra del 79*, pp. 194–202. The rest of Cáceres' campaign, the defeat at Huamachuco, the reorganization of a new army in Ayacucho, the peace treaty and so on, are not of relevance here. Information on them can be found in most of the sources on the war that are quoted in this chapter.

[53] Lynch, *Memoria*, II: 125; Cáceres, *La guerra del 79*, pp. 203–205; Ahumada Moreno, *Guerra del Pacífico*, VIII: 161.

[54] Ahumada Moreno, *Guerra del Pacífico*, VIII: 181–82.

[55] Tello Devotto, *Historia de Huancayo*, pp. 72–73.

[56] Ibid., p. 73.

[57] Ibid., p. 72; Nemesio A. Ráez, *Monografía de la Provincia de Huancayo (1898)* (Huancayo: Universidad Nacional del Centro del Perú, n.d.), p. 21.

This was the case because, despite the fact that Urriola's division was Chilean, the elite was willing to use its backing to repress the *montoneras* and ultimately to strip the peasant guerrillas of whatever legitimacy they still maintained as nationalist soldiers. The end result was simply that there was no longer any common ground for negotiation between the two classes. The elite viewed all action by the peasant guerrillas as racially or class-motivated pillage, whereas the peasants perceived elite attempts to protect their property as treachery to the national resistance. It is in this context, with class and national concerns intermingled and reverberating against each other, that the various land invasions and other actions in the area must be viewed.

By the time the war was completely over in early 1886, more than fifteen haciendas in the Huancayo area alone had been invaded by the peasants. Most of these properties belonged to people who had collaborated with the Chileans or with Iglesias: three to Luis Milón Duarte, four to the Valladares brothers, two to Jacinto Cevallos, and several to other "collaborators."[58] Both Duarte and Giráldez had been assassinated.[59] And in the Cerro de Pasco area, where the elite had also cooperated with the Chileans, the peasants had invaded a total of sixteen municipal properties and ten private haciendas.[60]

While the actual mechanics of many of these actions are not known, the general context in which they occurred is fairly clear. In the course of the various resistance campaigns against the Chileans (1882–1883) and against Iglesias (1884–1885), the peasants gained de facto control of the countryside. In the same way as the regular armies, the peasant guerrillas lived off the land, taking cattle and other supplies from the haciendas to feed themselves or, in some cases, to finance the purchase of arms.[61] Whenever they were faced with a superior force, the *montoneros* would retire to the high *puna* regions, which served as a nearly impenetrable defense.[62] But it was precisely in the high *puna*

---

[58] Tello Devotto, *Historia de Huancayo*, p. 79; APJ, "Juan E. Valladares y otros al Prefecto del Departamento," Huancayo, August 10, 1886; "Juan E. Valladares al Ministro de Gobierno," Lima, June 7, 1886; and "Ministerio de Gobierno al Prefecto del Departamento de Junín," August 3, 1886.

[59] Tello Devotto, *Historia de Huancayo*, pp. 76 and 79; AHM, "Memorias sobre la Resistencia de la Breña."

[60] APJ, "Subprefecto del Cerro de Pasco al Prefecto del Departmento," Cerro de Pasco, August 23, 1886.

[61] APJ, "Oficio de varios vecinos de Comas al Prefecto del Departmento," Jauja, September 9, 1887.

[62] This was true even into the Civil War of 1884–1885. See, for example, AHM, "Oficio del Prefecto de Junín Andrés Recharte al Ministerio de Guerra," Huancayo,

that most of the large properties were located. Since the *hacendados* were forced to remain in the cities throughout these campaigns, whether or not the peasants actually held the entire land surface of the various haciendas, they were the only force in the countryside with the power to control hacienda resources. Motivated by their newly developed combination of nationalist outrage and class hostility, they used the existing balance of power to expand and consolidate their hold over the elite's property.

Yet it is important to emphasize that the land invasions were not indiscriminate. For the most part, they occurred in areas where the elite had collaborated openly with the Chileans or with Iglesias. The victims were mainly the individual landowners known to have been the worst offenders in this regard. In areas where the Cacerista alliance had been maintained, on the other hand, most notably in the northern part of the Mantaro Valley, there were no invasions at all. Thus it seems necessary to take the testimony of the *hacendados* and other sources close to them, such as the Chilean commanders, foreign consular officers, or political authorities, with a rather large grain of salt.[63] While violent and racially motivated actions did occur, the generalized peasant mobilization in the central highlands was far from being an all–out racial war or the unleashing of some form of savage, atavistic barbarism. Quite the contrary, it was the Indian and *mestizo* peasants, rather than the elite, who were willing to subsume their class interests to a national resistance effort. They stopped doing so only once they realized that the elite was unable to accept them as patriotic soldiers.

But the heaviest blow to the peasant guerrillas' legitimacy was to come when Andrés Cáceres accepted the Treaty of Ancón. Signed in October 1883, the treaty changed the balance of power in the country as a whole by getting the Chilean army out of Lima and the Iglesistas into the presidential palace. Though it took Cáceres until June 1884 to acquiesce to the Ancón treaty, once he did so his entire view of the balance of forces in the central sierra underwent a transformation. Since the war with Chile was officially over, it was no longer necessary to fashion the broadest possible coalition to resist a foreign invasion.

December 10, 1884, Paquete 0.1884.6, Prefecturas; AHM, "Oficio del Prefecto Relayze al Oficial Mayor en el Despacho de Guerra y Marina, transcribiendo el oficio del Subprefecto de Huancayo," Cerro de Pasco, February 2, 1895, Paquete 1885 s/n.

[63] Both Bonilla, "The War of the Pacific," pp. 112, 115 and passim, and Favre, "Remarques," use these sources somewhat uncritically. It is from here, apparently, that they both get the interpretation that mobilization in the southern Mantaro region became an all-out racial war against the whites.

Indeed, given the broad and unpopular territorial concessions made to Chile by Iglesias, the issue became what type of alliance would be most successful in the impending and probably inevitable internal conflict between Iglesistas and Caceristas. And in that context the peasant guerrillas, with their control of elite property and their democratic pretensions, began to look increasingly less attractive to the leader of the La Breña campaign.[64]

On July 2, 1884, a mere month after he accepted the Ancón treaty, Cáceres ordered the execution of four peasant guerrillas in the Plaza Huamanmarca in Huancayo. Their leader Tomás Laimes, a noncommissioned officer from Huanta, Ayacucho, confessed to sacking the haciendas of Tucle, Laive, and Ingahuasi, and distributing the booty among his men. He also admitted that his followers had killed Giráldez, among others, but insisted this was because the victims were traitors to the *patria* and Chilean spies.[65] It is clear that, despite their recognition of guilt, the peasant guerrillas were confused and disoriented by what was happening to them. After all, the main reason they had entered Huancayo was to receive a supposed decoration from Cáceres in reward for their patriotism.[66]

The execution of Laimes and his men marked the beginning of a concerted campaign by the Cacerista authorities to repress peasant mobilization. Several weeks after that first incident, Cáceres' representative in Huancayo sent a letter to the governor of Comas urging that the *montoneros* return to Manuel Fernando Valladares the cattle, sheep, horses, and llamas that they had taken from his haciendas Runatullo, Pampa Hermosa, Curibamba, and Ususqui. "[T]his . . . general command gives the individuals from those communities every guarantee," he said,

> that they will not be persecuted or molested for the mistakes they have made; but [if they do not return what they have taken], . . . this office will dictate the most decisive and urgent measures in order to capture those delinquents, as the most excellent General

[64] For the events surrounding the Treaty of Ancón, see Basadre, *Historia*, 8: 448–68. For a similar interpretation of Cáceres' changing motivations, see Manrique, "La occupación y la resistencia," pp. 304–305, and *Campesinado y nación*, pp. 331–73.

[65] Tello Devotto, *Historia de Huancayo*, pp. 74–76; Ráez, *Monografía*, pp. 19 and 25.

[66] Bonilla and Favre, despite their "racial" interpretations of the mobilizations, agree on this point. See Bonilla, "The War of the Pacific," p. 114 (basing himself on Favre); and Favre, "Remarques," p. 65.

[Cáceres] has ordered, and impose upon them the severe and exemplary punishment that their grave crimes deserve.[67]

Thus the Comas guerrillas, who only a short time before had been the backbone of Cáceres' resistance, were suddenly defined as a group of common criminals. This change was not due to any particularly barbarous acts they had committed, however, but simply to the fact that, if Cáceres wished to make a bid for national power, it was no longer possible to leave the countryside in the hands of independently armed peasants.

As Luis Milón Duarte, Juan Enrique Valladares, Jacinto Cevallos, Dr. Giráldez, Manuel Fernando Valladares, and many other *hacendados* had known from the beginning, to base a resistance campaign on an armed, mobilized, and increasingly autonomous peasantry was a risky proposition. But Cáceres and his followers had made an even more dangerous mistake. Because the La Breña campaign did not have the support of the entire regional elite, the Caceristas had in effect given the peasants the power to decide which *hacendados* were traitors to the cause. Yet long before the civil war was over, it became clear to the hero of La Breña that, in order to build an alliance that would carry him to the presidential palace, he had to mend fences with the *hacendados* as a class, including those who had collaborated with the Chileans. The only way to do so was to give the *hacendados* what they wanted and repress the very guerrillas who had made the La Breña campaign possible in the first place. What was not clear until much later was that it would take the government twenty years to bring the countryside under control.

Aftermath

On November 30, 1886, the subprefect of Jauja, alarmed by the level of violence and disorder in his jurisdiction, wrote to the prefect of the department of Junín asking for reinforcements. "Bands of criminals are overrunning the villages of Orcotuna and Mito," he wrote,

> committing all kinds of excesses against peaceful and defenseless citizens, and the vigilance and power of the local authorities is not enough to contain them.
>
> The small force at my disposal, which is destined exclusively to guarding the jail and the capital, which is also alarmed by the pres-

[67] APJ, "Prefecto del Departamento al Gobernador del Distrito de Comas," Huancayo, July 31, 1884.

ence of bandits in the area, does not allow me to send a single gendarme to the districts of Mito and Orcotuna. Since this serious situation cannot be remedied without the efficient help of a respectable force that is able to chase the criminals in different directions until they are captured, I request that you send me, as soon as possible, a reinforcement from the Cavalry, or ask the Supreme Government to do so if the Department [of Junín] lacks the necessary men.[68]

When the prefect received the note in Tarma four days later, he wrote across the bottom of it: "Answer, then file in its proper place." And although a copy of the answer has not survived, it is not difficult to imagine what it said.

By the time Cáceres became president in May 1886, the central highland region was in a state of economic and political chaos. The peasantry, armed, mobilized, and still in control of an impressive chunk of elite property, was not ready to submit to authority without a struggle.[69] The regional elite, heavily indebted and with many of their haciendas either partially or totally invaded, was unable to assist in bringing the peasantry under control. The central government's representatives were therefore forced to take on the burden of pacifying the countryside. But the national treasury was not solvent either, and could not finance the necessary men and arms to carry out a successful campaign. Thus, when the prefect wrote back to his official in Jauja, the only thing he could tell the subprefect was to make do with what he had.

For local officials in the central highlands, the crux of the problem lay in a simple mathematical calculation: if an arms count had been carried out in 1886, the results would have probably shown that the peasantry held a number of weapons superior to those in the power of the authorities. And the national government was certainly aware of this. In January 1886, Colonel Bartolomé Guerra had been given a national commission to travel to the central highlands. One of his

[68] APJ, "Oficio del Subprefecto de Jauja B. S. Leyva al Prefecto del Departamento," Jauja, November 30, 1886.

[69] The general tone of life in the countryside at this time was one of violence and rebellion. See, for example, in APJ, letters from the subprefect of Jauja, B. S. Leyva, to the prefect on: November 30, 1886; December 7, 1886; March 1, 1887; November 21, 1888. Also, BNP, Document No. D8457: "Oficio del Subprefecto de Jauja, pidiendo más fuerzas para controlar bandidos," Jauja, January 4, 1887; No. D7095: "Expediente sobre proceso criminal de juicios sobre sucesos en la hacienda 'Chinche,'" Cerro de Pasco, November 5, 1887; No. D6963: "Documentos relativos a la captura y prisión de bandoleros," Jauja, November 25, 1888.

main tasks was to collect all weapons in the hands of private citizens, especially those in control of the peasant guerrillas. Guerra, a prominent landowner from the village of Chupaca, general commander of the guerrillas in the department of Junín, and one of Cáceres' most trusted officers, was clearly the logical choice for the job. Despite the good reputation he enjoyed in the central sierra, however, he was cautioned to be extremely careful because, according to the official who informed him of his duties, the task required "the greatest sagacity and prudence . . . it is necessary to carry it out without provoking resistance."[70] Yet in the final analysis, no matter how prudent or sagacious Guerra was, he could not pacify the population singlehanded.

Forced to rely on local authorities, Guerra was caught in the same bind as they were: they could not gain control of the countryside because they lacked funds, and they lacked funds because they could not control the countryside. During and immediately after the war, departmental authorities had relied on the collection of local taxes, especially the *contribución personal* (Indian head tax), to cover their expenses. In practice, however, this meant very little, since the disorganization caused by the war had made collection virtually impossible.[71] Once the central government was reorganized, moreover, it ratified this de facto situation by approving the decentralization of the country's budget.[72] Thus local officials could not proceed with pacification until they had collected the *contribución*. But because Cáceres had exempted the guerrillas from payment of the tax, and because the productive sector had suffered extensive damage during the war, it was impossible to collect the *contribución* in 1886 without risking widespread rebellion in the villages.[73]

Despite the problems they posed for the elite and political authorities, however, the peasants were far from united at the regional level. The very structure of the peasant society and economy—the pursuit

[70] APJ, "Oficio del Ministerio de Gobierno al Prefecto del Departamento de Junín," Lima, January 18, 1886. For Guerra's position in Chupaca, see Carlos Samaniego, "Peasant Movements at the Turn of the Century and the Rise of the Independent Farmer," in Norman Long and Bryan Roberts (eds.), *Peasant Cooperation and Capitalist Expansion in Central Peru* (Austin: University of Texas Press, 1978), p. 52.

[71] Basadre, *Historia*, 9: 50.

[72] Ibid., pp. 151–52.

[73] BNP, Document No. D4399: "Oficio de la Prefectura de Junín al Ministerio de Hacienda y Comercio," Tarma, May 23, 1885; APJ, "Ministerio de Guerra al Prefecto del Departamento de Junín," Lima, July 8, 1886; "Subprefecto de Huancayo al Prefecto del Departamento," Huancayo, August 24, 1886; and "Subprefecto de Jauja al Prefecto del Departamento," Jauja, October 26, 1886.

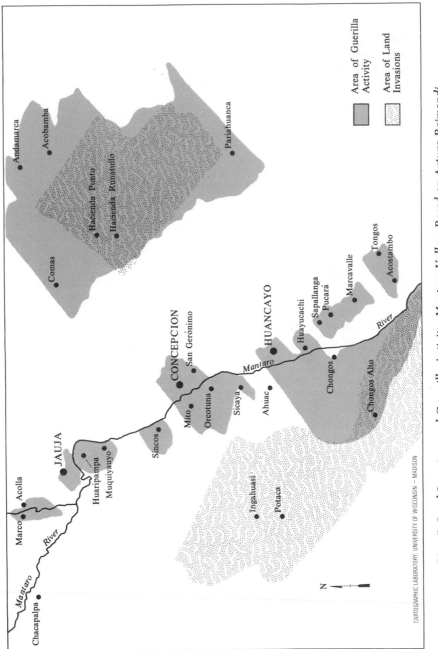

Map 5. *Land Invasions and Guerrilla Activity, Mantaro Valley. Based on Arturo Raimondi,*
"Mapa de la Región Central" (Paris, ca. 1880).

Area of Guerrilla
Activity

Area of Land
Invasions

Andamarca
Acobamba
Hacienda Punto
Hacienda Runatullo
Pariahuanca
Comas
Tongos
Acostambo
Marcavalle
Sapallanga
Pucará
HUANCAYO
Huayucachi
CONCEPCION
San Gerónimo
Mantaro River
Chongos
Mito
Orcotuna
Sicaya
Ahuac
Chongos Alto
JAUJA
Sincos
Huaripampa
Muquiyauyo
Acolla
Marco
Mantaro River
Chacapalpa
Ingahuasi
Potaca

N

of household self-sufficiency, the system of land tenure, the tendency toward intra- and intercommunity conflict—militated against the extension of peasant unity beyond the confines of the village. In the period before the war, the intensification of commercial penetration had increased the level of class tension between peasants and *hacendados*, but it had also exacerbated existing tensions between communities. During the war, the use of patron-client relations in the organization of the *montoneras* had tended to tie the peasant guerrillas from each village more closely to merchants and other prestigious outsiders than to *montoneros* from other communities. Although the process of negotiation would prove a long and tortuous one, therefore, the government's strategy was fairly clear. By promising rewards and benefits to cooperating villages, the authorities could use patronage and clientele networks to exploit intercommunity conflicts and rivalries. Essentially, it was a policy of "divide and conquer" through integration into the national political system.

Perhaps the most attractive reward that the government could offer a peasant village was the attainment of political district status. After independence, when political districts evolved from the colonial parishes, many villages were left in the subordinate position of *anexos* vis-à-vis neighboring communities or towns. The capital of a political district had control over all revenues and access to labor for public projects, and it was not uncommon for the villages within a district to finance the development of the capital—the construction of schools, roads, public buildings, and so on—and get very little in return. Since the district council also controlled political apppointments, frequently village officials were either from outside the community or indebted in some way to the municipal power structure.[74] Thus intercommunity rivalries were often channeled into competition between the district seat and the most populated and prosperous *anexos*, providing an excellent inroad for government negotiators.

The policy of district creation worked extremely well in several cases. Muquiyauyo and Acolla, for example, villages that had participated actively in the guerrilla effort, became capitals of new districts. The former, located on the western bank of the Mantaro River, had been completely subordinate to the neighboring village of Huari-

[74] On the problem of *anexos* and district capitals, see especially Richard N. Adams, *A Community in the Andes: Problems and Progress in Muquiyauyo* (Seattle: University of Washington Press, 1959), pp. 29–32; and Bravo Guzmán, *La segunda enseñanza*, pp. 158–59.

pampa since independence.[75] The situation in the Yanamarca Valley
was even more onerous, since the entire valley had continued to be
subject to the authority of the district capital in Jauja. Representatives
from both communities had applied for district status before the war,
arguing that their villages were far too populated and commercially
active to continue being administered from the outside.[76] One of the
local notables in Acolla had gone as far as to spend his wife's entire
dowry on the application effort, and the village as a whole had shocked
ecclesiastical authorities by mortgaging *cofradía* properties to finance
trips to Lima and other expenses.[77] Thus, when the two villages became district capitals on October 26, 1886, it was the culmination of
a prolonged campaign. But contrary to what might have been expected at first glance, the granting of district status did not benefit
the population as a whole.

As part of a system of patronage controlled by Cáceres' government, the creation of political districts followed the channels already
established by the La Breña campaign, benefiting the richer peasants
and merchants who were in touch with the peasant communities. In
Muquiyauyo, for example, it would take close to twenty years before
more than one Indian, or poorer member of the community, would
serve on the municipal council. For that entire time, local government would remain exclusively in the hands of *mestizos*—richer peasants, merchants, and other prominent citizens—many of whom had
settled in the village only a few generations before.[78] And in the Yanamarca Valley, although the district seat was founded in Acolla, it was
the *mestizos* and richer peasants from Marco who would dominate the
municipal council for nearly two decades.

Since before the war, much of the endemic conflict between Marco
and Acolla had been directed into a battle over which village should
control the district seat. The three or four powerful merchant families
in Marco, because they had excellent connections to the local elite in
Jauja, had never doubted that their village would receive the district
seat, just as it had received the parochial seat. During the war, the
same four families, using their close personal relationship to José María
Dianderas, parish priest of Jauja and related to Cáceres by marriage,
had dominated the guerrilla effort in the Yanamarca Valley. No one

---

[75] Adams, *Community in the Andes*, pp. 29–32.

[76] Ibid., p. 30; and conversation with Moisés Ortega, Acolla, 1977.

[77] Conversation with Moisés Ortega, Acolla, 1977; Archivo SINAMOS, cc 205 (Marco),
"Expediente sobre la reivindicación del molino de propiedad comunal," 1939, 134–36v.

[78] Adams, *Community in the Andes*, p. 37.

was more angered or surprised than they when Fidel Crespo, a sub-lieutenant in the Jauja Battalion of the National Guard and related by marriage to the Ortega family of Acolla, went directly to Cáceres' sister and managed to claim the district capital for Acolla.[79] Yet in the end the event was of little consequence: by the time the first district council was inaugurated in 1887, although the *Acollino* José de la Rosa Ortega was mayor, the rest of the seats on the council were dominated by rich *Marqueños* and a smattering of smaller *hacendados* from the upper Yanamarca Valley.[80] This situation would not change until 1907, when Marco became capital of a separate district.

Although it did not completely pacify the countryside, the policy of district creation was successful because it gave political backing to precisely that sector of the village population that could best control local life and mediate between the community and the government. It was no coincidence that this same sector had mediated between the peasant guerrillas and the Cacerista high command during the war. Thus the La Breña campaign, and the political negotiations that followed, strengthened the position of the merchant and *mestizo* elite within the peasant villages and established this group as a dominant force in municipal government. The ultimate success of the patron-client alliance between the *mestizo* elite and the national government was assured because, given the centralized nature of the Peruvian state, municipal officials were either designated, or had their local election approved, by the central government's representative.[81]

Successful cooptation was, however, limited to the northern part of the Mantaro Valley, where the ties of patronage and clientele that gave rise to the guerrilla organizations survived relatively unscathed. In the south, the emergence of class conflict amidst the ruins of the nationalist front militated against the formulation of a workable *"pax andina."* On the *punas* of the Mantaro River's western bank, as well as in northern Huancavelica, mobilized guerrillas still controlled elite property. To the east of the valley, in the Comas area, *montoneros*

[79] For the activities of the *Marqueños* during the La Breña campaign, see APJ, "Informe de la Subprefectura de Huancayo al Prefecto del Departamento," Huancayo, February 17, 1897, and Bravo Guzmán, *La segunda enseñanza*, p. 302. For the process by which Acolla received district status, see Hutchinson, "Sociocultural Change," pp. 29–30. Also, conversation with Moisés Ortega, Acolla, 1977.

[80] BNP, Document No. D6954: "Nuevo Personal de los Concejos Distritales, Junín," June 1888.

[81] Control over local political office was, at least in theory, particularly strong during the Cacerista years. Only when Nicolás de Piérola took power in 1895 were local elections restored. See Frederick B. Pike, *The Modern History of Peru* (New York: Frederick A. Praeger, 1967), p. 173.

refused to make good on the cattle they had removed from the haciendas and continued to hold on to the properties themselves.[82] In none of these areas would the peasants have considered paying the *contribución personal*. By 1888, it became clear that more drastic measures would be necessary to bring the recalcitrant guerrillas back into the national fold.

On October 29, 1888, Cáceres created a special commission to return the haciendas in the department of Junín to their "legitimate" owners. "There have been several disagreements," the resolution said,

> between various Indian communities that are in de facto possession of some lands in the department of Junín, and the people who possessed those same lands in the past and claim to be the legitimate owners: . . . it is convenient, for the tranquility of that department, to resolve these questions and give back to the true owners the possession of their lands: . . . in order to do so, it is necessary to examine impartially and carefully the titles that both sides present, so that it is possible to judge correctly which side has the legitimate right.[83]

Cáceres therefore appointed Emiliano A. Carvallo special commissioner in the department of Junín to carry out this mission, and invested him with all the necessary powers.[84]

Between November 1888 and May 1889, Carvallo heard a number of land cases in the southern Mantaro Valley and in northern Huancavelica. He examined the titles on both sides, walked the disputed borders with representatives from the two parties, heard both arguments, and then usually found it impossible to decide between the two. In most cases, Carvallo left things just as he found them—with the peasants in control of the land through de facto rights of possession—and gave the landowners the right to pursue the matter in an ordinary court.[85] There were two main reasons for this. First, since

---

[82] At the end of his article, "The War of the Pacific," Bonilla speculates on the terms and forms of the *"pax andina"* after the war (pp. 114 and 118). Ultimately, he is at a loss to explain the process through which the peasantry was brought under control. Favre has the same problem. I would argue that both of them have difficulty explaining the process of repression, because neither has adequately understood the process of mobilization. On the *montoneros'* refusal to return the cattle, see APJ, "Oficio de varios vecinos de Comas al Prefecto del Departamento," Jauja, September 9, 1887.

[83] APJ, "Ministerio de Gobierno al Prefecto del Departamento de Junín," Lima, November 12, 1888.

[84] Ibid.

[85] BNP, Document No. D8207: "Comisión especial del Supremo Gobierno, Decretos sobre Potaca y Chongos Alto vs. Antapongo, Chupaca vs. Aliaga," April 1889; Docu-

Carvallo did not have the military backing he needed to enforce a change of possession, it was most advisable for him not to tamper directly with the situation unless the balance of forces allowed him to do so. Secondly, most land titles were extremely unclear, especially for someone not familiar with the terrain. This meant both parties were free to interpret the boundaries any way they wished, and did not allow Carvallo to fulfill his role of "impartial" arbitrator.[86]

Despite the overall lack of concrete results, particularly from the *hacendados'* point of view, Carvallo's commission was important because it brought the communities and the landowners back to the negotiating table. This was a crucial first step in the pacification of the area, since by listening to a representative of the government the villagers were, in effect, recognizing the legitimacy of the authorities. And until it was possible to regain a monopoly over the means of violence, the only way to reestablish government control in the region was through negotiation. Yet it would be easy to overestimate the effectiveness of Carvallo's mission.

The success of negotiation in Chongos Alto, Huasicancha, and northern Huancavelica was due less to Carvallo's skill than to the fact that the area had already been subjected to selective repression by Cáceres during the civil war. Tomás Laimes and the other leaders executed in Huancayo during July 1884 were precisely from these villages. Later on in the year and into 1885, the same villages were invaded by Iglesias' "Pacification Army" and given little choice but to play a central role in the Cacerista resistance, this time under the more dependable leadership of Father Peñalosa and Colonel Bartolomé Guerra.[87] Thus by the time Carvallo arrived there three years later, the guerrillas had already undergone both a process of repression and of selective remobilization which predisposed them to accept the legitimacy of the Cacerista authorities. Had he ventured into the region around Comas, which had neither been repressed nor seen much direct action in 1884 and 1885, Carvallo would have had much more difficulty. Indeed, from the government's point of view, the

ment No. D12846: "Oficio de Emiliano Carvallo al Director de Gobierno," Tarma, March 10, 1889.

[86] BNP, Document No. D12844: "Nueva petición de Chongos Alto sobre linderos con Antapongo," May 13, 1889.

[87] See, for example, AHM, "Oficio del Prefecto de Junín," December 10, 1884; "Oficio del Prefecto Relayze," February 2, 1885; and "Parte del Coronel Eduardo Jessup, Comandante General de la Primera División, al Comandante General en Jefe del Ejército del Centro," Huancayo, May 12, 1885, Paquete 0.1885.2.

situation in the Comas district clearly necessitated the use of military force.

In September 1888, the central government ordered the prefect of Junín to use the necessary troops from the Callao Battalion of the National Guard in an expedition to occupy the haciendas Punto and Callanca, which had been invaded by peasants from the Comas area. It was not until December 10, however, that the expedition, composed of the Callao Battalion and a few villagers whom the interested *hacendados* had enlisted through patron-client ties, was actually able to leave Huancayo. Although the subprefect, Andrés Freyre, had orders to use violence only after all attempts at conciliation had failed, when he arrived on the hacienda Punto three days later he found that the balance of forces was somewhat different from what he had expected. After a short battle with a group of peasants guarding the entrance, the troops managed to reach the main house safely. In the days that followed, the peasants, using guerrilla techniques they had learned during the La Breña campaign, occupied the surrounding hills and kept up a constant fire on the troops below. Every time the soldiers attempted to drive them away, the guerrillas would leave for the moment, only to return a few minutes later and continue firing down. After several days, it became clear that the peasants, protected by their knowledge of the terrain and by the rain and fog typical of the season, could not be defeated. Freyre was forced to order the retreat of his troops.[88]

With the failure of the expedition, the authorities realized that the subjugation of Comas would take a long time. The national government had certainly been aware of the special qualities of the Comas case since the end of the war. That part of the Mantaro Valley region, including the villages of Comas, Canchapalca, and Acobamba, had constituted the vanguard of the resistance against the Chileans. It had developed the most active, militant, and independent guerrilla organizations. It was the *montoneros* from Acobamba who had written to Jacinto Cevallos, accusing him of treachery and threatening revenge. It was the Comas guerrillas who had taken Concepción from the Chileans in 1882. When the minister of the interior (Ministro de Gobierno) ordered a military expedition sent to the area, therefore, he was perfectly conscious of the exceptional circumstances involved. And in one sense at least he was right about Comas' uniqueness.

In contrast to other mobilized areas in the central sierra, the peas-

[88] BNP, Document No. D11466: "Parte Oficial sobre la expedición a 'Punto,' " Huancayo, January 15, 1889.

ants in Comas and the surrounding communities had developed a consciousness of themselves as a class that extended far beyond the confines of the individual village. More than other communities, they had been left to their own devices during the La Breña campaign and forced to collaborate with each other to resist the Chileans. During four years of guerrilla warfare, they had lived off the land, battled the enemy, and tested the boundaries of their own unity and strength. They learned that the local *hacendados* were not willing to treat them like patriotic soldiers because they were only peasants. When the Chileans left Peruvian territory, the guerrillas also learned that Cáceres, symbol of resistance under whose name they had fought, would not treat them as equals once he no longer needed the *montoneros* to help him. Thus, by 1887, the *Comasinos* and their neighbors had drawn a clear line of division between themselves as a class and all the *hacendados*. They included within their definition of the enemy all those from Cáceres' government who attempted to tamper with the situation in the countryside.[89] And yet they did so not because they were antinationalist in any absolute sense, but because they felt they had been cheated out of the recognition and rewards they deserved for having contributed to the war effort.

On January 25, 1888, several municipal officials from Comas sent a letter to the nearby community of Uchubamba. "The inhabitants of Comas with its *caseríos* [dependent villages or *anexos*] Cochas, Canchapalca, Mucllo, Todos Santos, Runatullo, and those from Punto, Acobamba and Andamarca, have decided to form a confederation or alliance of districts," they wrote,

in order to defend ourselves and to improve our commerce, industry, education, and administration of justice, and we count on a judge from Ica who has already lived a year in Jauja, and who now has decided to come and live among us forever. He has already given us proof of his loyalty to us, and is well known as a reformer. This gentleman is already known in Lima for the articles he has

[89] It is interesting to note that, despite the fact that the officials of the Cáceres government in the central highlands had often fought with the *montoneros* during the La Breña campaign, the guerrillas did not hesitate to attack them if they proved hostile to peasant interests. Thus Guillermo Ferreyros, who as Cáceres' prefect in Huancayo in 1884 had urged the *Comasinos* to return the cattle they had taken from Manuel Valladares, had one of his haciendas invaded for his pains (APJ, "Juan E. Valladares y otros al Prefecto del Departamento," August 10, 1886). And Andrés Freyre, previously Commander of the Pucará Battalion at the Battle of Concepción in 1882, was forced to retreat from Punto in December 1888.

written in the newspapers asking for reform. And we also have other competent people to help us.

If you wish to form a district of our Federal State, you will be free, you will govern yourselves, elect your own authorities, and no one will be able to attack you, without the whole Federal State coming to your defense. In return, you will also be obligated to come with your weapons when we need you. For some time already we have taken up our weapons, we have achieved things, and we will achieve much more very soon. We will know how to contain your enemies if you will join our confederation if you agree send a representative, that is one of your principal citizens to negotiate with us, and everyone will benefit. Those who come should bring a power of attorney so they can contract properly in the name of all of Uchubamba.[90]

What is most striking about this letter is that, in the midst of planning for a defense against the *hacendados*, the peasants continued to be concerned with legalism and reform. The federation, composed of both hacienda and village peasants, would not only provide for a common defense, but also improve local government, commerce, and education. In order that the alliance should be considered legitimate, it would be advised by a judge from Ica and other competent specialists, and the representatives of each community would have to receive a power of attorney from the other inhabitants before they were allowed to negotiate.

Thus the alliance did not necessarily constitute a revolutionary threat to the established order. As was true of other peasants in the central highlands, the Comas guerrillas had originally mobilized in alliance with landowners, merchants, and political authorities. In return, they had expected the benefits accruing to legitimate patriotic soldiers: at the very least, a recognition of their contribution to the defense of the *patria*. Had the government been willing to provide a minimal level of services, benefits, and political participation to their villages, the peasants in the Comas region would certainly have been willing to lay down their weapons. But instead, given the balance of forces in the southern Mantaro Valley, the authorities chose to take a hard line. By 1888, then, the peasants were convinced that the Cáceres government had abandoned them. Rather than wait for aid that would never come, they decided to form an alliance among themselves and

[90] APJ, "Autoridades de Comas a las autoridades de Uchubamba," Comas, January 25, 1888.

rely on their own resources. What made the alliance unacceptable was that, for a government based on the support of an *hacendado* elite, any attempt by peasants to organize independently constituted a major threat. For the peasants, the ultimate irony was that, in order to struggle for benefits and demands whose content was eminently reformist, they were forced to take a stand that was, for all intents and purposes, revolutionary.

The 1888–1889 Freyre expedition was the first test of the Comas federation and it brought out the major contradictions on both the peasant and government side over how to handle the confrontation. Among the peasants, there was ambivalence over whether to negotiate or to fight. Thus, even though the guerrillas ultimately carried the day by expelling the invaders during the December campaign, a sector of the community of Canchapalca initially attempted to negotiate separately with the troops.[91] On the government side, Freyre's return to the area in January 1889, during which he attempted to co-opt the peasants into submission, was evidence of a willingness to negotiate. But in this case, it is important to remember that negotiation was attempted only after violence had failed.

On January 4, 1889, Freyre arrived at the hacienda Llacsapirca, near the rebellious villages, and sent letters to the communities of Acobamba, Yanabamba, Canchapalca, and Comas, asking to speak with them and guaranteeing immunity if they cooperated in bringing the rebellion to an end. In the conference that followed, Jacinto Cevallos offered to sell the hacienda Punto to the communities. Representatives from Acobamba and Comas, Cevallos, and Freyre actually signed a contract before a notary public, in which the village of Comas received a portion of the hacienda located in the Paliacancha Valley in exchange for 250 head of cattle three years old. Acobamba received the rest of the hacienda, and was obligated to pay 2,000 head of cattle the same age. Cevallos also promised to drop all civil and criminal charges against the peasants, while both villages agreed to respect the rights and boundaries of surrounding haciendas, and to help keep order in case of future difficulties. In a further attempt at co-optation, Cevallos gave the neighboring hacienda of Callanca to three peasants from Comas who had not participated in the guerrilla actions, with the condition that they take an inventory of the property and be ready to turn the hacienda over to Cevallos at any time in the future.[92]

As was clear from the agreement made on Callanca, not to mention

[91] BNP, Document No. D11466: "Parte Oficial sobre la expedición a Punto."
[92] Ibid.

the unequal partition of the hacienda Punto, Cevallos and the government representatives were attempting a sophisticated "divide and conquer" strategy. By offering the hacienda, they appealed to growing land hunger among village peasants. By dividing the property unequally, they hoped to break the unity of the Comas federation. But most important, Cevallos' demand that the peasants pay in cattle for the purchase of the hacienda proves that the offer was never sincere in the first place. To expect the *Comasinos* and their neighbors to pay such an elevated price, not only in mature cattle but so soon after the devastation of the war, was patently ridiculous, and probably reflected Cevallos' belief that the peasants had accumulated much livestock during their wartime "pillaging" expeditions.

Not surprisingly, Comas never handed over a single cow or steer, whereas Acobamba paid a total of 130 young cattle after two months. As a result, a court in Huancayo ordered that the debt be paid within a specified time or the hacienda returned to Cevallos.[93] Yet in the end, Cevallos' attempt to create a more compelling legal justification for the return of his property proved a failure. The only way to actually enforce the court order was by sending another military expedition, something the financially pressed Cacerista government could not do. Completely disregarding the court in Huancayo, and more than ever in control of the area's haciendas, the peasants lived in peace for the next seven years.

Precisely because there were no attempts by the government to break up the Comas alliance during these years, it is extremely difficult to get information on events in the area between 1889 and 1896. From scattered evidence, it seems that some of the hacienda lands were parceled out to individual families and cultivated within the household economy.[94] We also know that several of the original guerrilla leaders continued to play a central role in the alliance and in community affairs.[95] Completely cut off from the authority of the Peruvian government, the villages in the federation elected their own

[93] BNP, Document No. D12845: "Expediente sobre la propiedad de la hacienda 'Punto,' Provincia de Huancayo," May 8, 1889.

[94] APJ, "Oficio de las autoridades de Canchapalca al Subprefecto de la Provincia de Jauja," Canchapalca, June 28, 1902; "Aurelio Ponce al Prefecto del Departamento," July 19, 1902.

[95] APJ, "Oficio del Subprefecto de Huancayo al Gobernador de Comas," Hacienda Punto, June 23, 1902; "Oficio de Juan C. Aparicio, Pedro N. Cárdenas y Baltazar Chávez a los ciudadanos del caserío de Canchapalca," June 30, 1902; "Junta de vecinos de Comas al Prefecto del Departamento," Comas, July 7, 1902; AHM, "Memorias sobre la Resistencia de la Breña."

officials, administered their own justice, and paid no taxes.[96] Through a contraband cattle trade with local merchants, they maintained their access to new weapons and ammunition.[97] All in all, the Comas federation looked very much like an independent peasant republic, and at least for a few years the central government seemed content to let it stay that way. As it turned out, however, the federation was so attractive to other peasants that it became too dangerous for the authorities to ignore.

At some point in August 1896, the peasants of the hacienda Llacsapirca, with the aid of peasants from Punto, took over Llacsapirca from its owner. Domingo Argote, the subprefect of Huancayo, travelled to the area and attempted to negotiate. The rebels, while meeting with the authorities in apparent acquiescence, made arrangements to ambush Argote on his way out of the valley. According to Argote's report, the only thing that saved him was that one of the peasants accepted a bribe in return for information on the ambush. Argote then ended his report on a somber note, commenting that it was necessary to send a powerful military expedition to the area in order to protect the rights of the *hacendados* and assure the application of the law:

Judging by the attitude of the Indians I saw and by the constant exchange there is of a head of cattle for a rifle or a carbine, and of a sheep for four or five cartridges of ammunition, with irresponsible merchants whose conduct it is impossible to condone, the movement that took place on the hacienda Punto years ago, extended today to Llacsapirca and Patalá, will undoubtedly extend itself further, and unless radical repressive measures are taken, will take on truly alarming proportions.[98]

In addition to the objective danger that the alliance presented for the elite and the local authorities, it was also a source of grave embarrassment for the new central government in Lima. Nicolás de Piérola, the caudillo who had organized the disastrous defense of the capital during the War of the Pacific, had taken power in a coup d'état in 1895. Backed by a group of progressive Civilista intellectuals, Piérola initiated a campaign to modernize the country, build roads, extend the educational system, and generally provide a decent climate

[96] APJ, "Memoria Administrativa del Subprefecto de Jauja Andrés Freyre al Prefecto del Departamento," Jauja, June 3, 1893.
[97] BNP, Document No. D5041: "Sucesos en la hacienda Llacsapirca," August–September 1896.
[98] Ibid.

for investment.[99] Since part of his plan was to "civilize" the Indians, the existence of such a large pocket of peasant rebellion was definitely a thorn in his side. But it was also a source of friction for the anti-Cáceres landowners in the central highlands, particularly Jacinto Cevallos and the Valladares brothers, who had supported Piérola's campaign with the hope that they might finally get their haciendas back.[100] Thus, in November 1896, the minister of the interior financed a large expedition to the Comas region with the intention of finally winning the rebellious communities back into the national fold.[101]

Although he traveled to the Comas area at the head of a column of cavalry, the prefect of Junín, Ramón Valle Riestra, was under strict orders to follow a policy of conciliation. In contrast to Freyre's attempt seven years earlier, Valle Riestra was empowered by the central government to offer the villages concrete benefits, especially funds for education and public works, in exchange for their willingness to submit to the authority of the government. He therefore held meetings with the political and religious authorities in the different villages, inquiring as to each community's most urgent needs, and emphasizing "the general goals of the Supreme Government in what concerns the order and progress of the country and especially the honest desire of his Excellency the Chief of State for the progress of the Indian race."[102]

Because he individualized the negotiation process, tailored the benefits he offered to each community's specific needs, and had the enthusiastic backing of the Lima government, Valle Riestra was a great deal more successful than his predecessors. Authorized by the respective ministers in Lima, he was able to offer the district of Comas between 150 and 200 soles to finance a school and textbooks, set up a municipal council, and initiate a program of public works. In exchange, the authorities from the district signed a document proclaim-

[99] Pike, *Modern History*, pp. 159–75; and Chapter IV of this book.

[100] Some of the evidence on this point is indirect, such as the fact that neither Cevallos nor the Valladares brothers appeared on the list of Caceristas elaborated by the subprefect of Huancayo, Aurelio M. Solís, in 1897 (APJ, "Informe del Subprefecto de Huancayo al Prefecto del Departamento," Huancayo, February 17, 1897). Also, one of the activists in the anti-Cáceres elitist plots that immediately preceded Piérola's takeover in 1895 was named Jacinto, and there is a good possibility that it was Cevallos. See BNP, Document No. D7334: "Disturbios y detenciones en Jauja y Huancayo," April 1894.

[101] BNP, Document No. D5051: "Pacificación de Comas y Acta de Adhesión al Supremo Gobierno," Tarma-Jauja, November 21–23, 1896.

[102] Ibid.

ing their loyalty to Piérola's government.[103] In the case of Andamarca, Valle Riestra was able to play on the latent rivalry between that village and the district seat. In a statement denying their complicity with Comas in the rebellion, Andamarca agreed to respect the central government in exchange for independent district status, and entrusted the success of their petition to the prefect himself.[104]

Even though Valle Riestra succeeded in having the communities sign documents of adherence to Piérola, the Comas rebellion was far from over. There is no evidence that the agreements about additional services and district status, despite their extremely limited nature, were ever honored. The guerrillas, still organized and by that point experienced in the ways of negotiation and local politics, were not placated by pending promises. By 1898, the guerrillas from Andamarca were making bold incursions into nearby towns, thereby endangering the government's colonization effort in Pampa Hermosa.[105] In the same year, the merchants and *hacendados* of Concepción formed a volunteer police force, at least in part because they feared the incursions of the *Comasinos*.[106] In fact, not until 1902, when Jacinto Cevallos himself led an expedition to the area, was the Comas alliance finally brought to its knees.

In June 1902, Jacinto Cevallos used his power as subprefect of Huancayo to launch his own personal campaign against the villages of the Comas alliance. Having received an order from the national government to once again attempt a pacification of the area, Cevallos formed an expedition which included, according to some accounts, soldiers drafted through *enganche* in the village of Chupaca.[107] After entering the hacienda Punto on June 22 without resistance, he spent four days exchanging letters with the authorities of the various vil-

---

[103] Ibid.

[104] BNP, Document No. D5046: "Pacificación de Andamarca—Acta de adhesión al Supremo Gobierno," Tarma-Andamarca, November 23, 1896.

[105] APJ, "Subprefecto de Jauja, Dulanto, al Prefecto del Departamento," Comas (Pampa Hermosa), July 9, 1898; "Subprefecto de Jauja al Prefecto," Andamarca-Pampa Hermosa, July 14, 1898; "Subprefecto de Jauja al Prefecto," Andamarca, July 25, 1898; "Subprefecto de Jauja al Prefecto," Jauja, August 4, 1898; "Subprefecto de Jauja al Prefecto," Andamarca, August 11, 1898; "Vicente A. Pando y Brígido Bocanegra al Prefecto del Departamento," Cárcel de Huancayo, September 12, 1898; "Varios vecinos de Andamarca al Prefecto del Departamento," Andamarca, November 24, 1898, and attached report by surveyor Víctor Enzián, Concepción, January 14, 1899.

[106] APJ, "Acta de Formación de la Guardia Urbana de Concepción," Concepción, September 10, 1898.

[107] APJ, "Jacinto Cevallos al Gobernador de Comas," Huancayo, May 26, 1902; "Pedro A. Cárdenas al Gobernador de Comas," Jauja, June 21, 1902; "Alcalde de Comas al Prefecto del Departamento," Comas, July 8, 1902.

lages, offering to come to terms peacefully if they would send representatives for a conference.[108] Faced with repeated refusals, however,
Cevallos decided to take more direct action.[109] In the days that followed he sent small groups of his retainers to different villages, sacking, looting, stealing cattle, burning houses, taking prisoners and beating
them severely. In fact, his repressive campaign became so vindictive
that protests from the area's villages forced the prefect of the department, Bruno Bueno, to intervene.[110]

On July 12, Bueno issued a proclamation emphasizing the existence
of the habeas corpus law and warning both private citizens and political authorities against its infringement. Two days later, the governor
of Comas communicated the proclamation to the village of Canchapalca.[111] Bueno also sent Cevallos a letter ordering him to stay on the
hacienda Punto, and by July 18 had arrived personally on that property.[112] In a letter he addressed to Canchapalca from the hacienda,
Bueno said that his purpose in traveling to the area was to inform
himself of the communities' principal necessities, and to help provide
the peasants with an environment of peace within which they could
work and progress undisturbed.[113]

Although Bueno intended his policy as a counterforce to Cevallos'
violence, the ultimate success of his conciliation efforts depended precisely on the efficiency of Cevallos' previous repression. As an *hacendado* native to the area, Cevallos knew the Comas geography very
well, and the guerrilla strategies that had worked against previous
expeditions were ineffective against him. In the month before the

[108] APJ, "Jacinto Cevallos al Gobernador de Comas," Punto, June 23, 1902; "Jacinto
Cevallos a las autoridades y personas notables del pueblo de Canchapalca," Punto, June
25, 1902; "Jacinto Cevallos a autoridades y notables de Canchapalca," Punto, June 25,
1902, two separate notes; "Jacinto Cevallos a los vecinos de Canchapalca," Punto, June
26, 1902.
[109] APJ, "Autoridades de Canchapalca al Subprefecto de Jauja," Canchapalca, June
28, 1902; "Junta de vecinos de Comas al Prefecto del Departamento," Comas, July 7,
1902; "Alcalde de Comas al Prefecto del Departamento," Comas, July 8, 1902; "Oficio
de los ciudadanos y notables de Canchapalca al Prefecto del Departamento," Canchapalca, July 18, 1902.
[110] See all the documents in footnote 109, plus APJ, "Subprefecto de Jauja, Pedro A.
Cárdenas, al Gobernador de Comas," Jauja, July 6, 1902.
[111] APJ, "Bando de Bruno Bueno, Prefecto del Departamento de Junín," Jauja, July
12, 1902; "Oficio de Juan C. Aparicio al Teniente Gobernador de Canchapalca," July
14, 1902.
[112] APJ, "Oficio de Jacinto Cevallos al Prefecto del Departamento," Punto, July 14,
1902; "Oficio de Bruno Bueno al Teniente Gobernador de Canchapalca," Punto, July
18, 1902.
[113] APJ, "Oficio de Bruno Bueno al Teniente Gobernador de Canchapalca," Punto,
July 18, 1902, and also on July 28, 1902.

prefect arrived on the scene, Cevallos had matched the peasants both in cunning and knowledge of the terrain, winning a battle against them on the hacienda Callanca.[114] He was also successful at disorganizing the resistance effort, both by informing one village of the supposed surrender of another, and by holding several of Comas' political authorities hostage.[115] In the end, it was the combination of effective violence and intimidation that split the peasant leadership and provided a vulnerable point for Bueno's negotiation efforts.

The most important split that developed within the Comas leadership was between José Benito Gil and Baltasar Chávez, the only two surviving members of the original *montonera*. Central figures in the Sierra Lumi ambush in early 1882 and participants in the takeover of Concepción later the same year, Chávez and Gil continued to have widespread prestige in the Comas area.[116] Yet events during the Cevallos campaign led to a serious misunderstanding between them. Almost from the beginning of the expedition, Gil, justice of the peace in Comas and previously the general secretary of the Comas guerrilla organization, was held prisoner on the hacienda Punto.[117] Chávez, aware that the quickest way to get rid of the expedition was to reach an agreement, initially joined with the governor of Comas and the subprefect of Jauja in attempting peaceful negotiation, then opted for an appeal to the prefect to halt Cevallos' violence.[118] Despite the success of his appeal, however, criminal charges were brought against Chávez for having led the *montoneros* of Cochas and Canchapalca, and an order was put out for his arrest. Chávez understandably blamed Gil—the only other surviving *montonero*—for having betrayed him while in captivity, and decided to organize a violent resistance to Cevallos.[119]

By the time the prefect arrived in the Comas area, however, it was too late to plan a concerted resistance to the authorities. From the

[114] APJ, "Jacinto Cevallos a los vecinos de Canchapalca," Punto, July 28, 1902.

[115] APJ, "Jacinto Cevallos al Gobernador de Comas," Huancayo, May 26, 1902; "Jacinto Cevallos al Gobernador de Comas," Punto, June 23, 1902; "Junta de vecinos de Comas al Prefecto del Departamento," Comas, July 7, 1902.

[116] AHM, "Memorias sobre la Resistencia de la Breña"; APJ, "Oficio de Juan C. Aparicio, Pedro N. Cárdenas y Baltazar Chávez a los ciudadanos del caserío de Canchapalca," June 30, 1902; "Alcalde de Comas al Prefecto del Departamento," Comas, July 7, 1902.

[117] APJ, "Junta de vecinos de Comas al Prefecto del Departamento," Comas, July 7, 1902.

[118] APJ, "Oficio de Juan C. Aparicio, Pedro N. Cárdenas y Baltazar Chávez a los ciudadanos del caserío de Canchapalca," June 30, 1902; "Alcalde de Comas al Prefecto del Departamento," Comas, July 8, 1902.

[119] APJ, "Baltazar Chávez a las autoridades y notables," Comas, July 15, 1902.

beginning of the rebellion, the guerrillas had been caught in a bind between their desire for legal, fairly limited reforms, and their inability to get them without fighting an armed battle against the landowners. The central government, rather than ally with the peasants and grant them the reform they desired, had chosen to ally with the landowners. As the years progressed, the villages of the federation had been forced to face a number of military expeditions which, even if they promised reforms, did not expect to deliver on those promises. Yet it was difficult for the peasants to resist being tempted by negotiation, particularly after Cevallos instituted a successful "burnt-earth" policy against the guerrillas.

Given the overwhelming odds that the peasants faced, it is not surprising that, once the leadership split, the federation was quickly broken. A number of the region's peasants began to petition the prefect individually for redress of grievances.[120] At least one inhabitant of Comas joined with a Jauja merchant in presenting to the authorities a set of documents "proving" the guilt of various peasant leaders.[121] A group of peasants from the village of Acobamba disavowed their complicity in the movement, arguing that they had been forced to take part under threat of violence by the "famous criminals" from Comas.[122]

As often happens with the losing side in a historical confrontation, documentation on what finally happened to the *Comasinos* is extremely thin. We know that a few of the leaders were taken to Jauja and tried for military crimes.[123] The majority of the peasants had little choice but to submit peacefully in exchange for government promises. In order to avoid similar problems in the future, the central government located one of its first rural police outposts in Comas and neighboring Pariahuanca.[124] And it is with the establishment of this outpost that the epilogue on the Comas alliance, along with the broader peas-

---

[120] See, for example, APJ, "Varios vecinos de Apata al Prefecto del Departamento," Macon, July 18, 1902; "Castulo Muñoz al Prefecto del Departamento," Comas, July 20, 1902; "Ciudadanos de Canchapalca al Prefecto de Departamento," Canchapalca, July 18, 1902; "Aurelio Ponce al Prefecto del Departamento," Comas, July 19, 1902; "Justo Sánchez al Prefecto del Departamento," Comas, July 21, 1902.

[121] APJ, "Santiago Motto al Sr. Pablo Apolinario, Comas," Jauja, July 22, 1902.

[122] APJ, "Autoridades y principales de Acobamba al Prefecto del Departamento," Puntu, July 29, 1902.

[123] APJ, "Baltazar Chávez a las autoridades y notables," Comas, July 15, 1902; "Oficio de varios presos en la cárcel de Tarma al Prefecto del Departamento," Tarma, September 25, 1902.

[124] BNP, Document No. E197: "Memoria del Subprefecto de Jauja Carlos E. García," July 4, 1905.

ant movement that it represented and superseded, can most fittingly be written.

The Comas federation did not succumb to the strategy of combined negotiation and repression that so successfully pacified the rest of the central highland mobilizations. Instead, it fell only when confronted with a concerted counterinsurgency policy on the part of Jacinto Cevallos and his troops. In one sense, there can be no higher tribute to the level of consciousness and unity of the *Comasinos* than to point out that their independent peasant federation survived for fourteen years. Yet equally important, we must remember that their primary purpose was not to wage war against the central government, but simply to gain access to the benefits and recognition which, as patriotic soldiers, they felt they deserved.

In fact, it seems clear that the peasants of the central sierra in general, and those of the Comas alliance in particular, were in some sense "available" for organization by a reformist nationalist coalition. Had a national party with an antilandowner platform of some sort emerged in Peru at this time, almost surely it would have been successful in a bid for their support. It probably would have mattered less whether that group was a party of the national bourgeoisie (such as the Mexican Constitutionalists of the 1910 revolution) or a party of the nationalist left (such as the Chinese Communist party of the 1930s and 1940s), as long as it took an antilandlord position. For, as the *Comasinos* and their neighbors discovered through bitter experience, it was impossible for the peasantry to get access to even the most limited reforms as long as the state depended, for its very survival, on an alliance with the *hacendados*.[125] In Peru, however, the central

[125] I do not mean to suggest here that the alliance between the Constitutionalists and the peasant armies was an equal one during the Mexican Revolution. Quite the contrary, both Zapata and Villa ended up fighting against the Constitutionalists once the fragile alliance between them broke down. In addition, the Constitutionalists were extremely adept at using the working class to repress the peasants and then ultimately repressing the workers. Still, at least initially the Constitutionalists and peasants had some common ground upon which they could agree, since they both opposed the alliance of landlords and foreign capital upon which Porfirio Díaz based his régime. And agrarian reform was, after all, at least a plank in the platform of both groups, even if each meant something quite different by it. In China, given the fact that the Kuomintang was deeply compromised with the landlord class, the only party that addressed the issue of agrarian reform and changing relationships in the countryside was the Communist party. On the Mexican Revolution, see especially John Womack, Jr., *Zapata and the Mexican Revolution* (New York: Random House, 1968), and John H. Hart, "The Urban Working Class and the Mexican Revolution: The Case of the Casa del Obrero Mundial," *Hispanic American Historical Review*, 58:1 (February 1978), 1–20. On China, see Lucien Bianco, *Origins of the Chinese Revolution, 1915–1949* (Stanford: Stanford University Press, 1971), for an overview of some of the important issues.

sierra peasantry's readiness to accept a nationalist coalition occurred at a time when the emergence of such a coalition was a historical impossibility. Given the elite's continued identification with traditional agriculture, it was not interested at this point in putting together an antilandlord, national-bourgeois platform. The other possible alternative, a party of the national left, would be a long time coming. The peasants of the central highlands, it seemed, were out of step with class formation in other parts of the country.

Only in the twentieth century would a process of industrialization and national integration bring to the fore the classes and political groups capable of formulating a nationalist program. With the construction of roads and railroads, investment in production and industry, and the incorporation of wider areas of the highlands into a national market for goods and labor, peasants in other parts of the country would begin to demand reforms similar to those the *Comasinos* had put forward several decades before. In the central sierra, however, the same period would witness the investment of foreign capital directly in production, the development of an industrial mining economy, and, ultimately, the proletarianization of a sector of the region's population. Thus, once the conditions for a national-reformist alliance came into existence, the central highland peasantry would no longer be internally homogeneous enough to participate as one class. Their confrontation with industry would have irrevocably changed the conditions of their existence, as well as the reforms they considered relevant to their daily lives.

PART II

The Peasants Confront Industry, 1895–1930

*What the hell, I've barely / found metal in the pasture, / and
already the gringo arrives, takes it, / and leaves
nothing but a gaping hole.*

—Patricio Manns, "Ya no somos nosotros."

CHAPTER FOUR

The Piérola Years: A National Attempt

at Modernization

Incredible things are happening in the world . . . while we

go on living like donkeys.[1]

Writing about the War of the Pacific in 1882, the Peruvian intellectual Luis Esteves called it a costly experience that "has shown us, perhaps, that each nation is solely responsible for its failures."[2] Only through hard work, imagination and investment, he argued, would it be possible to redeem the country from past mistakes and move forward to meet the future. There were markets in Europe just waiting for Peruvian goods—it was a question of knowing how to take advantage of them, and how to make Peru's negotiating position stronger. By developing an independent system of commerce, elevating the price of native raw materials through industrialization, and not mortgaging the country's future to a single export product, Peru would prosper beyond the wildest expectations, and that prosperity would attract much-needed colonists from Europe to populate the countryside. "This is the future that awaits us," Esteves concluded, "if we listen to reason, and allow ourselves to be led by the first of human virtues—hard work."[3]

Published while Peru was still occupied by Chilean troops, Esteves' book turned out to be the first expression of a feeling that was to become generalized among the country's various elites. In the years that followed, a number of entrepreneurs, eager to put the war's defeats behind them, initiated projects of reconstruction both on the coast and in the highlands. Economic sectors whose activities had been totally interrupted by the war began to recover and consolidate.[4]

[1] Gabriel García Márquez, *Cien años de soledad* (Buenos Aires: Editorial Sudamericana, 1969), p. 15. Translation by the author.

[2] Luis Esteves, *Apuntes para la historia económica del Perú*, 2d ed. (Lima: Centro de Estudios de Población y Desarrollo, 1971), p. i.

[3] Ibid., p. 157.

[4] Rosemary Thorp and Geoffrey Bertram, *Peru 1890–1977: Growth and Policy in an Open Economy* (New York: Columbia University Press, 1978), pp. 32–33; Peter F. Klarén, *Formación de las haciendas azucareras y los orígenes del APRA*, 2d ed. (Lima:

This recovery was particularly evident in the central sierra, where the devastation of the La Breña campaign had reversed a prosperous trend in production and commerce. In the mining sector, for example, an alliance of local mineowners and Lima entrepreneurs and technicians began to revive production by the mid-1880s.[5] In addition to reconstruction efforts, there were attempts at innovation in technology and organization of the industry. Several mining engineers from the first graduating class of the School of Engineering in Lima were hired as managers of mines and one of them, Ismael Bueno, organized a school for mining foremen.[6] After numerous tests with British metallurgical technology, Pedro Dávalos y Lissón, supervisor of the Rayo mine in Casapalca, perfected a method to amalgamate silver in two hours instead of the usual forty days.[7] And in 1889, the American engineers Jacob Backus and J. Howard Johnston, principal shareholders in the mining company Sociedad de los Andes, constructed the first custombuilt smelter at Casapalca.[8]

Efforts at revival were also apparent in subtropical agriculture. After several large haciendas resumed production of *aguardiente*, construction of the Tarma-Chanchamayo road, a project financed through a tax on the liquor sold outside the valley, began again for the first time since 1881.[9] Between 1883 and 1886, representatives from Switzerland, Italy, and Spain visited Chanchamayo to ascertain its potential for colonization.[10] The Swiss went so far as to form the Swiss-Peruvian Colonization Company, and petitioned the Peruvian government on two separate occasions to grant them an exclusive concession to colonize the region.[11] Yet no matter how numerous the individual efforts at reconstruction, and whether the initiative came from local or for-

Instituto de Estudios Peruanos, 1976), pp. 49–51; and Jorge Basadre, *Historia de la República del Perú*, 6th ed., 17 Vols. (Lima: Editorial Universitaria, 1969), 9: 38–47.

[5] RPI, *Sociedades*, I: 1–58; UNI, Tesis de Minería, No. 10–12, Federico Villarreal, "Memoria sobre Yauli"; No. 13, Germán Remy, "Informe sobre Yauli"; No. 14, Ismael Bueno, "Informe sobre Huarochirí"; No. 16, Rafael Muñoz, "Informe sobre Cerro de Pasco"; and Pedro Dávalos y Lissón, *Cómo hice fortuna*, 2 Vols. (Lima: Librería e Imprenta Gil, 1941–42), II: 23–36, 44–50, 55–58, 72.

[6] Dávalos y Lissón, *Cómo hice fortuna*, II: 50–51, 55, 83; APJ, "Oficio de Ismael Bueno al Prefecto del Departamento," Cerro de Pasco, February 1891.

[7] Dávalos y Lissón, *Cómo hice fortuna*, II: 71.

[8] Ibid., pp. 47, 76; Thorp and Bertram, *Peru*, p. 73.

[9] APJ, "Oficio del Encargado de la Junta Constructora del Camino a Chanchamayo al Ministerio de Gobierno," Tarma, May 1, 1886.

[10] BNP, Document No. D3913, "Expediente sobre las concesiones solicitadas por la compañía Suizo-peruana de colonización al Chanchamayo," Lima, December 1883; and *U.S. Consular Reports*, Vol. 20, No. 70 (October 1886), 57.

[11] BNP, Document No. D3913, "Expediente sobre las concesiones."

eign capital, it soon became clear that they would not go far without some kind of assistance from the central government.

The need for government support was particularly obvious in the case of the labor problem. Both on the northern coast, where the Chilean invasion had led to the rebellion of the Chinese coolies and the destruction of many plantations,[12] and in the central highlands, where mine- and landowners struggled with recalcitrant peasants to maintain a labor force on their properties, the acquisition and retention of workers necessitated a fairly high degree of political influence. Certainly this was the case when laborers were imported from the outside, and it was necessary to work out contracts with foreign governments. But it was also true when entrepreneurs relied on local supplies of workers.

Because they were dependent on seasonal labor from peasants with access to means of production in their villages, businesspeople continued to advance money through merchants in order to indebt peasants and force them to work off the debt on their mines or plantations. Yet *enganche* was not a dependable or efficient way to obtain or retain workers. In the first place, it was extremely expensive. Not only was it necessary to tie up a great deal of money simply in the acquisition of workers, but often an equal or greater amount was spent chasing runaways. Even more important, the ultimate success of *enganche* depended on access to power at two levels: within the community, and in the larger society. Within the community, local merchants or wealthier peasants tapped personal networks of patronage and clientele that had been built up over generations of interaction and asymmetrical reciprocity to gain access to peasant labor. But once this exchange of labor was no longer part of the ongoing, face-to-face ties of community life, the merchant could not enforce all contracts personally. Thus it became necessary to call on judicial and political institutions in the larger society, using the formal existence of a debt as the means to legally compel peasants to finish their work terms. Ultimately, therefore, control over labor depended on how effectively local and regional elites could call on the state apparatus to back them up.

Another bottleneck needing government attention was the question of infrastructure, particularly roads and railroads. Throughout the Peruvian interior, the lack of adequate means of transportation drove up the cost and risk of commercial activity. In the 1860s, for example,

[12] Heraclio Bonilla, "The War of the Pacific and the National and Colonial Problem in Peru," *Past and Present*, No. 81 (November 1978), pp. 92–118.

the cost of shipping freight from Jauja to Lima, a distance of approximately 160 miles, was eighty pesos per ton; or, according to an informed observer of the day, four times higher than the maritime freight from Callao to either Liverpool or China.[13] Not surprisingly, this type of ratio could lead to extremely unusual price relationships. With regard to the plight of coffee cultivators in Chanchamayo, for example, Michael McNulty, U.S. consular agent in Cerro de Pasco, commented in 1886:

> The complaint of the cultivators was and is that they have speculated to [sic] far in the business for the very logical reason that owing to have to pack their produce on mule back for a distance of from 80 to 150 miles to the present terminus of the Oroya Rail Road [sic] at Chicla then the train freight to Lima unables [sic] them to compete with Costa Rica on the Pacific Coast.[14]

And the same problem affected many sectors of the economy. Indeed, most highland entrepreneurs would have probably agreed with McNulty's conclusion that until a railroad was nearby, there was little chance of making coffee, or any other commercial crop for that matter, a profitable business in the interior.[15]

Between 1886 and 1890, the Caceristas attempted to implement a program that would give the necessary state aid to entrepreneurial efforts by encouraging investment, production, and commerce, expanding the construction of infrastructure, revitalizing the exploration and colonization of the jungle, and reforming the system of education. A number of specific policies, including the abolition of most export duties and the creation of property registers, chambers of commerce, mortgage banks, and insurance companies, were designed to stimulate internal investment and production.[16] But as had been the case before the war, the government continued to rely mainly on foreign capital to revitalize the Peruvian economy and expand infrastructure.[17]

Throughout their first three years in power, the Caceristas struggled to attract foreign capital to Peru once again. Although the country had emerged from the war even more heavily in debt than before

[13] Manuel Pardo, *Estudios sobre la provincia de Jauja* (Lima: Imprenta de la Epoca, 1862), p. 23.
[14] YC, U.S. Consulate, Callao, Miscellaneous Correspondence Received, Microfilm Reel 22, "McNulty to H. M. Brent," Cerro de Pasco, January 5, 1888.
[15] Ibid.
[16] For the various specific policies that were instituted under the first Cáceres government, see Basadre, *Historia*, 9: 103, 105, 107–190.
[17] Thorp and Bertram, *Peru*, p. 23.

and the loss of valuable nitrate territories to Chile made repayment even more difficult, foreign investment still seemed the only effective path to reconstruction. Thus, in an effort to reestablish Peru's credit abroad and provide an attractive climate for investors, the Caceristas recalled the devalued wartime paper currency and began negotiations with the bondholders against whom the Peruvian government had defaulted in the 1870s.[18] The result of these negotiations was the Grace Contract, signed in 1889. In exchange for cancellation of the 1869, 1870, and 1872 loans, the Peruvian government relinquished control of all its railroads, gave the bondholders the remaining guano exports and free navigation rights on Lake Titicaca, and agreed to pay eighty thousand pounds sterling per year over a period of thirty-three years. In 1890, the bondholders formed the Peruvian Corporation to enforce the terms of the contract and were given an additional grant of two million hectares of land in the Ene-Perené region of the central jungle.[19]

Despite these sizable concessions, however, the Peruvian government was unable to gain the lasting confidence or interest of foreign capital. After an initial rash of enthusiastic investment in several sectors, including oil, sugar, mining, and cotton textiles, the fall of silver prices on the international market in 1892 destabilized Peruvian currency and caused a serious economic recession. Equally important, the Caceristas were unable to put together the kind of hard-hitting policy that would discipline labor and pacify those sectors of the lower classes still in rebellion after the War of the Pacific. Thus, as the brief postwar economic recovery and the even briefer renewal of foreign investment came to an end, so did the internal political alliance that had backed Cáceres' candidacy. On the national level, the progressive Civilistas retired their support and Congress challenged the validity of the Grace Contract concessions. At the regional level, local elites chafed at the central government's inability to revive the economy or provide them with the backing they needed to reestablish control over labor.[20]

Nowhere was the erosion of the Cacerista alliance more evident

---

[18] Ibid.

[19] Ernesto Yepes del Castillo, *Perú 1820–1920: Un siglo de desarrollo capitalista* (Lima: Instituto de Estudios Peruanos-Campodónico Ediciones, S.A., 1972), pp. 138–39.

[20] On the recession, the problems with foreign capital, and the protests over the Grace Contract, see Thorp and Bertram, *Peru*, pp. 23–24. On the problems with labor and pacification, see above, Chapter III; on the lack of a labor policy, see Basadre, *Historia*, 9: 219–34, 255–58; and Agustín Barcelli S., *Historia del sindicalismo peruano*, 2 Vols. (Lima: Editorial Hatunruna, 1971), I: 33–36, 55–58, 109.

than in the central highlands. As we have already seen, continued Cacerista control of the area was predicated on an alliance between the regional elite and the *mestizos*, petty merchants, and rich peasants in the villages who had benefited most from the postwar Cacerista policy of district creation. Because the La Breña campaign had a differential effect on the various subregions of the central sierra, however, this alliance had never worked smoothly except in the area immediately around Jauja. Perhaps the best proof of this is a confidential document, compiled after Cáceres' defeat, that listed approximately sixty Caceristas in the province of Jauja important enough to be considered potentially dangerous to the new government. The same document found only thirty active supporters of Cáceres in the province of Huancayo. Of those listed for Huancayo, none were prominent members of the landowning elite. Finally, of all the Caceristas listed for either province, none were from the city of Concepción, the main residence of the wealthiest *hacendado* group. Clearly, therefore, it was mainly the Jauja merchants who controlled social and political influence in the region during the Cacerista government.[21] Yet the very narrowness of this political base prevented a number of groups, both within the elite and in the villages, from taking part in or benefiting from reconstruction policy.

Perhaps the most powerful of these groups was the merchant and *hacendado* elite in the southern Mantaro Valley, particularly in Concepción. Since it was here that most of the land invasions had occurred during the La Breña campaign, several *hacendados* were in danger of permanently losing their properties to recalcitrant peasant guerrillas.[22] Others, who had borrowed copiously from merchants immediately before or during the war, found that defaulted loans were threatening their lands.[23] All landowners, their haciendas reduced to mere shells by the incursions of Chileans, Caceristas, and Iglesistas, were forced to tighten their belts, and the worst of it was that no one knew how long it would last. Even the Concepción merchants who

[21] APJ, "Subprefecto de Huancayo al Prefecto del Departamento," Huancayo, February 17, 1897.

[22] See above, Chapter III. Also, ANF, Protocolos Notariales, Luis Salazar, Book 3: October 7, 1888, 144–44v.

[23] ANF, Protocolos Notariales, Manuel Víctor Morales, Book 13: November 19, 1887, 34v–35; Luis Salazar, Book 2 (1886): 8v–9, 61v–62, 73–73v, 88v; Book 3 (1890): 112v–13v, 172–73; Book 4 (1892): 336–39, 339–40v; Book 5 (1893–94): 28v–29v, 270–72, 353v–54v; Book 7 (1897): 174v–76, 176–77v. AGN, Protocolos Notariales, Manuel Orellana, Protocolo 540, April 9, 1883; Mariano E. Terrazas, Protocolo 958, May 10, 1889; Felipe S. Vivanco, September 20, 1888, 793v–94v; Juan Ignacio Bernizón, July 16, 1892; José Ramón Valdivia, Protocolo 994, 99v–102v, 138–39v, 145–46.

had emerged relatively unscathed, or even profited, from the La Breña campaign, could not break through the political monopoly of the Jauja Caceristas to consolidate and expand their commercial and productive interests.[24] As the Cacerista program ran into problems at the national level, therefore, it was only natural that the Concepción merchants and *hacendados* should begin to celebrate the possibility of Cáceres' downfall.

Another faction that opposed Cáceres was a new group of merchants who had settled in Jauja immediately before or after the war. Interested in exploiting the incipient markets for goods and labor that were being created in the various productive sectors of the regional economy, these Peruvians and recent immigrants established contacts in mining and subtropical agriculture.[25] By offering loans to peasants in the area's communities and representing them in their legal conflicts over land, the merchants began to forge networks of patronage and clientele through which they hoped to provide mines and haciendas with laborers.[26] But as long as the Cacerista merchants continued to control the main channels of access to social, economic, and political influence, the new group could expect only limited success in its efforts. Of the nine new merchants identified for Jauja, for example, none held an important political position between 1886 and 1894. Of

[24] The combination of the Jauja merchants' good connections with the central government, and Cáceres' policy of reprisals against those who had opposed him in the La Breña campaign, made it extremely difficult for a number of Concepción merchants. See, for example, ANF, Protocolos Notariales, Luis Salazar, Book 5: September 23, 1894, 355v–65v, and Book 6: March 28, 1896, 269v–70v; and APJ, "Solicitud de varios notables de Concepción al Prefecto del Departamento," Concepción, October 19, 1892. Also, since Jauja was the capital of the province to which Concepción belonged, it made the Cacerista merchants' dominance a great deal simpler. In May 1890, for example, when elections for both president and senators were held in the province, all the principal electors and observers were Jauja Caceristas. APJ, "Elección de senadores propietarios por el departamento," and "Elección del presidente de la República," Jauja, May 13, 1890.

[25] Examples of this group are: José G. Andía, Apolinario Bardales, Eugenio Barraillier, Dionicio Bravo Vial, Tomás Hovispo, Santiago Motto, Gerónimo and José Silva, and Manuel E. Rojo. See ANF, Protocolos Notariales, Luis Salazar, Book 5: August 25, 1893, 167–68v; ANF, Expedientes y Libros Judiciales, Libro de Juicios Verbales, Jauja, 1891 (various documents), and Libro de Juicios Verbales, Acolla, 1891–1892, especially 2–2v, 3v–4v, 5v–6, 10–11, 11v–12, 12v–13; APJ, "Expediente de Manuel E. Rojo al Subprefecto de la provincia de Jauja," Jauja, November 20, 1890, and "Expediente de diez enganchadores al Subprefecto de Jauja," Jauja, February 27, 1893; and Dávalos y Lissón, *Cómo hice fortuna*, II: 29.

[26] ANF, Expedientes y Libros Judiciales, Libro de Juicios Verbales, Jauja, 1891 (various documents), and "Comunidad de Concho contra Tomás V. Hovispo sobre tierras," March 23, 1897; ANF, Protocolos Notariales, Manuel Víctor Morales, Book s/n: May 1, 1891, 42–42v; Luis Salazar, Book 4: March 9, 1892, 208–209; Book 5: April 23, 1893, 69v–71v, and August 25, 1893, 167–68v; Dávalos y Lissón, *Cómo hice fortuna*, II: 29.

the same group, only four had any political participation at all, and always at a secondary level. And this low level of political influence could not help but lessen the effectiveness of the group as *engancha-dores*. Thus it is hardly surprising that they welcomed the possibility of both a local political shake-up and Cáceres' fall from power.[27]

The third group that was willing to ally with the anti-Cáceres forces was, ironically enough, a faction of peasants from several villages in the Jauja area. Though they had all been passionately Cacerista during and directly after the La Breña campaign, the contradictory process of district creation and the tendency for merchants, *mestizos*, and rich peasants to monopolize the newly created political offices had thrown many peasants into the opposing camp. In Acolla, for example, the peasants' enthusiastic support for Cáceres during the La Breña campaign had earned them independent district status in 1886.[28] But several rich and powerful families from the neighboring village of Marco, who happened to have excellent connections with the Cacerista merchants and officials in Jauja, immediately took over the district apparatus and monopolized municipal office.[29] By the 1890s, therefore, the *Acollinos* had moved to the opposite side of the political struggle in an effort to break the political stranglehold of the *Marqueños*.[30]

When Nicolás de Piérola and his recently formed Democratic party initiated a civil war against Cáceres in 1894, then, they found broad support in the central highlands. For a number of reasons, some connected directly to broader issues of national power and development, others obeying a much more localized dynamic of class struggle, a wide coalition of sectors joined together to oust the Cacerista clique. And to a certain extent, everyone got what they wanted. For the new merchants in Jauja, the political decline of the Caceristas at the local

[27] On the group's low level of political participation, see APJ, "Bando político en Jauja," March 13, 1886; "Acta," Jauja, March 13, 1886; "Cuadro del personal y empleados del Honorable Concejo Provincial de Jauja," June 20, 1887; "Personal de la Junta Directiva del H. Concejo Provincial de Jauja, 1890–1891," Jauja, December 15, 1890; "Copia de las elecciones, Parroquia de Jauja," Tarma, April 22, 1890; "Personal de la H. Junta Directiva del Concejo Provincial de Jauja," January–April 1893; "Elección de senadores propietarios y suplentes," Jauja, June 26, 1894. On their lessened effectiveness as *enganchadores*, see APJ, "Manuel E. Rojo al Subprefecto de Jauja," Jauja, November 20, 1890; and "Diez enganchadores de Jauja al Subprefecto," Jauja, February 27, 1893.

[28] See above, Chapter III.

[29] BNP, Document No. D6954, "Nuevo Personal de los Concejos Distritales, Junín," June 1888; APJ, "Personal de los Concejos Distritales de la Provincia," Jauja, March 27, 1893. The patron-client relations between this group and the Jauja Caceristas emerge clearly from ANF, Expedientes y Libros Judiciales, "Concho contra Hovispo."

[30] Conversations with Moisés Ortega, Acolla, 1977.

level opened up new vistas for the consolidation of their patronage networks.[31] For the peasants, the changing balance of power among the various elite factions provided some needed room to move and allowed for a realignment of forces at the district level.[32] For the Concepción *hacendados* and merchants, renewed access to national influence meant they could finally emerge from the wartime depression, reclaim their lands, and reestablish control over the lower classes.[33] But most important for the region as a whole, the Pierolista development strategy generated an economic boom that came close to changing the very nature of the central highland economy and society.

National Modernization and Regional Development

On March 17, 1895, in the midst of a thick fog, Nicolás de Piérola and his troops battled inch by inch into downtown Lima. Two days later, they took power at the head of a reconstructionist coalition.[34] In the years that followed, the Pierolista coalition initiated a program of modernization that included the building of roads, the extension of public services, the institution of a system of protective tariffs that encouraged national industrialization, the creation of a credit and finance network to foment investment in mining and other productive sectors, the colonization of the jungle, and the so-called "civilization and incorporation" of the Indian.[35] Through what was essentially an

[31] APJ, "Oficio de Bartolomé Guerra al Prefecto del Departamento Jacinto Cevallos, pidiendo garantías," Huancayo, July 30, 1895; "Razón de las personas que pertenecen al partido constitucional," Huancayo, February 17, 1897; "Lista de gobernadores de Jauja y Acolla," Jauja, February 28, 1897; "Expediente sobre irregularidades en el gobierno municipal de Jauja," Jauja, August 2, 1900; and BNP, Document No. D4597: "Correspondencia de la Junta Patriótica Nacional," Lima, 1898, 1–2, and Jauja, August 29, 1898; Document No. D5039: "Expediente sobre fondos recolectados para el rescate de Arica," Jauja, June 11, 1896.

[32] In the case of Acolla, for example, the people who had previously controlled local government were identified by the new authorities and marginalized to a large degree. See APJ, "Lista de Caceristas en Jauja," Huancayo, February 17, 1897, and "Lista de Gobernadores de Jauja y Acolla," Jauja, February 28, 1897. Of course, the battle over power between Cacerista and Pierolista factions continued at the local level, adding an extra layer of complication to many other conflicts. See, for example, ANF, Expedientes y Libros Judiciales, "Concho contra Hovispo."

[33] ANF, Protocolos Notariales, Luis Salazar, Book 6: March 28, 1896, 269v–70v; Book 7: April 23, 1897, 92v–94; May 23, 1897, 124v–26v; Book 8: August 24, 1898, 536–37; Book 9: August 16, 1899, 220v–22v; APJ, "Expediente sobre enganche para la montaña del Pichis," Jauja, October 30, 1898.

[34] Frederick B. Pike, *The Modern History of Peru* (New York: Frederick A. Praeger, 1967), p. 158.

[35] Thorp and Bertram, *Peru*, pp. 24–25; Basadre, *Historia*, 10: 213–44, 259, 269–74,

attempt to create a national market for goods, capital, and labor, the Pierolistas succeeded in giving a stake in the regime to a wide variety of elite groups. For the first time, coastal sugar *hacendados* and Civilistas, emerging industrialists and merchants, and several of the commercial and landowning elites in different regions of the Peruvian highlands joined together to back a government they hoped could create new opportunities for investment while at the same time increasing their economic and political control over the lower classes.[36]

The reconstructionist coalition's strategy for national development was both the only alternative the Peruvian government had left, and an extremely viable one under the circumstances. After the willingness of foreign investors to invest in Peru declined precipitously in 1892, there was nothing left to do but rely on internal capital accumulation. As it turned out, however, this was an attractive possibility in the last years of the nineteenth century. As Europe and the United States entered the truly industrial phase of capitalist development, the nature and structure of demand for both raw materials and foodstuffs changed dramatically.[37] Several of Peru's export products, including sugar, wool, cotton, and coffee, were ideal for the expanding consumer markets overseas. Others, such as the extensive deposits of industrial minerals—including copper, zinc, and lead—were just waiting to be exploited for a booming industrial market. And as long as production occurred within Peruvian borders, the devaluation of the currency that began in 1892 could only serve to cheapen production and increase the profitability of exports.[38]

Thus, by making government support to local initiative the central plank of their reconstruction program, the Pierolistas turned a new combination of circumstances on the international market to their advantage. Rather than depend on massive infusions of foreign capital to initiate a few large development projects, they relied on internal accumulations of resources and skill to carry out a variety of smaller, more modest efforts.[39] As a result, the Peruvian economy underwent a dramatic expansion and diversification between 1895 and 1900. Us-

---

287–302; and BNP, Document No. D5051: "Pacificación de Comas y Acta de Adhesión al Supremo Gobierno," Tarma-Jauja, November 21–23, 1896.

[36] For an analysis of Piérola's support on the coast, see Basadre, especially 10: 102–143, and Pike, *Modern History*, pp. 168–86. For an analysis of the political importance of the Piérola years in the southern highlands, see Karen Spalding, "Estructura de clases en la sierra peruana, 1750–1920," *Análisis*, No. 1 (January–March 1977), pp. 25–35.

[37] For an elaboration on this argument, see Yepes del Castillo, *Peru*, pp. 143–49.

[38] Thorp and Bertram, *Peru*, pp. 26, 29–30.

[39] Ibid., pp. 32–36; Pike, *Modern History*, pp. 160–68.

ing increased earnings from several export products, including sugar, copper, and coffee, entrepreneurs invested in the expansion of agricultural and mining production, urban manufacturing, public utilities, and credit networks.[40] At the regional level, merchants, mineowners, and landowners responded to government requests by contributing labor, money, and supplies to the construction of roads that would tie their areas more closely to the national and international markets. Some answered government queries on how to discipline and accustom peasants to the rigors of proletarian labor.[41] For the first time in Peruvian history, a modernizing state was providing the context within which the various innovative regional elites could come together and forge a national bourgeoisie.

Given the substantial advances made in mining, subtropical agriculture, and the colonization of the jungle, the central highlands became somewhat of a showcase during the Piérola years. Throughout the latter half of the 1890s, businesspeople from Lima and other parts of Peru moved into the region and, either singly or in partnership with local entrepreneurs, invested in commerce, mining, and agriculture. The top echelons of the regional elite were finally able to recover from the War of the Pacific, expanding and diversifying their holdings, innovating in the various sectors of the regional economy.

Nowhere was this boom more evident than in mining. Although the precipitous fall of silver prices on the world market in 1892 had caused a major crisis in the industry, the rapid rise of copper prices throughout the 1890s made the exploitation of copper a viable alternative.[42] To supply the expanding industrial market in Europe and the United States with copper was quite a different matter from supplying a luxury market with silver, however. The volume of the trade could not be handled simply with llamas and mules. For the shipping of the ores to be profitable, the copper content had to be relatively high; and while it was possible to make initial windfall profits on the richest surface ores, sooner or later it would become necessary to smelt them before export. Thus copper production needed a much

[40] Thorp and Bertram, *Peru*, pp. 32–36.
[41] APJ, "Oficio del Cónsul Francés Sr. Prugue, al Prefecto de Junín Jacinto Cevallos," Hacienda Bellavista, Valle de Chanchamayo, July 7, 1895; "Albino Carranza, de la Administración Municipal de Tarma, al Prefecto del Departamento," Tarma, December 20, 1897; "Nemesio D. Jorquiera, administrador de la Hacienda Naranjal, al Prefecto del Departamento," Hacienda Naranjal, Valle de Chanchamayo, July 3, 1902; and "Emilio Prugue, Cónsul Francés en Chanchamayo, al Prefecto del Departamento," Hacienda Bellavista, Valle de Chanchamayo, July 5, 1902.
[42] Yepes del Castillo, *Perú*, p. 147.

broader infrastructure and investment network than traditional silver production. And it was only after the arrival of the Central Railway in La Oroya in 1893, and the beginning of copper matte production at the Backus and Johnston smelter in 1894, that the initial outlines of such a network became available.[43]

Starting in 1895, and especially after 1897, the extraction of copper ores, both for direct export and for sale to the Backus and Johnston smelter, increased dramatically. Particularly in Morococha, which was very close to the railroad and to Casapalca, copper became extremely profitable.[44] In fact, given the high copper content of the ores, most mineowners in Morococha and its surrounding districts preferred to export them directly rather than accept the comparatively low price that Backus and Johnston were willing to pay at the smelter.[45] Even in Cerro de Pasco, a hundred miles away from the railroad station at Oroya, the extraction of high-grade copper ores from already existing silver mines and their direct shipment by llama to Oroya remained profitable for about two years. After that, the short supply of freight animals pushed up the cost of transportation while the copper content of available ores declined, forcing entrepreneurs to build their own smelters in the area.[46]

In this context, one of the truly pioneering businessmen was Eulogio E. Fernandini. Between 1897 and 1898, Fernandini constructed a *fundición* (smelter) to smelt ore at his mineral hacienda, Huaraucaca. Initially, this modest facility used the lexiviation method and functioned partially on machinery that had already existed on other mineral haciendas in the central highlands. One machine, a mill from the hacienda La Esperanza, was brought to Huaraucaca piece by piece on the backs of fourteen mules.[47] Eight years later, however, Huaraucaca had been transformed into a smelter and concentration plant that

[43] Ibid., pp. 147–48; Thorp and Bertram, *Peru*, pp. 77–78; BCIM, No. 25, Manuel G. Masías, *Estado actual de la industria minera en Morococha* (Lima: Imprenta "El Lucero," 1905), p. 22.

[44] Thorp and Bertram, *Peru*, p. 77; BCIM, No. 25, p. 22.

[45] BCIM, No. 25, pp. 22–23; BCIM, No. 5, M. G. Masías, *Informe sobre los trabajos efectuados en el asiento mineral de Yauli* (Lima: Imprenta Torres Aguirre, 1902–1903), pp. 33–34; BCIM, No. 14, J. A. Loredo, *Estadística Minera del Perú en 1903* (Lima: Imprenta de la Escuela de Ingenieros, 1904), pp. 39–40.

[46] Thorp and Bertram, *Peru*, pp. 77–78; BCIM, No. 14, p. 39.

[47] AFA, Documents Fernandini: Minas, Documentos Varios, "Contrato de Arrieraje de Gregorio Oldana y Pablo Estrella con Eulogio E. Fernandini," 1898, and various letters and other documents concerning the sale of the mill, November 1897–April 1898.

rivaled the most modern in the region.[48] And over time, Fernandini would have the unique distinction of being the only national capitalist to hold out against the Cerro de Pasco Corporation. But that is getting ahead of our story.

Fernandini was but one notable example of a general trend toward modernization in the central highland mining industry. At every level, entrepreneurs were taking advantage of the copper boom to accumulate and modernize. Between 1897 and 1900, seventeen small-scale copper smelters were built in the Cerro de Pasco area.[49] By the first years of the twentieth century, some of the wealthier Lima business-people were discussing the possibility of building a large central smelter in the region.[50] From the largest joint stock company that combined capital from Lima with the more modest resources of local entrepreneurs, to the smallest individual mineowner, the emphasis was on local capital and initiative. And although this trend was most dramatic in the mining industry, the same tendencies could be seen in other sectors of the regional economy.

East of the highland region the entire *ceja de selva*, from the Perené Valley in the north to Pampa Hermosa in the south, was a new frontier waiting to be explored by enterprising individuals. The Chanchamayo and Monobamba Valleys, which lay roughly at the center of the *ceja* area, had been substantially settled before the war; but there were still many plots of land to be claimed in both. In Chanchamayo and the neighboring Vítoc Valley, large haciendas dedicated to the production of sugarcane bordered on smaller properties that produced rice, coca, tobacco, and fruit for local consumption.[51] In Monobamba the same pattern held true, although the tendency was more toward the smaller plot with diversified production for the local market.[52] Further to the north in the Perené Valley, the Peruvian Corporation

[48] BCIM, No. 30, Carlos E. Velarde, *Reglamentaciones mineras para el Cerro de Pasco* (Lima: Tipografía de "El Lucero," 1905), p. 19; BCIM, No. 41, M. A. Denegri, *Estadística Minera del Perú en 1905* (Lima: Imprenta la Industria, 1906), pp. 29–31; BCIM, No. 54, Germán Klinge, *Estadística Minera del Perú en 1906* (Lima: Imprenta la Industria, 1907), pp. 32–37.

[49] Thorp and Bertram, *Peru*, p. 78; BCIM, No. 14, p. 39.

[50] Thorp and Bertram, *Peru*, p. 78.

[51] See Manuel María del Valle's letters from Chanchamayo (1876), in Municipalidad de la Merced, *Los pioneros* (1969), pp. 36–90; Bureau of International Republics, *Monthly Bulletin*, November 1899 (French edition), pp. 782–83; Great Britain, *Diplomatic and Consular Reports*, Annual Series, No. 2807, "Report on the Trade of Peru," 1901, pp. 30–31; No. 3079, "Report on the Trade of Peru," 1902, pp. 17–18; APJ, "Solicitud de Marcos Melo al Prefecto de Junín," Tarma, January 16, 1901.

[52] ANF, Protocolos Notariales, Luis Salazar, Book 6: August 4, 1895, 108–109; Book 7: May 3, 1897, 104v–106; Book 9: April 10, 1899, 73–75v.

encouraged the settlement of colonists on small- to medium-sized individual plots.[53] And in Pampa Hermosa, the jungle region due east of Huancayo, members of the regional elite staked out land claims, planting sugar cane and using native labor to collect rubber from the wild hevea trees. The rubber was then fashioned into large balls and sent by mule to Oroya, by train to Callao, and to Liverpool through the Graham Rowe commercial house.[54]

Yet of all the agricultural or subtropical products, it was coffee that made the most headway as an export crop in the late 1890s. Particularly after 1896, the volume of coffee being exported to Europe shot up dramatically. In 1902, when they reached their highest peak, exports were almost four times the volume they had generally been in the decade between 1884 and 1894.[55] And, at least according to the reports of British and American consular agents, the bulk of this production came from the Perené and Chanchamayo Valleys.[56]

In contrast to both subtropical agriculture and mining, the central sierra livestock sector did not progress notably in this period. The main reason for this stagnation was, of course, the intense decapitalization that most haciendas had suffered during the War of the Pacific. In several cases, moreover, battles with invading peasants dragged on for many years, making it even more difficult for *hacendados* to invest scarce resources in refurbishing their properties. Thus, rather than risk yet another debacle on the livestock haciendas, it was a great deal more efficient for landowners wishing to invest to do so in other productive sectors or in commerce, where the profits were larger and more secure.[57]

That there were large profits to be made in commerce should come as no surprise. The boom in agriculture and mining production generated a rapidly expanding demand for freight animals and labor. Though the railroad to Oroya lessened the need for mule traffic to Chicla, the greater carrying capacity of the trains intensified traffic

[53] BNP, Document No. D7254, "Annual Report, Peruvian Corporation," December 4, 1893, 8; Great Britain, *Diplomatic and Consular Reports*, Annual Series, No. 1538, "Callao: Report on Trade and Commerce," 1894, p. 8; *U.S. Consular Reports*, Vol. 47, No. 175 (April 1895), p. 550.

[54] Interview with Hernán Valladares, Huancayo, June 3, 1977.

[55] Thorp and Bertram, *Peru*, pp. 330–31.

[56] Great Britain, *Diplomatic and Consular Reports*, No. 1538, pp. 7–8; No. 1866, pp. 15–16; No. 2807, p. 30; and *U.S. Consular Reports*, Vol. 47, No. 175, pp. 549–51.

[57] In fact, the debts built up around the War of the Pacific led to several haciendas changing hands. See, for example, AGN, Protocolos Notariales, José Ramón Valdivia, Protocolo 994, July 12–July 19, 1886; Mariano E. Terrazas, Protocolo 958, May 10, 1889; Juan Ignacio Bernizón, Minuta 704, July 16, 1892.

along all the *arrieraje* routes that served Oroya. In the specific case of the mining industry, increased industrial activity and the greater bulk and weight of copper ores generated a sharply rising demand for freight animals that the existing *arriero* population could not always handle successfully. This shortage was further exacerbated by the need to transport coal for the new smelters in the Cerro de Pasco area, and transportation costs skyrocketed. A similar bottleneck was created in the labor supply. Since several productive sectors were expanding at once, it was extremely difficult to meet the demand for workers with a supply of seasonal labor from peasants who still had access to land in their villages. The overall result, then, was that transportation and labor became extremely expensive, and since wages remained low in this period it was the intermediaries providing the mines and landowners with workers or mule drivers who profited most from the situation.[58]

A number of merchants and landowners, both established members of the regional elite and recently arrived "upstarts" from the coast, took advantage of this conjuncture. Rather than actually invest in production, they simply reorganized commercial and credit relations and used them in the service of mineowners and *hacendados*.[59] Some, such as the landowner and merchant Julio C. de Castañeda, began companies that specialized in mule and llama transportation.[60] Others, such as Braulio Llanos of Junín, the Silva brothers in Jauja, or José Andía in Llocllapampa—to name only a few—used their commercial establishments to build influence in peasant communities and provide

[58] On the development of bottlenecks in the mining industry, see Thorp and Bertram, *Peru*, p. 78. On wage levels in this period, see UNI, Tesis de Minería, No. 10–12: Federico Villarreal, "Memoria sobre Yauli," 1885, 8, 13v, 16; No. 14: Ismael Bueno, "Informe sobre Huarochirí," 1887, 22; "Informe sobre Cerro de Pasco," 1887, 13; No. 16: Rafael Muñoz, "Informe sobre Cerro de Pasco," 1887, 2–3; No. 43: Alberto Noriega, "Informe sobre Aguas Calientes (Huarochirí)," 1891, 27–28; No. 50: Francisco R. Del Castillo, "Informe sobre Huarochirí y Yauli," 1891, 9; No. 57: Carlos I. Lissón, "Informe sobre la Hacienda Mineral Párac," 1894, 12; No. 58: Santiago F. Marrou, "Memoria sobre Huarochirí," 1894, 10; and AFA, Documentos Fernandini, Minas, Documentos Varios, 1887–1899.

[59] An excellent example of this is a contract between José G. Andía, a merchant living in Llocllapampa, and Pedro A. Espinoza, a rich peasant from Marco. Andía lent Espinoza the substantial quantity of 900 soles in silver at 3 percent interest a year, which Espinoza was to pay back in two installments: one after six months, and another after a year. Both of these payments, the contract explained, could be made either in money, "or in workers for the mines in which case we will abide by the existing laws on the *enganche* of workers." Thus, a common loan was used as a way of initiating a relationship of a completely different nature. ANF, Protocolos Notariales, Luis Salazar, Book 5: August 25, 1893, 167–68v.

[60] ANF, Protocolos Notariales, Luis Salazar, Book 10: April 7, 1901, 94–96v.

workers or *arrieros* for the mines and haciendas.[61] Yet because these activities merely strengthened existing networks of local power and patronage by manipulating them for new ends, they could not ultimately solve the bottleneck problems of the regional economy. Increasingly, therefore, entrepreneurs turned to the government to help them deal with the difficulties of labor and transportation.

Between 1896 and 1900, the central government finally put into effect a project that had been in the minds of progressive intellectuals for several decades—the construction of a central highway that would connect the rubber-producing jungle region of the Ucayali River, through the Pichis and Chanchamayo Valleys, down the mountain passes of the central sierra, to the coastal port of Callao.[62] When he appointed Joaquín Capelo, author of the impressive two-volume *La vía central del Perú*, head of the new Office of Development (Fomento),[63] Piérola proved that road construction in the central sierra was high on his list of priorities. And in keeping with the general spirit of infrastructure expansion, several projects for subsidiary roads were also accepted.[64] Rather than depend on foreign capital or technology, all these projects relied on local resources and initiative. A number of the region's most prestigious merchants and landowners contributed coca, dynamite, tools, *aguardiente*, or money to the construction.[65] Petty merchants and political officials advanced the government's money in the area's villages in order to provide workers.[66]

[61] AFA, Documentos Fernandini, Correspondence between Braulio Llanos and Eulogio E. Fernandini, 1897–1898; ANF, Protocolos Notariales, Luis Salazar, Book 6: November 30, 1895, 197–98v; Book 9: March 25, 1899, 53–55; September 10, 1899, 247–48v; APJ, "Solicitud de diez enganchadores de Jauja al Subprefecto," February 27, 1893; and ANF, Protocolos Notariales, Luis Salazar, Book 5: August 25, 1893, 167–68v.

[62] Basadre, *Historia*, 10: 261–65; Joaquín Capelo, *La vía central del Perú*, 2 Vols. (Lima: Imprenta Masías, 1895).

[63] APJ, "Contrato entre Francisco Egoavil, Teniente Gobernador de Palca, y el Teniente Coronel Enrique Vigil, Subprefecto de Tarma," Palca, September 3–5, 1896. The Office of Development was one of two subdivisions in the new Ministry of Development (Fomento), created in January 1896. Basadre, *Historia*, 10: 258–59.

[64] APJ, "Expediente iniciado para la apertura de un camino de Ulcumayo a Chanchamayo," June 1889–April 1897; "Planilla de tareas del pueblo de Cacas de los operarios que han trabajado en el camino carretero de la cección [sic] de Tambo Colorado al Cerro de Pasco," Junín, February 1899; "Planilla de tareas del pueblo de Pari de los operarios que han trabajado en el camino carretero de la cección [sic] de Tambo Colorado al Cerro de Pasco," Junín, February 6, 1899; and "Resolución del Congreso Nacional sobre la Construcción de carreteras en el Departamento de Junín," October 23, 1901.

[65] APJ, "Relación de los que contribuyen al camino en el Cerro de Pasco," April 7, 1897, in "Expediente . . . de Ulcumayo a Chanchamayo."

[66] APJ, "Pedro Verástegui, enganchador de Sicaya, al Subprefecto de Huancayo,"

In several agreements, peasant communities contributed money and labor to road construction in exchange for land or for having the road pass through their village.[67] Yet despite the varied and imaginative strategies used, the projects for expansion of infrastructure in the central highlands could not surmount a crucial problem: the constant struggle of the engineers to maintain anything resembling a stable labor force on the construction site.

Although several villages had been inspired by the promise of increased commerce or land to volunteer their labor for the central highway, the actual presence of workers on the road was something else again. Working conditions—regimentation, subtropical heat, disease, the craggy nature of the terrain, the inevitable shortages of supplies, the abuses of the engineers and foremen—were nightmarish, and it did not take long for this fact to circulate in the villages of the region. Many of the peasants who went to work on the road returned as fugitives, telling hair-raising stories of disease, abuse, and near-starvation.[68] Others refused to go, even though the government offered the highest wage in the region.[69] Again and again, work on the

April 16, 1898; "Eliaso Castillo, enganchador de Palca, al Prefecto del Departamento," Tarma, April 21, 1898; "Actas de los notables de Huaripampa, Muquiyauyo, Sincos, Mito, Orcotuna, Concepción, Apata, Acolla y Llocllapampa, comprometiéndose a ayudar en el enganche al Pichis," May 1898; "Contrato entre Francisco Egoavil, Teniente Gobernador de Palca, y Enrique Vigil, Subprefecto de Tarma, sobre enganche de operarios," Palca, September 3–5, 1896; and passim.

[67] APJ, "Recibo de contribución de la comunidad de Carhuamayo para el camino de Ulcumayo a Chanchamayo," August 27, 1897; "Relación de los que contribuyen," April 7, 1897, in "Expediente . . . de Ulcumayo a Chanchamayo"; "Acuerdo entre la comunidad de Ulcumayo y el Gobernador del distrito de Carhuamayo," January 4, 1898.

[68] In the APJ there are numerous documents concerning the bad treatment of workers and the problem with runaways. See, for example, "Oficio del Subprefecto de Tarma al Prefecto del Departmento sobre la fuga de operarios enganchados a Chanchamayo," Tarma, December 12, 1896; "Rafael F. Samaniego, enganchador de Sicaya, al Subprefecto de Huancayo," Huancayo, April 16, 1898; "Pedro Verástegui, enganchador de Sicaya, al Subprefecto de Huancayo," Huancayo, April 16, 1898; "El enganchador M. Zambrano al Subprefecto de Huancayo," Huancayo, April 18, 1898; "Eliaso Castillo, enganchador de Palca, al Prefecto del Departamento," Palca, April 21, 1898; "Celestino Camacho, enganchador de operarios al Pichis, al Prefecto del Departamento," Tarma, April 22, 1898; "Toribio Rodríguez, enganchador de Sicaya, al Subprefecto de Huancayo," April 30, 1898; "El Subprefecto de Tarma y el Comisario de Chanchamayo, al Prefecto del Departamento, sobre problemas con el pago de peones en el camino a Chanchamayo," May 2, 1898; "Oficio del Comisario de Chanchamayo al Prefecto, sobre pago de peones," September 23, 1898; "Vecinos de Acobamba en contra del contratista del camino a Chanchamayo, sobre falta de pago a peones," October 29, 1898; "José M. Beraún, vecino de Tarma, al Subprefecto de la Provincia, sobre entrega de soles a ex-peones en el camino al Pichis," November 4, 1898; and "Martín Cabezas y Pablo Cabezas, peones enganchados, al Prefecto del Departamento," San Luis de Shuaro, April–May 1901.

[69] APJ, "Cancelaciones de haberes para treinta operarios en la Vía Zapata, por el

highway had to be stopped while the government and its agents carried out a new wave of *enganches* in the villages.[70] Over and over, the political authorities and merchants who acted as *enganchadores* returned with fewer laborers than they had promised, explaining that the peasants had developed a terror of life on the *vía central* and preferred to retire to the hills rather than submit to an *enganche*.[71]

Yet no matter how horrendous working conditions actually were, they constituted at best a partial explanation for peasant recalcitrance. Official government *enganche*, coming at a time of general economic expansion in the region, simply brought into sharper focus a problem that had existed for a long time. As long as the labor supply was restricted to peasants with substantial access to means of production, the control and discipline of a work force would be extremely problematic. This was particularly evident in the second half of the 1890s, when the demand for labor in various sectors of the economy was increasing, and different industries ended up competing with each other for a seasonal labor pool that simply did not expand rapidly enough to keep up with demand. Clearly, drastic measures were needed to socialize workers into proletarian rhythms and habits. Since it was impossible in the short run forcibly to separate peasants from the land, the government did the next best thing; it passed laws, and it used force.

Throughout the Piérola years, government officials experimented with different modes of labor control. Between 1895 and 1901, for example, political authorities in the department of Junín considered three separate projects for legislation on the issue of *arrieraje* that, in addition to providing for the registration of individual *arrieros*, legislated on such questions as the size and nature of loads, the relationship between merchants and mule drivers, who was liable for what kind of damage, and how animals should be handled on the road.[72] In

Subprefecto de Jauja y el gobernador de Carhuamayo," Jauja, April 19, 1898; "Subprefecto de Jauja Manuel Fernández, Decreto sobre enganche a Chanchamayo," February 28, 1897.

[70] See, for example, APJ, "Oficio del Comisionado del Gobierno, Francisco F. Urbieta, al Prefecto del Departamento," August 30, 1896; and "Antonio Graña, Ingeniero en Jefe del Campamento No. 8, al Prefecto, pidiendo urgentemente nuevos enganches," September 6, 1896.

[71] See especially APJ, "Subprefecto de Tarma Pedro Días al Prefecto del Departamento," Tarma, August 18, 1896; "Subprefecto de Jauja al Prefecto del Departamento," April 19, 1897; and "Subprefecto de Jauja a varios notables de los distritos de la provincia," October 30, 1898.

[72] APJ, "Decreto de Germán S. Herrera, Prefecto Accidental de Junín," Cerro de Pasco, November 27, 1895; "Reglamento de Arrieraje por Domingo F. Argote, Subprefecto de Jauja," Jauja, September 5, 1897; and "Proyecto de Reglamento de Arri-

the same period, the prefect polled landowners and other entrepreneurs on how best to establish a code for the *enganche* and control of workers.[73] The result was, in 1902, the elaboration of a complex code of regulations for workers in subtropical agriculture, including the registration of contracts and their enforcement by local political authorities.[74] Then in 1903, the central government passed a general labor code for the mining industry that authorized political officials to chase fugitive workers.[75] And despite variations in the specific nature of the projects, or types of workers covered, all the labor codes had one thing in common: they relied on the interconnected system of state officials at the national, regional, and local levels to enforce the provisions of the law.

This system, extending from the appropriate ministries in Lima down through the prefect and subprefects to influential merchants and landowners and judicial and political authorities at the district level, and then on down to petty merchants and officials in the area's villages, was first used in an extensive and systematic way during the construction of the central highway. At that time, a special government *enganche* office was created to act as intermediary in advancing money to local officials. Each district governor, mayor, and justice of the peace was given a certain quota of men to fill. Because of the vital character of the project, all prominent citizens were urged to cooperate. Peasants were assured that they would labor under decent conditions and get paid a high wage. And if government propaganda did not convince prospective workers, the state's selective use of violence certainly did.[76]

eros, presentado por varias compañías mercantiles de la Oroya," Oroya, February 16, 1901.

[73] APJ, "Oficio del Cónsul Francés Sr. Prugue, al Prefecto de Junín Jacinto Cevallos," Hacienda Bellavista, Valle de Chanchamayo, July 7, 1895; "Albino Carranza, de la Administración Municipal de Tarma, al Prefecto del Departamento," Tarma, December 20, 1897; "Nemesio D. Jorquiera, administrador de la Hacienda Naranjal, al Prefecto del Departamento," Hacienda Naranjal, Valle de Chanchamayo, July 3, 1902; and "Emilio Prugue, Cónsul Francés en Chanchamayo, al Prefecto del Departamento," Hacienda Bellavista, Valle de Chanchamayo, July 5, 1902.

[74] APJ, "Oficio de José Rivera, Comisario de Chanchamayo, al Prefecto," La Merced, October 19, 1902, and accompanying "Reglamento de operarios elaborado en La Merced, con la aprobación de los propietarios de La Merced y Perené," October 19, 1902.

[75] APJ, "Oficio de varios enganchadores al Subprefecto de Jauja," Jauja, May 28, 1910, and Dora Mayer de Zulen, *La conducta de la Compañía Minera del Cerro de Pasco* (Callao: Imprenta del H. Concejo Provincial, 1914), p. 7.

[76] For empirical examples of the state's use of violence see below, this chapter. On the government's *enganche* program as a whole, see APJ, "Oficio del Subprefecto de Tarma al Prefecto del Departamento," Tarma, April 28, 1896; "Oficio del Subprefecto de Jauja al Prefecto del Departamento," Jauja, February 2, 1897; "Oficio del Encargado

In the end, however, neither government regulation, nor the use of state power in the *enganche* itself, were able to make labor recruitment function smoothly. While the state's alliance with local elites managed to forcibly expand the labor pool available to the various sectors of the regional economy, not even the use of state-controlled violence was able to bring about a significant advance in the proletarianization of the peasantry. Consistently, tenaciously, and militantly, the peasantry resisted government and elite efforts to expand the market for labor. Through a variety of tactics, including passive resistance, running away, and even pitched court battles, peasants were a thorn in the side of the elite's modernization attempts. Indeed, it could be argued that peasant resistance constituted the single most important impediment to the transformation and development of the regional economy.

National Modernization and the Peasant Community

When the state's representatives in the department of Junín registered the male population in the Yanamarca Valley for the purposes of military conscription in 1898, nearly 90 percent of the 443 men who registered defined their occupation as agriculture. The remaining 10 percent were fairly evenly divided between traditional artisans—

de la Oficina de Enganche al Prefecto del Departamento," Jauja, June 17, 1897; "Francisco Egoavil, Teniente Gobernador de Palca, al Subprefecto de Tarma," Palca, September 3–5, 1896; "Oficio de Francisco Urbieta, Representante del Supremo Gobierno para los Trabajos del Pichis, al Prefecto del Departamento de Junín," Tarma, October 7, 1896; "Oficio de Francisco Urbieta, Comisionado del Supremo Gobierno para los trabajos del Pichis, al Prefecto, agradeciendo la autorización para solicitar peones a los Gobernadores," Palca, November 12, 1896; "Oficio del Subprefecto de Jauja al Prefecto, confirmando su orden sobre los gobernadores y el enganche," Jauja, February 22, 1897; "Oficio de F. Urbieta, encargado de la Oficina de Enganches, al Prefecto del Departamento, acusando recibo de 1,000 papeletas impresas de enganche de operarios," Tarma, March 7, 1897; "Oficio del Subprefecto de Jauja al Prefecto, acusando recibo de 25 ejemplares del contrato de operarios," Jauja, March 18, 1897; "Oficio de F. Urbieta, comisionado del Gobierno, al Teniente Gobernador de Huasahuasi, explicando la creación de una exclusiva oficina de enganches," Tarma, February 10, 1897; "Oficio de Castamán y Cia., Contratistas de la Vía Central del Perú, a Celestino Camacho, pidiendo operarios," Palca, November 18, 1897; "Actas de los notables de Huaripampa, Muquiyauyo, Sincos, Mito, Orcotuna, Concepción, Apata, Acolla, Matahuasi y Llocllapampa, comprometiéndose a ayudar en el enganche al Pichis," various districts of Jauja province, May 1898; "Moisés Bohl, Teniente Gobernador de San Luis de Shuaro, expidiendo a dos operarios enganchados comprobantes de que han cumplido su enganche," San Luis de Shuaro, May 26 and October 17, 1898; "Oficio del Subprefecto de Jauja al Prefecto del Departamento, negando la verdad de un reclamo que se está mandando operarios al Pichis a la fuerza," Jauja, October 20, 1898; "Subprefecto de Jauja a los Gobernadores de los distritos, sobre el enganche al Pichis," Jauja, October 30, 1898.

carpenters, shoemakers, blacksmiths—and musicians, with a relatively small group dedicated to commerce, mining, and education.[77]
Of course, even though an overwhelming majority of the valley's population defined their main occupation as agriculture, most also participated in other activities during slow periods in the agricultural cycle.
But it is significant that, at the end of the nineteenth century, after
many waves of commercial penetration, after a good proportion of
village lands had been privatized and some of them sold to outsiders,
such a high percentage of the peasantry continued to earn their main
living on the land. For it was this fact that made the acquisition of a
stable labor force in mining, agriculture, or road construction so difficult.

Taken in isolation or uncritically, however, the conscription figures
tend to obscure some important trends that were beginning to emerge
in local society. For one thing, an aggregate analysis can hide occupational variation according to age. When the totals are broken down,
it turns out that 95 percent of the men thirty years of age or older
gave agriculture as their main occupation, whereas in the younger
groups (eighteen to thirty years), only 85 percent did so.[78] But most
striking is the fact that in an 1899 census of the Yanamarca Valley
which gave people the opportunity to list more than one form of employment, a significant minority of the village population considered
nonagricultural activities an important enough part of their lives to
list them separately as additional occupations. Thus over 40 percent
of the peasants in Acolla listed both agriculture and *arrieraje*, while
nearly 30 percent of the men in Tragadero migrated to the mines as
well as participating in agricultural production.[79] Clearly, something
was happening in the Yanamarca Valley in the last twenty years of the
nineteenth century that had begun to have an important effect on
occupational structures in the peasant villages.

To a large extent, the changes were directly traceable to the intensification of commercial and productive activity in the central highlands after the War of the Pacific. Starting in the early 1890s, and
particularly after 1895, peasants from the Yanamarca Valley participated increasingly as workers and *arrieros* in the expansion of commerce, mining, and subtropical agriculture.[80] In addition, the rising
levels of economic activity, the colonization of the jungle, and the

---

[77] APJ, "Lista de Inscripción Militar, Valle de Yanamarca," District of Acolla, 1898.
[78] Ibid.
[79] APJ, "Censo del Valle de Yanamarca, Distrito de Acolla," 1899.
[80] ANF, Expedientes y Libros Judiciales, Libro de Juicios Verbales, Jauja, 1891, and
Libro de Juicios Verbales, Acolla, 1891–1892; APJ, "Censo del Valle de Yanamarca."

construction of the *vía central* generated a growth of the regional market for foodstuffs and other agricultural products. As a result, both peasants and *hacendados* dedicated a greater part of their property to agricultural production for the market. Thus the commercial value of land, particularly in those areas with abundant water, easy access to *arrieraje* routes, or other advantages, increased. And conflict over land—both among haciendas and between haciendas and communities—also intensified.

Heightened conflict was particularly visible in the Jauja area. In contrast to the southern Mantaro Valley, this region had not witnessed a rash of land invasions or disputes during the War of the Pacific. But beginning in the last decade of the nineteenth century, a series of conflicts emerged, both between neighboring haciendas and between haciendas and neighboring communities. In most cases, these struggles were old disagreements that had festered and flared over many years. Yet whether or not they were old, the fact that they reemerged precisely in this period was due to increased opportunities for the commercial exploitation of land.[81]

Changes in the system of land tenure and utilization were not limited to larger properties. Throughout the 1890s there was also a trend toward the commercial utilization of smaller plots in the peasant villages. In some cases, this meant the actual transference of *chacra* ownership from local peasants to outside merchants. The Jauja merchant Luisa del Rivero, for instance, enumerated fifteen separate *chacras* in her last will and testament that she had bought from peasants in Acolla.[82] In other cases, it was the peasants themselves who

[81] For cases of land conflict within communities, see ANF, Expedientes y Libros Judiciales, Libro de Juicios Verbales, Acolla, 1891–1892, especially Rufino and Evangelista Basco vs. De la Cruz López, June 6, 1891, 7v–8; "División y partición de los bienes de Esteban Maita y Juana Esteban," October 18, 1891, 22–23; Manuel Félix Barzola vs. Manuel Idalgo and his wife Anselma Barzola, February 22, 1892, 30v–31v. For cases of land conflict between small to medium commercial properties, see Libro de Juicios Verbales, Acolla, 1891–1892, Julián Núñez vs. Agustina Remusgo, May 25, 1891, 4v–5; Julián Núñez vs. Anacleto and José Rivera, June 23, 1891, 14v–16; and APJ, "Expediente de Julián Núñez al Prefecto del Departamento," Jauja, 1892–1893; "Queja de Julián Núñez al Subprefecto de la Provincia," Jauja, August 3–10, 1896. For cases of land conflict involving communities and haciendas, see ANF, Expedientes y Libros Judiciales, "Comunidad de Concho contra Tomás Hovispo sobre tierras," began March 23, 1897; "María Magdalena Villanueva contra la comunidad de Yauli sobre amparo en posesión de unos terrenos de la hacienda Hualá," 1890–1893; "Segundino Valladares, propietario de la hacienda Cayán, contra las comunidades de Ricrán y Jajachaca sobre despojo de tierras," 1899; and ANF, Protocolos Notariales, Luis Salazar, Book 6: June 19, 1895, 83v–85; Book 9: June 13, 1900, 505–506, June 20, 1900, 510–11.

[82] ANF, Protocolos Notariales, Luis Salazar, Book 8: March 30, 1898, 389–90v.

bought additional land and dedicated it to market production. In 1900, Pío Quinto Rojas, a well-off peasant from the village of Acolla, sold to his children over seven hectares of good land, most of which he had bought since the death of his wife. As Rojas himself specified in the sale document, several of the larger and better *chacras* were dedicated exclusively to the production of wheat, a prime commercial crop.[83]

The expansion of agricultural production for the market spawned a series of important changes within the peasant economy and society. With the extension of commercial production beyond the mere sale of a surplus, there developed within the family economy a starker division between subsistence and market activities. The use of money in agriculture, such as purchasing seed rather than saving a portion of the crop for the next year's planting, increased.[84] The buying and selling of land and its use as collateral for loans—both between peasants and merchants and among the peasants themselves—became more generalized.[85] And with the expanding circulation of land, money, and products came yet another process of social and economic differentiation within the peasant community.

As had been the case before the War of the Pacific, renewed commercialization tended to heighten already existing differences within the village.[86] Because they operated with a surplus of resources, it

[83] ANF, Protocolos Notariales, Luis Salazar, Book 9: February 27, 1900, 394–96; and Expedientes y Libros Judiciales, Libro de Actas de Escrituras de Venta, 1891–1892, Acolla, for other examples of accumulation of agricultural property, especially 1-2, 3v–5, 7v–9, 11v–12v.

[84] Information on this point is difficult to find, except occasionally and incidentally. See, for example, ANF, Expedientes y Libros Judiciales, Libro de Juicios Verbales, Acolla, 1891–1892, "Eulalia Salazar viuda de Falconi contra Igidio Rosales," June 29, 1891, 18–19v.

[85] Documents on the increased circulation of land can be found throughout the ANF. See especially Protocolos Notariales, Luis Salazar, Book 7: June 27, 1897, 145–46v; Book 8: December 10, 1897, 301v–303, June 23, 1898, 486–87v; Book 9: October 4, 1899, 264–65v, October 12, 1899, 278v–79v, November 16, 1899, 294v–96, February 27, 1900, 394–96. Also, Expedientes y Libros Judiciales, Libro de Actas de Escrituras de Venta, Acolla, 1891–1892, passim, and "Demanda de Pablo Flores contra el Juez de Paz de Acolla Francisco Ortega," October 27, 1898.

[86] As often happens in these cases, systematic, historical, and quantitative data on household differentiation in the Yanamarca Valley are somewhat scarce. Aside from the 1899 Yanamarca Valley census, which provides but a partial view of income distribution for that one year, I have relied on an overall qualitative assessment of the data available in ANF, both notarial and judicial documents, and in interviews in the Yanamarca Valley on the process of migration (see especially the sources below in footnote 92). The intensification of differentiation in this period is also corroborated by other research done on the central highlands, such as Carlos Samaniego, "Peasant Movements at the Turn of the Century and the Rise of the Independent Farmer," in Norman Long and Bryan R. Roberts (eds.), *Peasant Cooperation and Capitalist Expansion in Central Peru* (Austin: University of Texas Press, 1978), pp. 45–71, and the editors' "Introduction,"

was the richer peasants who were in the best position to take advantage of new opportunities in agriculture or commerce by buying land or animals and producing for the market. Because they had no surplus to spare, it was always the poorer peasants who were most subject to the vagaries of market, debt, and climate. And it did not take much of a debt to ruin a poor peasant. At the customary rate of accumulated interest, which usually varied between 2 and 5 percent a month, an initially small loan could double in no time. If debtors were courageous or foolhardy enough to fight collection through the courts, they usually ended standing helplessly by while a judge auctioned off virtually all the property they possessed. Asunción Ñaupari, for example, a peasant woman from Acolla, lost four *chacras*, a house, and a corral for her animals in 1900, all as payment for a debt she and her deceased husband owed Luisa del Rivero, plus interest and court costs.[87] In fact, court costs were so onerous that it was probably cheaper in the end to cede a limited amount of land to a creditor before the case came to trial and so avoid losing a great deal more in the future. Yet for a peasant with only a little land to begin with, that was not much of a choice.[88]

For a rich peasant, on the other hand, there always seemed to be a way out. Santiago Espinoza, a prestigious *vecino* (citizen) from Marco, borrowed nine hundred soles from the Llocllapampa merchant José Andía in 1893. Although Espinoza promised to pay back the principal plus interest in either money or workers for the mines, Andía brought a case against him three years later for the total sum of 1,700 soles. Even then, however, Espinoza's position and access to resources saved him from total ruin. Not only was he able to get the debt reduced by nearly one half, but he also settled the remaining thousand soles in easy payments by mortgaging six commercial *chacras*—all of them for planting either vegetables or wheat—and a house.[89] Clearly, not every peasant had the resources to do the same.

especially pp. 28–30; and Gavin A. Smith, "Socioeconomic Differentiation and Relations of Production among Rural-Based Petty Producers in Central Peru, 1880–1970," *Journal of Peasant Studies*, 6: 3 (April 1979), 286–310.

[87] ANF, Protocolos Notariales, Luis Salazar, Book 9: February 15, 1900, 380–82.

[88] Information on debt, interest rates, court costs, etc. abounds in the ANF. See particularly Protocolos Notariales, Luis Salazar, Book 6: November 7, 1896, 414–16v, November 24, 1896, 426v–29; Book 7: April 24, 1897, 97v–99; Book 9: August 14, 1899, 215v–17, August 16, 1899, 218v–20v, September 13, 1899, 250–51, October 12, 1899, 278v–79v, February 15, 1900, 380–82.

[89] Because of the generally more fragile nature of most vegetable crops, land that is good for vegetables is usually in a favored location—more water and sun, more protected from frost and hail, and so on. ANF; Protocolos Notariales, Luis Salazar, Book 5: August 25, 1893, 167–68v; and Book 6: November 7, 1896, 414–16v.

Thus the accumulated effects of debt and market relations tended to widen the gap between rich and poor households in the peasant village. The same was true of what had traditionally been an occasional source of extra income: seasonal migration. No matter how large or small the pool of resources available to a peasant family, the spread of commercial relations increased a household's need for money. For a rich family, it was often a question of unexpected investment opportunities or short-term irregularities in income flow. For a poor family, it was usually a question of staying afloat. In either case, it was only a matter of time until the best way, or perhaps the only way, to get access to cash was through wage labor. Yet here again, the motivation, destination, length, and relative success of migration varied greatly between rich and poor households.

Whether it was caused by a disaster in the family or simply by a shortfall in the months right before harvest, a poor family's need for cash was dramatic and immediate. Merchants with connections in mining and subtropical agriculture were perfectly aware of this. Frequenting the villages during fiestas and before the final maturation of the crops, they profited from the fact that poor peasants, close as they were to the margin of subsistence, could not negotiate the conditions of a cash advance very successfully. By catching the villagers at their most desperate, these merchants contracted with laborers who could not afford to worry about where or how they would be forced to work off their debt. The result for the peasants was often a vicious circle of indebtedness, as the merchant's advances of food and tools at the mines and haciendas augmented the amount owed at the very moment the peasants expected to be working it off.[90] Over time, this process cut even more deeply into a family's access to means of production, and poor households, facing a constant struggle to balance a shrinking amount of land against a stable or expanding pool of family

[90] For the relationship between debt and wages, and the role of the merchant in the *enganche* process, see APJ, "Razón Detallada de los operarios que les adeuda sus alcances el contratista Señor Redencio Castamán," 1898; "Copia de los Libros de enganche y gastos de Dn. Santiago Vialardi," 1898; "Planilla de tareas del pueblo de Cacas de los operarios que han trabajado en el camino carretero de la cección [sic] de Tambo Colorado al Cerro de Pasco," Junín, February 6, 1899; "Planilla de tareas del pueblo de Pari de los operarios que han trabajado en el camino carretero de la cección [sic] de Tambo Colorado al Cerro de Pasco," Junín, February 25, 1899; "Planilla de tareas del pueblo de Ondores de los operarios que han trabajado en el camino carretero de la cección [sic] de Tambo Colorado al Cerro de Pasco," Junín, February 25, 1899; "Emilio Prugue al Prefecto B. E. Bueno," Hacienda Bellavista, July 5, 1902, and attached "Cuenta del Sr. Emilio Prugue con Jacinto E. Echegoyen por enganche de operarios, Chanchamayo, Enero 17 de 1902."

labor, began to send members forth on ever longer and more permanent migrations.

For rich households, on the other hand, the need for money was more negotiable and less immediate. Rather than accept any conditions a merchant offered, a wealthier peasant could afford to choose when and how to migrate, obtaining better jobs and developing a broader and more useful network of connections. Rather than cutting into a wealthy family's access to means of production, therefore, migration usually increased the existing surplus and allowed households to accumulate further. As they amassed land and livestock, the traditional balance between resources and family labor became less relevant for wealthier households. Needing to rely on outside labor, and able to gain access to it through kinship, patronage, and wage labor,[91] these families could often afford to send one or two members to seek their fortunes outside the village on a more permanent basis.

Migration, then, both at its most seasonal and its most permanent, obeyed a series of very different dynamics. When peasant men from the Yanamarca Valley registered for military conscription in 1898, therefore, the occupational structure that emerged tended to hide not only the increasing number of men with nonagricultural trades, but also the dramatically different processes that were contained within that increase. As all peasants struggled for greater revenue in an expanding regional economy, some came close to losing their access to means of production altogether. Others, accumulating land, wealth, and prestige, used their expanding social and economic base to consolidate a position of power within the community. And with the widening demand for labor and goods in the region's various productive sectors, shifting alliances of wealthy peasants and local merchants struggled to plug into the political system and hitch their wagons to the star of economic development.

For the wealthier peasants, the consolidation of power and prestige in the villages was a two-fold process. Economically, it meant a monopoly of the lands best suited for commercial agriculture, accumulation of large flocks of sheep or cattle, and control over local com-

[91] For information on labor relations, both in agriculture and more generally, see ANF, Protocolos Notariales, Luis Salazar, Book 7: July 26, 1897, 169–72v; Book 9: May 23, 1899, 139–40v, and October 4, 1899, 264–65v; ANF, Expedientes y Libros Judiciales, Libro de Juicios Verbales, Acolla, 1891–1892, 13v–14v, 16–20v; and APJ, "Protesta de Francisca Barzola, Lorenza Blancas, Norberta Oropeza y sus esposos Asencio Estevan, Mateo Barzola y Manuel Estevan, contra Justo Peralta, Germán Solís y Felipe Remusgo," Jauja and Tarma, February 4–15, 1898. For specific examples of the experience of wealthier households, see below, Chapter V.

merce.[92] Politically, it entailed the more or less permanent occupation of local office, particularly in the municipality and as justices of the peace.[93] Yet most importantly, their success was based on the use of traditional relations of reciprocity for new ends. By maintaining at least a symbolic reciprocal exchange with the community at large, the emerging elite within the village legitimated its political power, control over land and commerce, and access to the labor of its neighbors. And only insofar as this relationship remained legitimate could it actually continue to function.

Given their generally higher level of education, wider commercial and personal connections, and overall monopoly of political office, the most effective way rich peasants could vindicate their position vis-à-vis the rest of the village was by representing individuals, or the community as a whole, in their dealings with the outside world. In the years before the War of the Pacific, for example, José de la Rosa Ortega, son of a prominent *mestizo* family that was accumulating large plots of land on the fertile hillside behind Pachascucho, fought almost singlehandedly for Acolla's district status.[94] Between 1896 and 1898, José C. Hurtado and Felipe B. Rivas, among other prominent *vecinos* of Marco, played a leading role in contracting for the necessary artisans to build a new church for the village.[95] In the land conflict be-

[92] For the accumulation of land, see ANF, Protocolos Notariales, Luis Salazar, Book 6: June 18, 1896, 340–41v, November 2, 1896, 409–11, November 7, 1896, 414–16v; Book 7: October 12, 1897, 242–43v; Book 8: December 10, 1897, 301v–303, May 25, 1898, 459v–61v; Book 9: February 27, 1900, 394–96, May 17, 1900, 491–92v, June 13, 1900, 505–506, June 20, 1900, 510–11, July 19, 1900, 538–39v; and Provincia de Jauja, Matrícula de predios rústicos, Distrito de Acolla, 1901. For accumulation of livestock herds, see APJ, "Censo del Valle de Yanamarca," especially the community of Tragadero, and selected examples in Acolla. For the monopoly of commerce, see APJ, "Lista de Inscripción Militar," and ANF, "Concho contra Hovispo."

[93] For the monopoly of political office by wealthy peasants, see APJ, "Personal de los Concejos Distritales de la Provincia," Jauja, March 27, 1893; "Lista de los gobernadores de Jauja y Acolla," Jauja, February 28, 1897; "Manifiesto de ingresos y egresos de la Caja Municipal de Acolla durante los meses de Enero a Abril de 1896," Acolla, April 30, 1896; "Lista de Inscripción Militar"; "Manuel E. Landa al Prefecto del Departamento," March 23, 1899; and "Felipe B. Rivas, Alcalde Municipal del distrito de Acolla, al Prefecto del Departamento," November 14, 1900; ANF, Protocolos Notariales, Luis Salazar, Book 6: June 18, 1896, 340–41v, July 2, 1896, 353–54v; Book 10: May 10, 1901, 125–27; Expedientes y Libros Judiciales, "Queja de Buenaventura Tabraj contra los procedimientos del Juez de Paz de Marco José C. Hurtado," Jauja, 1898; "Queja de Andrea Mendoza contra el Juez de Paz de Acolla Pío Quinto Rojas," March 1, 1902; "Queja de José Palacios contra el Juez de Paz de Marco, Pedro Solís," July 10, 1902.

[94] For a more detailed account of José Rosa Ortega's role in the battle for district status, see Chapter III.

[95] ANF, Protocolos Notariales, Luis Salazar, Book 6: November 22, 1896, 424–26v; Book 8: October 30, 1898, 599v–601.

tween Tomás V. Hovispo and the community of Concho (1897–1899), Hurtado and Rivas were also among that village's most prestigious and supportive witnesses and representatives.[96] As was to be expected, however, the wealthy peasantry's mediation was a two-edged sword.

In addition to providing a vital service, mediation was a channel for strengthening and extending networks of patronage and clientele. By serving as intermediaries, rich peasants made themselves indispensable to both the poorer peasants in their village and the more prestigious merchants and landowners in the larger region. Acting as power brokers, they provided their clients with influence in land or debt disputes and their patrons with access to labor. Through ritual kinship ties, intermarriage, and commercial relationships, they reinforced bonds with small landowners, merchants, and other wealthy villagers. Through generosity and ritual kinship ties, they anchored poorer peasants more tightly into their patronage networks. The result was an intricately woven tapestry of mutual obligation and asymmetrical reciprocity that grew ever more complex and binding with the further expansion and commercialization of the regional economy.[97]

But the combined effects of peasant differentiation and the tightening bonds of patronage and clientele were not felt evenly from one community to the next. Since commercial penetration, social and economic differentiation, and the ever stronger hold of patronage and reciprocity relationships were all interdependent processes, they tended to progress further in communities with a history of commercialization than in those without. Thus in the Yanamarca Valley it was in the western villages, already known for the intensity of their commerce, the presence of more outside merchants and *cofradías* on the land, heavier seasonal migration, and a greater distance between rich and poor, that the burden of further differentiation and the consolidation of a peasant elite were most onerous. While the eastern villages wit-

[96] ANF, "Concho contra Hovispo."

[97] For relationships of patronage and clientele, mediation, and the role of intermarriage in extending the networks, see especially ANF, Protocolos Notariales, Luis Salazar, Book 6: November 2, 1896, 409–11; Book 7: February 14, 1897, 33–33v and pages inserted at the beginning; Book 8: December 10, 1897, 301v–303, November 23, 1898, 622v–24; Expedientes y Libros Judiciales, Libro de Juicios Verbales, Jauja, 1891; and "Concho contra Hovispo." For an analogous treatment of the relationship of marriage to patronage and peasant differentiation, see Kate Young, "Modes of Appropriation and the Sexual Division of Labour: A Case Study from Oaxaca, Mexico," in Annette Kuhn and AnnMarie Wolpe (eds.), *Feminism and Materialism: Women and Modes of Production* (London: Routledge and Kegan Paul, 1978), pp. 124–54, and her presentation at the symposium "The Development of Capitalism in Agriculture and the Peasantry: Theoretical Perspectives," Annual Meeting of the Latin American Studies Association, Pittsburgh, April 6, 1979.

nessed similar changes, both in terms of land accumulation by outsiders and wealthy peasants and the tendency for a new group of
merchants to settle directly in the village, the survival of a larger
middle sector within the peasantry tended to mitigate the worst effects of patronage and increasing poverty.

This diversity was keenly felt in the village household economy.
When the departmental authorities carried out their general census
of the Yanamarca Valley in 1899, they recorded especially carefully
the size of each family's livestock holdings and whether or not household members had occupations apart from agriculture. The records
that have survived, for the western community of Tragadero and the
eastern village of Acolla, show a dramatically different pattern in each
case. For Tragadero, there was extreme variation in size of livestock
herds among village households, with 45 percent of the families owning less than 100 head of sheep, 33 percent owning between 100 and
500 head, and 22 percent over 500 head. With regard to migration,
27 percent of Tragadero's male population—fairly evenly divided between different age groups—worked in the mines. In Acolla, on the
other hand, only 3 percent of the male population—all under thirty
years of age and unmarried—migrated to the mines. And although
livestock holdings were generally lower in Acolla, the variation in size
of herds between households was much less dramatic than in Tragadero, with 85 percent of the families owning less than 100 head of
sheep, and only 0.8 percent owning large herds.[98]

As economic patterns diverged, so did social and cultural interaction. In Marco, the larger community of which Tragadero was a subdivision, José C. Hurtado, Mateo Solís, Manuel E. Landa, and Felipe
B. Rivas headed the list of emerging small-town *gamonales* (local political bosses or patrons) who inhabited large, sumptuous houses, often
built with community labor, on the village plaza. They cultivated relationships with merchants, officials, and landowners in the Jauja area,
married among themselves, and often underlined their power by quite
openly maintaining relationships with several women at a time. Although they were clearly the proverbial large frogs in a small pond,
they consciously emulated the style and aura of the powerful *hacendado*, usually with a great deal of dramatic effect. When Manuel E.
Landa testified in favor of Concho in their land dispute with Tomás
Hovispo, for example, Hovispo accused him of having exploited Concho's community labor for his own personal domestic use. "I already

---

[98] APJ, "Censo del Valle de Yanamarca," communities of Acolla and Tragadero. For
a more complete description, see Appendix I.

have enough people to boss around in Marco," Landa responded haughtily.[99]

In Acolla, the emerging village elite had similar pretensions. Men like Manuel Ortega and Pío Quinto Rojas, prestigious *vecinos* who owned numerous commercial *chacras*, dominated municipal and judicial posts and intermarried with other wealthy peasant families, merchants, and small landowners. José Rosa Ortega, Manuel's son and leader of the battle for district status, developed quite a reputation for authoritarianism. Married to María Solís, daughter of a *gamonal* family in Marco, and close friends with several of the valley's merchants and landowners, José Rosa had strong opinions about the respect and deference supposedly owed him by other villagers.[100]

But despite the generally similar ambitions of wealthy *Acollinos*, a hierarchical style of interaction was much less successful than in Marco. When José Rosa Ortega was mayor in 1888, for example, he took a stick to the municipal agent, Faustino Barzola, because the agent refused to bring him a horse to ride. A friend of Barzola's informed Fidel Crespo, governor of the district, who ordered Ortega's immediate arrest. Though Ortega instituted judicial proceedings against Crespo for "insubordination," the court in Jauja took eight years to reach a verdict. And when the decision was finally handed down, it was in favor of the governor, who was by then no longer in office.[101]

Yet the fact that Acolla's rich peasants had less powerful connections in Jauja was only part of the picture. Because they faced a less differentiated, more independent peasantry, wealthy *Acollinos* simply could not use the same tactics. Had Faustino Barzola been a *Mar-*

[99] For the type and quality of relationships developed by the elite in Marco, see ANF, Expedientes y Libros Judiciales, "Concho contra Hovispo"; "José C. Hurtado contra los hermanos Onofre, Agustín Rafael y otros, por la muerte de Florián Hurtado," Jauja, 1918–1923; "Expediente de declaratoria de herederos de Antonio Onofre, iniciado por su madre Rosa Rivera," 1937; and William B. Hutchinson, "Sociocultural Change in the Mantaro Valley Region of Peru: Acolla, A Case Study," Ph.D. Dissertation, Indiana University, 1973, pp. 29–30. I also obtained information on this point through oral history, specifically through interviews with: Oscar Teófilo Camarena, Tragadero, November 29, 1977; Moisés Ortega, various talks throughout 1977; Francisco Solís, Tragadero, November 29, 1977; and Elías Valenzuela, Tragadero, October 22, 1977.

[100] For information on Acolla, I have relied on conversations with Moisés Ortega, throughout 1977; ANF, Protocolos Notariales, Luis Salazar, Book 8: October 21, 1898, 588–89v; Expedientes y Libros Judiciales, Libro de Juicios Verbales, Acolla, 1891–1892; "Juicio criminal seguido por Don José Rosa Ortega contra el gobernador de Acolla Don Fidel Crespo, por varios delitos," November 27, 1888; and all relevant documents listed above in footnotes 91, 92, and 96.

[101] ANF, Expedientes y Libros Judiciales, "Juicio criminal seguido por Don José Rosa Ortega . . . por varios delitos."

queño in a subordinate position to one of his town's *gamonales*, he would have agreed to bring the horse because, being more closely and hierarchically tied to his patron, he would have had a deal more to lose if he refused. Conversely, had José Rosa Ortega attempted to use community labor to build himself a house—as had several of Marco's prestigious citizens—he would have been laughed right out of the village.

The differences between village notables fed right into the battles that the region's various elite factions were fighting over national politics. The *Acollino* elite, struggling to regain control of the district political apparatus, joined with their patrons and clients in supporting Piérola after 1894. The *Marqueños*, on the other hand, in an effort to maintain the political hegemony they enjoyed under Cáceres, joined with the Jauja Caceristas in opposing the Democratic party's bid for power. When the Pierolista coalition took control of the state, Marco's *gamonales* suffered a substantial reverse at the level of political office.[102] Yet as we have seen, political positions were but the tip of the iceberg. Although the *Acollinos* and their patrons gained control of the district apparatus, they were unable to use this gain to consolidate and extend their influence within the local economy and society.

Despite their temporary exclusion from the top municipal positions, the Marco elite continued to use their patronage networks to dominate local commerce. In addition to maintaining their relationships with a number of important Jauja merchants and landowners, on several occasions they managed to control district tax collection by outbidding their competition in the various *remates de ramo*. Through tax collection, they further extended their networks of patronage and clientele among the merchants doing business in the area. They represented the valley's western communities in land disputes and other matters, lent money to those in need, rebuilt Marco's parish church, and cultivated good relations with the local priest and the *cofradías*. By monopolizing the more informal sources of village power and prestige, the *Marqueños* neatly sidestepped the *Acollinos'* bid for hegemony.[103]

---

[102] For the temporary decline of the *Marqueños* under Piérola, see above, footnote 32.

[103] ANF, Protocolos Notariales, Luis Salazar, Book 6: November 7, 1896, 414–16v, November 22, 1896, 424–26v, November 24, 1896, 426v–29; Book 8: October 30, 1898, 599v–601; Book 9: June 13, 1900, 505–506, June 20, 1900, 510–11, October 18, 1900, 648–50; APJ, "Expediente de Felipe B. Rivas al Prefecto," Jauja, November 14, 1900; "Expediente de varios vecinos y notables del caserío de Pomacancha pidiendo su separación del pueblo de Concho," Jauja, May 16, 1898; ANF, "Concho contra Hovispo";

Through their control of these sources of village power, the *Marqueños* also dominated the growing trade in seasonal labor that was being generated by the expansion of the regional economy. In exchange for money, influence, and aid of many kinds, they offered the use of their extensive webs of local patronage to the various *enganchadores* who were operating out of Jauja and its surrounding villages. In effect, they became involved in the commercialization of traditional relationships of reciprocity.[104]

Whether for the government's *vía central enganche* program, which was handled more formally through state institutions, or the *enganche* for the region's mines and haciendas, it was these increasingly commercialized traditional networks that provided the main channel for labor acquisition in this period. At a time when most peasants still had a relatively substantial access to land, these networks, because they were deeply rooted in local society and culture, were the most effective method for labor extraction. Yet the traditions governing reciprocity relationships also meant that wealthy peasants could push them only so far. The need to maintain a balance between extraction and legitimacy provided a perfect Achilles' heel that allowed poorer peasants to resist the increased incursions upon their subsistence base.

And resist is exactly what the peasants did. In the courts and on the land, in debt and labor disputes, they found the chink in the elite's armor. By playing one elite faction off against another, they used the double-edged nature of the patron-client relationship to their advantage. When that strategy did not work, they resorted to more direct action including, in some cases, violent confrontation.[105] Of course, the fact that peasants resisted debt, land expropriations, and labor extraction does not mean that they were successful in changing the system as a whole, nor would they have even thought about it in those terms. Although they managed a few notable victories, they also

Archivo SINAMOS, cc 205 (Marco), Inventory of church *cofradía* property and its uses, 1893, included in "Expediente sobre la reivindicación del molino de propiedad comunal," 1939, 134–36v.

[104] See sources in footnote 103.

[105] The most notable example of violent confrontation occurred in the 1890s in a land dispute between María Magdalena Villanueva, owner of the hacienda Hualá in the Jauja area, and the community of Yauli. Peasants from the villages of Yauli and Molinos attacked the judge, Villanueva, and several other representatives when they were in the process of delineating the boundary between the two properties. Although Villanueva's party retreated from the scene, the peasants followed them, brandishing sticks and stones. Five people were injured. See ANF, Expedientes y Libros Judiciales, "María Magdalena Villanueva contra la comunidad de Yauli, amparo en posesión de unos terrenos," 1890–1903.

lost many battles. When the Piérola years were over, the peasant household in the central highlands probably owned less land and was more dependent on migratory wage labor than before. But even if they ultimately could not stem the tide of commercial penetration, the peasants could, through their actions, help to shape the nature and limits of regional economic development.

In March 1897, Tomás V. Hovispo, *hacendado*, merchant, and *enganchador*, became involved in a dispute with the village of Concho over a fairly narrow strip of land on their common border. Through his marriage to Micaela Dianderas, descendant of one of Jauja's oldest and most prestigious Spanish families, Hovispo had come into possession of the hacienda Yanasmayo in the western part of the Yanamarca Valley. He argued that the piece of land claimed by Concho had always belonged to Yanasmayo. Concho, represented by the *enganchador* Manuel E. Rojo, demanded that Hovispo produce the titles to the hacienda. In the two-year battle that ensued, however, the interpretation of boundaries turned out to be the least important aspect of the dispute. Much more central were issues of power and patronage, with each party questioning the objectivity of the judges and each other's witnesses. And with good reason. Among those testifying in Hovispo's behalf were various *compadres* and dependents and several small landowners from nearby parts of the valley who owed favors to his father-in-law, Isidro Dianderas. Rojo brought in as witnesses several *enganchados* he was sending to work on the Pichis road, and it was his *perito* (expert witness), Manuel E. Landa, who was accused by Hovispo of having used community labor from Concho in the construction of his personal house. When the conflict was finally resolved in 1899, Hovispo agreed to "cede" the land to Concho in exchange for access to a specified amount of community labor—certainly no solution to the problem of who had the more legitimate claim to the land.[106]

The Hovispo-Concho dispute was but one example of the general tendency to confuse the boundaries (*linderos*) between different properties. As had historically been the case in periods of increased economic activity, judges and other legal authorities were caught in a bind between the increasing commercialization of the land and the consequent need for more objective, legally valid definitions of boundaries on the one hand, and the continuing use of custom and

---

[106] ANF, "Concho contra Hovispo." A *perito* is an educated person from the area of the conflict who is therefore familiar with the *parajes* being discussed in the document. The emphasis, in the definition of the word, is on expertise.

personal, informal knowledge in their actual definition on the other. Since most land titles referred to the *linderos* in terms of customary *paraje* names, only those familiar with the area could actually place the boundary. This made officials dependent on the definitions of the very people who were in conflict with each other—hardly an objective source. The resulting settlements usually had little to do with the actual justice of one boundary over another, and depended much more on how quickly or powerfully each side could muster influence and prestigious witnesses.[107]

In addition to disputing the ownership of an increasingly valuable asset, then, land conflicts became an arena for struggle over other issues. In the Hovispo-Concho case, the underlying problem was the competition for clients and access to labor among various merchants and *enganchadores*. In another conflict in this period, between Segundino Valladares and the *ceja* communities of Ricrán and Jajachaca, the issue below the surface was control of political institutions and land rights in an expanding subtropical economy.[108] Yet whatever the specific circumstances in each case, conflict over land was part of a more general struggle for power that was developing between elite and peasants in the region. At the root of the matter was the fact that the continued viability of the household economy provided peasants with a base from which to successfully resist elite strategies for the acquisition of labor. Insofar as access to land formed a central part of household autonomy, land disputes were a pivotal element in the elite struggle for hegemony. But so were the more direct battles over debt and *enganche* itself.

In February 1897, the subprefect of Jauja signed a decree on *enganche* for the Chanchamayo road. As he explained in the preamble, it had so far been impossible to make progress on the *vía central*

---

[107] In addition to "Concho contra Hovispo," see the other sources in footnote 81 above, and ANF, Expedientes y Libros Judiciales, "Luis Y. Ibarra contra la Obra Pía del Carmen sobre propiedad de los terrenos 'Putaj,'" began June 23, 1906. For a similar argument on the question of *linderos*, and how difficult their definition can be, see Juan Martínez Alier, *Los huacchilleros del Perú* (Paris and Lima: Ruedo Ibérico-Instituto de Estudios Peruanos, 1973), especially pp. 3–5.

[108] From other documents in addition to the Ricrán and Jajachaca vs. Valladares dispute, it is evident that a more general process of commercial penetration, and peasant resistance to it, had been going on in the area for some time. See, for example, APJ, "Solicitud de Francisco Abanto y Lorenzo Wissar al Prefecto del Departamento," Jauja, January 21, 1892; "Solicitud de varios comuneros de Ricrán al Prefecto del Departamento," Ricrán, June 11, 1892; "Expediente de Ricrán contra Víctor Odría sobre tierras," Ricrán-Jauja, October–December 1897; ANF, Protocolos Notariales, Luis Salazar, Book 9: April 10, 1899, 73–75v.

because the region's inhabitants, afraid of the abuses committed by some of the road's contractors, did not want to submit themselves to an *enganche* for the project. But at present, he continued, things were different. All those wishing to contract for work on the government's project in Chanchamayo would be guaranteed speedy and regular payment, good conditions, and a wage of a sol per day plus meals. Moreover, the subprefect promised,

> Every abuse committed by those in charge of those projects, both in the mistreatment of workers and the lack of payment of their wages, gives the workers the right to complain to the Prefect of the Department and to this office, so that these abuses can be severely punished.[109]

Perhaps the most salient aspect of the subprefect's decree was that the peasants, through their refusal to work for the *vía central* project, had forced upon the government important concessions. The state's *enganche* office had begun to pay the highest wage in the region and fired the previous road officials. The department's political authorities were offering workers the backing of state institutions if they were treated unjustly. Clearly, these measures were a response to the numerous protests of abuse and the many cases of fugitive workers that had occurred since the project's inception. But events in the next several years were to show that it would take more than a few concessions to convince the region's peasants to offer their labor voluntarily on the *vía central*.

As the governors of the districts of Acolla, Apata, Concepción, Huaripampa, Jauja, Llocllapampa, Matahuasi, Mito, Muquiyauyo, Orcotuna, and Sincos explained in a resolution they signed in April 1898, people just did not want to work on the government's project. "Despite the obligation contracted by the principal citizens of the villages," the governors wrote,

> it is impossible to locate volunteers for that project, both because of the panic they feel about that work, and because in this Province they all prefer to accept *enganche* for work in the mines, to which they are already accustomed.[110]

---

[109] For all the information in this and the following paragraph, see APJ, "Decreto del Subprefecto de Jauja Manuel Fernández, sobre enganche a Chanchamayo," Jauja, February 28, 1897.

[110] APJ, "Oficio de los gobernadores de Huaripampa, Muquiyauyo, Sincos, Mito, Orcotuna, Concepción, Apata, Acolla, Jauja, Llocllapampa y Matahuasi," Jauja, May 12, 1898.

And this sentiment was echoed by many other prestigious citizens in the region's villages. The answer, according to all, was the use of force, particularly against criminals and other noxious elements, to oblige them to work on the road. In the words of the authorities of Llocllapampa, "There is no other way to provide workers for the Pichis road than to forcibly apprehend the criminals and put them to work on that project."[111] Yet because the government's policy, in keeping with the progressive and "modern" aims of the reconstructionist program, was to use only voluntary labor, the situation created a rather embarrassing dilemma.

In fact, government officials were caught in an impossible situation. If they contracted for workers by force, the high runaway rate caused the state to lose both money and legitimacy. If they limited themselves to voluntary workers, they could not advance the project. This contradiction led to a series of disputes that were exploited both by opposing elite factions and by the peasants themselves.

In October 1898, there developed in Jauja an intense controversy over government *enganche* that involved peasants, political authorities, and various segments of the regional elite. The whole thing began when a group of *enganchados* from surrounding villages were brought into Jauja on their way to the Pichis road and kept under guard in the city jail for several days. On October 12th the mayor, a provincial deputy, and two municipal officials protested to the subprefect, saying they were aware that

> a high number of individuals were detained in the public jail of this city, who against their will were being sent to work in the jungle, and this cannot be tolerated because it is against all the rights and guarantees that our Constitution provides all citizens.[112]

In addition to petitioning the subprefect, the same municipal officials presented a formal request to a Jauja court that resulted in a judicial decree ordering the release of the workers. The subprefect then sent this decree, together with a petition from two of the *enganchados*, to

[111] APJ, "Oficio de las autoridades de Llocllapampa," Llocllapampa, May 19, 1898. See also APJ, "Oficio de las autoridades de Huaripampa," Huaripampa, October 30, 1898; "Colección de oficios que manda el Subprefecto de Jauja al Prefecto del Departamento," Jauja, October 31, 1898; "Oficio de los notables de Sincos," May 27, 1898; and "Oficio de los gobernadores de varios distritos."

[112] APJ, "Oficio del Alcalde de Jauja, Diputado Provincial, y demás autoridades al Subprefecto de la provincia, protestando el tratamiento dado a los enganchados al Pichis en la cárcel de esta ciudad," Jauja, October 12, 1898, included with "Oficio del Subprefecto de Jauja y varios notables al Prefecto del Departamento, haciendo relación de los hechos sobre los enganchados al Pichis," Jauja, October 30, 1898.

the prefect's office, asking for advice on how to resolve the question. Pressed further by the judge and the intensified protests of the *enganchados* themselves, however, the subprefect finally consulted the prefect by telegraph. Told to avoid violence and contract only for voluntary laborers, the subprefect decided to release all those workers who were not volunteers. "Before taking this step," he explained in a memorandum,

> we did everything we could to convince all of them that it was important that they contribute to the work on a project so important to the national interest. In addition, they were offered all sorts of guarantees as to good treatment, prompt payment, etc. But despite all our efforts, we were only able to get two volunteers.[113]

The events in Jauja were not an isolated incident. There were a number of instances in which an improbable alliance of peasants and members of the regional or village elite attempted to thwart the state's efforts to acquire a labor force. In the case of the peasants, motivation and interest in such an alliance were perfectly clear. By playing one sector of the elite off against another, they gave themselves some extra room in the battle against commercial penetration. Whenever they could, they accepted elite aid in confronting state agencies.[114] Under other circumstances, they asked for state intervention in counteracting the abuses of the elite.[115] Under all conditions, the peasants

[113] APJ, "Oficio del Subprefecto de Jauja . . . haciendo relación de los hechos sobre los enganchados al Pichis," Jauja, October 30, 1898.

[114] See, for example, APJ, "Oficio del Subprefecto de Jauja al Prefecto del Departamento, quejándose sobre las exigencias del comicionado de enganche," Jauja, April 19, 1897; "Oficio de Pedro Verástegui, enganchador de Sicaya, al Subprefecto de Huancayo," Huancayo, April 4, 1898; "Oficio de Rafael F. Samaniego, enganchador de Sicaya, al Subprefecto de Huancayo," Huancayo, April 16, 1898; "Oficio de Eliaso Castillo, enganchador de Palca [Tarma] al Prefecto," Palca, April 21, 1898; "Oficio de Celestino Camacho, enganchador de operarios al Pichis, al Prefecto," Tarma, April 22, 1898; "Oficio de Abraham Altamirano y Federico de la Fuente, comisionados para enganchar operarios a la montaña, al Subprefecto de Jauja," Jauja, May 13, 1898; "Oficio del Subprefecto de Jauja al Prefecto sobre el gobernador del distrito de Matahuasi," Jauja, May 19, 1898; "Oficio de las autoridades de Llocllapampa sobre las dificultades de conseguir operarios voluntarios para el Pichis," Jauja, May 19, 1898; and "Oficio del Subprefecto de Jauja M. B. Dulanto, al Prefecto del Departamento, negando la verdad de un reclamo de las autoridades municipales de Jauja de que se están mandando peones por la fuerza al camino del Pichis," Jauja, October 20, 1898.

[115] See, for example, APJ, "Oficio de F. Urbieta, encargado del gobierno en la oficina de enganche, al Tnte. Gobernador de Palcamayo, José Baldoceda," Tarma, February 11, 1897; "Oficio del Subprefecto de Jauja Manuel Fernández al Prefecto del Departamento," Jauja, February 28, 1897; "Decreto del Subprefecto de Jauja, Manuel Fernández, sobre enganche a Chanchamayo," Jauja, February 28, 1897; "Oficio de Simeón Bonifacio, Dionicio Espinoza y Félix Cruz, vecinos del pueblo de Palcamayo, al Pre-

exhibited a sophisticated knowledge of the workings of legal and political institutions, and often managed to manipulate patronage and clientele networks in such a way as to make those institutions work for them. But in the case of the regional and village elites, the motives for allying with peasants against the state were a great deal more contradictory and complex.

Although merchants, miners, and *hacendados* all needed state support in their effort to consolidate a hold over labor, the government's *enganche* program for the *vía central* tended to interfere with private concerns. In an expanding regional economy, road construction competed with other sectors for a limited supply of workers. The abuses committed by government representatives also made peasants less willing to migrate to mines and haciendas. Under certain circumstances, then, it was in the elite's interest to help the peasants in their battle against *enganche*. Thus in 1898 Francisco L. Alvariño, an important *hacendado* in the Chanchamayo Valley, represented the peas-

fecto del Departamento, quejándose de los enganches que está practicando el teniente gobernador," Tarma, November 5, 1897; "Oficio de Feliz Sanches [*sic*] al Prefecto, quejándose del enganche al Pichis," Tarma, August 26, 1898; "Oficio de Pedro Samaniego, vecino de Tarma, al Prefecto, quejándose del enganche al Pichis," Tarma, September 24, 1898; "Oficio de Luciano Baldoceda, vecino de Tapo, al Prefecto, quejándose de los enganches forzados a Chanchamayo que está haciendo el Teniente Gobernador Paulino Aliaga," Tapo, January 19, 1899; "Oficio de 58 vecinos de Palca al Prefecto del Departamento, protestando enganches forzosos para trabajar en la carretera entre Oroya y Cerro de Pasco," Palca, January 31, 1899; "Oficio de Paula García de Egoavil, vecina de Palca, al Prefecto, quejándose de los abusos del teniente gobernador de Palca contra su esposo," Palca, February 5, 1899; "Oficio de Pío Egoavil, de Palca, al Prefecto, quejándose del enganche forzado a Chanchamayo," Palca, March 1, 1899; "Oficio de Juan Casas, vecino de Palca, al Prefecto, quejándose del enganche forzado a Chanchamayo," Palca, March 1, 1899; "Oficio de Manuel Patilongo, Miguel Baldoceda, Gerónimo Galarza, Máximo Calderón y Apolinario Valdoceda, indígenas de Tapo, al Prefecto del Departamento, quejándose que el teniente gobernador Paulino Aliaga los obligó a la fuerza a aceptar un adelanto," Tapo, March 3, 1899; "Oficio de 22 vecinos de Quichuay al Subprefecto de Huancayo, quejándose de los procedimientos del gobernador de San Gerónimo Nicolás Gonzáles," Quichuay, August 15, 1899; "Oficio de 23 vecinos del pueblo de Ingenio, al Subprefecto de Huancayo, quejándose del gobernador de San Gerónimo Nicolás Gonzáles," Ingenio, August 19, 1899; "Oficio de 20 vecinos del pueblo de San Gerónimo al Prefecto del Departamento, quejándose del gobernador Nicolás Gonzáles," San Gerónimo, November 14, 1899; "Oficio de Nicolás Cajacuri, Ramón Guerrero, Manuel Martínez, Marcos Porras, José Cajacuri, Casimiro Pérez y Nicacio Aliaga, todos vecinos de Tupín, al Prefecto, quejándose del gobernador de Acobamba," Tarma, December 11, 1899; "Oficio de José María Castro, natural de Picoy, Acobamba, al Prefecto, quejándose de los procedimientos de Francisco L. Alvariño, en cuya hacienda ha sido hortalero," Tarma-Acobamba, February 9, 1900; "Oficio del Comisario Rural de Chanchamayo al Prefecto del Departamento, quejándose de abusos en el enganche de operarios," La Merced, October 9, 1902; and "Oficio del Comisario de Chanchamayo, José Rivera, al Prefecto del Departamento, quejándose de abusos en el enganche de operarios," La Merced, December 15, 1902.

ants of the village of Palca in a protest against a municipal official who was forcibly sending people to work on the Pichis road. "With the goal of returning to my clients the tranquility taken from them due to these events," he wrote,

> I went, on Sunday April 24, to the village of Palca, where the entire community was awaiting me, and I told them that the kidnapping of their neighbors, taken to the Pichis with military escort, obliged to work on tasks they do not accept voluntarily, was nothing more than an abuse of force . . . but that the individual guarantees that the Peruvian Constitution gives to all the country's inhabitants had not been erased for Indians, who are as free as anyone else, and that no one could impose on them work that they did not want to accept voluntarily.[116]

Yet despite the democratic and passionate tone of his petition, Alvariño was not really against all forced work for peasants. Less than a year later, two peasants from the same town of Palca presented petitions to the prefect of the department, protesting that the lieutenant governor and municipal inspector were forcing them to accept money to work on Alvariño's hacienda in Chanchamayo, and threatening them with imprisonment if they refused. The only possible conclusion is that Alvariño had allied with the peasants not because of some abstract principle, but because he wished to strengthen his own chances of gaining access to labor.[117]

In other cases, the village elite allied with the poorer peasants against the state because they feared a loss of legitimacy within traditional relationships. José C. Salgado, for example, governor of Matahuasi, resigned his post in May 1898 because of the pressures put on him to participate in *enganche* for the jungle. As the subprefect explained in a letter to the prefect, Salgado "saw himself in the situation of being

[116] APJ, "Solicitud de Francisco L. Alvariño al Prefecto del Departamento, sobre el enganche en Palca," Tarma, May 3, 1898.

[117] APJ, "Oficio de Pío Egoavil, de Palca, al Prefecto del Departamento, quejándose que la policía le obligó a aceptar 10 soles de adelanto para ir a trabajar a la hacienda de Francisco Alvariño en Chanchamayo," Palca, March 1, 1899; and "Oficio de Juan Casas, vecino de Palca, al Prefecto, quejándose que los ministriles [sic] de Palca, por orden del Teniente Gobernador Don Juan Lara, le han arrojado diez soles para obligarle á trabajar en la chacra de Don Francisco L. Alvariño en Chanchamayo," Palca, March 1, 1899. Another example of a similar contradiction is the case of Timoteo Sedano who, while protesting the sending of workers to Chanchamayo by force, also indebted workers in the mines. See APJ, "Oficio del Subprefecto de Jauja y varios notables al Prefecto del Departamento, haciendo relación de los hechos sobre los enganchados al Pichis," Jauja, October 30, 1898, and ANF, Protocolos Notariales, Luis Salazar, Book 9: March 27, 1899, 56–59.

accused by those he governed, or appearing negligent in the eyes of his superiors." And, the subprefect concluded, this governor was not the only one to find himself in this predicament.[118]

In the last years of the nineteenth century, a number of people in the central highlands found themselves trapped ever more tightly between the increasing demands of the regional economy and the desperate resistance of the peasantry. Though the advances of commercial penetration and differentiation within the peasant community in fact increased the size of the labor pool in this period, the much more dramatic expansion of regional economic activity meant that it remained impossible to detach enough *arrieros*, miners, and agricultural workers from the peasant household to keep pace with the labor needs of the various productive and commercial sectors. Despite more differentiation and indebtedness, therefore, the central sierra as a whole continued to experience a relative scarcity of laborers, which in turn generated much conflict between officials and peasants, local merchants and peasants, and officials and local merchants. As villagers took advantage of these struggles to limit the incursions of commercialization upon their subsistence base, entrepreneurs began to suffer serious setbacks. For as bottlenecks in production and transportation became progressively longer and more expensive due to the labor shortage, peasant resistance cut ever more deeply into the elite's possibilities for further modernization and development.

Accumulation, Hegemony, and Peasant Resistance

In 1902, the seemingly solid edifice of economic development in the central sierra came down around the regional elite's ears. Part of the problem was the changing conditions on the international market. After Peru went on the gold standard in 1897 and depreciation of the currency halted, the comparative advantage of production within Peruvian borders tended to disappear.[119] Between 1900 and 1902, a fall in copper and coffee prices reduced the profitability of mining and subtropical agriculture.[120] But there were also related technological and infrastructural problems.

[118] APJ, "Oficio del Subprefecto de Jauja al Prefecto, elevando la renuncia del Gobernador de Matahuasi," Jauja, May 16, 1898.

[119] Thorp and Bertram, *Peru*, pp. 32, 36–38.

[120] BCIM, No. 14, J. A. Loredo, *Estadística Minera del Perú en 1903* (Lima: Imprenta de la Escuela de Ingenieros, 1904), pp. 35–36; Thorp and Bertram, *Peru*, pp. 329–37; Great Britain, *Diplomatic and Consular Reports*, Annual Series, No. 2639 (1899–1900), pp. 18–19; No. 2807 (1901), pp. 30–31; No. 3079 (1902), pp. 17–18.

Starting in 1900, copper mines in Cerro de Pasco began to reach the water table. Their inability to extract high-grade ores below the water level, combined with the skyrocketing cost of transportation and the shortage of fuel, made continued production extremely difficult for local entrepreneurs. The state of the industry became even more problematic with the fall in copper prices, since the combination of higher production expenses and higher transportation costs made it impossible to go on exploiting available lower grade ores.[121] And a similar situation developed in subtropical agriculture once coffee prices fell. In 1901 and 1902, the British vice-consul in Chanchamayo reported on the alarming state of coffee production. "The prospects of coffee planters in Chanchamayo are not very encouraging," he wrote in 1901.

A great many of them have abandoned their plantations after getting in the crop, and if prices do not change for the better, many more will have to follow. Only those who have sufficient capital, and can afford to wait, will be able to remain.[122]

And he continued in the following year:

There has been no marked improvement in trade during the year, the prices of most of the agricultural products having been so low as to be barely sufficient to meet ordinary working expenses. Planters have for this reason been worse off than in previous years, for although they had good crops, they have had great difficulty in obtaining money to harvest them, even though disposed to pay the usual ruinous rate of 3 to 5 per cent. [sic] per month interest.[123]

In all sectors of the central highland economy, therefore, production met with increasing problems in the first years of the twentieth century. Yet what is most striking is not the problems themselves, but how quickly they led to a collapse of autonomous development. A recent study has argued, for Peru as a whole, that the rapidity of the collapse was due to the lack of a conscious, concerted program of national development. The only program that existed, moreover, was not carried out by a separate, committed class of industrialists who could have pressured the state to give them continued support through a new series of economic policies, but rather by merchants and landowners. Thus, once there were important changes on the interna-

---

[121] Thorp and Bertram, Peru, p. 78.
[122] Great Britain, Diplomatic and Consular Reports, No. 2807 (1901), p. 30.
[123] Great Britain, Diplomatic and Consular Reports, No. 3079 (1902), p. 17.

tional market and in local production conditions, the entrepreneurs who had invested in manufacturing, mining, and other new concerns could just as easily return to their previous activities, leaving the production sphere wide open to foreign capital.[124]

While this line of reasoning is convincing as far as it goes, it leaves out an extremely important factor: the resistance of the peasantry. In both production and transportation, inability to acquire a constant and dependable labor force increased the risk and cost of operations. Forced to finance their businesses on a shoestring, entrepreneurs were unable to accumulate sufficiently to either innovate technologically, or build the necessary infrastructure to transform the regional economy. Historically, the initial accumulation of capital has always been a difficult process. This was even more true for Peruvians at the turn of the century, when industrial developments in Europe had already raised the level of accumulation necessary to enter most industries.[125] Their need to spend large amounts of money in acquiring and retaining a labor force made accumulation only more problematic.

As Emilio Prugue, French consul in Chanchamayo, complained in 1902, *enganchadores* charged 10 percent commission on every day a laborer worked. They often used the mineowners' and *hacendados'* money for their own commercial transactions and were not prompt or dependable in their remissions of *enganchados*. Even if an entrepreneur was lucky enough to get workers, moreover, many of them ran away. "For three years I have informed all the Prefects of the department as to which of my workers are fugitives," Prugue continued, "and I have not managed to have even one returned to me; with the result that all of them [the workers] now think they can do the same."[126]

---

[124] Thorp and Bertram, *Peru*, especially pp. 36–38, 141–44.

[125] For an analysis of how the initial level of capital accumulation needed to enter an industry rises with industrial and technological development, see Karl Marx, *Capital* (New York: International Publishers, 1967), I: 626. For some considerations on how peasant resistance to proletarianization can limit accumulation, see Robert Brenner, "Agrarian Class Structure and Economic Development in Pre-Industrial Europe," *Past and Present*, No. 70 (February 1976), pp. 30–75; Robert Brenner, "The Origins of Capitalist Development: A Critique of Neo-Smithian Marxism," *New Left Review*, No. 104 (July–August 1977), pp. 25–92; and Maurice Dobb, *Studies in the Development of Capitalism*, rev. ed. (New York: International Publishers, 1963). For the pioneering attempt to apply these considerations to the Peruvian central highlands, see Juan Martínez Alier, *Los huacchilleros del Perú*, and "Relations of Production in Andean haciendas: Peru," in Kenneth Duncan and Ian Rutledge (eds.), *Land and Labour in Latin America: Essays on the Development of Agrarian Capitalism in the Nineteenth and Twentieth Centuries* (Cambridge: Cambridge University Press, 1977), pp. 141–64.

[126] APJ, "Oficio del Cónsul Francés en Chanchamayo Emilio Prugue, al Prefecto B. S. Bueno, acompañando una copia de su cuenta con Jacinto E. Echegoyen por enganche de operarios," January 17 and July 5, 1902.

And finally, even if the runaways could be found, prosecuting each one through the courts involved more time and expense than most mineowners or *hacendados* could afford.

In the final analysis, the regional elite was caught in a vicious circle. Because they could not accumulate, they could not set into motion the economic, social, and political changes necessary for the successful proletarianization of labor. Because they could not proletarianize labor, they were forced to use expensive and undependable networks of patronage and clientele to acquire workers, and could not accumulate. As peasants continued to use the double-edged nature of patron-client relationships to their advantage, it became clear once again that traditional mechanisms of labor acquisition simply could not create a supply of workers dependable enough to support a major transformation of the regional economy. Given that changing conditions on the international market continued to generate increasing pressures to innovate in production, it turned out that the easiest—and perhaps the only—way to transform the economy and proletarianize labor was through a renewed alliance with foreign capital.

CHAPTER FIVE

The Penetration of Foreign Capital:
The Manufacturing Period

[M]anufacture was unable, either to seize upon the production
of society to its full extent, or to revolutionize that production
to its very core.[1]

As he made his way up the hillside that divided the Jauja Valley from the Yanamarca Valley, Luis Salazar, Jauja's most prominent notary, must have wiped his brow in frustration. Although he was on horseback and it was still too early for the sun to spoil the freshness of the August morning, Salazar certainly had a right to complain. Squinting his eyes through the dust of the road, he considered the problem of the *protesto de letra vencida*.[2] Whether it was he or his secretary who made the trip to the various villages, it still took several hours out of the work in the office, and for something that never brought much of a profit. As long as it was an occasional thing, of course, it was worth the trouble, since it allowed Salazar to maintain good relations with the merchants in Jauja and the surrounding towns who did most of the moneylending. Yet especially in recent months, *protestos* had become an everyday business. And for some reason, merchants always seemed to indebt peasants who lived miles away over dusty, hilly roads.

Finally reaching the beginning of the broad, flat pampa of Yanamarca, Salazar turned his horse to the left and rode toward the red hills that framed the town of Chocón. At least today he only had to visit the first town in the valley. On other days, he was forced to travel the wide pampa of Acolla, where houses were few and far between, or even search out the small hut of an illiterate peon on the

---

[1] Karl Marx, *Capital* (New York: International Publishers, 1967), I: 368.

[2] In the *protesto de letra vencida*, a merchant who wished to collect on a debt that had fallen due requested that the notary go out to the address cited on the promissory note and serve legal and formal notice that the note was expiring. See ANF, Protocolos Notariales, Luis Salazar, Book 17 (1907–1908) and passim.

hacienda Yanamarca. Today he found the house of Gabriel Limailla with relatively little effort. Predictably, however, the woman who answered the door informed him that her son was working in the mines, and that she knew nothing of his debts. After leaving a copy of the *letra* and giving the usual speech about waiting until sundown for payment and charging damages for any delay thereafter, Salazar turned his horse back across the parched fields.[3] As he began his descent toward Jauja, bracing himself against the ever-strengthening glare of the sun, he shook his head. It had not always been like this.

Whether or not Salazar voiced his complaints in precisely this manner, he was certainly correct in perceiving the year 1908 as an important watershed in the commercialization and indebtedness of the peasant economy.[4] Although the penetration of commercial capital had been increasing dramatically for several decades, the arrival of the central railroad at Jauja in 1908 underscored the ever more rapid expansion of the market that had been taking place since the turn of the century. And in conjunction with the extension of the central railway had come momentous changes in the central highland mining industry.

In the second half of 1901 Alfred W. MacCune, a business associate of the American capitalist James B. Haggin, had traveled to Cerro de Pasco to ascertain the potential of developing and exploiting the region's mines. By November of that year MacCune had, together with Haggin, bought up 80 percent of the area's mining claims. Early in 1902 these two capitalists, along with several more of the United States' most prominent businessmen—James Pierpont Morgan, Henry Clay Frick, Darius Ogden Mills, Hamilton McKown Twombly representing the Vanderbilts, and Edward H. Clark representing the estate of George Hearst—formed the syndicate that would, in the space of a few short years, completely dominate mining in Peru's central sierra. On June 6th, they founded the Cerro de Pasco Investment Company, which functioned as a holding company for the mining and railroad interests the syndicate was acquiring. Within the next six years, this

[3] For examples of *protestos* on the hacienda Yanamarca, see ANF, Protocolos Notariales, Luis Salazar, Book 12: June 22, 1903, 185 and insert, and especially Book 21: October 1, 1910, 997 and insert. For examples of *protestos* on distant *parajes* in the pampa of Acolla, see Book 15: January 15, 1906, 607 and insert; and Book 19: February 26, 1909, 80v and insert. For the case of Gabriel Limailla, see Book 18: August 13, 1908, 635 and insert.

[4] Even a cursory glance at ANF, Protocolos Notariales, Luis Salazar, Books 16, 17, and 18, shows the dramatic change in quantity of *protestos* between 1907 and 1908.

company not only completed the Central Railway to Huancayo, but also controlled the majority of mines in Cerro de Pasco and Morococha.[5]

The effects of the Cerro de Pasco Company were quickly felt far beyond mining and transportation. Increased investment and economic activity generated an expanding regional demand for many products. The arrival of the railroad to Huancayo tied the central highlands more closely to the Lima and international markets. As members of the regional elite hastened to take advantage of these opportunities, livestock raising, subtropical agriculture, and small- to medium-scale commercial agriculture all underwent a new boom.

The generally high level of economic activity could not help but affect the peasant community. Labor migrations to the mines, livestock haciendas, and subtropical plantations, and to engage in petty commerce, became almost an everyday occurrence in many families. Social and economic differentiation proceeded apace. And when the Cerro de Pasco Company looked for allies in local society to help reorganize the mining sector and restructure the region's economic relationships, it found willing, zealous, and violent collaborators among the villages' wealthy peasantry.

Foreign Capital and the Regional Elite

In the first twenty years of its existence, the Cerro de Pasco Mining and Railroad Company was able to extend and consolidate its control over most mineral deposits and valuable infrastructure in the central highland provinces of Cerro de Pasco, Huarochirí, and Yauli. First in 1908 and again in 1915, it underwent a major restructuring of its corporate organization that reflected changes in its overall process and strategy of growth. By 1922, the company had gone through three distinct stages. The first (1902–1908) was a period of expanding property ownership and investment in infrastructure. The second (1908–1915) was a time for consolidation of investments and increased production. During the third stage (1915–1922), the company once again

[5] For data on the formation of the Cerro de Pasco Company and its initial activities, see Adrian DeWind, Jr., "Peasants Become Miners: The Evolution of Industrial Mining Systems in Peru," Ph.D. Dissertation, Columbia University, 1977, Ch. 1, pp. 8–11; Rosemary Thorp and Geoffrey Bertram, *Peru 1890–1977: Growth and Policy in an Open Economy* (New York: Columbia University Press, 1978), pp. 81–82; and Dirk Kruijt and Menno Vellinga, *Labor Relations and Multi-national Corporations: The Cerro de Pasco Corporation in Peru (1902–1974)* (Assen, The Netherlands: Van Gorcum, 1979), pp. 43–45.

expanded its property base into new districts and initiated new capital investments that would come to fruition in the second half of the 1920s.[6]

By the third decade of the twentieth century, then, the company had acquired all its major mining properties and had become the Cerro de Pasco Corporation, an industrial giant in the Peruvian countryside. Yet such a broad perspective in time tends to obscure the drama and magnitude of the day-to-day transformations the corporation set in motion. During its first period of growth (1902–1908) and under the name of the Cerro de Pasco Investment Company, *la compañía*—as it came to be known in the central highlands—brought 730 mining claims in Cerro de Pasco, built a new railroad between Oroya and Cerro, completed the railway to Jauja and Huancayo, bought over one hundred coal mine claims to the north of Cerro, and began acquiring properties in the Morococha area. The company also instituted important changes within the productive sector. It rationalized the system of mine tunnels, installed cars and elevators for the internal transportation of ores, built a system of iron tubes for ventilation below ground, developed water pumps to solve the ubiquitous flooding problem and, on the surface, devised an intricate network of cars and storage facilities that dumped the minerals directly on railroad cars for transportation to the smelter.[7]

And, of course, there was the smelter itself. The product of several years of investment and experimentation at the old mineral hacienda of Tinyahuarco, it was capable of processing a total of 1,000 tons of ore a day by 1907. When compared to the 100- to 200-ton per day capacity of the next three largest smelters, Tinyahuarco must have seemed huge to Peruvian miners of the day. Equally impressive was the size of the labor force which, at Tinyahuarco alone, reached between 1,500 and 2,000 workers in 1908. In an industry where the largest mines employed around 300 people, and where the other smelters had between 100 and 300 workers each, a concentration of 1,500 laborers in one place was quite a transformation.[8] But the best

[6] For a periodization of the company's early growth, see DeWind, "Peasants Become Miners," Ch. 1, pp. 9–14.

[7] For the company's acquisition of property and construction of infrastructure in this early period, see DeWind, "Peasants Become Miners," Ch. 1, pp. 11 and 17, and Thorp and Bertram, *Peru*, pp. 81–83. For changes in the productive sector, see BCIM, No. 30, Carlos E. Velarde, *Reglamentaciones mineras para el Cerro de Pasco* (Lima: Tipografía de "El Lucero," 1905), pp. 17–19; and Kruijt and Vellinga, *Labor Relations*, pp. 43–45.

[8] For information on the smelter, see BCIM, No. 61, Comisión del Cerro de Pasco, *Informe Anual sobre la Labor* (Lima: Imprenta Nacional de Pedro Berrio, 1907), pp.

way to gauge the effect of these changes is to let the Peruvian experts of the time speak for themselves. "Accustomed to the small *fundiciones* existing in Cerro de Pasco . . . ," wrote a panel of engineers commissioned to study the company's operations in 1907,

> the present smelter seems a gigantic installation, like a small hell visible at a distance of many kilometers. Seventy multicolored tongues of fire can be seen jumping from the furnaces for the manufacture of coke, while the spirals of smoke that emerge from the gigantic chimneys seem to disappear into the sky. The atmosphere saturated with sulphuric gases, the fire projected by a battery of converters, the immense cars transporting matte or ashes, the labyrinth of rails circulating in every direction, the murmur of compressed air, give such an appearance and level of activity to the previously silent plains of the old hacienda Tinyahuarco, that it seems to have been magically transported to a European country.[9]

Yet the drama of the transformation lay not in technological innovation, but simply in the size of the investment. Between 1904 and 1907, the company invested 12 million *libras peruanas* (Lp) in mines, railroads, and general infrastructure.[10] Within the space of five years, this allowed the foreign capitalists to solve the majority of the infrastructural and technical bottlenecks that had held up Peruvian miners, off and on, for over a century. In fact, having the funds available for such a large initial expenditure gave the Cerro de Pasco Company an incomparable edge. Small wonder that most Peruvian mineowners, floundering in the mire of capital and raw material shortages, were more than happy to sell out to the North Americans, even if the latter did not exhibit an initial technological superiority.

Some of the more solvent and committed Peruvian entrepreneurs tried to hold out. A few, such as Lizandro Proaño of Morococha, Eu-

---

38–41. For the comparative size of the various labor forces, and the capacity of the other smelters, see BCIM, No. 67, "Estadística Minera del Perú en 1907," pp. 40–43; BCIM, No. 65, Alberto Jochamowitz, "Estado Actual de la Industria Minera en Morococha (1907)"; BCIM, No. 76, Carlos P. Jiménez, "Estadística Minera del Perú en 1908," especially pp. 70–71; BCIM, No. 77, Carlos P. Jiménez, "Estadística Minera del Perú en 1909 y 1910," especially pp. 70–71; and BCIM, No. 78, Carlos P. Jiménez, "Estadística Minera del Perú en 1911," pp. 78–79.

[9] BCIM, No. 61, *Informe Anual sobre la labor*, 1907, pp. 40–41.

[10] Ibid., p. 40. In 1907, according to the British consul, the Peruvian pound (*Libra peruana*, or Lp) was on the same standard as the British pound: 1 Lp = 10 soles. See Heraclio Bonilla (ed.), *Gran Bretaña y el Perú, 1826–1919: Informes de los cónsules británicos* (Lima: Instituto de Estudios Peruanos, 1975), II: 143–83, 191; and III: 73–75. Kruijt and Vellinga calculate that Cerro de Pasco had $25 million in direct investments by the end of the first decade.

logio E. Fernandini of Cerro de Pasco, and Ricardo Bentín of Casa-palca, put up resistance individually.[11] Others did so in a group, par-ticularly the Empresa Socavonera del Cerro de Pasco. Formed in 1900 by a group of prestigious Lima capitalists, the Empresa had signed a contract with the government to construct the drainage tunnel so des-perately needed by Cerro de Pasco's mines. In exchange, the Em-presa was to receive a percentage of the ores extracted after the drop of the water level.

At first, the North American company did not see the Empresa Socavonera as a serious competitor. But the Cerro de Pasco Compa-ny's opinion changed in 1906, when the Empresa negotiated an ex-tension of its government contract, tunneled under one of the com-pany's mines, and claimed 20% of that mine's ores under the terms of the original agreement. A court battle began, and tensions esca-lated. The U.S. company dynamited one of the Empresa's water tanks, forcing the Peruvian government to send troops to the area to keep order. The North American capitalists also pressured the U.S. State Department to intervene in their favor with the Peruvian state. Then in 1908, one month after the Empresa had completed the drainage tunnel, the two companies reached a settlement. The Empresa re-nounced its right to a percentage of extracted ores, receiving 5 per-cent of an additional sixty million dollars in shares that the North Americans agreed to add to their operating capital.[12]

This obligatory restructuring resulted in the formation of the Cerro de Pasco Copper Company, which owned the stock of both the pre-vious mining and railway companies. The Empresa Socavonera re-ceived 5 percent in this new firm, with the remaining stock staying in the hands of the old Cerro de Pasco Investment Company. The claims the U.S. capitalists owned in Morococha, however, were in-corporated into the Morococha Mining Company so as to remain un-affected by the 1908 settlement.[13] And it was with the birth of the Cerro de Pasco Copper Company that the first stage of foreign capi-tal's expansion in the central sierra came to an end.

During its second stage of development (1908–1915), the Cerro de Pasco Copper Company followed a policy of consolidation. Between 1906 and 1908, the company had begun extracting coal locally from

[11] DeWind, "Peasants Become Miners," Ch. 1, pp. 18 and 21; Thorp and Bertram, *Peru*, pp. 83–84.

[12] For the most detailed account of the struggle between the Empresa Socavonera and the U.S. company, see DeWind, Ch. 1, pp. 11–12. See also Thorp and Bertram, *Peru*, pp. 82–83, and 368–69 (footnote 45).

[13] DeWind, Ch. 1, p. 13.

the deposits of Goyllarisquisga, Quishuarcancha, and Vinchuscancha, and had started to produce coke at Tinyahuarco. Concomitantly, production figures for coal at the national level had shot up from nearly 80,000 metric tons to over 310,000. As the mines the company had bought were refurbished, the increases in local coal and coke production provided the necessary background to the expanded output of copper, which rose from 20,000 to nearly 28,000 metric tons between 1908 and 1913. Along with the growth in overall production came a parallel increment in the size of the labor force, from 6,742 workers in 1908 to 10,400 in 1912.[14] Thus, although the Cerro de Pasco Copper Company did not engage in significant new purchases during these years, the development of the properties it already possessed intensified regional economic activity. Not only did new opportunities open up in the commercial sector that serviced the mining industry, but the augmentation of the mining labor force expanded the local market for foodstuffs and other products.

Members of the regional elite were quick to see, and make the most of, changes in the central highland economy. The livestock sector, for example, which had gone into a protracted decline after the War of the Pacific, began to expand once again in the first decade of the twentieth century. Encouraged by the new demand being generated by the mining economy and the new ease of railroad transportation to Lima, entrepreneurs began investing relatively large quantities of funds in modernizing cattle and sheep haciendas. Between 1905 and 1910 several *sociedades ganaderas*, each a firm comprising a series of separate properties, came into being. By joining a number of properties under the same administration, *hacendados* hoped to rationalize the system of production on a larger scale. By forming joint stock companies, they attempted to guard against the type of financial ruin that had occurred during the La Breña campaign.

One of the first firms of this type was the Sociedad Ganadera Junín. Launched on the hacienda Cónsac by the Olavegoyas and Alvarez Calderóns, important entrepreneurial families in Lima with connections in the central sierra and related to each other by marriage, the Ganadera Junín soon added the haciendas Pachacayo, Cochas, and Piñascocha.[15] Starting with an original capital of 30,000 Lp, the Socie-

---

[14] The production figures for coal and copper can be found in BCIM, Nos. 76, p. 14; 77, p. 10; 80, p. 11; and 81, p. 11. Labor force figures are in BCIM, Nos. 76, p. 73 and 81, p. 91. For the resumption of production in the company's mines, see DeWind, Ch. 1, p. 13.

[15] For evidence on the founding of the Sociedad Ganadera Junín and the connection

dad soon evidenced a commitment to transforming the nature of live-stock-raising in the area. In the first five years of its existence, the firm imported merino sheep to improve its flocks, constructed pens to enhance the care and condition of its animals, divided production carefully among its various units, and installed pasteurizing machinery on Cónsac. There were also attempts to systematize an annual budget for the entire enterprise that would rigorously account for all expend-itures, whether these were on means of production for the haciendas, on wages, or on the money and goods advanced to shepherds and other *colonos*.[16] Overall, then, the goal of the Ganadera Junín's op-erations was to profit from the changes in the regional economy by initiating a modern, efficient livestock industry.

The Sociedad Ganadera del Centro, founded in 1910, had the same general goal. The Olavegoya brothers, Demetrio and Domingo, were also among the principal stockholders in the Ganadera del Centro, contributing to its initial property base with their recently acquired haciendas Acopalca and Chamiserías. Juan E. Valladares, the only member of his once-powerful family not to be seriously affected by the War of the Pacific, contributed his hacienda Runatullo. The rest of the stockholders who contributed to the initial capital of 50,000 Lp were businessmen from Lima.[17] Between 1910 and 1920, the Gana-dera del Centro reorganized production in a similar way to the Gana-dera Junín. Its administrators constructed a complex system of pens and sheep folds on Acopalca, and bought merino sheep from the ha-cienda Cónoc in Cerro de Pasco. In 1925, the board of directors al-located 15 percent of yearly profits to the capitalization of the hacien-das and improvement of the flocks. By the end of the 1920s, the Ganadera del Centro had added the haciendas Acocra, Huari, Inga-

---

between the Olavegoyas and the Alvarez Calderóns, see ANF, Protocolos Notariales, Luis Salazar, Book 13: August 21, 1904, 693v–95; AGN, Protocolos Notariales, Gera-vasio Bustamante, Protocolo 124, December 31, 1886; and Felipe S. Vivanco, Protocolo 1049, December 24, 1889, 603v–607v. For the acquisition of other haciendas, see BCIM, No. 35, Enrique I. Dueñas, *Recursos Minerales de las provincias de Jauja y Huancayo* (Lima: Imprenta la Industria, 1906), p. 22; and Víctor Caballero, Research Notes: AFA, Sociedad Ganadera Junín, Correspondencia, 1906–1908, 83.

[16] Víctor Caballero, Research Notes: AFA, Sociedad Ganadera Junín, Corresponden-cia, 1908–1911, March 23, 1911, 210–13; April 3, 1911, 216–17, and passim.

[17] The Olavegoya brothers obtained the haciendas Acopalca and Chamiserías by in-debting Juan Enrique Valladares while he was trying to save his sister and brother from ruin after the War of the Pacific. See Chapter IV, footnote 23, and especially AGN, Protocolos Notariales, José Ramón Valdivia, Protocolo 994: July 12, 1886, 138–39v. For the initial list of stockholders in the Sociedad Ganadera del Centro, see Gerardo Ré-nique, Research Notes: Registro Mercantil, Lima, V:231, and XXIX:29.

huasi, Laive, and Siutucancha, and its total capital had risen to 250,000 Lp.[18]

The Ganaderas Junín and del Centro were but particularly dramatic examples of the rising profitability of livestock. Many mineowners, merchants, and *hacendados* developed individual haciendas in this period, or formed smaller, more family-oriented *sociedades*. Juan E. Valladares, even though he belonged to the Ganadera del Centro, also maintained a medium-sized property on the Mantaro Valley floor called San Juan de Yanamuclo, where he ran a dairy industry and improved his cattle by importing high quality livestock from Switzerland.[19] Even the Cerro de Pasco Copper Company owned at least three livestock haciendas by 1913.[20] Thus, whether supplying the local or Lima markets with milk, butter, hides, and wool, or exporting fibers to Europe's burgeoning textile industry, it seemed that the central highlands' sheep and cattle haciendas had finally come into their own.

There were similar trends in commercial agriculture. For properties of all sizes, swelling demand in an expanding economy provided almost unlimited scope for increased production. Some landowners, taking advantage of the economies of scale brought about by rationalizing production, specialized in a particular product for a particular purpose, such as alfalfa for the mule trade, wheat for the local mills, or wood for the mines. Others, tempted by the higher demand for crops previously grown within the self-sufficient household unit, simply sold a larger amount of subsistence products at the regional fairs.[21]

[18] Gerardo Rénique, Research Notes: AFA, Sociedad Ganadera del Centro, Correspondencia, Vol. II, 97; and AFA, Sociedad Ganadera del Centro: Hacienda Acopalca, Correspondencia, 1911–1918, September 3, 1911, "Carta de Carlos Alvarez Calderón a Manuel Valladares," 27.

[19] For Juan Enrique Valladares' experiments, see Interview with Hernán Valladares, Huancayo, June 3, 1977; and BCIM, No. 35, p. 22. For the formation of smaller *sociedades*, see APJ, "Memoria del Subprefecto de Yauli, 1907," Anexo 5, and Víctor Caballero, *Hacienda Conocancha: Desarrollo capitalista y proletarización*, Taller de Estudios Andinos, Serie: Andes Centrales No. 1 (La Molina: Universidad Nacional Agraria, 1975), pp. 1–19. For another example of innovation in the livestock industry, see Alejandro Garland, *Reseña Industrial de Perú* (Lima: Imprenta la Industria, 1905), p. 96.

[20] APJ, "Memoria del Subprefecto de Yauli, 1907," Anexo 5; and Dora Mayer, *La conducta de la Compañia Minera del Cerro de Pasco* (Callao: Imprenta del Concejo Provincial, 1914), p. 2.

[21] For how small properties were used, see ANF, Protocolos Notariales, Luis Salazar, Book 11: September 18, 1902, 619v–21; Book 13: August 31, 1904, 733–34v; Book 23: August 14, 1912, 991v–93; and passim. For how medium-sized properties were used, see ANF, Protocolos Notariales, Luis Salazar, Book 11: November 29, 1902, 691–95; Book 13: May 25, 1904, 573v–77; Book 16: December 13, 1906, 1156–57v; Book 18: March 24, 1908, 434–35v; and passim. On the subject of commerce and the distribution of products within the regional economy, see BCIM, No. 35, pp. 16–21, 29–31.

In either case, increased demand was the result not only of the expanding mining industry, but also of the new needs of the *sociedades ganaderas*. The Sociedad Ganadera Junín's administrators, for example, were always trying to find stocks of corn, barley, and other subsistence products they could buy to feed their shepherds and *colonos*. "If they are not given [their supplies] punctually every fifteen days," one administrator explained, "they eat the livestock."[22] And as the personnel of the Sociedad Ganadera del Centro discovered, the availability of provisions was closely tied to labor discipline. "I have been forced to give them [goods] from their monthly wages," wrote the administrator of Acopalca in 1917, "because they had nothing to eat and with the excuse of looking for food they will leave and not come back for many days."[23]

Not surprisingly, the auspicious conditions for agricultural production increased the value of land, and consequently the desirability of landownership. A number of the wealthier Jauja merchants, particularly those who were relative newcomers to the area, began to accumulate and improve commercial *chacras*. Thus in 1911 Carlos Sanguinetti, representing the commercial house and *enganche* firm of Sanguinetti Brothers, bought a *chacra* in Huaripampa that was valued at 500 soles in silver—a great deal of money, even for land dedicated to cereal production.[24] Not content with this purchase, Sanguinetti then proceeded, between 1911 and 1912, to accumulate land next to the Mantaro River in the town of Ataura. In addition to expanding his property through several separate purchases from the same extended family, he constructed an irrigation system out of stone which allowed him to grow several crops per year of certain products.[25] And other merchant-*enganchadores* followed similar patterns. R. Arístides Castro, a native of Callao living in Jauja, bought three *chacras* and a *cerco* (small, fenced-in property) from Custodio Huánuco, a peasant from the village of Pucucho, and over seven hectares of land from a peasant in Chucllú.[26] Pedro A. Aizcorbe, a merchant originally from Lima, signed a rental contract on a number of *chacras* in 1911. Located on

[22] Caballero, Research Notes: AFA, Sociedad Ganadera Junín, Correspondencia, 1908–1911, November 14, 1910, 160–61.

[23] AFA, Sociedad Ganadera del Centro, Hacienda Acopalca: Correspondencia, 1911–1918, March 1, 1917, 141.

[24] ANF, Protocolos Notariales, Luis Salazar, Book 22: April 26, 1911, 222–23v.

[25] ANF, Protocolos Notariales, Luis Salazar, Book 22: May 1, 1911, 234v–36v; Book 23: May 10, 1912, 846–48; and Book 24: October 11, 1912, 1125–26.

[26] ANF, Protocolos Notariales, Luis Salazar, Book 23: April 29, 1912; and Book 28: April 13, 1915, 228v–30.

the bank of the Mantaro River in the neighboring village of Tambo, these properties comprised a total of eleven hectares and were planted mainly with trees and alfalfa. Although Aizcorbe did not buy the properties outright, renting them for four years certainly allowed him to exploit their products commercially.[27]

The boom in land acquisitions, speculation, and market production was not limited to newcomers. A number of the villages' wealthy peasants also became involved. In 1909 Francisco Espinoza, from the community of Chocón, rented a *chacra* from the *cofradía* of the Lord of Souls (Señor de Animas) composed of nearly eleven hectares of fertile land around the temporal lagoon in the middle of the Yanamarca Valley.[28] Between 1911 and 1916 José C., Ezequiel, and Narcizo Hurtado first rented and then owned the hacienda Quishuarcancha, to the north of their home village of Marco, which in addition to being good for livestock, produced potatoes and barley for the market.[29] And in 1915, Martín Bonilla Collazos, a merchant and *enganchador* originally from the village of Ataura, bought two *chacras* from the church. The first, belonging to the Obra Pía of Santa Elena, was forty hectares large and located between the communities of Ataura and Viscap. The second, property of the Obra Pía of Santo Domingo, was composed of thirty hectares of irrigated land in Ataura. As the priest who sold the properties to Bonilla explained, these two sales were not an isolated case.

> Our constant experience through the years has proven that it is now time to simplify the administration of our pious foundations, which have become the source of constant difficulties and court battles, in grave detriment to the religious and spiritual interests of the faithful. . . . That this circumstance makes difficult the expansion of the city, which is required by the recent traffic of the railroad and the growth of the population, [and] converts the ecclesiastical administration into an impediment to local progress, also makes convenient the sale of some of our present properties, unproductive for the most part, or in imminent danger of being usurped.[30]

[27] ANF, Protocolos Notariales, Luis Salazar, Book 22: March 15, 1911, 145–46.

[28] ANF, Protocolos Notariales, Luis Salazar, Book 19: January 13, 1909, 15–17v.

[29] ANF, Protocolos Notariales, Luis Salazar, Book 22: April 18, 1911; Book 30: April 28, 1916, 1136v–38v, and August 17, 1916, 1418–19; and Expedientes y Libros Judiciales, "Santiago Motto vs. José C., Narcizo y Ezequiel Hurtado, sobre cantidad de soles," Jauja, November 15, 1917.

[30] ANF, Protocolos Notariales, Luis Salazar, Book 28: July 6, 1915, 443–46v. Literally a pious foundation, *obra pía* was the name given to some *cofradías* in an attempt to circumvent the late nineteenth-century law making their properties liable for government intervention.

In essence, the priest's comments referred to the fact that increased commerce, combined with Jauja's urban expansion, was driving up land values and increasing the number of land conflicts. Suddenly, properties that had lain fallow for years and whose boundaries had never been clearly defined took on a new attraction. As landowners struggled to legitimize their claims over newly desirable *chacras*, they often found that their titles—if indeed they had titles—were not legal, or were so old that no one could make out the references to landmarks or *parajes* that they contained. In some cases, other claimants had been in possession of the property for several generations, and would not give up without a court battle.[31] And since the *cofradías* and *obras pías* were important landowners in the region, many of these battles involved the church.

The repercussions of economic expansion were also felt in the subtropical *ceja de selva* region. The growth of local markets, particularly the industrial demand for wood in the mining sector and the consumer demand for coca and *aguardiente* in mines and haciendas, stimulated production from Oxapampa in the north to Pampa Hermosa in the south.[32] With the generally higher level of commercial activity, coffee production revived once again. And as was the case in the highlands, the growth of commercial agriculture in the *ceja de selva* occurred on properties of all sizes.

Especially among coffee growers, whose concern over persistently low prices continued, there seems to have been a strong move toward expanding the amount of land under cultivation and using more sophisticated machinery to process the beans. Francisco L. Alvariño, owner of the hacienda Santa Clara in Oxapampa, was a good example of this trend. In addition to building his own roads in and around the property, Alvariño constructed an elaborate system of terraces for planting coffee on the hillsides. This facilitated the expansion of cultivation and made possible the efficient use of fertilizers. The labor

[31] For some examples of land disputes in this period, see ANF, Expedientes y Libros Judiciales, "Juan Villar y otro contra los herederos del finado Juan Solís, sobre deslinde entre Tingo Paccha y Carampa," Jauja, November 7, 1906; "Luis Y. Ibarra contra la Obra Pía del Cármen, sobre propiedad de los terrenos 'Putaj,' " began June 23, 1906, especially Resumen de Actuados, 244–45v; "Felix R. Vílchez contra Benjamín Otero, Interdicto de retener unos terrenos," began September 18, 1914; AFA, Sociedad Ganadera del Centro, Hacienda Acopalca: Correspondencia, 1911–1918, July 3–September 16, 1911, 20–30; December 14, 1917, 292–93; APJ, "Belisario Orellana vs. Olavegoya: conflicto sobre terrenos para el Sanatorio Olavegoya, varios documentos," December 1906–April 1908, and "Comas vs. Sociedad Ganadera del Centro," April 1911.

[32] BCIM, No. 35, pp. 21, 29–30; ANF, Protocolos Notariales, Luis Salazar, Book 13: June 29, 1904, 621v–24; Book 26: May 26, 1914, 825–26; Book 32: June 15, 1917, 350–52v; BNP, Document No. E198, "Informe del Prefecto de Junín acerca de Chanchamayo," Tarma, January 31, 1904.

on Santa Clara was provided by a combination of resident peasant families called *mejoreros*, who worked for a limited number of years, and *enganchados* who supplemented labor needs in the heaviest periods of the year. In addition to being a great deal more efficient than relying solely on *enganche*, this combination was possible because the nature of coffee cultivation allowed resident families to plant subsistence crops between the rows of coffee. Finally, in keeping with the "modern" and "progressive" aims of his time, Alvariño provided an elementary school on the hacienda for the children of the *mejoreros* and other workers.[33]

In addition to Peruvian landowners, the tendency toward greater capital investment as a partial compensation for low coffee prices could be seen among the area's various communities of foreign colonists, such as the Germans in Oxapampa and the Perené colony run by the Peruvian Corporation. In the case of the latter's hacienda San Juan del Perené, moreover, the recent profitability of investment was dramatically evident. This hacienda had originally been developed by a group of Lima entrepreneurs who, after investing 100,000 soles, were forced to sell the property for 20,000. The second owner invested still more, but was unable to make the hacienda productive. He sold it once again, this time to the Peruvian Corporation for 10,000 soles. Not until 1904, after installing machinery and appointing an experienced administrator, did the corporation make a profitable enterprise out of San Juan del Perené.[34]

The profitability of subtropical agriculture was not limited to large or capital-intensive ventures. Particularly with local market crops such as coca and *aguardiente*, small- and medium-sized commercial properties were also viable. This was true not only in the areas of heaviest commercial activity, such as Oxapampa and Chanchamayo, but also in part of the *ceja* where peasant subsistence production was relatively important, such as Monobamba. There, Pedro and Leonardo Calderón formed a commercial society in 1908 to exploit twenty small properties they owned, planting sugar cane and some subsistence crops and installing a machine to distill *aguardiente*. The size of their initial capital—400 soles plus the value of the distillery—illustrates the relative modesty of their enterprise.[35] And the same was true of others. In 1905, for example, Pedro A. Espinoza, a wealthy peasant from Marco, bought a small property in Monobamba for forty soles to add

[33] BNP, Document No. E198, 2–4.
[34] Ibid., 4–5, 7–8.
[35] ANF, Protocolos Notariales, Luis Salazar, Book 18: April 17, 1908, 472v–74.

to another modest *chacra* he already owned in the area.[36] Six years later, Cenofio Rivera and wife, Francisca Oropesa, both peasants from the village of Pacapaccha, bought a cane-growing property in Mono-bamba for 100 soles.[37] Though none of these modest entrepreneurs could begin to compete with the larger *hacendados*, it was a tribute to the changing conditions on the regional market that they seemed able to prosper within the limits of their size.

In fact, what was most striking about the growth of the Cerro de Pasco Corporation in this period was the broad and multifaceted nature of the opportunities it created on the regional market. In sharp contrast to the circumstances generally considered to characterize an enclave economy,[38] the combined development of transportation networks and of a larger urban consumer population allowed local entrepreneurs to profit handsomely from foreign investment. Whether in livestock or sugar cane, hacienda or small *chacra*, the economic changes set into motion by foreign capital opened up new vistas for the commercial agriculturalist. At the local and regional levels, increased demand for labor and goods generated much prosperity for the area's merchants. Indeed, it was precisely the creation of a broad spectrum of economic alternatives for local elites that helped smooth the way for foreign capital's dominance of the regional economy, particularly in this early period. Even in the mining industry itself, where the direct and dramatic nature of national capital's expropriation inevitably generated a higher level of resistance, most Peruvian entrepreneurs made a surprisingly easy transition to investment in other sectors.

Of the twenty-two major mining enterprises that dominated the industry in Cerro de Pasco and Morococha at the turn of the century, twenty sold to the Cerro de Pasco Corporation without a struggle. Although about half of the owners apparently spent the money they

[36] ANF, Protocolos Notariales, Luis Salazar, Book 14: November 21, 1905, 499v–500v.

[37] ANF, Protocolos Notariales, Luis Salazar, Book 17: April 29, 1907. For other examples of subtropical commercial agriculture on a small scale, see BNP, Document No. E198, 9, 15–16.

[38] Kruijt and Vellinga (*Labor Relations*, pp. 25–26) have presented the most recent argument in favor of the enclave concept for the central sierra mining industry, insisting that the mining economy as dominated by the Cerro de Pasco Corporation remained isolated from the rest of the region. However, as is especially clear when one researches the development of sectors outside mining, the impact of foreign investment on the rest of the central highlands was indeed great and contributed, in the long run, to the transformation of forms and relations of production. Only by focusing on the mining industry in isolation is it possible to continue considering it an enclave.

received for their properties in increased consumption and luxurious lifestyles, a number also took advantage of expanded economic opportunities to invest their funds.[39] The Tello family, for example, descendants of the patriarch Agustín Tello who had accumulated an initial fortune in the salt trade, invested in electricity for the Cerro de Pasco region and bought land in Lima.[40] The Gallo brothers, originally Spain's consular agents in Cerro de Pasco, maintained their commercial house in that city and in Lima, and invested in banking and insurance houses.[41] And N. B. Tealdo Peri y Compañía, an Italian immigrant firm with commercial houses in Lima, Tarma, and Chanchamayo, kept up their various branches of commercial activity—from the marketing of coffee on the national level to the local financing of coffee planters and other landowners—and invested in subtropical agriculture.[42]

Even those who resisted the corporation's attempts to buy them out were successful precisely because they came to terms, in one way or another, with foreign capital. Eulogio E. Fernandini, for example, the only Peruvian entrepreneur in either Cerro de Pasco or Morococha to expand and invest after the arrival of the foreign company, did so through a complex combination of collaboration and competition. Though at one point he was rumored to have defiantly answered a corporation offer to buy him out by saying that he would buy *them* out instead,[43] he also knew when to work with the U.S. capitalists. Thus he leased several of his mines to the Cerro de Pasco Corporation, worked others in partnership with the company, and took advantage of their infrastructure whenever he could.[44] When the American Vanadium Company offered to buy his Ragra mine, moreover, Fernandini was more than happy to sell for ten thousand dollars cash and 10 percent of the shares.[45] And finally, in conjunction with his administrator Sixto Venegas, Fernandini profited from the general mining boom by staking claims on many new mines in the pastures of his developing livestock haciendas.[46]

[39] Thorp and Bertram, *Peru*, pp. 82–85, 92–93.

[40] Ibid., p. 92; Pedro Dávalos y Lissón, *Cómo hice fortuna* (Lima: Librería e Imprenta Gil, 1941–42), II:8–10.

[41] RPI, Sociedades, I:25; Thorp and Bertram, *Peru*, pp. 82 and 92; APJ, "Solicitud de los extranjeros residentes en Cerro de Pasco," June 1892.

[42] RPI, Sociedades, I:60–65 and 365–71; BNP, Document No. F198, 10–12, 14–15, 21; and Thorp and Bertram, *Peru*, p. 84.

[43] Interviews with Felipe Artica, I and II, Huancayo, June 1977.

[44] AFA, Documentos Minas Fernandini, Libro de Planillas Mina Peregrina, 1903–1906; Thorp and Bertram, *Peru*, pp. 81 and 370 (footnote 65).

[45] Thorp and Bertram, *Peru*, pp. 84–85.

[46] AFA, Negociación Ganadera Fernandini, 3.11: Denuncios de Minas, 1905–1923.

Even members of the regional elite who had been less directly involved in the mining industry were able to profit from the mining boom. Already in the first years after the corporation's arrival in Peru, expectations about the increased profitability of mining had led to a rash of *denuncios* (claims), particularly of coal mines. In Jauja province alone, eighty-eight coal mines had been claimed by 1905, and a number of companies were formed to exploit them.[47] The general tendency was for these firms to include, in addition to one or two mineowners or mining experts, several important merchants or *enganchadores* from the Jauja region. Thus the Jauja Coal Mining Company, formed in 1904 to exploit fifteen mines in the Jatunhuasi and Cónsac region, included as partners Juan Colareta and Justo Peralta, prominent mineowners, and Luis Bardales and Teodoro Grelland, both among Jauja's principal merchants and *enganchadores*.[48] The Sociedad Explotadora de Minas de la Provincia de Jauja, founded the next year, followed a similar pattern: Martín Bonilla Collazos, Carlos Sanguinetti, and José M. Silva, all merchant-*enganchadores* in the Jauja area, joined with Agustín Mármol and Manuel Terreyros, both considered experts in the *denuncio* and exploitation of mines.[49]

The ubiquitous presence of merchants and *enganchadores* as partners in these firms, combined with the generally modest quantities of capital invested and the usually short duration of each company, gave most enterprises of this sort a rather speculative character. As the years went on, this continued to be the case. In 1910, for example, Manuel J. Landa, Lizandro Bambaren, and Josué Ortiz de Foronda, all merchants in Jauja province, signed a contract with the C. Weiss y Compañía commercial house in Lima to market the waste from their mines in Chuquishuari and Tipillapa. The three Jauja merchants promised to deliver 6,000 tons, containing 55 percent lead and five *marcos* of silver per *cajón* (box), to the railroad station over the next four months. Weiss agreed to pay sixty cents per *quintal* of 120 pounds, or a total of 30,000 soles, for the shipments, and gave the merchants an advance of 6,000 soles.[50] Again, the four-month span of this contract points to the casual, short-lived quality of many investments.

[47] BNP, Document No. E199: "Anexo a la Memoria del Prefecto de Junín y Ancash," Tarma, 1905, Anexo 15. In addition to the companies listed below, several other firms started to consider exploiting mines in the Jauja area in this period. See, for example, RPI, Sociedades, I:365–71, 103–108; and ANF, Protocolos Notariales, Luis Salazar, Book 13: May 15, 1904, 539v–40v; Book 14: November 13, 1905, 477v–78v.

[48] ANF, Protocolos Notariales, Luis Salazar, Book 13: May 16, 1904, 560–60v and previous inserts.

[49] ANF, Protocolos Notariales, Luis Salazar, Book 15: December 2, 1905, 528–30v.

[50] ANF, Protocolos Notariales, Luis Salazar, Book 22: February 24, 1910, 624–27, and February 6, 1911, 70–75. A *marco* of silver is approximately eight ounces.

Yet it also points to the fact that local entrepreneurs were quick to see, and take advantage of, the opportunities that did arise.

In some cases, regional elite members served the mining industry on a more long-term basis. The Valladares family, one of the more powerful landowning families in the central highlands during the nineteenth century and member of the Sociedad Ganadera del Centro in the twentieth, was a case in point. In addition to his interests in large- and medium-scale livestock production, Juan Enrique Valladares exploited the first molybdenum mine in South America and exported the ores to Liverpool through the Graham Rowe commercial house.[51] His son, Hernán Valladares, discovered, claimed, and exploited copper and coal mines in the Cerro de Pasco area. For a number of years, Hernán sold anthracite from his mines as fuel to the Fernandini and Huarón Mining Companies, and then sold them the mines directly. Over the years, he also became known as an expert in designing blueprints for mining *denuncios*, drawing close to forty such blueprints for different mines during his lifetime.[52]

The overall boom in production also generated a boom in commerce. Several of the towns in the central highlands, particularly Cerro de Pasco, Oroya, Jauja, La Merced, Concepción, and Huancayo, served as depositories for a wide spectrum of goods and services. Through the developing system of weekly fairs, produce from local villages found its way into the urban market in exchange for commodities from other areas. Particularly after the arrival of the railroad to Huancayo in 1908, that city witnessed a spectacular spurt of growth as a clearing house for merchandise from distant places. At the weekly Sunday fair, products from as far south as Huancavelica and Ayacucho were redirected to Tarma, Chanchamayo, Yauli, Morococha, Cerro de Pasco, and Lima. Commodities from other parts of the highlands and from Lima were exchanged and transported by mule to the more distant sierra regions. Jauja performed a similar function a bit further to the north, directing the flow of commodities to and from the Chanchamayo area, through the mining sector, to the Lima market.[53] And

[51] Interview with Hernán Valladares. A lead-like metal that gives great strength to alloys, molybdenum became valuable only with the development of heavy industry.

[52] Ibid.

[53] Interview with Felipe Artica, I, Huancayo, June 7, 1977; Giorgio Alberti and Rodrigo Sánchez, *Poder y conflicto social en el Valle del Mantaro* (Lima: Instituto de Estudios Peruanos, 1974), pp. 40–44; Norman Long and Bryan Roberts (eds.), *Peasant Cooperation and Capitalist Expansion in Central Peru* (Austin: University of Texas Press, 1978), pp. 28–30; BCIM, No. 35, 29–31; BNP, Document No. E199, 17–18; and

whether they specialized on the Lima-Morococha-Jauja-Chanchamayo axis, or the Lima-Oroya-Huancayo-Huancavelica route, both large commercial houses and smaller local merchants profited greatly from this increased commercialization.

As was the case in other sectors of the regional economy, those who expanded their commercial interests in this period were a combination of old and new merchant families. On the one hand, many of the same merchants who had established themselves during the last two decades of the nineteenth century now emerged as dominant figures in the new commercial boom. José G. Andía, for example, a merchant from Arequipa who had settled in Llocllapampa after the War of the Pacific and developed a commercial and *enganche* business in the 1890s, expanded his firm and began buying merchandise directly from W. R. Grace and Company in Lima.[54] The Grelland brothers, originally from France but also operating in the area since the 1890s, established a new commercial partnership in 1907 and, in 1911, petitioned the prefect of Junín for the right to establish an electric company in Jauja and its surrounding districts.[55] In the same year, they joined with Juan Primo, another merchant in the same position, in starting a movie theatre.[56] On the other hand, some of the merchants who began to prosper between 1900 and 1915, such as Pedro Aizcorbe, Arístides Castro, and the Sanguinetti brothers, were recent arrivals in Jauja.[57] But the very fact that newer and older firms existed side by side lends credence to the picture of a rapidly expanding, ever more commercialized regional economy where many different types of investment and innovation could coexist and turn a profit.

ANF, Expedientes y Libros Judiciales, "José C. Hurtado contra los hermanos Onofre, Agustín Rafael y otros, por la muerte de Florián Hurtado," began in Jauja, August 20, 1918, especially 687 and 1284v.

[54] ANF, Protocolos Notariales, Luis Salazar, Book 20: December 8, 1909, 518v–20. For Andía's earlier activities, see Chapter IV, especially footnote 59.

[55] For proof of the Grelland presence in Jauja from the 1890s on, see ANF, Protocolos Notariales, Luis Salazar, Book 6: May 8, 1895, 50–51; Book 9: March 25, 1899, 53–55; and APJ, "Varios documentos sobre irregularidades en el gobierno municipal de Jauja," August 1900. For the formation of a new commercial firm, see ANF, Protocolos Notariales, Luis Salazar, Book 15: March 10, 1906, 698–99v; Book 17: March 20, 1907, 90v–93. For the petition to the prefect, see APJ, "Solicitud de Grelland Hermanos al Prefecto del Departamento," Jauja, December 9, 1911.

[56] On Juan Primo's history in Jauja, see APJ, "Various documentos sobre irregularidades," August 1900. For his business agreement with Grelland Hermanos, see ANF, Protocolos Notariales, Luis Salazar, Book 22: January 21, 1911, 33v–35.

[57] ANF, Protocolos Notariales, Luis Salazar, Book 21: August 8, 1910, 891–91v and inserts; August 29, 1910, 931v–33v; RPI, Sociedades, I: 261–62; and Pedro S. Zulen, "El enganche de indios: Informe del Comisionado de la Asociación Pro-Indígena," *La Prensa*, October 7, 1910, p. 4.

Until the 1920s, therefore, the central sierra economy exhibited a somewhat surprising combination of trends. On the one hand, a North American corporation was buying up most of the region's mines and engaging in strong-arm tactics with those who resisted,[58] investing large quantities of capital in revolutionizing transportation and the treatment of ores, and dramatically extending the regional markets for goods and labor. On the other hand the regional elite, while losing control of the region's economy as a whole to foreign capital, was in fact able to prosper greatly by developing livestock, agriculture, commerce, and urban services in the context of an expanding market. That the existence of the latter trend helped to facilitate the success of the former cannot be doubted. The regional elite's historical penchant for investment diversification was also important in this regard, since diverting funds from one economic sector to another was a change of emphasis rather than a radical disjuncture from previous patterns. Yet in the final analysis, the crucial element underlying the smooth relationship between the regional elite and foreign capital in this period was the lack of fundamental changes in the system of production and labor relations.

Throughout its initial expansion, the Cerro de Pasco Corporation operated in alliance with, and was ultimately dependent upon, local commercial capital. Rather than transform the system of mining, for example, the corporation relied on preexisting technology and labor relations for the extraction of ores. Through the use of *contrata*, the foreign company farmed out the actual mining to individual contractors—often petty merchants or wealthy peasants with previous experience in the industry—and paid them so much per meter or ton of mineral. The *contratistas* were thus responsible for all aspects of production, using their own tools and methods and obtaining their own labor force. Even in those parts of the industry where it was impossible, for whatever reason, to use *contratistas*, the corporation did not acquire a permanent or stable labor force. Instead, the company plugged into the *enganche* networks already developed by commercial capital, manipulating them for its own ends.[59]

Thus the first two decades of foreign capital's penetration in the mining sector can be seen as the "manufacturing period" of industrial

---

[58] See above, this chapter, and APJ, "Queja de Lizandro Proaño contra James B. Haggin," Morococha, October–December 1905.

[59] For a detailed analysis of the company's use of *enganche* and *contrata*, see below. For the historical antecedents of these practices, see above, Chapters II and IV.

mining.[60] Similar to what happened in the early years of European manufacturing, foreign capital in Peru did not revolutionize the system of production, but rather reorganized existing methods and labor processes to suit its own purposes. Because foreign investors remained dependent on local technology and social relations to make the enterprise work, they were also dependent, in the last instance, on the competence and connections of central highland miners and merchants. Yet despite the lack of fundamental change in the system as a whole, the speeding up of production and the partial transformations that did take place stretched existing relations to the breaking point. As these new tendencies played themselves out, the decisive battle turned out to be at the level of the individual peasant village.

Mining, Labor Migration, and the Peasant Community

In 1910, while he was representing Junín in the Senate, Joaquín Capelo received a telegram from Jauja denouncing the town's authorities for keeping a number of enganchados in jail. Pedro S. Zulen, one of the leaders of the Asociación Pro-Indígena, traveled to the central highlands on commission from the Senate to investigate the situation. He found that it was actually a group of fiadores who were being detained in the subprefect's office. They were being held because the workers whose enganche contracts they had guaranteed had run away from the mines, or never showed up at all. The fiadores and their relatives told Zulen horror stories of mistreatment by the enganchadores and their agents. Other peasants described the vicious cycle of indebtedness they entered upon accepting the first advance to work in the mines. Yet even more impressive than the individual dramas of the peasants he interviewed, Zulen discovered, was the depth and breadth of existing enganche networks.[61]

During the first decade of the twentieth century, enganche had moved from being a fairly profitable sideline activity to constituting big business in its own right. At the center of this transformation was, of course, the arrival of the Cerro de Pasco Company: the increased size of the mining labor force and the quickening pace of production necessitated a much larger and more constant supply of labor than

[60] My use the term "manufacturing period" has essentially the same meaning as Karl Marx's "manufacture," in that it denotes a reorganization of existing technology and labor relations through a more efficient division of labor and more centralized production. In no case, however, are there major technological breakthroughs at this stage. See Marx, Capital, I, especially 336–68.

[61] Pedro S. Zulen, "El enganche de indios," pp. 4–5.

ever before. In an attempt to solve the problems that *enganchadores* had previously encountered with peasant resistance, the state had passed the Reglamento de Locación de Servicios para la Industria Minera in September 1903. This law allowed, among other provisions, for political authorities from the various towns and districts to become involved in chasing runaway laborers. Thus, prompted by a larger and more regular demand for workers on the one hand, and by greater legal support for their transactions on the other, a number of merchants began to invest quite heavily in *enganche*. According to their own figures the main *enganchadores* had, by 1910, tied up well over half a million soles in advances to *enganchados*.[62] And the investment turned a nice profit. In addition to the 10 percent commission they charged the company per day's work (*tarea*) of each laborer, most merchants acting as *enganchadores* had stores in the mining centers where they sold merchandise to workers at inflated prices. In fact, the initial advances made to peasants were often at least partially in merchandise from the stores, or in *vales* (scrip) that were only redeemable at these stores.[63]

Yet despite its new size and efficiency, *enganche* in 1910 was still based on relationships and networks of dependency that had not changed, in any fundamental way, since the nineteenth century. In order to fulfill the quotas of workers they had agreed to send the company, the principal *enganchadores*, both newly arrived and somewhat more established merchants in Jauja, operated through agents called *subenganchadores*. Usually petty merchants or wealthy peasants from the area's villages, these agents were already accustomed to their role as social, economic, and political mediators between the

[62] Both for the actual amounts of money invested, and for the relationship between government decrees and the expansion of *enganche*, see APJ, "Queja de varios enganchadores al Subprefecto de Jauja," May 28, 1910.

[63] There are a number of descriptions of the *enganche* system, many of them polemical. For a good summary, see DeWind, "Peasants Become Miners," Ch. 3, pp. 6–10. A good critique of some of the literature is Alberto Flores Galindo, *Los mineros de la Cerro de Pasco, 1900–1930* (Lima: Pontífica Universidad Católica del Perú, 1974), pp. 37–43. Some examples of the more polemical materials are: Mayer, *La conducta*, pp. 3–4, and *Un decreto libertador*, Paper read at the Conference on *Enganche* organized by the "Centro Unión Hijos de Cajacay" (Callao), July 8, 1914 (Lima: Imprenta "El Inca," 1914), pp. 5–11; Zulen, "El enganche de idios," pp. 4–5; María Jesús Alvarado Rivera, *El aniquilamiento del aborígen por el sistema de enganche*, Paper presented at the Conference on *Enganche* organized by the "Centro Unión Hijos de Cajacay" (Callao), July 8, 1914 (Lima: Imprenta "El Inca," 1914), pp. 13–26; Marco Aurelio Denegri, "La crísis del enganche," Lecture given by the Asociación Pro-Indígena at the Sociedad de Ingenieros, Lima, August 12, 1911; and Francisco Mostajo, *Algunas ideas sobre la cuestión obrera (contrato de enganche)*, J.D. Dissertation, University of Arequipa (Arequipa: Tipografía Quiroz, 1913).

larger society and the peasant community. As had been the case during the nineteenth century, they used debt and relationships of patronage and clientele in the villages to gain access to labor for the commercial economy. Operating through their monopoly of political office, they collected the *enganchadores'* debts and "convinced" their own debtors to sign *enganche* contracts.[64] Once again, therefore, a modernizing regional economy ended up dependent on traditional relationships of asymmetrical reciprocity for its access to labor. The difference was that growing foreign investment began to transform the terms upon which local commercialization and economic integration could occur.

As existing networks of commercial capital in the villages were reorganized to meet the needs of a developing industrial mining sector, they became increasingly oppressive to the average peasant household. With the general economic expansion in the region, peasant families participated more extensively in market relations. This often led to higher levels of indebtedness, which wealthier peasants and merchants were more than happy to exploit for their own purposes. Within the village, the result was an ever-widening gap between rich and poor. And the rich used their connections to the mining industry or to other sectors of the regional economy to push differentiation even further, forcing their debtors to give up property and labor on a large scale.[65]

In one such case, Antonio Onofre, a rich peasant from the community of Tragadero, lent a poor peasant woman named Fidela Llacsa 400 soles in 1914. As Llacsa explained in the contract, rather than pay the interest in money,

> I promise to pay it with my personal labor and that of my children Emilio, twelve years old, Cecilia, ten years, and Maria Amalaya, five years; each one of us carrying out the tasks that the said Don Antonio Onofre has in his house, in proportion to our respective

[64] Zulen, "El enganche de indios," pp. 4–5; and ANF, Protocolos Notariales, Luis Salazar, Book 18: December 3, 1908, 841 and insert; Book 20: June 22, 1910, 799v and insert; Book 23: July 12, 1912, 934v and insert; and Book 32: February 12, 1917, 73–79.

[65] Increasing differentiation, indebtedness, and property sales are obvious trends in ANF, Protocolos Notariales. In addition to the pertinent documents listed below, see especially Luis Salazar, Book 16: December 21, 1906, 1164–67; Book 17: June 25, 1907, 161–62v, and November 8, 1907, 308v and insert; Book 18: October 2, 1908, 737v and insert, and December 3, 1908, 841v and insert; Book 19: February 26, 1909, 80v and insert; Book 20: November 17, 1909, 485v–86v; Book 22: January 9, 1911, 14v–16v; Book 28: April 6, 1914, 214–16v; Book 35: September 16, 1918, 1540–41; Book 41–42: March 5, 1921, 180v–82.

ages and strength. It is a condition [of this contract] that for no reason will I or my children abandon the house of Don Antonio Onofre, who will give us the food and clothes we need for the duration of this contract and until we return the money we have received and in the eventuality that we should break this agreement, we shall submit ourselves to the legally constituted authorities so they may force us to comply with the rigors of the law, for which I renounce the *fuero de mi domicilio*.[66]

Even though it was a contract for domestic service, the agreement between Onofre and Llacsa read like an *enganche* contract in several ways: the promise to pay back a debt with personal labor, the submission to the legally constituted authorities, and the renunciation, before the fact, of the *fuero de domicilio*. Yet in other ways, it was even more onerous than an *enganche* contract. In the first place, Llacsa agreed to give Onofre not only her own labor, but also that of her children. In addition, they were all to be dependent on Onofre, in a day-to-day fashion, for their subsistence. But worst of all, Llacsa and her children were prohibited by the contract from paying back the money in less than eight years. In a sense, Onofre need not have bothered to write that clause into the agreement since, given the rest of the conditions, it did not seem likely that they would be able to pay the money back at all.[67]

Despite its extremely oppressive nature, this contract is a good illustration of the general fabric of social relations that was developing in this period. Fidela Llacsa was a good example of a very small but growing stratum of peasants who lost all they had to the incursions of commercial capital. Forced to sell their property first, they were then slowly and inexorably reduced to selling their labor power and that of

---

[66] *Fuero de domicilio* is the provision of Peruvian law under which each citizen is guaranteed immunity from arrest and prosecution while he/she is within her/his house.

[67] ANF, Protocolos Notariales, Luis Salazar, Book 26: August 7, 1914, 955v–56v. For its similarities with *enganche* agreements, see the contracts reproduced in Zulen, "El enganche de indios," pp. 4–5; and ANF, Expedientes y Libros Judiciales, "Revisorio referente a la demanda verbal seguida ante el Juez de Paz de Segunda Nominación de esta Ciudad por Don Manuel Núñez Salinas, apoderado de Don Nicanor Galarza contra D. Pablo M. Hinostroza, sobre cantidad de soles," Jauja, 1904–1906. Also, it is particularly interesting, given the contribution that feminist literature has made to relating sexual and economic oppression, that four years after signing the contract, Llacsa was Onofre's mistress in Morococha. Though it is unclear whether Onofre thought that Llacsa's debt and promise to serve him naturally included sex, or Llacsa hoped to improve her position by becoming Onofre's mistress, in either case the relationship between the two kinds of oppression holds. See ANF, Expedientes y Libros Judiciales, "Hurtado contra Onofre," 824v.

their children. Antonio Onofre, for his part, was one of the three sons of Vicente Onofre, a peasant who had made his fortune in the mines during the nineteenth century. Antonio had followed his father to the mines while still in his teens, gaining valuable experience in the industry. With the arrival of the Cerro de Pasco Company, he and his brother Jacinto progressed very naturally to becoming *contratistas* in the company's mines at Morococha.[68]

Onofre's contract with Llacsa was just one example of the increasingly violent and oppressive exactions that wealthy peasants, in alliance with foreign capital and regional commercial capital, were committing against their poorer neighbors. In fact, it was precisely their alliance with foreign capital that gave peasants of Onofre's ilk the power and resources to tighten their networks of extraction. Although they had acted as brokers and intermediaries in the past, they had been forced to work within more narrowly and traditionally defined limits of legitimacy. Only with the arrival of the North American company did it became both possible and necessary to increase the oppressivo ness of these traditional networks.

Through the various concrete forms that commercial capital took in local society, wealthy peasants fulfilled their role as the handmaidens of foreign capital and its Peruvian allies. Some dedicated themselves to the accumulation of land, buying out the peasants who bordered on their best *chacras*, improving the properties through irrigation, channeling a greater part of their production to the market.[69] Others engaged in livestock-raising on a medium scale, farming out their cattle or sheep to poorer peasants who cared for them *al partir*.[70] Still others specialized more fully in commerce and moneylending, dominating the trade in potato, barley, and other seeds that developed with the commercialization of agriculture, working part-time as *subenganchadores*.[71] Whether or not they actually contracted laborers,

[68] In addition to Llacsa's case, see ANF, Luis Salazar, Book 26: November 27, 1918, 502–503v; Book 39: August 26, 1920, 1965v–67v; Book 41–42: January 7, 1921, 3–5, and February 11, 1929, 89v–91. For the story of the Onofres, see below.

[69] For the case of the Hurtados, see below. Such was also the case with the Palacios family of Chocón. See, for example, ANF, Protocolos Notariales, Luis Salazar, Book 15: January 2, 1906, 590–91v; Book 28: July 23, 1915, 479v–81; Book 29: December 31, 1915, 846v–47v; Book 32: April 18, 1917, 216–18; Book 33: November 3, 1917, 736–37v; and Book 35: December 24, 1918, 1850–51v.

[70] This was the case with the Espinoza family of Chocón. ANF, Expedientes y Libros Judiciales, "Pedro Blancas vs. Manuel S. Espinoza y otros, sobre robo de ganado," 1918.

[71] This was the case with Gregorio Bravo and Agustín Rafael, both merchants resident in Acolla. For Bravo, see ANF, Protocolos Notariales, Luis Salazar, Book 23: June 21, 1912, 896–97v; Book 31: October 23, 1916, 1605v–1607; Book 32: March 2, 1917,

they sped up the process of social and economic differentiation by monopolizing a greater proportion of the resources available at the village level, thus generating a more constant supply of seasonal labor for the productive sectors of the regional economy.

As we have seen previously, most wealthy peasant families had been rich for several generations, marrying among themselves and consolidating a position of social and political influence in their respective communities. But it was only with the beginning of foreign investment in the central highlands, and the resulting economic and commercial boom, that a number of them became the type of petty tyrants that are commonly referred to as *gamonales*. In addition to widening their access to land and wealth, they attempted to establish hegemony over entire villages or groups of villages. If they could not enforce and reproduce their authority through the manipulation of political and judicial institutions, they did not hesitate to use intimidation and physical violence. Of course, when their networks of patronage worked well, these newly emerging *gamonales* maintained a sense of generosity and reciprocity that guaranteed them the loyalty, and even sometimes the admiration, of their followers. Yet increasingly, village life developed a current of violent and almost ruthless exploitation that was never far below the surface. It was this darker, more hidden side of community life that tended to differentiate a peasant's existence in the early twentieth century from what had been possible in the nineteenth. But perhaps the only way to make this clear is by examining the historical development of these relationships at the local level by means of case studies. Among the several wealthy families who lived in the Yanamarca Valley at this time, two are particularly interesting: the Onofres, a mining-merchant family from Tragadero who worked as *contrastistas* in Morococha; and the Hurtados, merchants and commercial agriculturalists who lived in Marco and served as *subenganchadores* for several of the *enganche* firms in Jauja.

According to legend, the Onofres were not originally from the Yanamarca Valley. Available historical evidence would seem to bear this out, since the first reference to the family name is the presence in Tragadero, around the mid-nineteenth century, of Toribio Onofre.

103–104v; Book 34: February 6, 1918, 1023v–30; Book 36: February 10, 1919, 111v–13v; Book 46: October 24, 1922, between 2200 and 2201; APJ, "Solicitud de varios hijos y vecinos del Distrito de Acolla al Prefecto," Acolla, February 7, 1906. For Rafael, see ANF, Protocolos Notariales, Luis Salazar, Book 18: December 3, 1908, 841v and insert; Book 29: February 8, 1916, 920v–22, and February 28, 1916, 975v–77v; Book 39: August 31, 1920, 1995–96v; Book 41–42: March 4, 1921, 178–79; Expedientes y Libros Judiciales, "Hurtado contra Onofre," 917–23v.

Toribio apparently settled down in the valley, marrying a local woman by the name of Manuela Ortega. Little else is known about the couple, except that among their surviving children was a son, born in 1849, whom they named Vicente. At the age of thirty, Vicente Onofre married Rosa Rivera, daughter of *colonos* on the hacienda Cachicachi. They probably met, if one were to hazard a guess, while Vicente was plying the commercial route that, passing right through Cachicachi, connected Lima and Oroya to Tarma and Chanchamayo.[72]

Whatever the actual mechanics of the process, it is clear that the Onofre-Rivera household managed to accumulate a fair amount of wealth through labor migrations. By the turn of the century they had a flock of 400 sheep, and Vicente had spent enough time working in the mines to consider mining one of his occupations. Their teenage son, Antonio, had already migrated to the mines with his father on several occasions. Commerce was also an important activity for the family. Not only did they own three mules, but Vicente had developed personal contacts with several of Jauja's important merchants.[73] Thus, by the time the Cerro de Pasco Company arrived in the central highlands, the Onofres were already well established as miners and merchants. Yet after a mere five years of collaboration with the company, their former fortunes would pale by comparison.

As *contratistas* for the Morococha Mining Company at the San Francisco mine, Antonio and Jacinto Onofre were responsible for the entire production process. Aside from a few improvements in the transportation system, such as the use of small railway cars to transport the mineral within the mine and the installation of *jaulas* (elevators) to move the ore from one level to another, the labor system remained very similar to that of the nineteenth century. A group of workers called *perforadores* opened holes in the wall to put in dynamite. Then the workers left the mine until all the explosions had been accounted for. When they entered once again, the *lamperos* used picks and shovels to break up the loosened mineral, and the *carreros* loaded the small railway cars and directed them to the nearest *jaula*. Aside from this primitive division of labor, there were a few super-

[72] ANF, Expedientes y Libros Judiciales, "Rosa Rivera Vda. de Onofre contra el Ministerio Fiscal, Declaratoria de herederos del que fué don Antonio Onofre Rivera," April 24, 1937, especially 14; Interview with Elías Valenzuela Soto, Tragadero, October 22, 1977.
[73] APJ, "Censo del Valle de Yanamarca: Comunidad de Tragadero," 1899; ANF, Protocolos Notariales, Luis Salazar, Book 14: March 15, 1905, 77v and insert, April 4, 1905, 115–16v, and May 9, 1905, 178 and insert.

visors or foremen whose only claim to expertise was their friendship or special patron-client relationship with the Onofres.[74]

In general, therefore, the Morococha Mining Company simply planted itself at the top of a traditional production structure, reaping the benefits in the form of copper and silver ores, but without interfering in the process by which those ores were extracted. The Onofres, for their part, took advantage of the company's willingness to leave well enough alone. Since the company paid them by the ton, they made large profits in production by paying low wages, intensifying work rhythms, and lengthening the working day. Through their various stores in Morococha, they advanced food and other commodities to their workers and discounted an inflated price from wages. Thus they were able to repocket, through commerce, much of what they paid out. And they invested these resources in the accumulation of land, wealth, and power in Yauli and the Yanamarca Valley, insuring themselves a continued supply of labor for their enterprise.[75]

At the village level, the Onofres made use of every opportunity to drive a wedge into the peasant household economy. On the many occasions during the year when peasants needed money—at the marketplace, right before harvest, after a fiesta, when there was a death in the family—the Onofre brothers were always the first to offer cash advances. Not surprisingly, a condition followed almost immediately: "Please do me the favor of paying it back as a worker in the mines." At other times, the Onofre brothers generously offered to serve as intermediaries in a political or judicial problem, such as the forced drafting of a son into the army. But here again, generosity was short-lived. If the parents could not "reciprocate" with labor, they were forced to do so with land. And the effects of both kinds of "reciprocity" were clearly evident in Tragadero by the second decade of the twentieth century.[76]

Every Monday and Thursday, a dynamite explosion in the nearby hills signaled the departure for the mines. Most families had at least one relative who migrated, often to pay back a debt they had contracted on a previous trip, or because they had served as *fiadores* for

[74] Interview with Oscar Teófilo Camarena, Tragadero, November 29, 1977.

[75] Interviews with Elías Valenzuela Soto, Oscar Teófilo Camarena, and Francisco Solís Camarena, Tragadero, November 29, 1977; and a series of documents in ANF, Protocolos Notariales: see below, footnote 78.

[76] Interviews with Elías Valenzuela Soto and Francisco Solís Camarena, and Moisés Ortega Rojas, Acolla, February 6, 1978.

friends or relatives who had not kept their *enganche* obligations.[77] And the Onofres' *gamonalismo* was also visible on the land itself. Between 1907 and 1918, at the office of notary Luis Salazar alone, Antonio Onofre signed contracts on properties amounting to over 6,600 soles. Included within this were approximately thirty-five hectares of good land in various *chacras*, seven houses (one of them in Jauja and valued at 1,900 soles), and nearly ten small urban properties (*corrales* and *solares*). Of the nineteen separate contracts this represented, eleven were with peasants who seemed to be in need of money, most dramatically several widows who had to pay off the debts of their late husbands.[78]

According to some of the Onofres' opponents, by 1918 the brothers were in almost complete control of Tragadero and were threatening to turn the entire Yanamarca Valley into their personal hacienda.[79] Although this is somewhat of an exaggeration, the Onofres had achieved, in little more than a decade, a truly impressive level of wealth and dominance. The sons of an illiterate, upwardly mobile petty trader and the daughter of hacienda peons, Antonio and Jacinto had never acquired the polish of the well-established among the village elite. Indeed, Antonio was himself close to illiterate, and had engaged an aged and haughty local schoolteacher—whom everyone nicknamed Marcos "Tieso" (stiff)—to teach him the rudiments he needed to carry on his business.[80] That two such peasants could climb the ladder of success in a mere ten years smacks of Horatio Alger transplanted to the highlands of Peru. And perhaps it is only fitting, since it was a U.S. company that provided the favorable circumstances in which the Onofres could prosper. But none of this explains how the Onofres, once presented with the opportunity, were actually able to take ad-

[77] Interviews with Oscar Teófilo Camarena and Elías Valenzuela Soto; ANF, Protocolos Notariales, Luis Salazar, Book 18: April 14, 1908, 468 and insert, December 5, 1908, 841v and insert, December 29, 1908, 895v and insert; Book 20: May 2, 1910, 712 and insert; Book 23: June 20, 1912, 891v–92 and insert; Book 29: October 17, 1915, 638–39; and passim.

[78] ANF, Protocolos Notariales, Luis Salazar, Book 17: November 18, 1907, 323–24v; Book 18: March 11, 1908, 412–14, March 19, 1908, 428v–30v, March 30, 1908, 450–51v, April 18, 1908, 475v–76v, June 26, 1908, 562v–64, July 28, 1908, 611–12; Book 20: May 17, 1910, 739v–40v; Book 22: January 10, 1911, 20–21v; Book 26: December 10, 1913, 523–24v, April 18, 1914, 750–51v; Book 32: January 23, 1917, 42–43v, April 18, 1917, 220–21v, July 25, 1917, 438v–40; Book 33: August 20, 1917, 506v–508, August 20, 1917, 508–10, January 18, 1918, 954–55, January 19, 1918, 956v–58; Books 33–34: January 30, 1918, 1000–1001v.

[79] APJ, "Solicitud de las comunidades indígenas de los Distritos de Marco y Acolla y otros al Presidente de la República," Marco, June 12, 1918.

[80] Interviews with Elías Valenzuela Soto and Francisco Solís Camarena.

vantage of it, both establishing and maintaining a position of power in local society. When one looks carefully at the intricate fabric of local life, there seems to be only one answer to that final and most important question. They did it through violence.

On December 6, 1914, a poor peasant from Acaya named Juan Rafael presented a complaint to the subprefect of Jauja. According to his story, he had been on his way home from Jauja the night before when Santiago and Tiburcio Misari, well-off merchants and agriculturalists from the community of Tragadero, had come up to him on horseback, somewhat drunk, and tried to take his money. When Rafael resisted, Tiburcio Misari had hit him with some stones, and then both brothers had beaten him into unconsciousness. It was only thanks to five travellers who came by just then, Rafael concluded, that he survived the attack, for the Misari brothers were at that point ready to kill him. At five o'clock the next morning, while Tiburcio Misari was still in bed in Tragadero, he was arrested by Antonio Onofre and brought to jail in Jauja. As the trial progressed, the connection between the Onofre brothers and Rafael became more and more obvious.

Although in many court cases it is difficult to establish the actual facts, the following explanation, put together on the basis of several sources, seems the most reasonable. Previous to Rafael's accusation, Tiburcio Misari had been involved in a conflict with Aurelio Onofre, Antonio and Jacinto's half-brother, over a *chacra* in Tragadero's Curicancha neighborhood. On one occasion the two had actually come to blows, with Misari winning the fight until Jacinto Onofre intervened. At that point the tide turned against Tiburcio, and he was left with both eyes swollen, his face distorted, and the top of his right ear torn away from his head. It was in this context, with Tiburcio still in bed from the attack he had suffered, that Rafael accused him and his brother of attempted murder. Yet as soon as Rafael made the initial accusation, he disappeared from view and left the entire prosecution up to Antonio Onofre.

Onofre brought Rafael's witnesses before a judge in Morococha and, according to the Misaris, used his influence with Yauli's political and judicial authorities to fake a number of the testimonies. As it turned out, moreover, Rafael was himself a debtor and servant of the Onofres and, at least in the version of several witnesses, had suffered the blows he attributed to the Misaris at the hands of Aurelio and Jacinto Onofre. As the same witnesses explained, Rafael had allowed himself to be beaten by the Onofres so that they would cancel a debt of 200 soles he owed them. In exchange, he promised to accuse the Misaris of having perpetrated the attack.[81]

It is here that we begin to understand most clearly how the Onofres reproduced their power at the local level. Because the Misaris had an independent position of wealth in Tragadero and had come into direct conflict with the Onofres, they could not go unpunished. Both through direct physical violence, and by embroiling them in costly and lengthy court battles, the Onofres hoped to beat the Misaris back into line. But most importantly, this battle was not an isolated case. Through a seemingly endless web of litigation—complaints to the political authorities, court cases, and documents of various kinds—the Onofres attempted to expand and reproduce their networks of patronage. Using their debtors, clients, workers, and servants as witnesses, they wove such convoluted tales of intrigue, wrongdoing, and violence that even the most impartial judge had difficulty disentangling the various pieces of conflicting evidence. If their clients refused to testify, or if the witnesses for the opposing side seemed too convincing, the Onofres did not hesitate to use direct intimidation or even brute force to turn around the various testimonies. And these were the gentlest tactics for, in a number of instances, the brothers showed a complete lack of respect for life and limb, beating up servants, blowing up their own houses, even injuring or killing their own mistresses, in order to blame the actions on one of their enemies.[82]

Yet no matter how graphically violent these relationships were, they

---

[81] ANF, Expedientes y Libros Judiciales, "Juan Rafael contra Santiago y Tiburcio Misari, por asalto en despoblado, flagelaciones, intento de robo y homicidio a mano armada," began in Jauja, December 6, 1914; Interviews with Elías Valenzuela Soto and Francisco Solís Camarena.

[82] On the Misaris' independent position of wealth, see ANF, Protocolos Notariales, Luis Salazar, Book 14: March 28, 1905, 92–93v; Book 17: October 18, 1907, 282v–84; Book 20: November 18, 1909, 486v–88v; Book 22: January 25, 1911, 46–47, February 15, 1911, 94–95v; Book 24: August 26, 1912, 1017v–19, December 12, 1912, 1226v–27v; Book 29: December 14, 1915, 793v–94v. For the general tenor of the Onofres' social relations, see ANF, Protocolos Notariales, Luis Salazar, Book 25: September 29, 1913, 394v–95; Book 32: June 26, 1917, 371–72; Expedientes y Libros Judiciales, "Rafael Contra Misaris;" and "Hurtado contra Onofre,"especially 1135–35v, 1276–80; APJ, "Queja de varios ciudadanos del pueblo de Marco, dirigida al Prefecto del Departamento, en contra del gobernador de Marco Lucio Galarza," Marco, September 20, 1910; "Oficio del Senador Villarán al Ministro de Estado en el Despacho de Gobierno," Lima, May 18, 1918; "Oficio de las comunidades indígenas de los Distritos de Marco y Acolla," Marco, June 12, 1918; "Oficio de varios vecinos de la provincia de Jauja defendiendo a los Onofre," Jauja, June 20, 1918; "Oficio de varios vecinos de Janjaillo, distrito de Marco, acusando a los Hurtado de falsedad," Janjaillo, June 26, 1918; interviews with Elías Valenzuela Soto and Francisco Solís Camarena, and conversations with Moisés Ortega in Acolla, throughout 1977.

also rested on a more peaceful, everyday manipulation of influence and patronage. In addition to the bevy of clients with whom they wielded the iron fist, the Onofres also maintained a select group of friends and retainers to whom they showed mainly the velvet glove. Such was the case, for example, with several judges in Jauja and Yauli, as well as numerous district or provincial political authorities. It was true in the case of José T. Ampuero, Laureano and Elías Maita Saavedra, all *tinterillos* in Jauja who, in exchange for economic and political favors, would keep their patrons informed of the proceedings in specific court cases or advise them on the legal niceties of enforcing debts, writing documents, or buying lands.[83] And there were also a number of petty merchants from Tragadero and Marco, including Oscar and Higinio Camarena, Raimundo Romero, and Julián Mandujano, who owed most of their prosperity to the Onofres. Oscar Camarena, for example, the son of a very poor family in Tragadero, had migrated to work in Morococha and caught the eye of the brothers. They promoted him to foreman of *lamperos* and *carreros*, and finally gave him one of their stores to administer. More than fifty years later, even after a number of problems, Camarena would still maintain his loyalty to the Onofres. Such dedication could not be acquired or maintained exclusively through violence.[84]

For the Onofres, then, it was on the cutting edge between unbridled violence and bland generosity that they sharpened their weapons and reproduced their power. Those who cooperated with them received protection and the opportunity to participate in the profits generated by an expanding regional economy. Those who resisted, or merely seemed too independent, suffered the full weight of vengeance in the form of political or judicial proceedings, violence, and even death. When the system worked smoothly, generosity was allowed to dominate over force. When the relationships seemed to falter, violence came to the fore. Ideally, of course, the mere threat of violence should have been enough to enforce existing networks. Yet as the second decade of the century came to a close, it seemed that the Onofres were increasingly called upon to make good on their threats.

One important reason for increased conflict in the Yanamarca Valley was an ever more direct contest for hegemony between the Onofres of Tragadero and the Hurtados of Marco, whose history has been

[83] A *tinterillo* is someone versed in the legal process, whether a lawyer or not, who profits from—and therefore tends to instigate or encourage—litigation.

[84] In addition to all the sources on the Onofres cited in footnote 82, interview with Oscar Teófilo Camarena.

traced in earlier chapters. Like the Onofres, the Hurtados were not originally from the valley. At some point during the nineteenth century an ancestor had settled in Marco, most probably a petty trader from Jauja or Concepción, and married into village society. Yet by the time the second generation married and began to have children in the 1870s and 1880s, the Hurtados were nicely integrated into the stratum of village notables. Closely tied to many important merchants in Jauja, the members of this stratum profited greatly from their position as intermediaries and, by the end of the nineteenth century, were already controlling local politics and engaging in commercial agriculture. The Hurtado clan quickly rose to a position of prominence within the village elite, and their fortune expanded even further after the arrival of the Cerro de Pasco Company in 1903. Yet rather than serve directly as employees of the foreign company, the Hurtados dedicated themselves to profitable subsidiary activities within the village economy.

The different ways in which the Hurtados and Onofres took advantage of the favorable conjuncture created by foreign capital are, of course, related to their previous histories of accumulation. In contrast to the Onofres, the Hurtados were not nouveaux riches. Because the first Hurtado to arrive in Marco already had some resources, at least by village standards, the family was not forced to migrate in search of wealth. Instead, the Hurtados concentrated on extending and reproducing their fortune within village society. Particularly through the "exchange of women"[85]—quite literally the exchange of marriageable women between lineages with the purpose of strengthening the bonds between men—the Hurtado clan developed kinship ties with many of the wealthiest peasant families in Marco and Tragadero. These links were then extended even further through the selective use of ritual kinship. The final result was an extensive web of personal relations that served to firmly root the family, both politically and economically, in the community. And it was these relationships, rather than any migration or mining experience, that the Hurtados could most successfully exploit in the context of foreign investment.[86]

[85] This concept is developed theoretically in Gayle Rubin, "The Traffic in Women: Notes on the 'Political Economy' of Sex," in Rayna R. Reiter (ed.), *Toward an Anthropology of Women* (New York: Monthly Review Press, 1975), pp. 157–210; and Kate Young, Presentation at the symposium "The Development of Capitalism in Agriculture and the Peasantry: Theoretical Perspectives," Annual Meeting of the Latin American Studies Association, Pittsburgh, April 6, 1979.

[86] The following sources provide an overview of the Hurtado family's position and relationships in Marco: ANF, Protocolos Notariales, Book 17: January 13, 1908, 361–

Between 1905 and 1910 the Hurtado family, in alliance with other wealthy peasants, moved to consolidate its position on the western side of the Yanamarca Valley. As had been the case during previous periods of commercialization, the economic boom generated by the arrival of foreign capital led to an intensification of competition between the valley's eastern and western communities, particularly Marco and Acolla. One of the main reasons for the conflict was the emergence in Acolla, around the turn of the century, of a newly prosperous group of merchants. Anxious to extend their hegemony within the village economy, these traders had seized control of local municipal posts. Because this presented a direct challenge to the *Marqueños'* historical dominance in district politics, rising tensions between the two communities naturally focused on the question of Marco's status within the political district.[87] But the underlying issues had much more to do with control of labor and access to political power at the provincial level.

In the first months of 1907, a group of wealthy peasants from Marco and Concho wrote two letters to the prefect of Junín, protesting the actions of Acolla's governor, Gregorio C. Bravo. According to the plaintiffs, Bravo was forcing people from the villages to travel to Oroya with their animals and bring back to Jauja construction materials that were needed for a school. When the lieutenant governor of Concho refused to provide the men Bravo had requested, he was sent to jail in Jauja. Then Bravo's agents travelled through the communities, leaving small amounts of money at the doors of the houses. This was clearly abusive, the peasants wrote, not only because it tried to give the appearance of legality to an exploitative practice, but also because in Oroya there were plenty of *arrieros* ready and eager to transport the materials for a fair price. Moreover, since the prefects had already issued many decrees against forced servitude, both by individuals and

62; Book 26: February 5, 1914, 608–609v; Book 31: December 1, 1916, 1689v–91v; Book 33: September 26, 1917, 621–24; Expedientes y Libros Judiciales, "Hurtado contra Onofre," especially 835, 836–36v, 884–85, 1087v–92; "Rafael contra Misaris," especially 147, 201–203v; "Santiago Motto vs. José C., Narcizo y Ezequiel Hurtado," especially 39; APJ, "Queja de varios ciudadanos de Marco," 1910; "Oficio de varios vecinos de la provincia de Jauja," 1918; "Oficio de varios vecinos de Janjaillo," 1918; interviews with Elías Valenzuela Soto, Francisco Solís Camarena, Oscar Teófilo Camarena; and conversations with Moisés Ortega.

[87] For the merchants in Acolla, in addition to the sources in footnote 70, see AMA, Libro de Correspondencia, 1908–1934, pp. 54, 80, 99. For the battle over district status, see ANF, Protocolos Notariales, Luis Salazar, Book 14: July 16, 1905, 271v–74, September 15, 1905, 375v–78; Book 15: April 12, 1906, 769v–71v; Book 17: August 11, 1907, 192–94.

communities, it was no longer possible to ignore the illegality of the practice. Thus, the petitioners concluded, the district authorities should conform to the law:

> The villages of Marco, Concho and others that compose the district of Acolla, do not wish to serve as instruments for transporting, in the old style, those materials, as has been decided by the whim of privileged people . . . they should celebrate their contracts in a way that is accessible to justice and to equality before the law.[88]

Not surprisingly it was the Hurtado clan, along with other well-off villagers, who signed this document of protest. They also headed the subsequent effort, in August of the same year, to formally break off from Acolla and found their own district. As they explained in the contract giving power of attorney to Juan de Dios Salazar, national deputy for the province of Jauja, "It is completely impossible for our town to remain in the condition in which it presently finds itself."[89] And their strategy proved successful. On October 28, 1907, the village of Marco became the capital of a new district, taking with it the *anexos* of Acaya, Concho, Curicaca, Huashua, Janjaillo, Pomacancha, and Tragadero. The *Marqueños* had established their own private sphere of influence.[90]

The Hurtado family, along with their relatives, associates, and other village notables, dominated Marco's municipal council during its first decade of existence. Since according to municipal law the district council had access to revenue and community labor drafts from all the *anexos*, control of political office gave the *Marqueño* elite the resources necessary to expand and reproduce their prestige and hegemony. One way to increase prestige, for example, was by initiating a program of public works that, under the unwritten laws of traditional reciprocity, distinguished its organizers as generous, concerned members of the community. Thus Narcizo Hurtado managed, during his two years as mayor, to regularize the system of public lighting in the plaza, clean and repair the irrigation ditches, and begin constructing the tower for the village chapel. His brother Ezequiel, who succeeded him in the post, led a battle against the exactions of the parish priest and took

[88] APJ, "Queja de varios vecinos de Marco y Concho al Prefecto del Departamento, sobre los procedimientos del gobernador del distrito de Acolla," Marco, January 15, 1907.

[89] ANF, Protocolos Notariales, Luis Salazar, Book 17: August 11, 1907, 192–94.

[90] APJ, "Cuadro de Gobernadores de la provincia de Jauja," Jauja, December 11, 1914; AMM, Libro de Actas del Concejo Muncipal, I (1907–1918): 14.

control of the local cemetery after many of the district's citizens complained that the priest charged too much for burials.[91]

As had been the custom in the nineteenth century, such accumulations of "social capital" could easily be privatized at some future date. Just as Manuel E. Landa had used Concho's commmunity labor to build his house in the 1890s, so José C. Hurtado used community labor from Pomacancha in 1916 to make six thousand adobe bricks for his new residence in Jauja.[92] Four years later, the village of Marco granted Narcizo and Ezequiel free usufruct of the community lands of Azapampa for an entire year, as recompense for "the important services they have performed, especially in the judicial defense and recuperation of these same lands of Azapampa."[93] But in addition to providing new ways for rich peasants to engage in relationships of asymmetrical reciprocity, control of the district council opened up more direct and immediate channels for the accumulation of wealth.

During their consecutive terms as mayors of Marco (1909–1915), the Hurtado brothers found two particularly fruitful paths for accumulation. The first of these was the urbanization of the village, which entailed opening up a series of new streets and blocks near the center of the population and naturally led to a rise in land values in the area. Both immediately before and after he initiated the urbanization program, therefore, Narcizo also engaged in a little private speculation, buying up several *chacras* in the center of town.[94] But the reorganization of the irrigation system proved to be a more lasting investment for the brothers. After the ditches were repaired in 1910, Narcizo proposed to the municipal council that a special water inspector be appointed to give tickets to each owner of irrigated property, specifying the time and length of irrigation for each *chacra*. Since the hours of water available to each property owner were proportional to the number or size of the *chacras* they had to irrigate, the establishment of a working system for irrigation control favored those who were substantial owners of irrigated property. And the Hurtados certainly belonged in that group: of the fifteen land purchases in Marco district

[91] AMM, Libro de Actas del Concejo Municipal, I:3–5, 18, 19, 23, 28–29, 30–31, 33–35, 38–40, 44–47, 49–54, 62–63, 65–66, 76, 94, 121–22, 144, 166–74.

[92] For Manuel E. Landa's case, see above, Chapter IV. For José C. Hurtado, see ANF, Protocolos Notariales, Luis Salazar, Book 31: December 1, 1916, 1689v–91v.

[93] ANF, Protocolos Notariales, Luis Salazar, Book 40: December 3, 1920, 2382v–84v. The trial was brought by the neighboring community of Janjaillo. See Book 26: February 5, 1914, 608–609v; Book 33: September 26, 1917, 621–24.

[94] AMM, Libro de Actas del Concejo Municipal, I, July 10, 1911, pp. 52–54; ANF, Protocolos Notariales, Luis Salazar, Book 21: December 10, 1910, 1155v–57; Book 24: November 13, 1912, 1169–70v; Book 26: May 15, 1914, 806v–808.

that the Hurtados made at the Salazar notarial office between 1908 and 1918, thirteen were irrigated.[95]

In contrast to the Onofres, therefore, the Hurtados began their alliance with foreign capital from a strong position of local social and political power. In this context it was only natural that the family concentrate on developing their activities and connections within the village economy; for, as we have seen, the purpose and effect of foreign investment in this initial period was not to transform the mode of production, but to use, strengthen, and reorganize existing relationships within local society. Thus the Hurtados, rather than working as *contratistas*, became *subenganchadores*. Through their family's relationships of patronage and clientele and their control of district politics, the Hurtado brothers encouraged the signing of *enganche* contracts, collected on *enganche* debts for Jauja merchants, and served as agents in the prosecutions and property auctions that followed non-payment.[96] Yet despite its profitability, *enganche* never became more than a sideline for the Hurtados. Much more central to the overall family enterprise was the development of commercial agriculture.

While the Onofre and Hurtado families both viewed the acquisition of landed property as important to the reproduction of power and prestige, the Hurtados also purchased land out of more purely economic motives. This difference emerges very clearly from a comparison of the Onofre and Hurtado land contracts that were celebrated at Salazar's notarial office between 1908 and 1918. Of the eighteen transactions involving Onofre, only one specified that the land had irrigation, and one concerned a property that bordered on the buyer's land. Of the twenty transactions involving the Hurtados, on the other hand, eleven were on irrigated properties and six on lands that had a common boundary with other Hurtado properties. And the two categories

[95] For the reorganization of the irrigation system, see AMM, Libro de Actas, I, April 28, 1910, 33–35; June 19, 1911, 49 and 51; July 3, 1912, 65–66. For the Hurtados' land purchases, see ANF, Protocolos Notariales, Luis Salazar, Book 18: October 13, 1908, 757–58v; Book 21: December 10, 1910, 1155v–57; Book 22: July 21, 1911, 371v–73; Book 23: August 16, 1912, 996v–98, 998–99; Book 24: November 13, 1912, 1169–70v; Book 26: May 15, 1914, 806v–808; Book 27: November 26, 1914, 1190–91v; Book 31: September 7, 1916, 1501–1502v, October 13, 1916, 1577v–79, November 11, 1916, 1637–38v; Book 32: January 25, 1917, 50v–51v, March 5, 1917, 107–108v; Book 34: February 18, 1918, 1062v–64; Book 35: October 18, 1918, 1655v–57.

[96] ANF, Protocolos Notariales, Luis Salazar, Book 13: September 19, 1904, 764–65v; Book 20: June 22, 1910, 799v and insert; Book 32: February 12, 1917, 73–79; Expedientes y Libros Judiciales, "Hurtado contra Onofre," 938–38v; Interview with Oscar Teófilo Camarena; Conversations with Moisés Ortega.

were closely related: of the six properties that the Hurtados purchased to add on to lands they already owned, five had irrigation.[97]

What is significant about this pattern, however, is not simply that the Hurtado family used their land for commercial purposes. As we have already seen, the trend toward commercialization in agriculture had been obvious among the wealthy peasantry during the nineteenth century. Nor did commercial production by itself differentiate the Hurtados from the Onofres, since even a cursory glance at Antonio Onofre's purchases—the size of the properties, what crops they were used for, and where they were located—makes clear that he was also using his land, at least in part, for market crops.[98] The real difference, then, was not the accumulation of land for commercial production viewed in the abstract, but rather the rationale behind it.

As is evident from the pattern of land contracts, the Hurtados did not accumulate land for its own sake, but to rationalize their system of land tenure. Over and over, they purchased land in clumps. In August 1912, for example, Ezequiel Hurtado bought two small pieces of land from the Yupanqui brothers in the *paraje* of Jatuncorral. In addition to having irrigation, these two *chacras* bordered on lands already belonging to Ezequiel. Then in October 1914 and September 1915, Ezequiel made two ten-hectare purchases in Tingo Paccha, an hacienda undergoing a process of fragmentation through inheritance. Although neither property was irrigated, the fact that they bordered on each other and were for cereal production suggests the beginnings of more rational commercial agriculture. And most importantly, in December 1916, Narcizo Hurtado bought half of the hacienda Quishuarcancha, a total of 7,000 hectares, which included 2,500 irrigated hectares for quinoa and potatoes and 1,500 hectares of irrigated pasture for dairy cattle.[99] Thus for the Hurtados, the overall purpose of land accumulation seems to have been the more efficient exploitation of commercial properties. But it would also be a mistake to overstate the importance of this trend.

Despite the very real difference in their patterns and styles of ac-

[97] For the contracts involving Onofre, see footnote 78. For those involving Hurtado, see footnote 94 and ANF, Protocolos Notariales, Luis Salazar, Book 27: October 19, 1914, 1094v–96; Book 29: September 9, 1915, 584–85v; Book 31: December 6, 1916, 1711–15; Book 33: January 21, 1918, 968–69; Book 34: March 18, 1918, 1148–49v.

[98] See especially ANF, Protocolos Notariales, Luis Salazar, Book 18: April 18, 1908, 475v–76v; Book 20: May 17, 1910, 739v–40v; Book 26: December 10, 1913, 523–24v, April 18, 1914, 750–51v; Book 32: January 23, 1917, 42–43v.

[99] ANF, Protocolos Notariales, Luis Salazar, Book 23: August 16, 1912, 996v–98, 998–99; Book 27: October 19, 1914, 1094v–96; Book 29: September 9, 1915, 584–85v; Book 31: December 6, 1916, 1711–15.

cumulation, the Onofre and Hurtado families were essentially two variations on a single theme. Though they were clearly interested in the more rational use of their lands, the Hurtados continued to exploit their properties with labor acquired through debt and compulsion. Like the Onofres, they signed contracts condemning peasants and their families to long-term personal servitude. In one particular case, Ezequiel went as far as literally to buy the person and services of the one-year-old illegitimate child of a poor peasant woman.[100] And while the Hurtados could rely on established networks of patronage and constant control of local political institutions to enforce and reproduce their hegemony less harshly than the Onofres, their dominance still rested on the ultimate capacity to use force. Thus, when Florián Hurtado returned from Lima with a university education and *indigenista* ideas concerning equality and rights for the Indian, he had several confrontations with his older brothers Narcizo and Ezequiel over their complicity in the *enganche* system. As a result, Narcizo's brother-in-law apparently fired a gun at Florián on several occasions.[101]

Whether or not extraction was accomplished elegantly, it generated a process of social and economic differentiation that had increasingly onerous repercussions within the peasant society and economy. On one side were the wealthy peasants, of whom the Onofres and Hurtados were only the most dramatic examples, accumulating land, profiting from commerce, extending their webs of patronage and power. On the other was a growing stratum of poor peasants being pushed slowly and inexorably to the brink of landlessness. In the middle, the majority of peasants were forced to migrate more and more regularly to keep the family economy afloat. And yet, despite these developments, peasant households were successful at using a variety of strategies to partially stem the tide of proletarianization.

Peasant Resistance in the "Manufacturing Period"

Particularly after two explosions at Goyllarisquisga claimed numerous lives in 1910, a group of Lima intellectuals, including progressive

[100] The particular case of the peasant woman and her child appears in ANF, Protocolos Notariales, Luis Salazar, Book 41–42: February 11, 1921, 89v–91. For other cases, see Book 39: August 26, 1920, 1965v–67v; Book 41–42: January 7, 1921, 3–5; Book 43: August 12, 1921, 671–73; Book 44: November 30, 1921, 1081v–82v; Book 46: December 12, 1922, 2331v–32v.

[101] Conversations with Moisés Ortega; AMM, Libro de Actas del Concejo Muncipal, I, February 21, 1918, pp. 166–74; ANF, Expedientes y Libros Judiciales, "Hurtado contra Onofre," 1145.

politicians, members of the *Asociación Pro-Indígena*, and some mining engineers, protested against the abuses of the Cerro de Pasco Company. According to Peruvian law, they pointed out, the safety of the workers was the company's responsibility. Yet local and national authorities were so partial to the North American corporation that it was impossible to enforce compliance. In addition to the lack of safety precautions, progressives also condemned other aspects of the company's treatment of the workers: *enganche*, poor housing, no schools, payment in scrip, the company store, lack of compensation, and inadequate medical care. Many saw the solution to all these problems in increased government regulation and a less servile attitude toward foreign investors.[102] But although the Civilista governments in the early twentieth century had certainly thrown their lot in with foreign capital, many of the specific problems in the mining sector had to do with the particular stage of development in which the industry found itself.

Since in this early period the Cerro de Pasco Corporation did not invest in transforming the system of production, it depended for its profits on a bountiful supply of cheap, unskilled labor. It was not in the interest of the company, therefore, to invest money in providing safety equipment, schools, medical care, or any other benefit to a labor force that was transitory and, because it had no special skills, expendable. The best thing the company could do, from its own point of view, was to continue to employ seasonal migrants who had other means of subsistence in their communities. Not only did this help to keep wages low, but it also minimized labor unrest, since most peasants considered their main interests to be elsewhere.[103]

In fact, it was because most peasants remained in the mines for only a short period of time, rather than because they were inherently conservative or "prepolitical," that there were few manifestations of working class consciousness among miners in this period. There was

---

[102] For some examples of the progressive literature protesting working conditions and abuses in the mining industry, see Mayer, *La conducta*, and *Un decreto libertador*; Alvarado Rivera, *El aniquilamiento*; Denegri, "La crísis del enganche"; Mostajo, *Algunas ideas*; Zulen, "El enganche de indios," pp. 4–5; APJ, "Oficio del Director de Fomento E. Habich al Prefecto del Departamento," Lima, July 5, 1910; "Oficio del Director de Fomento E. Habich al Prefecto del Departamento," Lima, August 29, 1913; "Oficio del Director de Salubridad Pública Olaechea al Representante de la Empresa Minera," Lima, August 9, 1918; and BCIM, No. 25 and No. 65.

[103] For other examples of this line of reasoning, see DeWind, "Peasants Become Miners," Chapter 3 and passim; Florencia E. Mallon, "Microeconomía y Campesinado: Hacienda, comunidad y coyunturas económicas en el Valle de Yanamarca," *Análisis*, No. 4 (January–April 1978): especially pp. 48–50.

no reason to face repression, loss of job, or any other risk that mobilization entailed, for something that occupied a marginal position in one's life. Moreover, since most people were transients, there were few opportunities to develop the kind of community among workers that could provide support in case of strike or other forms of protest. Often, the closest most miners came to a sense of group solidarity was with their fellow villagers. It is therefore not surprising that the earliest spontaneous protests seemed to be organized along community lines. In 1908, for example, after a horrible explosion in the Peña Blanca mine in Cerro de Pasco, the entire contingent of workers from Chongos, a village in the Mantaro Valley, left en masse and returned home.[104] But in addition to these spontaneous outbursts, a number of more defined strikes broke out before 1920. They pointed to the fact that, given half a chance, peasants were willing to confront the company on its own terms.

The location of these early strikes tends to support the hypothesis that a certain level of commitment to location, job, and fellow workers must exist before it seems reasonable to engage in serious, planned protest. Although the general population of miners did strike in April 1912, demanding that the company pay for the carbide consumed by their safety lamps,[105] the other mobilizations mentioned in the documents were usually concentrated among workers in the more industrialized sectors of the company's operations, particularly the coal mines, railroad, and smelter. In all these cases, there seems to have been a higher level of skill and job stability. Indeed, even the recruitment policy in these sectors was different: the company seemed to prefer people with more extensive mining and urban experience for jobs in transportation and smelting, while preferring recent rural migrants for the heavier and unskilled work in the mines themselves.[106]

The demands presented by workers in the more industrialized sectors also reflected their greater interest in permanence and job stability. In 1909, for example, the stokers at the Cerro de Pasco Railway Company not only demanded higher wages, but also a nine-hour working day and consideration of seniority when the company gave promotions—hardly the demands of a transient labor force.[107] In 1917, when the coalminers from Goyllarisquisga and Quishuarcancha, the machinists, stokers, and other workers from the railroad, and the la-

---

[104] Mayer, *La conducta*, p. 53.
[105] Ibid., p. 55.
[106] Kruijt and Vellinga, *Labor Relations*, pp. 62–63.
[107] Mayer, *La conducta*, pp. 53–54.

bor force at the smelter went out on strike, their delegations demanded, in addition to higher wages and shorter hours, the extension of free medical care and the provision of food and other subsistence needs at cost.[108] Even in those mobilizations with broader participation, the special position and militance of workers from the more industrialized sections of the company was evident. Thus, when the *comisario* of Morococha sent a letter to the prefect reporting on local plans for a general strike in 1921, he mentioned specifically that it was being organized, instigated, and led by the railroad workers who, in his opinion, were "an element always disposed toward that sort of movement."[109]

But these actions, and the high levels of repression that accompanied them, were not the rule at this point.[110] Until the 1920s, the majority of the labor force was composed of seasonal *enganchados*, much of the mining was done by *contratistas*, and strikes remained harbingers of things to come. Of course, this did not mean that there was no resistance. But because most mineworkers were still more peasant than miner, they continued to use the weapons for class struggle they had developed in their communities.

[108] APJ, "Oficio de la Comición de los Trabajadores de los Talleres de Mecánica de la Cerro de Pasco Railway Company al Prefecto del Departamento de Junín," Cerro de Pasco, May 29, 1917; "Informe del Subprefecto de Pasco al Prefecto del Departamento," Cerro de Pasco, June 1, 1917; "Conclusiones acordadas entre los delegados de los Obreros de la Sección Minas de la Cerro de Pasco Mining Company y el Representante de Esta," Cerro de Pasco, June 1, 1917; "Conclusiones Acordadas entre los delegados de los obreros de las minas de Goyllarisquisga de la Cerro de Pasco Mining Company y el Representante de Esta," Goyllarisquisga, May 31, 1917; "Conclusiones Acordadas entre los delegados de los obreros de la Cerro de Pasco Railway Company de las secciones Casa Redonda y Departamento de Carros y el Representante de la Expresada Compañía," Cerro de Pasco, June 1, 1917; "Conclusiones acordadas entre los delegados de los fogoneros, carboneros y brequeros de la línea de la Cerro de Pasco Railway Company y el Representante de esta compañía," Cerro de Pasco, June 1, 1917; "Conclusiones acordadas entre los delegados de los obreros de las minas de Quishuarcancha de la Cerro de Pasco Mining Company y el Representante de Esta," Quishuarcancha, June 1, 1917; "Acuerdo entre el Superintendente del Smelter y los delegados nombrados debidamente por los trabajadores," La Fundición, November 29, 1917.

[109] APJ, "Oficio del Comisario de Morococha al Prefecto del Departamento," May 28, 1921. A *comisario* is similar to a chief of police. There were, of course, other movements and strikes in the mining centers in this period, most of which tend to confirm the differences among various sectors of the labor force, depending on all the factors mentioned. For a good summary of other mobilizations, see Flores Galindo, *Los mineros*, pp. 67–78.

[110] Although repression would get much worse later on, there were already several examples of deportations and framing of militants in this early period. See, for example, Mayer, *La conducta*, p. 54; and APJ, "Informe reservado del comisario de policía al Subprefecto de Pasco, sobre los antecedentes de don Horacio Mieses," La Fundición, October 11, 1921.

Even though the peasant sector in the central highlands had historically been quite permeable to the penetration of commercial capital, it also turned out to be extremely resistant to complete proletarianization. In a sense, both tendencies coexisted within the structure of the household economy. Because agriculture was seasonal and yields fluctuated greatly, peasants had, from early in the colonial period, participated in market relations and worked in other sectors or tasks during parts of the year. This made households extremely open to the incursions of commercial capital, and led easily to the internal differentiation of peasant communities. Yet at the same time, the open nature of the family economy protected it from ultimate destruction. Because the family unit combined income from a variety of activities, it could continue to survive, even as it lost access to land and other means of production, by changing the balance of income provided by the different economic sectors. In many cases, moreover, it was possible to transfer income from one sector to another, using money earned in handicraft production, commerce, or wage labor to buy land or, as many migrants did, taking animals and crops to the mines to keep expenses down and aid in accumulation.[111]

Thus, although the first two decades of the twentieth century witnessed a general trend toward the impoverishment and expropriation of the peasantry, the peasant household was able to remain viable through the shrewd manipulation of alternatives and the careful and thorough exploitation of available resources. In the end, this entailed a constant, day-to-day confrontation between the peasantry and the modernizing sectors of the regional economy. And even though the struggle was often defined in terms of backwardness versus modernity, or conservatism versus rationality, at bottom it was a battle over income, labor, and means of production. For the peasants, it was not a question of tradition, but simply of survival.

There were many instances in which a struggle over subsistence seemed to the uninformed observer to be merely resistance to change. In 1908, for example, a North American engineer reported that work-

---

[111] For the operation of the household economy during commercialized parts of the colonial period, see Steve J. Stern, *Peru's Indian Peoples and the Challenge of Spanish Conquest: Huamanga to 1640* (Madison: University of Wisconsin Press, 1982). For examples of transference of income from one sector to another during the nineteenth and twentieth centuries, see above, Chapter II, and below, Chapter VII; BCIM, Nos. 25 and 65; Carlos Samaniego, "Peasant Movements at the Turn of the Century and the Rise of the Independent Farmer," in Long and Roberts (eds.), *Peasant Cooperation*, pp. 45–71; the editors' "Introduction," pp. 3–43; and their "Peasant Coooperation and Underdevelopment in Central Peru," pp. 297–328.

ers in the mines had refused a company offer to work six eight-hour shifts per week instead of nine ten-hour shifts per week, despite the fact they would be paid the same amount in wages. "These customs are . . . deeply rooted in the minds of an ignorant people," the engineer concluded. "This is merely one example of the stupidity of the native miners."[112] Yet, as a recent study has pointed out, if we keep in mind that most workers were peasants who had been hired by the shift, a different explanation emerges:

> It seems that the *enganchados* preferred to finish more shifts a week, even if this meant longer hours, rather than to work fewer shifts per week and prolong the time which they had to stay in the mines.[113]

The same pattern could be seen in other sectors of the regional economy. In 1917, the administrator of the Sociedad Ganadera del Centro was frustrated in his attempt to rationalize the system of payment to the workers by substituting cash for their daily ration of coca. "The workers do not accept the five cents per day that we give them," he wrote,

> because they say they can do nothing with the money; and because they were complaining that they were not getting their coca ration, I was forced to send someone to Huancayo, where it is selling for 34 soles per *arroba* [approximately 25 pounds], which is very expensive and without the coca they refuse to work, so that I think it convenient to order Sr. Salazar to send an *arroba* of coca per week which I will reserve only for the workers.[114]

As is clear from this quotation, the peasants did not resist payment in cash out of attachment to their traditional rights, but because prices were going up extremely rapidly. Not only was the cash they were offered insufficient, but continuing to receive payment in kind would serve as insurance against further inflation.

In fact, peasants became extremely adept at using "traditional rights" as a weapon in the battle against expropriation. Perhaps the best documented case of this is the shepherds, or *huacchilleros*, on the livestock haciendas of the various *sociedades ganaderas*. According to a series of recent studies, the demand for long fibers in the European

[112] As cited in DeWind, "Peasants Become Miners," Ch. 3, p. 18.

[113] Ibid., Ch. 3, pp. 18–19.

[114] AFA, Sociedad Ganadera del Centro, Correspondencia Hacienda Acopalca, 1911–1918, October 26, 1917, 248.

textile industry resulted in the ever more urgent need to improve existing flocks on the various central highland haciendas. Yet the importation of choice sheep from England, the United States, or Australia was not enough. Because the shepherds pastured their own sheep, or *huacchas*, along with the hacienda flocks, it was impossible to control the reproduction process. Thus the *sociedades* attempted to substitute wages and other benefits for grazing rights, in the hope that the shepherds would willingly give up their *huacchas*. But the ensuing battle lasted for many decades, and the *hacendados* were never able to win a clear-cut victory. Aside from a few prize-winning sheep that continued to come from abroad, the quality of the flocks remained unchanged.[115]

As several authors have argued, the underlying motivation for the *huacchilleros'* struggle was not only their continuing access to means of production on the hacienda, but also the preservation of that access for other members of their village. In addition to pasturing their own sheep, many *huacchilleros* contracted themselves as shepherds for relatives, neighbors, and other villagers from their communities of origin. In exchange for extra income, whether in the form of money, labor, or livestock, the *huacchillero* gave other peasants the opportunity to expand the resources available to their family economies by using means of production belonging to the hacienda. Consequently, the attempt to proletarianize the *huacchilleros* was in effect a broader attack on the viability of the family economy in the surrounding villages. The peasantry perceived it, and confronted it, in those terms.[116]

[115] In addition to the pioneering study of Juan Martínez Alier, *Los huacchilleros del Perú* (Paris-Lima: Ruedo Ibérico-Instituto de Estudios Peruanos, 1973), see the excellent studies of Víctor Caballero on the Sociedad Ganadera Junín, and Gerardo Rénique on the Sociedad Ganadera del Centro. See also Víctor Caballero, *Hacienda Conocancha: Desarrollo capitalista y proletarización*, Taller de Estudios Andinos, Serie: Andes Centrales No. 1 (La Molina: Universidad Nacional Agraria, 1975); Florencia Mallon, Gerardo Rénique, et al., *Lanas y Capitalismo en los Andes Centrales*, Taller de Estudios Andinos, Serie: Andes Centrales, No. 2 (La Molina: Universidad Nacional Agraria, 1977); Gerardo Rénique, *Sociedad Ganadera del Centro: Pastores y Sindicalización en una Hacienda Alto Andina. Documentos 1945–1948*, Taller de Estudios Andinos, Serie: Andes Centrales, No. 3 (La Molina: Universidad Nacional Agraria, 1977); and Gerardo Rénique, *Comunidades Campesinas y "Recuperaciones" de Tierras. Valle del Mantaro*, Taller de Estudios Andinos, Serie: Andes Centrales, No. 4 (La Molina: Universidad Nacional Agraria, 1977–1978).

[116] Martínez Alier develops the concepts of "asedio interno" vs. "asedio externo"—that is, internal siege or pressure vs. external siege or pressure—which relate to this general analysis, in *Los huacchilleros*, pp. 2–7. Also, Don Felipe Artica, who worked as an accountant for the Sociedad Ganadera Tucle, described graphically in his second interview with me how the size of the shepherds' flocks was a daily struggle between them and the administration, with the latter realizing all along where the sheep in the

The utilization of hacienda and community resources within a single household economy was not limited to the haciendas of the *sociedades ganaderas*. In other localities, while the practice of giving livestock to hacienda peons or shepherds existed, there was also a broader exchange of labor, land, and money, usually along kinship lines. In the Yanamarca Valley, for example, peons from the haciendas in the northern section often gained access through purchase, inheritance, or marriage to lands in the villages. When these *chacras* were added to the land assigned to them on the hacienda, many peons ended up having rather substantial access to means of production. Yet because most had to labor three to four days per week on the lands of the *hacendado*, they often faced a shortage of labor when tending their own crops. Through reciprocity relationships with village peasants who faced a shortage of land and a surplus of labor, therefore, hacienda peons could once again bring their family economy into balance.[117]

Thus through migration, kinship, and reciprocity, peasants combined a wide variety of resources within the household economy in an effort to limit the shrinkage of their subsistence base. Just as the Cerro de Pasco Company reorganized existing labor relations, technology, and networks of commercial capital to meet their new needs, so the peasants used traditional institutions and relationships to begin a new chapter in their struggle against proletarianization. Yet in addition to the more purely social or economic weapons available to them in the context of village and household life, the peasants had also developed, in the context of previous confrontations, an arsenal of political techniques that would serve them well in the new situation. The most important among these were the exploitation of elite factionalism, the use of the courts, and the manipulation of patron-client relationships.

As had been true in previous times, peasants in the early twentieth

---

huacchilleros' flocks actually came from and not being able to do anything about it. See Interview with Felipe Artica, II, Huancayo, June 1977.

[117] For examples of the hacienda-community connection in the Yanamarca Valley, in terms of labor, income, and means of production, see ANF, Protocolos Notariales, Luis Salazar, Book 10: February 7, 1902, 383–84v; Book 14: January 23, 1905, 18v–20; Book 26: August 4, 1914, 947v–48v; Book 27: November 2, 1914, 1125v–26v; Book 28: January 15, 1915, 608v–10v; Book 32: May 1, 1917, 255–56v, June 18, 1917, 356v–58; Book 33: August 28, 1917, 527v–29, Book 39: August 30, 1920, 1000–01v; Book 43: October 29, 1921, 953v–55; Book 46: December 21, 1922, 2363–64v; Expedientes y Libros Judiciales, "Félix R. Vílchez vs. Benjamín Otero," began September 18, 1914; "Pedro Blancas vs. Manuel S. Espinoza y otros," 1918; APJ, "Solicitud de varios peones de la hacienda Yanamarca, sobre exoneración de la contribución de predios rústicos," Jauja, January 18–29, 1921.

century were keenly aware of existing conflicts of interest within the ranks of the regional elite. The central dispute in this period, at least from the peasantry's point of view, was competition for labor. Although this problem had existed for many years, foreign investment in the mining industry and the consequent expansion of the mining labor force had exacerbated it dramatically. Since the peasantry continued to resist proletarianization, the labor supply again did not keep up with widening demand. The peasants took advantage of this fact, playing elite factions off against each other, moving among the various productive sectors competing for labor,[118] and trying to turn village relationships of asymmetrical reciprocity against those who manipulated them. Because they successfully resisted the complete loss of their means of production, they forced the Cerro de Pasco Corporation and its Peruvian allies to find new strategies for acquiring a permanent labor force.

[118] As was true in Europe, it is often in the manufacturing period of capitalist development that we find the most problems with labor discipline. At bottom, the reason seems to be that capital is unable to take full control of the worker's labor time. In other words, labor is not yet completely proletarianized. See Marx, *Capital*, I:367–68. For more examples of peasant resistance, see below, Chapter VI.

CHAPTER SIX

The Penetration of Foreign Capital:
The Industrial Period

. . . you will want to be innocent, that night you did not choose,

you did not choose, that night.[1]

Around six-thirty on the moonlit night of August 19, 1918, eight men came out of Gonzalo Lino's house to join another group already waiting for them on the pampa of Marco. Dressed in motley military gear and armed with rifles, revolvers, and shotguns, the men conferred briefly, then separated into two bands of approximately a dozen each. One band began to move stealthily along the village's tree-lined avenue toward the plaza. The other group took the road from Tragadero to Marco and moved in the same direction. As both bands approached the town square, their guns glistening in the moonlight, the leaders signaled to each other by blowing on police whistles.

Meanwhile, on the plaza, there seemed to be a great deal more activity than was usual on a cold August night. Their *mantas* and ponchos shrugged high against the frosty air, a group of people had gathered at the window of the local boys' school to watch a rehearsal in progress. Inside the building the schoolteacher, Florián Hurtado, was leading a group of students in a literary presentation he was preparing for the forthcoming springtime fiesta. Also present were Florián's brother, Narcizo; Lydia Arroyo, the teacher at the girls' school; and many other women, men, and children.

When the two bands of men reached the plaza, they gathered in front of the school. A man on a black horse, later identified as Antonio Onofre, gave the order to fire directly into the building. Florián Hurtado fell to the floor, his body riddled with bullets, and Lydia Arroyo was badly injured. In the ensuing panic and confusion, the assailants allowed the women and children to leave; but when several boys and men attempted to do the same, shots rang out once again. A student

---

[1] Carlos Fuentes, *The Death of Artemio Cruz*, trans. Sam Hileman (New York: Farrar, Straus & Giroux, 1964), p. 118.

named Procopio Lino fell dead near the door, bullets lodged in his chest and head.

As he later testified at the trial, it was at this point that Víctor Fabián, lieutenant governor of the district, arrived at the square. Sending one of his companions to ring the church bell and summon the townspeople, Fabián made his way along the back of the municipal building and pulled himself up to the second floor. From his hiding place he saw six men trying to leave the building, and heard Jacinto Onofre call after them: "Cowards, where are you going?" This prompted the group to return and resume shooting. At the sound of the bells in the church tower, however, the assailants left the school, regrouping at the corner of the plaza. Only once the villagers began arriving in answer to the bells did the assassins flee in various directions, shooting as they went.

When Fabián and others were finally able to enter the school building, they found the corpses of Procopio Lino and Florián Hurtado. According to the coroner who later issued the certificates of death, Hurtado's body had seventeen separate bullet holes. From the angle of perforation, it was clear that only some of the bullets had been fired while Florián was still standing. His murderers had continued to empty their firearms into his body after he was already dead.[2]

The nightmarish, bloodthirsty quality of this nocturnal raid sent shock waves through the entire Jauja region. The Jauja newspaper *El Porvenir* took great interest in the case, demanding a speedy trial and careful administration of justice. The fact that the Onofres were known as oppressive *contratistas* in Morococha fueled the already blazing fires of protest against *enganche* and *contrata*. People in the Yanamarca Valley would continue to talk about the incident for decades to come.[3] After Florián Hurtado's funeral, the *comuneros* of Marco rioted, sweeping through Tragadero, burning Jacinto Onofre's house in the Curicancha neighborhood, and destroying Antonio's store on the plaza.

[2] The entire description of the incident is based on the *expediente* of the court case against the Onofres. See ANF, Expedientes y Libros Judiciales, "José C. Hurtado contra los hermanos Onofre, Agustín Rafael y otros, por la muerte de Florián Hurtado," began in Jauja, August 20, 1918, 897–900, 910–12v, 913v–14v, 1025–26v, 1076–77v, and passim.

[3] For data on the reaction in Jauja, see William B. Hutchinson, "Sociocultural Change in the Mantaro Valley Region of Peru: Acolla, A Case Study," Ph.D. Dissertation, Indiana University, 1973, pp. 39–40. For the deep impression the incident made on people in the valley, see especially: Interview with Elías Valenzuela Soto, Tragadero, October 22, 1977; Interview with Francisco Solís Camarena, Tragadero, November 29, 1977; Interview with Oscar Teófilo Camarena, Tragadero, November 29, 1977; and Conversations with Moisés Ortega throughout 1977 and early 1978.

According to an eyewitness, the straw in the adobes continued to smolder for fifteen days.[4]

In addition to the intensely dramatic events that surrounded the case, the murder was of crucial importance because it marked the end of an era. While Antonio and Jacinto Onofre were never brought to justice, they were also never able to return to the Yanamarca Valley.[5] In the next ten years, through a power of attorney he gave his mother, Rosa Rivera, and with the help of other relatives and friends, Antonio sold off most of his property in Tragadero and its environs.[6] Even more quickly than they had built their empire, the Onofres watched it tumble about their ears. For the people in the Yanamarca Valley, it was the material and symbolic end of *contrata*. Like buzzards feasting on a carcass, former clients crowded in to settle old debts.[7] Yet despite the sudden, violent, and dramatic quality of their final downfall, the storm against the Onofres had been gathering for quite some time.

Two months before the tragic raid on Marco, a coalition of officials from Jauja and wealthy peasants, merchants, and political authorities from the villages of Acolla, Chocón, Concho, Marco, Pachascucho, Pomacancha, and Tragadero sent a petition to the president of the Republic asking for guarantees against the abuses of the brothers Antonio and Jacinto Onofre. "The Onofre brothers are merchants in the mining centers of Yauli, Morococha and Casapalca," they wrote,

> and as such have been perpetrating a series of exactions, particularly against the unfortunate Indians they have under their control as workers in the mines, tied [to them] by means of unfair contracts, paid minimal wages, enslaved and treated almost like animals, forced to give false testimony in criminal trials that the Onofres have invented against other unfortunates who have tried to defend themselves and ask for justice.

[4] Interview with Elías Valenzuela Soto; RPI, Registro de Propiedades, Tomo 52, Inscripción No. 94, p. 273.

[5] ANF, Expedientes y Libros Judiciales, "Hurtado contra Onofre," especially 1278–81, 1301–1301v, 1305, 1311, 1312, 1314, 1327–30v; Hutchinson, "Sociocultural Change," p. 40; APJ, "Acta entre Víctor Rafael y Antonio Onofre, sobre amenazas y usurpación," Oroya, May 30, 1930.

[6] RPI, Registro de Propiedades, Tomo 52, Inscripción Nos. 92, 93, 94, 95, pp. 269, 271, 273, and 275, respectively; ANF, Protocolos Notariales, Luis Salazar, Book 36: February 4, 1919, 94–96; Book 37: October 8, 1919, 862v–65, October 8, 1919, 868–69v; Book 38: April 19, 1920, 1496v–99; Book 40: October 27, 1920, 2242–44v; Book 43: October 31, 1921, 961v–64; Book 46: September 14, 1922, 2001–2003v; Book 65: March 24, 1930, 1251–52, March 27, 1930, 1260v–62.

[7] ANF, "Hurtado contra Onofre," 962–62v, 1135–35v, 1267–67v, 1276–80.

In addition, the petitioners continued, the brothers had indebted people to the point of reducing them to the status of beggars. They had taken away people's land and animals, forced others to sign blank pieces of paper, and even chased several completely out of their villages. Unless the Onofres were stopped, they would turn the entire Yanamarca Valley into their private domain. "Justice therefore demands," the letter concluded,

> that a resolution in harmony with existing law give back to the destitute Indian race what rightfully belonged to them; that authorities be established in the mining centers to intervene in favor of the Indian in the contracts they might celebrate, so that they are not exploited or deceived; that the unjust workers' contracts for the mines be punished and stopped; that the Indian's social condition be improved, changing him from an outcast into a free man; that his lost rights, his freedom, his property, his personality be returned to him; . . . that . . . the Indian race more than any other sector of our population needs constant and effective guarantees and justice in order that we may all live in peace and serve our country; and finally that the perpetrators of the horrible crimes that we denounce should be brought to trial.[8]

Given the passion and poetry of the document, one might expect it to be signed by at least one or two members of an *indigenista* organization, but this was not the case. Instead, the signatures heading the list belonged to men whose activities did not differ all that much from those of the Onofres: Manuel Velasco, head of Jauja's provincial council and known for his *enganches* to Monobamba; José C. Hurtado; Francisco J. Espinoza, a wealthy *gamonal* from Chocón; and Manuel Camarena 5th, a rich peasant from Tragadero, a relative of the Hurtados and a member of Marco's district council.[9] Rather than pointing to the sincere reformist spirit of its signers, then, the petition evidenced their sharp political common sense. By using the progressive language of the *indigenista* movement, they hoped to portray

[8] For the petition, see APJ, "Oficio de las comunidades indígenas de los distritos de Marco y Acolla pidiendo garantías contra los abusos de los hermanos Antonio y Jacinto Onofre, " Marco, June 12, 1918.

[9] For the identification of Velasco, see interview with Elías Valenzuela Soto, Tragadero, October 22, 1977. For Espinoza, see ANF, Protocolos Notariales, Luis Salazar, Book 25: January 16, 1913, 20–22, November 21, 1913, 484–85v; Book 29: February 19, 1916, 948–49; Book 36: May 7, 1919, 385–86v. For Camarena, see interviews with Francisco Solís Camarena and Oscar Teófilo Camarena, Tragadero, November 29, 1977; and AMM, Libro de Actas del Concejo Municipal, I, 1908–1921, 166–74.

themselves as the champions of the peasant's cause and win support, both in local society and from the national government, for their battle with the Onofres over labor and patronage. But the Hurtados and their allies were not the only ones who understood the niceties of petitions and progressive language.

In a response to the original petition, signed by a number of their retainers and clients, the Onofres turned the accusations around, claiming that the Hurtados and their allies had acquired signatures by force. "Even though their accusations are false," they wrote,

> the Hurtados take advantage of their influence in Marco to obtain signatures, influence which they have gained through fear and all kinds of abuses, to which end they have monopolized all the administrative and judicial posts.

Moreover, they charged, the only reason for the original accusation was envy:

> Since the Onofres are well-established citizens of Tragadero, which belongs to the district of Marco, certain people cannot stand the fact that they have become wealthy, and, tormented by jealousy, try to ruin the reputation of such respectable people, with petitions presented to you [the president of the Republic] and the Minister of the Interior, to see if they can humiliate the Onofres before the authorities by slandering them.[10]

These particular charges and countercharges were only the last and most passionate in a long line of documents, court trials, and battles that pitched the Onofres against the Hurtados, and more generally one faction of wealthy peasants against another, in the Yanamarca Valley. Especially between 1915 and 1918, the level of overt violence and conflict soared dangerously. As each side openly courted allies among the valley's inhabitants, it was no longer possible to remain neutral. Every disagreement, no matter the subject or size, fed into polarization. If peasants were in competition with each other for any reason, they would hasten to join opposing factions. If an ally of one group felt slighted, it was simple enough to move to the opposing camp.[11] And as each conflict fed into the next, and the battle lines

---

[10] APJ, "Oficio de varios vecinos de la provincia de Jauja, a favor de los Onofre," Jauja, June 20, 1918.

[11] Peasants opposing each other by joining opposing factions included, within the Onofre faction, Agustín Rafael of Acolla, Manuel E. Landa of Marco, and Higinio Camarena of Marco. Within the Hurtado faction: Santiago and Tiburcio Misari of Tragadero, Pedro Camarena of Tragadero, Julio Córdova and Teodoro Ortiz of Acolla. Those

became clearer and clearer, it was as if the fuse had been lit on a keg of dynamite.

What made the situation so explosive was the worsening shortage of labor in the regional economy. As the mining industry continued to expand, foreign capital's allies at the local level were forced to use increasingly violent methods to secure an adequate supply of workers. This was particularly true because other sectors were expanding also, especially livestock and subtropical agriculture. The end result was that *enganchadores* employed by the Cerro de Pasco Corporation competed ever more fiercely with each other. And the peasants, quick to see the weakness in the *enganchadores'* position, attempted to turn the situation to their advantage.

As Pedro Zulen reported in 1910, *enganchados* were very skilled at exploiting the labor shortage by playing one *enganchador* off against another. After having taken out a loan with one *enganchador*, a peasant would borrow from a second to pay back the first, then from a third to pay back the second, and so forth, until his scheme was discovered. Even if he was then forced to report to the mines, he had achieved free access to cash for a number of weeks. This strategy worked even better across sectors of the regional economy. If a peasant began by indebting himself to a mining *enganchador*, then moved on to an *enganchador* working for subtropical haciendas, then finally to one serving the *sociedades ganaderas*, the resulting confusion could keep him safe for a long time.[12]

Peasants also used the competition for labor as a negotiating point in labor disputes. This was particularly effective on the haciendas, since the mining industry paid a higher wage and was always looking for workers. On the haciendas belonging to the *sociedades ganaderas*, for example, peasants would threaten to go to work in the mines unless a particular demand was met. And in the region as a whole, there

---

changing factions due to a disagreement included Lucio E. Galarza, Daniel Solís, and Manuel E. Landa. See ANF, Expedientes y Libros Judiciales, "Hurtado contra Onofre"; "Juan Rafael contra Santiago y Tiburcio Misari, por asalto en despoblado, flagelaciones, intento de robo y homicidio a mano armada," began in Jauja, December 6, 1914; APJ, "Queja de varios ciudadanos del pueblo de Marco, dirigida al Prefecto del Departamento, en contra del gobernador de Marco Lucio Galarza," Marco, September 20, 1910; and AMM, I, 1908–1921, 3–4, 166–74.

[12] Pedro S. Zulen, "El enganche de indios: Informe del Comisionado de la Asociación Pro-Indígena," *La Prensa*, October 7, 1910, p. 4; AFA, Sociedad Ganadera del Centro, Correspondencia Hacienda Acopalca, 1911–1918; Gerardo Rénique, Research Notes: AFA, August–September 1976; ANF, Protocolos Notariales, Luis Salazar, Book 21: December 28, 1910, 1188–88v and insert. I use the pronoun "he" deliberately, since women were prohibited by law from taking part in formal *enganche* contracts.

is reason to believe that *hacendados* offered a substantial access to means of production to their *colonos*—as much as four to five hectares of land at a time when smallholding peasants usually controlled between one and two—at least partially because they had to compete with other sectors, especially mining, for access to labor.[13]

The strategy of playing one *enganchador* or economic sector against another was often used in conjunction with running away or never reporting at all. During 1910, Zulen calculated, there were 4,903 runaways or delays among the workers with whom the three main *enganche* firms had already contracted. Even supposing that the Cerro de Pasco Company obtained all its workers from these three firms, which it did not, the runaway rate was nearly half of the total labor force.[14] And the livestock industry had the same problem. Between 1910 and 1918, the correspondence of the Sociedad Ganadera del Centro is full of complaints about workers: *enganchados* who never showed up; others who arrived, worked two days, and left; some who decided to go to the mines after already contracting for the hacienda; and many who refused to work more than a couple of shifts a week.[15]

Precisely because the problem was so widespread, it was impossible to prosecute more than a handful of runaways through the courts. Of the 2,369 workers who were in violation of their contracts at the Arístides Castro firm in 1910, for example, only 71 were being prosecuted.[16] Part of the reason for this was the heavy expense involved. As a group of *enganchadores* complained in 1910, "the expenses that we would incur would reach such levels that it would be unreasonable to risk them, given the long process of litigation that is customary in our courts, and that we would have to prosecute thousands of cases."[17] But peasants also tended to be good at manipulating litigation. In a

[13] Figures on size of landholdings are based on the situation in the Yanamarca Valley. See Florencia E. Mallon, "Microeconomía y Campesinado. Hacienda, comunidad y coyunturas económicas en el Valle de Yanamarca," *Análisis*, No. 4 (January–April 1978), pp. 39–51, especially 39–43. For a more general argument along the same lines, see Juan Martínez Alier, *Los huacchilleros del Perú* (Paris–Lima: Ruedo Ibérico-Instituto de Estudios Peruanos, 1973), especially pp. 43–96.

[14] The runaway rate for the industry is calculated on the basis of extrapolation of labor force size from the figures for 1908 and 1912. See BCIM, No. 77, Carlos P. Jiménez, "Estadística Minera del Perú en 1909 y 1910," especially pp. 70–71; and BCIM, No. 80. For the total number of runaways, see Zulen, "El enganche de indios," pp. 4–5.

[15] AFA, Sociedad Ganadera del Centro, Correspondencia Hacienda Acopalca, 1911–1918; and Rénique, Research Notes.

[16] Zulen, "El enganche de indios," pp. 4–5.

[17] APJ, "Solicitud de varios enganchadores al Subprefecto de Jauja," Jauja, May 28, 1910.

number of cases they managed to overturn, on the basis of legal technicalities, a lower court decision in favor of the *enganchadores*.[18]

Finally, peasants continued to be extremely adept at managing the two-edged sword of reciprocity and patronage. Although they were unable to break the influence or dominance of the wealthy village elite, they recognized the fissures and weaknesses in the system and exploited these for their own ends. Thus in the Yanamarca Valley a number of peasants from Tragadero, though unable to oppose the Onofres directly, allied with the enemies of the brothers, particularly the Misaris and the Hurtados. Some of the peasants from Marco, feeling especially slighted or mistreated by the Hurtados, allied with the Onofres. Even if these strategies fed into the system rather than attacking it, they did force the village elite to take the balance of forces into account, and at times even to make some very real concessions.[19]

Ultimately, of course, while the peasants won some battles in the struggle against proletarianization, they lost the war. But what is central to the entire process is that, while they were losing, they forced the Cerro de Pasco Corporation to change its strategy. Because peasant resistance converted labor acquisition into an expensive, violent, and embarrassing confrontation, both *enganche* and *contrata* became increasingly less attractive to the foreign corporation.[20] This was es-

[18] See, for example, ANF, Expedientes y Libros Judiciales, "Queja de Pedro Ramos contra el Juez de Paz de Masma, Juan M. Soto, sobre el juicio que Vicente Cairampoma ha instituído contra el primero sobre pago de cantidad de soles provenientes de una fianza," Jauja, May 15, 1903; "Revisorio referente a la demand verbal seguida ante el Juez de Paz de Segunda Nominación de esta Ciudad por Don Manuel Núñez Salinas, apoderado de Don Nicanor Galarza contra D. Pablo M. Hinostroza, sobre cantidad de soles," Jauja, 1904–1906; "Pablo Stucchi contra Francisca Ortega, por cantidad de soles provenientes de una fianza," began October 12, 1906.

[19] For a closer look at the intricacies of these patron-client networks, see ANF, Expedientes y Libro Judiciales, "Rafael contra Misaris," and "Hurtado contra Onofre;" Protocolos Notariales, Luis Salazar, Book 26: February 5, 1914, 608–609v; Book 31: December 1, 1916, 1689v–91v, December 28, 1916, 1756–58v, 1758v–60; APJ, "Queja de various ciudadanos de Marco contra el gobernador Lucio Galarza," September 20, 1910, and subsequent individual legalizations of the various signatures; "Oficio del Senador Villarán al Ministro de Estado en el Despacho de Gobierno," Lima, May 18, 1918; "Oficio de las comunidades indígenas de los distritos de Marco y Acolla y otros, contra los hermanos Onofre," Marco, June 12, 1918; "Oficio de varios vecinos de la provincia de Jauja a favor de los hermanos Onofre," Jauja, June 20, 1918; "Oficio de varios vecinos de Janjaillo a favor de los hermanos Onofre," Janjaillo, June 26, 1918; Interviews with Elías Valenzuela Soto and Francisco Solís Camarena; AMM, I, 1908–1921, passim, especially 166–74.

[20] The peasants were, of course, helped in this social war by events in Lima and on the northern coast, where the period between 1910 and 1920 was one of intense labor unrest and strong pro-Indian agitation by sectors of the urban middle class. This agi-

pecially true because, despite the lack of major technological innovations, the sheer size and complexity of the company's operations began to demand a more skilled and stable labor force. By 1917, moreover, the company's comparative technological disadvantage on the international market, combined with the high price of copper, had prompted the decision to construct a new and more sophisticated smelter at Oroya.[21] "At a given stage in its development," a prominent theorist on European capitalism has written, "the narrow technical basis on which manufacture rested, came into conflict with the requirements of production that were created by manufacture itself."[22] Such was the case with the central highland mining industry. And as the Cerro de Pasco Corporation prepared to enter its more truly industrial phase, it also prepared to break off its alliance with local commercial capital. For those wealthy peasants in the area's villages whose fate was most closely identified with foreign capital, the signs of impending doom were already there.

The Transformation of Mining and the New Balance of Power

By 1918, the Cerro de Pasco Corporation had decided to change the very basis upon which the mining industry was organized. As the corporation had expanded its holdings, the capacity and location of its smelter at Tinyahuarco proved an obstacle to the rationalization and integration of the enterprise. In the first place, expanded production at Casapalca, Morococha, and Cerro de Pasco had combined to make

tation was at least partially responsible for the repeal of the 1903 Mining Labor Law in 1914, and for the general discrediting of *enganche* and of mine labor conditions in this period. See especially Dora Mayer, *Un decreto libertador*, Paper read at the Conference on *Enganche* organized by the "Centro Unión Hijos de Cajacay" (Callao), July 8, 1914 (Lima: Imprenta "El Inca," 1914), pp. 5–11; Peter Klarén, *La formación de las haciendas azucareras y los orígenes del APRA*, 2d ed. (Lima: Instituto de Estudios Peruanos, 1976), pp. 73–109, 165–95; and Alberto Flores Galindo, *Los mineros de la Cerro de Pasco, 1900–1930* (Lima: Pontífica Universidad Católica del Perú, 1974), pp. 67–77. There is also evidence that the peasants knew exactly who their allies were at the national level, and exploited the relationship to the hilt. Interview with Oscar Teófilo Camarena; APJ, "Oficio de las comunidades indígenas de los distritos de Marco y Acolla," 1918.

[21] Adrian DeWind, Jr., "Peasants Become Miners: The Evolution of Industrial Mining Systems in Peru," Ph.D. Dissertation, Columbia University, 1977, Chapter 1; Julian Laite, "Industrialisation and Land Tenure in the Peruvian Andes," Paper presented at the Symposium on Landlord and Peasant in Peru, Cambridge, 1972, ms.; and Julian Laite, "Processes of Industrial and Social Change in Highland Peru," in Norman Long and Bryan R. Roberts (eds.), *Peasant Cooperation and Capitalist Expansion in Central Peru* (Austin: University of Texas Press, 1978), pp. 72–98.

[22] Karl Marx, *Capital* (New York: International Publishers, 1967), I: 368.

Tinyahuarco inadequate as a smelting facility. Secondly, transporting the ore north from Morococha and Casapalca to Tinyahuarco, only to send the metal back south so that it could be shipped to Lima, was highly inefficient and increased production costs. The town of Oroya, therefore, located at the crossroads of the various railroad lines, seemed most indicated as the site for a larger and technologically more advanced smelter.[23]

More than any other single event, the planning and construction of the Oroya smelter symbolized the changing realities of the mining industry in the central highlands. Its smokestacks billowing acrid smoke, the smelter became the technological hub of the company's entire operation, reorganizing the flow of minerals and metals and imparting a new rhythm and rationale to the extraction process. On the one hand, the increased smelting capacity at Oroya multiplied the demand for ores and generated an overall speedup in the mining sector. On the other hand, the new technology made possible, for the first time, the commercial production of new metals such as lead and zinc.[24] Ten years after the smelter had started operations, the Cerro de Pasco Corporation had earned a reputation for being one of the most efficient and low-cost copper producers in the entire world.[25] Yet in addition to the technological transformation it symbolized, the Oroya smelter represented a new phase in the company's labor relations, and consequently the end of its alliance with local commercial capital.

The alliance with local merchants had become both expensive and embarrassing for the company. Expensive, because in order to maintain a labor force large enough to meet the needs of production, it was necessary to advance large sums of money to the *enganchadores* and endure a runaway rate of 50 percent. Furthermore, the presence of middlemen tended to cut into the company's profits, since both the *enganchadores* and *contratistas* received sizable commissions and the right to expand their earnings through commercial activities. And the alliance was embarrassing because the constant abuses of *enganchadores* and *contratistas* came back to haunt the foreign company. As was clear from the case of the Onofres, the ever-present violence

[23] DeWind, "Peasants Become Miners," Ch. 1, p. 22.

[24] Dirk Kruijt and Menno Vellinga, *Labor Relations and Multinational Corporations: The Cerro de Pasco Corporation in Peru (1902–1974)* (Assen, The Netherlands: Van Gorcum, 1979), p. 37.

[25] DeWind, "Peasants Become Miners," Ch. 1, p. 35. Laite, in "Industrialisation and Land Tenure" and "Processes of Industrial and Social Change," presents another description of the process and implications of the construction of the Oroya smelter.

needed to reproduce networks for labor acquisition was, beyond a certain point, more troublesome than the networks were worth.[26]

In addition to reasons of profit and prestige, there were also strictly technological motives for putting an end to the company's dependence on local commercial capital. With the increasing rationalization, centralization, and efficiency of the enterprise, the *contratista*'s control over production and the intensely seasonal nature of *enganche* labor became obstacles to further modernization. For one thing, it was more difficult to centralize operations that were under the direction of *contratistas*. In addition, the new demands of the Oroya smelter made it necessary to convert several seasonal mining camps, which had operated successfully with *enganche* labor, into full-time operations whose labor needs were more constant and could no longer be met in the same way.[27]

But perhaps most important, the nature of *contrata* and *enganche* militated against the creation of a skilled labor force. As an acute observer commented as early as 1908,

> the system of *enganche* has, among other inconveniences, the fact that the mines and principally the smelters, cannot form a skilled labor force, because even though the Indian learns rapidly, he leaves once his contract expires, and it is necessary to replace him with more unskilled personnel.[28]

In fact, during the years before the construction of the smelter, the need for more stable and skilled personnel was already being felt in various sectors of the company's operations. In an attempt to meet this demand, the corporation began to hire a number of workers directly, without going through the *enganchadores*. Called *maquipureros*, these workers were paid a higher wage than the *enganchados*, and the differential increased as time went on.[29] But it was not until

[26] For a similar argument in the case of the sugar industry on the northern coast, see Klarén, *Formación de las haciendas*, especially pp. 55–57.

[27] Kruijt and Vellinga, *Labor Relations*, p. 63.

[28] BCIM, No. 72, Celso Herrera, *Estado actual de la minería en la provincia de Huarochirí* (Lima: Imprenta La Industria, 1909), p. 47. For a similar argument, see Kruijt and Vellinga, *Labor Relations*, p. 63.

[29] For an analysis of the *maquipuro* system, see DeWind, "Peasants Become Miners," Ch. 3, pp. 14–16. Apparently, *maquipureros* were used even before the arrival of the Cerro de Pasco Corporation, though in much smaller numbers. See UNI, Tesis de Minería, No. 50: Francisco R. del Castillo, "Informe sobre Huarochirí y Yauli," 1891. Interestingly, the only mention of *maquipureros* occurred with reference to the mineral hacienda Tuctu, one of the largest and most modern in the region.

after the construction of the smelter that direct hiring began to overtake *enganche* as the main method of acquiring a labor force.

Such a substantial shift in company policy could not help but affect the alternatives open to central sierra merchants. Some, such as the Onofres, were unable to move with the changing tide. Because they were in occupations that depended more directly on the foreign company, or because they had not diversified their investments among several sectors of the regional economy, this group suffered an inevitable and fairly precipitous decline in the 1920s. For those whose relationship with the company had been more tangential, however, or who had possessed sufficient foresight or luck to invest broadly, it was possible to survive and even prosper further by changing their emphasis toward commercial agriculture. Thus the Hurtados, despite the murder of their youngest brother, continued to accumulate land and develop their hacienda Quishuarcancha.[30] And Pedro Aizcorbe, owner of Jauja's largest *enganche* firm, bought the hacienda Pancán in the fertile and well-watered *paraje* of Putaj. In addition to planting eucalyptus trees, he managed to raise a loan with the Banco Agrícola del Perú for 30,400 soles in 1933 in order to further develop the property.[31]

Yet in the end, the area most directly affected by the new wave of changes in the mining industry was Oroya itself. Since 1893, when the central railway reached Oroya and converted the town into an important commercial entrepôt for goods from the entire central region, landowners and merchants in the area had been speculating in urban and rural land. The Santa María family, for example, originally from Tarma and important landowners in the Chanchamayo Valley, had owned the hacienda Huaymanta, which bordered on the community of Oroya Antigua, since the mid-nineteenth century. In 1892, the family formed a limited liability company with a capital of 100,000 soles to exploit Huaymanta. Calling the firm the Compañía Mercantil de la Oroya, the Santa Marías advertised in the Lima newspapers that

[30] ANF, Protocolos Notariales, Luis Salazar, Book 36: April 3, 1919, 276–77v; Book 37: June 23, 1919, 534–35v; Book 38: December 15, 1919, 1078–79v, February 26, 1920, 1300–1302; Book 39: May 10, 1920, 1565–67v; Book 41–42: February 11, 1921, 91–93v, May 6, 1921, 380–81v; Book 43: October 19, 1921, 909v–11, October 24, 1921, 931–32v; Book 44: January 4, 1922, 1204v–1206; Book 46: November 24, 1922, 2252v–53v; Book 50: May 5, 1924, 1951v–54; Book 51: September 5, 1924, 2358v–60; Book 53: March 4, 1925, 211v–13; Book 55: January 12, 1926, 1160v–62, February 8, 1926, 1246v–48; Book 59: August 4, 1927, 675v–77, September 26, 1927, 884–85v; Book 66: November 16, 1930, 1802–1803v.

[31] RPI, Registro de Propiedades, Tomo 59, Inscripción No. 30: Asientos 4, 5, 6 (1928–1933).

their aims were "to rent land, construct hotels, offices and markets and exploit commercial opportunities."[32] The alienation of communal land in Oroya Antigua also increased notably with the arrival of the railroad. According to a recent study, seventy-seven land contracts between 1900 and 1920 resulted in the concentration of land belonging to forty-three peasants in the hands of fourteen people, eleven of whom were recent migrants to the area.[33]

If we compare these trends to what happened after the construction of the smelter, however, they are less dramatic than they seem at first glance. By 1920, the Cerro de Pasco Corporation had bought out the Santa María family for approximately 55,000 soles and had begun construction of their new smelter. Two years later, in November 1922, the furnaces began to operate. Because of financial problems the company had suffered after the collapse of copper prices in late 1920, the smelter was built in a hurry and without any apparatus to screen the smoke. Since the corporation was also somewhat desperate to begin paying back the debts it had accumulated during the construction, it quickly brought the smelter up to full capacity. As a result, between 100 and 125 tons of arsenic, sulphur dioxide, lead, bismuth, and other poisons began to fall each day on neighboring villages.[34]

In the community of Oroya Antigua, the barley planted on seventeen hectares of land immediately opposite the smelter was completely destroyed from one day to the next. Within the first two years, the village's representatives claimed that 278 cattle, 3,874 sheep, and almost 200 horses and mules were killed by the smoke. Many of the townspeople also suffered. According to some of the inhabitants, the acid smoke and ash stuck to the skin, causing irritation and loss of hair.[35]

The effects of the smoke were felt for many miles. The hacienda Pachacayo, twenty-five miles downwind from Oroya, reported the destruction of its entire barley crop. Fifty miles downstream in the Mantaro Valley, livestock owners found flakes of pollution in the stomach linings of their animals. In Chacapalpa, a village of farmers, herders, and *arrieros* in the upper Mantaro Valley, peasants could do nothing but stand helplessly by while their sheep and cattle died off one by one, and their crops came up useless at the end of the growing season.

[32] Laite, "Processes of Industrial and Social Change," p. 78.

[33] Ibid., p. 79.

[34] Ibid., pp. 81–83; DeWind, "Peasants Become Miners," Ch. 5, pp. 2–4. For a more detailed analysis of the extent of the smoke damage, see Appendix 2.

[35] Laite, "Processes of Industrial and Social Change," p. 84; DeWind, "Peasants Become Miners," Ch. 5, pp. 3–5.

As Felipe Artica, the son of a wealthy peasant from Chacapalpa, remembered fifty years later,

> when the smoke was very strong, my fellow villagers planted their crops. They produced, but very small potatoes, and they had a gritty consistency. They would grab [the plant]—and the potato would come out, rotting. And the animals . . . they became very thin and contracted diarrhea. The cattle. And the sheep also. The horses, on the other hand, would turn around and around, fall over a rock or precipice, and die right there . . . they would roll down [the hillsides] . . . or bang themselves against the sides [of the precipice], trying to hold on by their teeth. Poor animals—it was enough to make us despair. I tell you this because I saw it with my father's animals. Especially the horses . . .[36]

The Cerro de Pasco Corporation had anticipated some difficulties with the smoke before the smelter began to operate. Company representatives had bought land in the surrounding area, putting sheep and cattle on it to see what would happen. They had attempted to bargain with neighboring villages ahead of time. But it is doubtful that the corporation knew beforehand how devastating and far-reaching the effects would actually be. By 1924, thirty communities had begun proceedings against the company for smoke damage including, from the Yanamarca Valley, Acolla, Curicaca, Janjaillo, and Pomacancha. Twenty-eight *hacendados* also petitioned the government for damages. Indeed, between 1924 and 1928, in order to settle some of these claims, the Cerro de Pasco Corporation bought thirteen haciendas, comprising over 200,000 hectares and including the entire Sociedad Ganadera Junín.[37]

Whether or not the company actually predicted what would happen because of the Oroya smelter, its operation had, by the late 1920s, significantly altered the agrarian economy and the system of land tenure in the central highlands. In the hacienda sector, the Sociedad Ganadera Junín and numerous individual proprietors were wiped off the face of the map. The majority of the good high pastureland outside the immediate vicinity of the Mantaro Valley passed to the North American company for a rock-bottom price. Even though at the be-

[36] Laite, "Processes of Industrial and Social Change," p. 84; Interview with Felipe Artica (I), Huancayo, June 7, 1977.

[37] DeWind, "Peasants Become Miners," Ch. 5, pp. 5–9. Flores Galindo, *Los mineros*, p. 49; and ANF, Protocolos Notariales, Luis Salazar, Book 60: December 8, 1927, 1175v–77, and December 8, 1927, 1177–78v.

ginning the land seemed close to useless, in the long run the installation of Cottrell systems to screen the smoke in Oroya would combine with the natural adaptation of vegetation and animals to make
the haciendas profitable once again. It was on these lands that the
Ganadera Division of the Cerro de Pasco Corporation, succeeding
where all others had failed, would create a new breed of sheep, the
Raza Junín, with the highest productivity of wool and meat in the
country. It was also off these lands that the Cerro de Pasco Corporation managed to provide meat to its labor force at below market price,
helping to keep wages low and profits high.[38] But in the final analysis,
the most far-reaching repercussions were felt in the villages.

When Felipe Artica's father saw what the smoke was doing to his
animals, he refused to sell them. Beside the fact that he felt a great
deal of affection for his flock, there was really very little he could do
with the animals in a practical sense, whether they were alive or dead.
The sheep's wool simply fell off their hides in brittle clumps. The
cattle's hides were so thin they were useless. In the hope of salvaging
something, Artica decided to take advantage of a connection he had
by marriage with Teodoro Valladares, owner of the hacienda Cayán.
Since Cayán was to the east of Jauja, it had not been affected by the
smoke. Packing up what he needed, Artica left Chacapalpa with his
livestock and his two sons and, passing through the Yanamarca Valley,
reached Cayán in two days. Once there, however, the Articas' flock
contracted hoof-and-mouth disease.

By the time the epidemic was over, the already weakened flock had
been decimated. Tired of traveling back and forth from Chacapalpa to
Cayán in order to care for the few remaining animals, Felipe Artica
decided to migrate in search of work. In 1925, he joined the swelling
ranks of displaced and proletarianized peasants who were looking for
employment in the mining sector. But because his father was a prestigious member of village society, Felipe managed to use family connections to avoid proletarian status.

Felipe Artica became a white-collar worker and, in time, a self-
taught accountant. By the time he was seventy years old, he had
worked at Goyllarisquisga, Malpaso, Cerro de Pasco, Chanchamayo,
and, finally, for the Sociedad Ganadera Tucle in the Mantaro Valley.
He owned a house in Huancayo, and most of his family lived in Lima.
When I spoke to him in 1977, he told me that the Cerro de Pasco

[38] For the development and function of the Ganadera Division, see especially DeWind,
"Peasants Become Miners," Chapter 5; El Serrano (Cerro de Pasco), XVIII: 224 (August 1968), 4–8; and Interview with Fortunato Solís, Acolla, Jan. 20, 1978.

Corporation had been, for the inhabitants of the central sierra, "like a great school."[39] But not everyone could use family influence to snatch victory from the jaws of defeat.

Because smoke damage cut drastically into the productivity of village flocks and fields, the construction of the Oroya smelter contributed directly to the proletarianization of the central sierra peasantry. As had always been the case, it was the poorer peasants, with fewer options to fall back on, who suffered most severely. Certainly the process was helped along by the previous three to four decades of social and economic differentiation that had set the scene, at the community level, for a major transformation of class relations. Even though foreign capital's alliance with wealthy peasants and petty *gamonales* had outlived its usefulness, therefore, it had played an invaluable role by increasing the proportion of the village population for whom the wage was an inescapable part of the struggle for survival. This fact, when combined with the ecological effects of the Oroya smelter, helped to create just the kind of labor force needed by a changing mining industry.

Indeed, as it inaugurated the more heavily industrial phase of its development, the Cerro de Pasco Corporation also began to transform relations of production. In the mines, the division of labor and supervision of the work process were intensified. *Contrata*, no longer used in the extractive process, was relegated instead to construction and the reinforcement of mining shafts, and brought under closer company control. The new production rhythms and relations demanded by the Oroya furnaces increased the need for a skilled and stable labor force. *Enganche* began to disappear as an organized form of labor acquisition.[40]

By the time the 1920s were over, the seasonal migration pattern that had predominated in the previous period had come to occupy a secondary position, both in terms of demand and supply, on the mining labor market. A series of measures adopted by the company during that decade—building schools, houses, and hospitals; paying bonuses at retirement to long-term workers; and facilitating the learning

[39] Interviews with Felipe Artica, I and II, Huancayo, June 1977.

[40] On the increasing division of labor and complexity of labor relations in the mines, see Ricardo Martínez de la Torre, *Apuntes para una interpretación marxista de la historia social del Perú* (Lima: Compañía Impresora Peruana S.A., 1949), I:343–45; and APJ, "Informe de las condiciones de vida i explotación de los obreros del Cerro de Pasco [Parts I and II]," Cerro de Pasco, November 7, 1930. For the end to *enganche* relationships, I have relied on interviews with Germán Maita, Acolla, February 7, 1978, and Fortunato Solís; and on Hutchinson, "Sociocultural Change," pp. 39–40.

of new skills—encouraged workers to remain in the mines. In the villages, the declining size of agricultural plots in the hands of pauperized peasant households, as well as the greater use of outside labor by wealthier families, freed the labor of some members year round and created a more flexible and willing labor pool. The number of people employed on a monthly basis declined noticeably, even in the more traditional mining camps. Migrations lengthened to the point where they tended to last for several years at a time.[41]

In one way, the construction of the Oroya smelter and related changes in production and labor relations were in accordance with a general tendency emerging in Peru as a whole. At the national level, Augusto B. Leguía's eleven-year dictatorship, known as the Oncenio (1919–1930), represented the Peruvian state's nearly unconditional surrender to foreign capital.[42] One important manifestation of this was the broad facilities Leguía offered North American investment in the productive sectors of the Peruvian economy. In the central highlands, Leguía's government was accused of consistent bias in favor of the Cerro de Pasco Corporation in the many legal actions following the smoke damage of the Oroya smelter.[43] After signing an agreement with Leguía in 1922, the International Petroleum Company (IPC), a division of Standard Oil, firmly established its position in the Peruvian oilfields. Among other provisions, the agreement granted IPC an extremely low tax rate.[44] In yet another case, the Foundation Company, a U.S.-based construction firm heavily involved in infrastructure expansion and urban building during the Oncenio, received generous encouragement to expand into glass, cement, and slaughterhouse ven-

[41] For the changes instituted by the company, see Kruijt and Vellinga, *Labor Relations*, p. 64. For the lengthening of migration, see also Flores Galindo, *Los mineros*, p. 61.

[42] Descriptions of the role of foreign capital during the Oncenio can be found in Frederick B. Pike, *The Modern History of Peru* (New York: Frederick Praeger, 1967), pp. 228–29; Steve Stein, *Populism in Peru: The Emergence of the Masses and the Politics of Social Control* (Madison: University of Wisconsin Press, 1980), pp. 53–55; Rosemary Thorp and Geoffrey Bertram, *Peru 1890–1977: Growth and Policy in an Open Economy* (New York: Columbia University Press, 1978), pp. 100–102, 109–110, 121–24; and Ernesto Yepes del Castillo, *Perú 1820–1920: Un siglo de desarrollo capitalista* (Lima: Campodónico Ediciones, 1972), pp. 279–87.

[43] Using the Jauja newspaper *El Porvenir*, Hutchinson argues that, despite energetic and numerous protests in the first years of smoke damage, the government dragged its feet in helping those affected with their claims; see "Sociocultural Change," pp. 41–44. For a detailed account of the negotiations between the company, the government, and the local inhabitants, see Laite, "Processes of Industrial and Social Change," pp. 84–95.

[44] Thorp and Bertram, *Peru*, 109–10.

tures during the same period.[45] And finally, Peru's dependence on
the United States for direct financial support increased notably. Between 1918 and 1929 the country's foreign debt, most of which was
owed to the U.S., rose from about ten million to one hundred million
dollars.[46]

A more controversial question, perhaps, is the extent to which the
Cerro de Pasco Corporation's drive to create a proletarianized labor
force and transform relations of production during the Oncenio was
part of a general transition toward the predominance of capitalism in
the Peruvian social formation as a whole. Some authors maintain that
Leguía had no consistent plan favoring national development and
modernization, but simply borrowed copiously in order to expand the
bureaucracy and enrich those near him through massive graft and
corruption. Those programs that did succeed, such as the rebuilding
of Lima and the construction of roads into the interior, are seen as
cosmetic attempts to create a modern veneer rather than substantive
policies. The stagnation or decline of manufacturing over the decade,
and the expansion of the foreign-owned export sector, merely dem-
onstrate that growth in this period was mainly the result of the inter-
nationalization of the Peruvian economy and had few implications for
sustained internal development or the transformation of relations of
production.[47]

By contrast, other analysts maintain that, particularly during the
second half of his regime, Leguía consciously supported the national
industrial bourgeoisie. They point to his tariff and credit policies as
proof of this support, and emphasize the expansion of the construction
industry, urban services, and public works. They argue that, even if
the changes going on during the Oncenio did not lead to the growth
of industry per se, they did result in urbanization, greater wage employment, and a widening of the internal market. Indirectly, all these
developments favored the expansion of capitalism.[48]

If we see the Oncenio as the period in which the form of capitalism
peculiar to Peru began to consolidate, the two arguments are not
necessarily contradictory. As had been true in the central highlands,
national capital's problems with accumulation and labor facilitated the
dominance of foreign investment in the development of Peruvian cap-

[45] Ibid., pp. 121–22; Stein, Populism in Peru, pp. 55–56.
[46] Pike, Modern History, pp. 228–29; Baltazar Caravedo M., Clases, lucha política y
gobierno en el Perú (1919–1933) (Lima: Retama Editorial, 1977), pp. 69–79.
[47] Thorp and Bertram, Peru, especially pp. 118–31, and more generally pp. 39–144.
[48] Caravedo, Clases, pp. 71–79.

italism more generally. Peru's dependent position on the international market, moreover, meant that the most profitable forms of investment—for both foreign and national investors—were in the export sector. Rather than give priority to national manufacturing, therefore, the role of the Peruvian state was to provide the infrastructure and services that facilitated continued investment and expansion of exports. It is in this context that Leguía's policies during the Oncenio must be viewed.

Whether or not he did so consciously, over the 1920s Leguía laid the foundation for the Peruvian state's supportive and mediating role in a capitalist society and economy. Though many of its articles were not enforced, the 1920 constitution provided the institutional framework for this role. It established the equality of foreigners and nationals in private enterprise and property ownership. It gave the government a central role in the reproduction of a healthy economy by involving it in the development of essential services, such as education, health, and public works. It set the legislative groundwork for state mediation between labor and capital, and declared the government responsible for social welfare. But perhaps most important for the peasant sector in general, the 1920 constitution made the state the key intermediary in political and property relations between Indian communities and the larger society. Because it also made peasants dependent on the government to settle internal disputes over politics and resources, the legal recognition of Indian communities would in the long run accomplish more than any other law to integrate the peasantry into the developing capitalist economy.[49]

In addition to the potential contained in the new constitution, some of the programs carried out during the Oncenio evidenced strong state support for capitalist development in Peru. The modernization of Lima was a case in point. Especially since the turn of the century, Lima's increasing importance as a service center for a growing export sector, as well as the expansion of manufacturing and of the working-class population, had transformed the Peruvian capital into a thriving commercial, bureaucratic, and industrial city. The construction, urban rationalization, and provision of vital services carried out during the 1920s brought the infrastructure up to the city's needs, making Lima

[49] On the 1920 constitution, see especially Jorge Basadre, *Historia de la República del Perú*, 6th ed., 17 Vols. (Lima: Editorial Universitaria, 1969), 13: 41–46; and Pike, *Modern History*, pp. 220–21. On the recognition of Indian communities, see also Thomas M. Davies, *Indian Integration in Peru: A Half Century of Experience, 1900–1940* (Lincoln: University of Nebraska Press, 1974), pp. 69–70, 76–77.

an efficient urban complex that could fulfill its various functions smoothly and effectively. Moreover the very same modernization process, because it generated a greater demand for labor in construction and other services, brought a huge wave of rural migrants into the city and set into motion yet another cycle of urban expansion.[50]

Even more vital for an expanding capitalist economy was the improvement in communications and transportation. Through a program of labor recruitment known as the *ley de conscripción vial* (highway conscription law), which required that all male residents of Peru between the ages of eighteen and sixty work on road construction and maintenance for a period of six to twelve days a year, the political authorities of the Leguía regime extended the network of highways into the furthest reaches of the country.[51] Sympathetic sources estimate that over 11,000 miles of road were built between 1919 and 1930.[52] But the highway conscription program also came under heavy criticism for its abuses. Some critics argued that the provincial Juntas Viales, composed of the local justice of the peace, the mayor, and the subprefect, had conflicts of interest, and that conscripted labor was used for private purposes or to build public works that had nothing to do with roads. Others criticized the lack of an overall concept and the poor organization of the program as a whole. Still others described the ill-treatment of peasant conscripts, who were forced to walk long distances without food and work many times their legal share.[53] But whatever the specific accusations, it is evident that the highway system, and with it the internal market for labor and goods, were dramatically extended during these years. It is also clear that, given the many exemptions granted and the possibility of buying one's way out, the labor obligations of highway conscription were borne almost exclusively by the peasantry.[54]

In the last analysis, the Oncenio was an important turning point because it blocked out the roles to be played by foreign and national capital in a dependent capitalist economy. Financed directly by foreign loans, the state emerged as an important mediator between sectors, creating the necessary infrastructure and a positive climate for further foreign investment. In the central highlands, these developments were felt in the form of the Oroya smelter and in the *conscrip-*

[50] Stein, *Populism in Peru*, pp. 55–57, 65–66, 69–73.
[51] Basadre, *Historia*, 13: 254–55; Caravedo, *Clases*, pp. 78–79, 85–95; Hutchinson, "Sociocultural Change," pp. 45–46; Stein, *Populism in Peru*, pp. 58–62.
[52] Basadre, *Historia*, 13: 257; Pike, *Modern History*, p. 227.
[53] Basadre, *Historia*, 13: 255–56.
[54] Ibid.

ción vial program. The many roads built in the 1920s not only facilitated migration to the mines and to Lima, but also tied the villages more closely to the developing urban markets. Because road construction made commercial agriculture both viable and profitable, it facilitated a process of internal transformation in the communities.[55] It thus formed part of the general trend toward the dominance of capitalism in Peru as a whole. And as another part of this transition, the decade of the 1920s would also witness the emergence of new political alternatives, both for workers and peasants, in the central highlands and in the country in general.

National Modernization, Proletarianization, and Peasant Politics

In addition to its promotion of foreign investment, urbanization, and capitalist development, Leguía's Oncenio was characterized, at least in the early years, by the emergence of new alternatives for peasant politics. Between 1919 and 1922, in an effort to break the political hegemony of the Civilistas, Leguía courted the support of the lower classes and certain sectors of the petty bourgeoisie, instituting, among other measures, a series of policies that favored the peasants. We have already seen that the 1920 constitution provided for the legal recognition of peasant villages and protected the integrity of communal lands. Between 1920 and 1922, Leguía and the Congress also created several organizations to investigate land claims and protect the status of the Indian. These included the Roca Commission that investigated land titles in Puno; the Sección de Asuntos Indígenas (Bureau of Indian Affairs) in the Ministry of Development (Fomento), headed by the *indigenista* Hildebrando Castro Pozo; and the Patronato de la Raza Indígena, a series of local and regional delegations centralized under the control of the Lima archdiocese whose function was to take the Indians' side against *gamonal* abuse. An Indian Congress was held in Lima in 1921, also under government auspices. Attended by delegations from a variety of communities, this Congress gave rise to the Comité Pro Derecho Indígena Tahuantinsuyo (Tahuantinsuyo Committee in Favor of Indian Rights), the first national *indigenista* organization with participation by the peasants themselves.[56]

[55] For a more detailed analysis of this transformation, see below, Chapters VIII and IX.

[56] Basadre, *Historia*, 13: 308–309; Pike, *Modern History*, p. 222; Davies, *Indian Integration*, pp. 76–78.

Predictably enough, there was a large gap between the letter of the law and its application. Since Leguía only wished to court the lower classes until he could break the Civilista alliance,[57] the *indigenista* organizations were abolished as soon as they began to suggest real changes. When the Roca Commission submitted a legislative proposal for Indian protection to Congress, for example, it was immediately dissolved under landowner pressure, and its suggestions permanently shelved. In 1923, Hildebrando Castro Pozo was exiled for his attempts to make the Sección de Asuntos Indígenas into an effective organization.[58] And in 1927, the government abolished the Comité Pro Derecho Indígena Tahuantinsuyo because its leaders were supposedly "exploiting" the Indian race.[59]

Yet despite the quick reversal of Leguía's progressive tendencies, the brief arousal of expectations in the early 1920s was enough to generate, within various sectors of the lower classes, a degree of ferment and mobilization that went far beyond the initial intentions of official policy. At the third Indian Congress in 1923, the delegates condemned the *conscripción vial* law and declared openly for the separation of church and state. A group of them also formed the Federación Obrera Regional Indígena (Regional Indian Workers' Federation), an organization dedicated to the application of anarcho-syndicalist principles to struggles in the countryside.[60] In fact, the government abolished the Comité Pro Derecho Indígena in 1927 and exiled its leaders largely because its radicalism was increasing at a frightening rate. Besides, if the situation in the central sierra was any indication, this radicalism was not going unnoticed among the country's peasants.

On August 18, 1921, according to the president of Jauja's Junta Vial, a group of "corrupt" people raised a red flag in that city's central plaza. Having attracted a considerable crowd, they marched to the area between the town of Tambo and the Huaripampa bridge, to the northwest of Jauja, which had been designated as a gathering place for those who would be working on the highway project. The leaders talked to a group of conscripts and convinced them to leave, disrupting the Junta Vial's activities. In the afternoon, they led a large demonstration through the center of town, protesting the highway conscription law and denouncing the abuses of the subprefect and the

[57] Caravedo, *Clases*, pp. 59–69.
[58] Pike, *Modern History*, p. 222.
[59] Basadre, *Historia*, 13: 312.
[60] Basadre, *Historia*, 13: 311–12; Agustín Barcelli S., *Historia del sindicalismo peruano*, 2 Vols. (Lima: Editorial Hatunruna, 1971), I: 172–79.

provincial council. Several days later, when the Junta tried once again to gather workers for the road, the same group passed out leaflets demanding freedom for the Indian race and proclaiming the sacredness of individual liberties. "We are not political revolutionaries," the leaflet concluded. "We simply want the freedom of our race. Down with slavery!"[61] And though the local political authorities accused the group of professional agitation and subversion, they were actually Jauja's Sub-comité Pro Derecho Indígena, composed of peasants, artisans, petty merchants, and small landowners who lived in Jauja but were originally from the surrounding villages.[62]

The economic transformations of the period lent a new urgency not only to what was happening in Jauja and nearby communities, but also to peasant struggles on the haciendas. Starting in the early 1920s, for example, Wenceslao Grandes, *arrendatario* (lessee) of the hacienda Yanamarca, attempted to limit the size of his *colonos'* flocks by charging grazing rights and to increase the intensity of peon labor on hacienda lands. Grandes' goal was to expand production for the market, but the peasants perceived these measures as a direct attack on their ability to use hacienda resources to increase their access to means of production and thereby resist total proletarianization. By limiting their flocks, the *hacendado* was limiting their ability to make extra money through grazing other peasants' animals. By intensifying work rhythms on hacienda lands, he was reducing the family's time to work their own fields. Almost continuously between 1922 and 1930, therefore, the *colonos* on Yanamarca were involved in court cases, strikes, petitions, and other battles over what they perceived as Grandes' challenge to their subsistence.[63]

[61] APJ, "Informe del Presidente de la Junta de Servicio de Caminos Provincial al Prefecto del Departamento, sobre sucesos en Jauja," Jauja, September 3, 1921, and accompanying leaflet "La ley de caminos," Jauja, August 1921.

[62] Ibid.; Barcelli, *Historia del sindicalismo*, pp. 172–79; Conversations with Moisés Ortega, throughout 1977 and early 1978, especially November 6, 1977; and Conversation with Sixto Miguel, Jauja, January 30, 1978.

[63] APJ, "Copia del Fallo Arbitral en el juicio entre los peones de la hacienda Yanamarca y el arrendatario Wenceslao Grandes," Huancayo, December 15, 1923; "Oficio de Wenceslao Grandes al Prefecto del Departamento," Jauja, December 17, 1923; "Oficio del Subprefecto de Jauja al Prefecto del Departamento," Jauja, January 21, 1924; "Solicitud de Wenceslao Grandes al Subprefecto de la provincia," Jauja, January 25, 1924; "Oficio del Director del Colegio Nacional de Jauja al Subprefecto de la provincia," Jauja, January 17, 1924; "Solicitud de Wenceslao Grandes al Prefecto del Departamento," Jauja, March 31, 1924; "Solicitud de Enrique Morales, como apoderado de los operarios de la hacienda Yanamarca, al Prefecto del Departamento," Jauja, April 16, 1924; "Solicitud de Isaías R. Grandes, administrador de la hacienda Yanamarca, al Subprefecto de la Provincia, pidiendo licencia para rodeo de pastos," Jauja, December

The congruence in dates between the construction of the Oroya smelter and the first strike of *colonos* on the hacienda is clearly nothing more than a coincidence. But it is also true that the narrowing of peasant alternatives, best symbolized by the extensive smoke damage the smelter caused, made work on some haciendas—especially those offering significant access to means of production—appear more attractive. Rather than going elsewhere, therefore, the Yanamarca peons decided to stay and fight for their rights within the hacienda system. In this context, it is interesting to note that the worst punishment the *hacendado* could give the movement's leaders was to expel them from the hacienda, replacing them with other peasants eager to take their place.[64]

On the haciendas as well as in the villages, then, the 1920s was a time of increasingly bitter struggles against proletarianization. The Oroya smelter, the highway conscription law, the further commercialization of agriculture[65]—all these combined to increase the pressures of change in the peasant sector. But in addition to their similarities as struggles against proletarianization, the battles in the central highlands had something else in common. They marked the first appearance on the historical stage of a new political alliance between the peasantry and an emerging stratum of urban radicals.

Even before Jauja's Sub-comité Pro Derecho Indígena raised the red flag in the central plaza in 1921, a sector of the rural and urban petty bourgeoisie—tailors, printers, farmers, and teachers—had decided to throw in their lot with the lower classes. In alliance with the peasantry, they supported an end to government labor extractions, the abolition of *gamonalismo*, the separation of church and state, and the return of *cofradía* properties to the villages. Initially influenced by anarcho-syndicalism and *indigenismo*, the same people would, by

29, 1927; "Oficio de Isaías R. Grandes al Ministro de Fomento," Jauja, December 10, 1930; "Solicitud de Isaías Grandes al Prefecto del Departamento," Jauja, January 30, 1931; "Solicitud de Pablo Estevan, Clemente Osorio y Simón Barzola, indígenas personeros de los operarios de la hacienda Yanamarca, al Ministro de Gobierno," Lima, January 19, 1931; "Solicitud de Pablo Estevan, indígena personero de los operarios de la hacienda Yanamarca, al Presidente de la Junta Nacional de Gobierno," Lima, June 12, 1931; "Resolución del Ministerio de Fomento sobre el conflicto entre los yanaconas y el conductor del fundo Yanamarca," Lima, April 8, 1931; "Oficio del Director del Colegio Nacional de San José de Jauja al Director de Bienes, Rentas y Cuentas Escolares," Jauja, November 10, 1930. For more on the underlying rationale of the battle, see Florencia E. Mallon, "Microeconomía y Campesinado," pp. 39–51.

[64] APJ, "Solicitud de Wenceslao Grandes al Prefecto del Departamento," Jauja, March 31, 1924.

[65] For a detailed consideration of agricultural commercialization in the 1920s, see below, Chapter IX.

the end of the decade, be drawn into the ranks of newly formed leftist organizations such as the Alianza Popular Revolucionaria Americana (APRA) and the Communist party. Throughout the period, they provided a new and invaluable source of support for peasant groups resisting specific exactions and abuses.[66]

For the duration of their case, for example, the peons on the hacienda Yanamarca received legal and strategical advice from Max E. Cordero and Víctor Graciano Mayta. Though they were both lawyers who served on Jauja's municipal council, Mayta and Cordero were also part of the first radical Aprista generation to emerge in the central highlands. Along with other members of the local petty bourgeoisie, they participated in a number of the battles against labor exactions and provincial council abuses that took place in Jauja over the decade. When Leguía fell in 1930, both were arrested and sent to Lima as political agitators. Among the most conclusive evidence presented by their captors was that they had "instigated" the rebellion of the *colonos* on Yanamarca.[67]

What made Cordero and Mayta dangerous to the government, however, was not only that they "incited" peasants to rebel, but also that they were developing connections with the first national leftist organizations. Along with other provincial radicals, they would become effective middle-level cadres in APRA or the Communist party, serving as an important link between the national leadership and the local constituencies. Decades later, after the parties to which they belonged had substantially modified their platforms, some members of this first generation still held fast to their initial ideals, proving that

[66] APJ, "Informe del Presidente de la Junta de Servicio de Caminos," and accompanying leaflet; "Oficio de la Confederación Regional del Centro al Prefecto del Departamento de Junín, defendiendo a la comunidad de Pancán," Lima, December 2, 1929; Barcelli, *Historia del sindicalismo*, pp. 172–79; Conversations with Moisés Ortega, Acolla, throughout 1977 and early 1978, especially November 6, 1977; Conversation with Sixto Miguel, Jauja, January 30, 1978; Interview with Oscar Teófilo Camarena, Tragadero, November 29, 1977; and ANF, Protocolos Notariales, Luis Salazar, Book 21: August 8, 1910, 891–91v and insert at end of book, for an example of a member of the Jauja merchant elite who disagreed with *enganche* and later sympathized with APRA. For a comparative look at the rise of local radicalism and *indigenismo*, see Luis E. Valcárcel, *Memorias* (Lima: Instituto de Estudios Peruanos, 1981).

[67] In addition to the many accusations of "outside agitation" made by Wenceslao and Isaías Grandes (see sources in footnotes 63), see especially APJ, "Oficio del Subprefecto de Jauja al Prefecto del Departamento, sobre las actividades políticas de Víctor Graciano Mayta," Jauja, December 12, 1930; "Oficio del Subprefecto de Jauja al Prefecto del Departamento, remitiendo a los detenidos Víctor Graciano Mayta y Estevan Pavlevitch," Jauja, December 12, 1930; and "Oficio del Subprefecto de Jauja al Prefecto Mayor Santiváñez, remitiendo al detenido Max E. Cordero," Jauja, December 19, 1930.

the highland masses could remain a great deal more radical than their urban, coastal leaderships.[68] But the link between peasant mobilization and the emerging national parties was not always felicitous or productive.

Of all the struggles in which peasants and newly formed radical groups collaborated, none was more dramatic or ill-fated than the two-year battle between the Cerro de Pasco Corporation and its mining labor force (1929–1930). In 1928, after the inundation of several mine tunnels under the Morococha lake had killed at least twenty-eight miners, the group around José Carlos Mariátegui that published the magazine *Labor* in Lima began to establish contacts with workers in the central mines. In addition to circulating *Labor* at the mines, Mariátegui and his collaborators began a correspondence with several mineworkers. By February 1929, this initiative had led to the founding of the Sociedad Pro-Cultura Popular (Society in Favor of Popular Culture) in Morococha. Naming Ricardo Martínez de la Torre its representative in Lima, the Sociedad continued to communicate with Mariátegui's group and to emphasize the importance of worker's education and culture.[69] With the beginning of the world depression, however, this cultural interchange soon took on political overtones.

The precipitous decline of copper prices on the world market after 1929 turned the short-term financial problems of the Cerro de Pasco Corporation into a major crisis as it could no longer keep up with payments on the loans that had financed a number of its large construction projects over the 1920s. In an attempt to recoup its losses, the company cut production, laid off large numbers of workers, and forced those remaining to take a cut in pay. This precipitous decline in the miners' standard of living greatly facilitated the formation of unions, which sprang up in a number of mining centers between late 1929 and early 1930. Unionization also received an important boost

[68] In addition to the sources in footnote 66, see APJ, "Oficio del Comisario de Jauja al Subprefecto de la Provincia, informando sobre actividades Apristas," and attached leaflet announcing APRA's candidates for the election, September 29–October 2, 1931; "Oficio del Alcalde Municipal al Prefecto del Departamento de Junín, denunciando las actividades Apristas en su distrito," Chongos, January 8, 1934, and attached leaflet; "Oficio del Subprefecto de Jauja al Prefecto del Departamento, remitiendo información sobre ocho detenidos apristas y comunistas," Jauja, August 24, 1935; "Oficio del Juez de Paz de Acolla, acusando al Gobernador del distrito de ser aprista," Acolla, October 15, 1934; "Informe del Alferez Jefe de Línea de Jauja al Subprefecto de la Provincia, sobre propaganda aprista en Acolla," Jauja, February 19, 1935; "Oficio del Subprefecto de Jauja al Prefecto del Departamento de Junín, informándole sobre detenidos apristas en Acolla," Jauja, February 19, 1935.

[69] DeWind, "Peasants Become Miners," Ch. 7, pp. 8–9; Flores Galindo, *Los mineros*, pp. 78–79; Martínez de la Torre, *Apuntes*, IV: 5–6.

from the successful strike of October 1929 in Morococha, which was organized by a committee in touch with Mariátegui's group (recently reconstituted as the Partido Socialista).[70]

Spurred on by its early successes, the relationship between the Socialist party and the miners' unions continued to flourish. But after Mariátegui's death in April 1930, the general orientation of the group and its connection with the miners began to change. Rather than continue to emphasize education and the gradual construction of a working-class movement, the party moved closer to the line held by the Communist International in America and began to emphasize strong leadership and the immediate espousal of an internationalist proletarian line. By October 1930, it had affiliated with the International and had become the Peruvian Communist party (PCP). In the mines, these changes in orientation at the national level were felt almost immediately in the actions and attitude of the political organizers.[71]

From the beginning of their collaboration, the intellectually and politically more sophisticated members of the Lima group had felt frustrated by what they perceived as the lack of political understanding and "opportunism" of their contacts in the mines.[72] As long as the party had emphasized the gradual approach, organizers had been forced to curb their impatience, recognizing the enduring connection of miners to the peasant sector and seeing their task as including elements of both workers' and peasants' organization.[73] Once the party took a harder line toward "petty-bourgeois deviations," on the other hand, it was easy for the leaders to blame all problems on the lack of a strong leadership, to trust the "proletarian instinct" of the miners, and to make themselves believe that the "final battle" of the revolution was just around the corner.[74]

This change in organizing style and strategy, however, accomplished precisely the opposite of what had been intended. When combined with the extreme hardships suffered by the mining labor force in 1929 and 1930, pressure from political organizers led to the rapid and superficial creation of militant unions. These newly formed, politically naive organizations then took on a company that not only could fall back on sophisticated and effective methods of labor control

[70] DeWind, "Peasants Become Miners," Ch. 7, pp. 9–10; Flores Galindo, *Los mineros*, pp. 79, 82–88; Martínez de la Torre, *Apuntes*, IV: 6–19.

[71] Flores Galindo, *Los mineros*, pp. 86–90, 96–104.

[72] Martínez de la Torre, *Apuntes*, IV: 5–32.

[73] Ibid., p. 31.

[74] DeWind, "Peasants Become Miners," Ch. 7, pp. 12–15; Flores Galindo, *Los mineros*, pp. 91–93; Martínez de la Torre, *Apuntes*, IV: 28–76.

developed in the mines of the North American West, but also had the support of the Peruvian state.[75] The result of this suicidal confrontation was massive repression, with little gained in terms of better conditions or lasting political consciousness.

The actual sequence of events is too intricate to reproduce here, and at any rate has been well summarized elsewhere.[76] Suffice it to say that, by the end of 1930, the impatience of the newly formed Communist party had combined with the high level of ferment in the mines to produce a series of bloody confrontations between the miners and the police. The rapid escalation of conflict reached its peak on November 12, with a massacre of workers at the newly constructed hydroelectric plant of Malpaso and the declaration of a state of siege for the departments of Lima and Junín.[77] After providing the authorities with carefully detailed lists of all known "agitators,"[78] the Cerro de Pasco Corporation's officials sat back to weather the depression.

In the end, the entire series of events proved a blessing in disguise for the company. After a month-long lock-out, the corporation rehired only those workers who, both for economic and political reasons, were considered "safe." Between 1929 and 1932, its entire labor force was reduced from nearly 13,000 to approximately 4,300.[79] Not only did this allow the corporation to cut its depression losses, but it also served

[75] For a discussion of the labor control techniques developed in the American West, see Kruijt and Vellinga, *Labor Relations*, pp. 80–81. The support of the Peruvian state for the company is clearly evidenced by the surveillance and quick repression of the mineworkers. See sources in footnotes 77 and 78, and Flores Galindo, *Los mineros*, pp. 104–107.

[76] DeWind, "Peasants Become Miners," Chapter 7; Flores Galindo, *Los mineros*, pp. 79–109; Martínez de la Torre, *Apuntes*, IV: 33–126; A. J. Laite, "Miners and National Politics in Peru, 1900–1974," *Journal of Latin American Studies*, 12: 2 (1980), 327–28.

[77] For the declaration of a state of siege, see BNP, Document No. D1130, "Decreto-Ley No. 6927, Declaración de Estado de Sitio en los Departamentos de Lima y Junín," Lima, November 12, 1930; and APJ, "Informe que presenta el Prefecto del Departamento de Junín, Mayor J. Santiváñez, al Señor Ministro de Gobierno, sobre el Congreso minero en Oroya," n.d., 21. For the massacre at Malpaso, see DeWind, "Peasants Become Miners," Ch. 7, p. 23; Martínez de la Torre, *Apuntes*, IV: 111, 113–15; "Informe que presenta . . . Santiváñez," 23–24; and Interview with Felipe Artica (I), Huancayo, June 1977.

[78] See, for example, APJ, "Lista de dirigentes huelguistas, Morococha," 1930; "Lista de dirigentes huelguistas, Oroya," 1930; "Lista de dirigentes huelguistas, Cerro de Pasco," 1930; "Lista de dirigentes huelguistas, Malpaso," 1930; "Lista de los activos en la huelga, Goyllarisquisga," 1930; "Lista de los activos en la huelga, Casapalca y Bellavista," 1930; "Otra lista de la Corporation de los activos en la huelga," Morococha, 1930; "Lista de los activos en la huelga, Mahr Tunel e Hidroeléctrica," 1930; "Lista general de los activos en la huelga, a nivel de la Compañía entera," Oroya, December 5, 1930.

[79] DeWind, "Peasants Become Miners," Ch. 7, pp. 9 and 24.

as a kind of "spring cleaning." Years later, when the firm resumed hiring, it was a great deal more careful and selective. And for whatever reason, unions did not reemerge until 1945.[80]

For the peasants, the effects of the 1930 mobilizations are somewhat more difficult to assess. Both the PCP and the authorities expected the mineworkers to give free reign to their "proletarian instincts," but both were disappointed.[81] While they were making the transition to permanent wage laborers, the peasant-miners still had one foot in the industrial sector and one foot in the countryside. Because the PCP cadres did not take this into account, the rapidly formed unions never took firm root in the miners' consciousness.[82] Thus the peasants, a militant complained bitterly, "in general, before suffering reprisals or reductions in wages on the part of the company, prefer to abandon the mining centers and go back to the agricultural or livestock sectors."[83] What with the lockout and the depression, that is exactly what many miners did.

When the peasant-miners returned to their communities of origin at the beginning of the 1930s, they did not find the same villages they had left a decade before. Intensified social and economic differentiation, the formation of a new village elite, the further pauperization of an important sector of the peasant population—together these factors had combined to close off some of the alternatives available to the peasant family economy. As both rich and poor discovered new alliances outside the community, class conflict increased and village solidarity declined. The alliance of wealthy peasants with foreign capital, the ever more numerous and permanent migrations of villagers to the mines, foreign capital's direct incursion into the peasant sector through the smoke damage of the Oroya smelter, and the modernization and road construction of the Oncenio, had all helped to set the scene for what was to come. And yet the transformation of class relations within the community was only at an embryonic stage.

What the union organizers in the mines failed to realize was that migration, in and of itself, would not proletarianize the central high-

[80] Flores Galindo, Los mineros, pp. 107 and 114.
[81] On the authorities' expectations, see APJ, "Informe que presenta . . . Santivá-ñez"; on the PCP's expectations, see Martínez de la Torre, Apuntes, IV: 33–137; Flores Galindo, Los mineros, pp. 101–104; and DeWind, "Peasants Become Miners," Ch. 7, pp. 14, 16, 25–26.
[82] DeWind, "Peasants Become Miners," Ch. 7, pp. 25–26; Flores Galindo, Los mineros, pp. 99–100; Kruijt and Vellinga, Labor Relations, pp. 103–105.
[83] Martínez de la Torre, Apuntes, IV: 114–15. Also cited in DeWind, "Peasants Become Miners," p. 26.

land peasantry. Insofar as proletarianization meant allegiance to one's condition, and a commitment to act on a common interest with others in that same condition, the effects of migration were at best contradictory. On the one hand, by forcing some peasants to depend more fully on the wage and providing others with an avenue of accumulation, migration could speed up the development of capitalism at the local level. But on the other hand, if it provided an additional source of income that aided in the reproduction of the peasant household or supported the purchase of land, migration could slow down or reverse the process of proletarianization. As long as a return to the village economy continued to be a viable choice for migrants, therefore, their class loyalties would remain divided. And the impetus for closing off that choice had to come from within the village itself.

PART III

The Peasants Confront Poverty:
The 1930s and Beyond

*The land gave birth to my grandfather, / to my father
and my mother, / but the children of the third generation /
don't have even a dog / to keep them warm at night.*

—Patricio Manns, "Ya no somos nosotros."

CHAPTER SEVEN

Migration and the Peasant Community

From mineral to mineral and mine to mine / I am bound by fate

to go; / In this endless walking and wandering / I will live out

my sad life.[1]

At any point after 1870, a traveler entering the Mantaro or Yana-marca Valleys would have probably been hard pressed to find a village where people did not migrate for at least a few weeks out of the year. Especially during the slow points in the agricultural cycle, men worked as miners, muledrivers, herders, or at whatever occupation they could find. When they were not busy with additional household tasks, such as spinning, knitting, or caring for the animals, women might engage in commerce, selling surplus agricultural produce or small amounts of handicraft in the nearby towns. Significant variation existed between villages as to length or type of migration, depending on the degree of commercial penetration and the nature of social relationships at the local level. But despite these variations, most migration patterns had one thing in common: they were tightly integrated into the family economy of the individual peasant household.

Migration fulfilled two important functions for the peasant family. First, given the eminently seasonal nature of agricultural work, it helped to keep household labor gainfully occupied during most of the year. Secondly, by providing a source of cash, it contributed to whatever emergency needs a subsistence economy might not otherwise be able to handle, such as fiesta expenses, church fees, a death in the family, or a court case. The decision to migrate, therefore, was made as part of the household's overall calculations and could not easily be separated from other family activities. And the migration process itself clearly reflected this.

Especially when going to the mines or subtropical haciendas, where it was customary to remain for several months, migrants tended to travel with relatives and share expenses. Living in a single dwelling,

---

[1] From "Desdenes," a *huayno* (popular folksong) written by M. Gutiérrez in 1930, cited in Heraclio Bonilla, *El Minero de los Andes* (Lima: Instituto de Estudios Peruanos, 1974), p. 11.

they often took a young or unmarried female relative with them to handle domestic chores. Each household also provided their migrant with several animals and bags of food from the village, so that he or she would not have to spend unnecessary money on subsistence while away. If the stay was long, another member of the migrant's family might later bring additional food, clothing, or other necessities, perhaps taking advantage of the trip to engage in a bit of commerce on the side. Once the migratory cycle was over and all hands were needed in the agricultural sector, everyone would return home and take up their customary tasks in planting or harvest.[2]

Rather than being motivated by the loss of means of production, then, seasonal migration in the central sierra seemed to provide insurance precisely against that type of loss. Since it served both to channel surplus labor out of the village and to bring extra income in, it was an extremely adaptable safety valve. It could diffuse population pressure on the land, or enable a land-poor family to purchase property. At its best, seasonal migration had a kind of timelessness: no matter how commercialized the regional economy, how fast the local population grew, or how many times *chacras* were subdivided by inheritance, a peasant could always migrate, bring the family economy into balance, and avoid proletarianization. While there might be differences in individual experience between families or time periods, the importance of the process seemed to lie in its general continuity. Whether it occurred in the 1890s or the 1920s, seasonal migration evoked images of dust hanging over mountain roads as peasants and their families, backs bent beneath bags of broad beans, barley and potatoes, drove their sheep before them on their way to work in the mines.

This vision of migration corresponds to a particular approach to the study of the peasant household. When analyzing the household as a unit of production and consumption, many scholars have emphasized family ties and life-cycle considerations as the crucial variables in understanding the dynamics of the peasant economy. In this context,

---

[2] This general picture of migration emerges from a wide variety of sources cited throughout this book, including interviews with ex-migrants, Protocolos and Libros Judiciales in the ANF, the Tesis de Minería in the UNI, and some secondary sources on mining and migration, such as Bonilla, *El Minero*; Adrian DeWind, Jr., "Peasants Become Miners: The Evolution of Industrial Mining Systems in Peru," Ph.D. Dissertation, Columbia University, 1977; Alberto Flores Galindo, *Los mineros de la Cerro de Pasco, 1900–1930* (Lima: Pontífica Universidad Católica del Perú, 1974); and Julian Laite, *Industrial Development and Migrant Labour in Latin America* (Austin: University of Texas Press, 1981).

differential access to resources is not a manifestation of permanent class differentiation in the peasant village, but rather of families at various moments in their life cycles attempting to keep a balance between household labor and available land and animals. Migration is merely an additional means to occupy family labor, to be used permanently to rid the agrarian household of extra hands, or to accumulate money to buy extra land. The important variable in migration decisions, therefore, is not the action of commercial capital and class differentiation on local society, but the changing needs of families as they move through their life cycles. And while this approach does not present a totally static picture of peasant society, certainly from a historical perspective the image that emerges is one of continuity rather than transformation, of timelessness in the larger sense, since variation occurs within rather than between generations.[3]

The main advantage of such an approach is that, by using the household as a unit of analysis, it is easier to understand how peasant society could successfully survive centuries of commercial penetration. In the central sierra, more than anything else, it was the constant adaptability of the family economy that allowed it to resist proletarianization while remaining permeable to commercialization. By manipulating the various sources of income open to them, peasants repeatedly met labor and other demands from the commercial sector but managed to resist total expropriation. Even if this strategy ultimately led to the shrinkage of the peasantry's subsistence base and the superexploitation of family labor, it still left a broader range of alternatives for the reproduction of the household. And in the battle over land and labor, the availability of alternatives was the peasant's strongest weapon.[4]

But because it stresses continuity in local society to the exclusion

[3] The classic formulation of this approach is, of course, A. V. Chayanov, *The Theory of Peasant Economy,* ed. Daniel Thorner, Basile Verblay, and R.E.F. Smith. Published for the American Economic Association (Homewood, Ill.: R. D. Irwin, 1966). For an interesting summary of the household approach to the peasant economy, and some of the debates surrounding the transformation of peasantries, see Teodor Shanin, "The Nature and Logic of the Peasant Economy: A Generalisation," *Journal of Peasant Studies,* I: 1 (October 1973), 63–80 and especially 77–78. For work which applies these concepts to the central highlands, see Norman Long and Bryan Roberts (eds.), *Peasant Cooperation and Capitalist Expansion in Central Peru* (Austin: University of Texas Press, 1978), especially pp. 3–44 and 297–328; Julian Laite, *Industrial Development and Migrant Labour,* especially pp. 95–119 and 194–209; and A. J. Laite, "Industrialisation, Migration and Social Stratification at the Periphery: A Case Study of Mining in the Peruvian Andes," *Sociological Review,* XXVI (November 1978):859–88.

[4] For other formulations of the same general point, and a more extensive discussion of the battle over land and labor, see above, Chapters II, IV, V, and VI.

of other trends, the household approach can easily overlook broader tendencies toward change that become apparent with a historical or class analysis.[5] In the central highland villages and even within a single time period, there were striking differences in migratory experience between rich and poor households. As we have already seen, while it was certainly possible for a poor migrant to accumulate some money, perhaps build a house or buy some property, the cases in which a family could climb the social ladder through migration were few and far between. In general, because their families could afford to send them more subsistence goods and usually had better connections and personal relationships in the commercial sector, wealthy migrants got higher paying jobs and could save more. The poorer peasants, by contrast, did not have special skills or education and could not afford to take large amounts of goods with them. If they stayed longer than expected, became ill, or for some other reason built up a debt with the company or hacienda, they could easily lose money on the experience. Thus, even though migration could turn back the tide of pauperization, it could also broaden the distance between rich and poor.[6]

The migration process varied even more across time. While it was often the same people who migrated in the 1920s as in the teens, or in the teens as in the 1890s, the general context in which these labor flows occurred was changing dramatically. In the first decades of the twentieth century, the central highlands witnessed a massive infusion of foreign capital in the mining industry, the creation of the *sociedades ganaderas*, and the modernization of production in subtropical agriculture. At the same time, population growth in the villages, increasing commercialization, and internal social and economic differentiation all intensified the pressure of people on the land and expanded the need for seasonal migration. By the 1920s, even if the migrants were not proletarians in the strict sense of the word, their reasons for seeking work elsewhere, as well as the conditions they found when they arrived, were completely different from those that had prevailed at the turn of the century.

In the 1880s and 1890s, when labor migrations first became more frequent in the villages around Jauja, they were almost exclusively

---

[5] A more detailed treatment of the pitfalls of a microeconomic household approach that excludes larger historical trends is presented in Florencia E. Mallon, "Microeconomía y Campesinado: Hacienda, comunidad y coyunturas económicas en el valle de Yanamarca," *Análisis*, No. 4 (January–April 1978), pp. 39–51.

[6] See above, Chapters IV and V.

seasonal and of short duration. This arrangement served the interests of both peasants and commercial enterprises, since the state of technology was too low for the mines to be exploited productively all year round and the period of heaviest work on the subtropical haciendas could be arranged so that it did not coincide with the busiest days of the village agricultural cycle.[7] In order to attract peasants who might otherwise be content to remain in their communities, mineowners and *hacendados* used *enganche*, sending merchants to visit the villages and offer money in exchange for a promise to work the debt off at a set rate in the haciendas or mines. As long as the labor needs of the commercial sector did not expand too rapidly, and peasants did not find that their migrations cut into the time necessary to care for their crops, this system worked well as a mode of labor acquisition. The conditions under which people worked, however, were quite horrendous.

Given the primitive division of labor, the mineowners tried to extract from the workers the maximum amount of work in the shortest amount of time. They did not provide even the most elementary facilities, such as ventilation or ladders for the mineworkers to enter and leave the mine. The migrants were also forced to pay for their own supplies, especially candles, out of wages, and to work *guaraches*—thirty-six hours without stopping. And finally, particularly in the last decades of the century, wages were further lowered by the fact that employers continued to pay in paper money during a very heavy devaluation.[8]

Starting in 1895, the mining industry converted to copper to meet the expanding demand on the international market, while coffee cultivation boomed in the *ceja de selva*. At the same time, the government instituted its own *enganche* program to construct the central highway. The delicate balance between demand and supply on the region's incipient labor market was thrown off, and labor shortages developed. In the end, the peasantry's resistance to increased labor exactions, combined with problems of technology and capital scarcity,

[7] In terms of the agricultural cycle, since the subtropical haciendas produced mainly sugar cane, they had a fair amount of flexibility as to when to start cutting. Once the harvest began, moreover, the pace had to be quick and it was all over relatively quickly. For the nature of mine work in this period, see above, Chapters II and IV.

[8] For a more detailed description of mining conditions in this period, see Florencia E. Mallon, "Minería y agricultura en la sierra central: Formación y trayectoria de una clase dirigente regional, 1830–1910," in Florencia E. Mallon, Gerardo Rénique, et al., *Lanas y Capitalismo en los Andes Centrales*, Taller de Estudios Andinos, Serie: Andes Centrales No. 2 (La Molina: Universidad Nacional Agraria, 1977), pp. 1–12; and above, Chapter II.

prompted a reorganization of the mining industry under the auspices of foreign capital. This, in turn, affected other sectors of the regional economy, and changed the conditions under which seasonal migration could occur.[9]

In the first two decades of the twentieth century, foreign investment in mining and the expansion of commercial agriculture and livestock raising increased the range of work opportunities available to migrants. On the one hand, intensified commercialization and the extension of *enganche* networks under the auspices of foreign capital led to further pauperization and the increase of migrations motivated by need. Yet on the other hand, the competition of various sectors for the available labor supply gave peasants some room to negotiate, and many of them consciously used one sector against another in their struggle for better conditions. Thus on both subtropical and highland haciendas, owners were sometimes forced to provide more benefits than they would have liked—whether in access to land, grazing rights, additional payments in kind, working hours, or even schools—because the laborers, attracted by the higher wage in the mining centers, might otherwise have left.[10] But it would be wrong to overestimate the effectiveness of this type of pressure.

Especially in the mines, where the wages were highest, living and working conditions did not improve much. The lack of safety precautions, the use of dynamite, and the long shifts most people had to work contributed to an alarmingly high accident rate. In addition to the catastrophes caused by explosions or flooding, some of which took nearly one hundred lives, intense work rhythms and dangerous levels of fatigue resulted in many smaller accidents involving machinery: an arm lost here, a hand cut there, one or two deaths at a time. Whether in cases of rapid death or mutilation by accidents, or in the slower, more insidious death caused by lung diseases, the company rarely provided anything resembling just compensation.[11] And the opportunities for death or serious illness did not stop at the door of the mine.

Located above the timberline at around 15,000 feet or higher, most

[9] For a more extended treatment of these issues, see above, Chapter IV.

[10] See above, Chapters V and VI.

[11] Dora Mayer, *La conducta de la Compañía Minera del Cerro de Pasco* (Callao: Imprenta del H. Concejo Provincial, 1914), pp. 26–37; APJ, Various reports on work accidents: January 9, 1917; February 7 and 24, 1917; March 4 and 10, 1917; March 17, 1917 (2); April 15, 1917; May 2, 1917; June 15, 18, 21, 1917; July 2, 4, 11, 26, 1917; August 9, 24, 1917; September 2, 23, 28, 1917; October 17, 25 (2), 26, 29, 1917; November 28, 29, 1917; December 27, 1918; February–April, 1919 (7); July 7, 1919; and passim.

mining centers in the central highlands were dank and dismal places to live. The housing available for migrants, small rooms averaging twelve feet by twelve feet, did nothing to mitigate the harsh conditions. Because prices in most mining towns were around 40 percent higher than in Lima, it was common practice for a group of migrants from a single village to arrive together and live in a single hut, where overcrowding and lack of sanitation could easily lead to serious illness. As one shocked observer commented with respect to the quarters of workers in Morococha,

> They are extremely messy and dirty, and those who live in them exist under the most promiscuous [sic] conditions. The rooms serve simultaneously to house an entire family, with various kinds of animals, and even at times as a place to relieve one's most basic necessities. This complete lack of hygiene is surely a powerful factor in the spread of disease.
>
> Typhus has claimed many victims, and children are especially prone to contracting fatal diseases, particularly bronchitis, bronchial pneumonia, influenza, measles, and convulsive coughs. These epidemics have, on occasion, claimed more than one hundred small children, which given the size of the population is an extremely high number.[12]

As we have already seen, an important reason for the persistence of these conditions was that the Cerro de Pasco Corporation did not invest in transforming the system of production in these first decades. From the point of view of the company, therefore, it was not necessary to invest in safety precautions, medical care, schools, or any other benefit if the labor force was transitory and unskilled. It was more profitable to farm out the mine work to *contratistas* or pay an *enganchador* to provide a constant supply of cheap labor. But the company soon found that violent confrontations between recalcitrant peasants on one side, and *contratistas* and *enganchadores* on the other, made these methods more expensive and problematic than they seemed at first glance.[13]

Continuing problems with labor, as well as the need to compete technologically on the international market, again forced a transformation of the mining industry in the 1920s. With the construction of

[12] BCIM, No. 65, Alberto Jochamowitz, "Estado Actual de la Industria Minera en Morococha," 1907, pp. 65–66. See also BCIM, No. 25, Manuel G. Masías, "Estado actual de la industria minera en Morococha," 1905, pp. 62–66.

[13] See above, Chapters V and VI.

the Oroya smelter, the corporation generated a need for a permanent and more highly skilled labor force. At the same time, the combination of smoke damage and internal differentiation cut off alternatives for peasants in their villages. Thus the conditions, motivation, and permanence of labor migrations changed dramatically.[14]

Indeed, if one were to choose a decade in which significant progress was made toward proletarianization, it would have to be the 1920s. Before then, even though migration had been going on for a long time and the arrival of the Cerro de Pasco Corporation had increased its frequency and length, neither the form of labor acquisition nor the seasonal nature of migration had varied substantially. In the 1920s, on the other hand, *enganche* for the mines began to disappear, migration became "voluntary," and people stayed away from their communities for years at a time. Some men took their families with them on a stable basis, returning to their villages only for a few days around harvest or planting, or else leaving the care of their fields to relatives. Most male migrants depended on wives and other female relations to tend the agricultural side of the household economy, often with the aid of occasional wage labor.[15]

Yet, as is clear from an examination of the 1929 strikes, even this decade witnessed only the first halting steps toward the creation of a proletariat in the central highlands. Because miners still had real or potential access to land in their villages and a sense of loyalty to their communities, their allegiances were divided. The process of proletarianization was contradictory, varying across time and by individual household. It was not only a material, economic experience, but also a cultural, psychological one.[16] And nowhere were the contradictions of this process clearer than in the actual life histories of migrants.

Migration and the Individual Household

In June 1925, Teodoro Colca, native of Acolla, fell into an irrigation ditch at the Tamboraque smelter, property of Lizandro A. Proaño, and died as a result of the injuries he suffered. His son Manuel, apparently working with him in Tamboraque, made out the official accident report and certificate of death. Ten years later, when Colca's

---

[14] See above, Chapter VI.

[15] See the case studies of migrants, below, this chapter.

[16] On the length and complexity of the proletarianization process, see Adrian DeWind, Jr., "From Peasants to Miners: The Background to Strikes in the Mines of Peru," *Science and Society*, 29:1 (Spring 1975):44–72; and Flores Galindo, *Los mineros*, especially pp. 15–16, 99, 112–14.

widow, Lucía Núñez, began proceedings to dispose of the inheritance, she listed a number of properties the couple had acquired during their marriage. These included a four-room house in Acolla, in the *paraje* of Huayllachupa; around one-and-a-half hectares of land in Acolla, divided into six *chacras*; about one-half hectare in Marco, composed of two *chacras*; a small urban property (*solar*) on the northeast corner of Acolla's plaza; and Lot 28 on Block 12 of the Rímac housing development in Lima, which the couple had been paying off in installments. As part of the evidence needed in such cases, Núñez also produced a copy of their marriage certificate, registered in Oroya, which stated that on December 25, 1902, Teodoro Colca, native of Acolla residing at the mineral hacienda Tucto, had married Lucía Núñez, native of Ataura living in Cajoncillo. According to the document, they were both twenty years old at the time of the wedding; that would have made Teodoro Colca forty-three at the time of his death.[17]

Because it spanned over twenty years, Colca's migration experience is a good illustration of what was happening to migrants from the central highland villages during the first three decades of the twentieth century. Born out of wedlock to an *Acollino* father and a mother from Arequipa, he probably began migrating early in his youth out of economic need. He met and married his wife while working at the mineral hacienda Tucto, where he almost certainly witnessed its transfer of ownership from the Pflücker family to the Morococha Mining Company, subsidiary of the Cerro de Pasco Corporation. Lucía Núñez, if one were to hazard a guess, had migrated from her home village of Ataura in the company of a male relative, and divided her time in the mining center between domestic chores and some form of petty commerce in order to supplement the family income. Given this previous experience in a migratory household, she was certainly prepared to make Colca an excellent partner.

As the years passed, Colca seemed to spend more and more time in the mines. In 1923, he was present at the founding of the first miners' association for natives of Acolla in Morococha.[18] When the time came, his son began to migrate with him. But the reorganization of the industry prompted by the inauguration of the Oroya smelter seems to have affected him adversely; by 1925, he was no longer

[17] All the information in this paragraph, as well as all other information on Colca in the next three paragraphs not separately footnoted, comes from ANF, Expedientes y Libros Judiciales, "Lucía Núñez viuda de Colca, sobre declaratoria de herederos de Teodoro Colca," began August 1935.

[18] "Acta de Fundación del Comité Pro-Acolla en Morococha," August 19, 1923, Archivo Personal de Germán Maita, Acolla, 1v.

working in Morococha. Instead, he met his death at Tamboraque, a smelter belonging to one of the few Peruvian families that did not sell out to the North American corporation.

Perhaps the most interesting part of Colca's experience, however, is the mixture of attitudes that emerges from the pattern of his property purchases. The fact that he bought a lot in a Lima housing development implies that he wished to pursue the more urbanized, modern lifestyle to which he was exposed in the mining centers. Had he finished paying off the lot, he would have certainly built a house there. And yet he did not give up the land or his village roots. Quite the contrary, he accumulated agricultural property in the Yanamarca Valley, bought a house, and probably dreamed about retiring there when he was no longer fit for mine work. In the end, it was this one-foot-in-each-world ambivalence, no matter how long they actually stayed in the mines, that most characterized the migrants of Colca's generation. The only difference in Colca's case was that he did not live long enough to give the conflict some form of personal resolution.

Though he felt the same kind of ambivalence, Fortunato Solís, also from Acolla, managed to resolve the conflict several times and in several different ways in the course of his long life. Born in 1907 to a poor mother, he migrated to the mines for the first time when he was eleven years old. Travelling with a neighbor, he went because he needed the money to go to school. While his neighbor worked as a *perforador* (drill operator) in Casapalca, young Fortunato found a job at the Backus and Johnston smelter making bricks from the dust that emerged as a waste product. It was not a full-time job, of course; he usually worked about three days a week, depending on how often the stocks of powder accumulated. And he was paid between 0.50 and 0.60 soles per day.[19]

At some point between the ages of twelve and fifteen, Fortunato Solís finally entered school. In the ensuing years, he was able to work in the mines only during vacations, but he still managed to migrate numerous times. Once he was done with his education he married Asunción Castro, daughter of the man he had migrated with for the first time. He continued migrating to the mines and, when Casapalca resumed hiring after the depression, he decided to stay permanently. From 1934 until he was fired in 1953 before reaching retirement, he worked at a number of different jobs, some on the surface and some

---

[19] The identification of Solís' neighbor was made through AMA, "Censo del Primer Cuartel," 1934. All the rest of the information in the paragraph comes from Interview with Fortunato Solís, Acolla, January 20, 1978.

underground. Despite his status as a permanent laborer, however, don Fortunato never made more than three soles per day because he never learned any of the skilled occupations. Thus he was not able to bring his family to live with him in a more permanent way.[20]

Asunción Castro migrated with her husband in the first few years after they were married, but she was soon forced to return to Acolla and take care of her growing family. Because her husband did not earn a high wage, and because they did not have much money to begin with, it was necessary for her to take care of the agrarian side of the family economy. With the help of her children, brothers, and other relatives, doña Asunción sowed the fields, took care of the animals, and hired the necessary wage workers to help with the harvest. Then she or her husband would make the trip to Casapalca carrying produce—barley, broad beans, peas, potatoes, wheat flour—to help reduce the price of subsistence. Yet even in this way, it was difficult for the Castro-Solís household to save much. Because doña Asunción did not live with her husband, he paid for the preparation of his meals as well as for a room. Since he worked in the mines permanently, a good deal of what he made in wages during harvest and planting went out to pay for the additional laborers his wife had to hire in the village, and to buy the food, coca, cigarettes, and *aguardiente* that went along with the actual pay. In fact, it was only through the superexploitation of their own family labor, including that of their oldest child, Lydia, that Asunción Castro and Fortunato Solís were able to save enough to build their home.[21]

Lydia Solís was eight years old when she went to the mines for the first time. Her mother accompanied her on the train, and stayed several days to teach her how to prepare her father's meals and send them down into the mines. When doña Asunción left, however, Lydia was frightened. She remembers having cried for several days, afraid that she would never learn how to prepare the food in time for the meal whistle. When her father was on the night shift and she had to stay alone in the room, she often fell asleep with the light on, exhausted after so much crying. It took her a long time to become accustomed to the mining area, but accustomed she finally became. For the next thirteen years, until she was twenty-one years old, she trav-

[20] The identification of Asunción Castro was made through AMA, "Censo del Primer Cuartel," 1934. The rest of the information in the paragraph comes from Interview with Fortunato Solís.

[21] Interview with Fortunato Solís; Interviews with Lydia Solís de Maita, I and II, Acolla, 1977.

elled for two or three months at a time to help her father and to cook, clean, and sew for her uncle. Toward the end, she also began engaging in commerce, taking blankets and *mantas* from the textile factories and selling them in Casapalca on pay day. When she was back in Acolla, she helped her mother with the planting, harvesting, and other agrarian tasks.[22] In the end, she played a major role in the reproduction of her household's economy.

Indeed, a striking similarity between the Colca and Solís life histories is the important role played by the family in the migration process. To begin with, both men married women with family migration experience. In both households, the children began to migrate with their fathers while the mothers tended to stay home and care for the fields. And these are not isolated cases. Of the sixty-two miners listed in a census of Acolla's first *cuartel* (subdivision) in 1934, comprising over 40 percent of the *cuartel's* economically active male population, twenty-six (41 percent) migrated with other members of their families. Together they made up twelve separate family groups, and half of them had a female relative listed as migrating with them.[23] Thus, despite the proletarianizing tendency of the 1920s and the increasingly permanent nature of migration patterns, the process itself continued to be family-oriented.

Equally important, however, and once again borne out by both the life histories and the census data, there seems to have been a connection between economic need and the migration of more than one household member. Migrants who began with nothing found it difficult to accumulate money, or to get the kind of training that would assure them a higher paying job. Thus they continued to be more dependent on a combination of various types of income through the family economy. In addition to tending flocks and fields, women from the poorer families more often engaged in petty commerce between the mining centers and the community in order to supplement household earnings. Boys might migrate with fathers or uncles on a seasonal or occasional basis. Many female children, particularly if they were unlucky enough to be among the eldest, were forced to sacrifice their education and any independence in order to pull their family through the lean years. Lucía Núñez never learned to sign her name.[24] Lydia

[22] Interviews with Lydia Solís de Maita, I and II.
[23] Calculations are based on an analysis of AMA, "Censo del Primer Cuartel," 1934. For a more complete breakdown, see Appendix 3.
[24] ANF, Expedientes y Libros Judiciales, "Lucía Núñez viuda de Colca, sobre declaratoria de herederos," 3.

Solís never finished primary school. "I wanted to continue studying," she told me in 1978,

> but my father said no. "Who will help your mother, with the harvest, the planting, the animals? Your brothers and sisters certainly won't." Because I was the oldest, there was no one else to help my mother. And that is why I stopped studying. But my brothers and sisters have all finished primary, secondary—some have gone to the university.[25]

Male migrants from poorer households paid a heavy price also. Those who could not choose to migrate for a limited number of years, and worked underground in a period before the improvement of safety standards, are no longer around to tell their story. Victims of miners' lung disease, many died with swollen bodies, coughing blood. Others, such as Teodoro Colca, died in an accident before they could contract the dreaded disease. To this day, a census of the older generation in Acolla and other villages will yield a strongly skewed male-female ratio. Seventy-one years old in 1978, Fortunato Solís was still unsure as to why he had survived. "All my compañeros are dead," he explained.[26]

When we turn to examine the cases of wealthier migrants, we find a somewhat different pattern. While it is true that all mineworkers in the second and third decades of the century were especially vulnerable to occupational disease because of lax safety standards, the wealthier peasants had more choice with regard to occupation or length of migration. Some worked in managerial or office jobs, completely avoiding the problems of health or safety caused by the mines.[27] Others migrated for only a few years, just long enough to accumulate some money to invest in agriculture or learn a white-collar occupation. And even if migration continued to involve the household in some capacity, the well-off were less dependent on income from other sources to make ends meet. Thus, if they took their crops or animals to the mines, it was in order to accumulate more rapidly. If their families

---

[25] Interview with Lydia Solís de Maita, I.

[26] The quote comes from Interview with Fortunato Solís; the information on miner's lung disease comes from Interviews with Fortunato Solís and Lydia Solís de Maita (I), and from William B. Hutchinson, "Sociocultural Change in the Mantaro Valley Region of Peru: Acolla, A Case Study," Ph.D. Dissertation, Indiana University, 1973, pp. 41 and 85.

[27] Interview with Fortunato Solís; Interview with Felipe Artica (I), Huancayo, June 1977.

migrated with them, it was usually to accompany them for the length of their stay.

The case of Felipe Artica, which we have already discussed briefly, provides a good example of some of these differences. Don Felipe's father, a prosperous herder and *arriero* from the village of Chacapalpa, had business relationships with several prestigious merchants in Huancayo and was related by marriage or friendship to some of the lesser *hacendados* in the Jauja area. He was able to send his son to study in the Colegio San José in Jauja, where the young Felipe rubbed elbows with the sons of Jauja's elite. The elder Artica also served as mayor of his community. When Felipe Artica first migrated after the family flock was decimated by smoke damage, therefore, he went with two initial advantages: he had a secondary school education, and his father was well-connected. His first job experience proved how important these advantages could be.

Once in Cerro de Pasco, don Felipe went to visit Máximo Gamarra, a friend of his father's who owned property near Chacapalpa, to see if he could get a job recommendation. Coincidentally, Gamarra had a cousin who owned a large business and coal mine in Goyllarisquisga, and don Felipe was hired immediately. Three months later, he was promoted to head of the bookkeeping section when the accountant in charge resigned. His secondary school education must have certainly come in handy as he pored over the books at night, desperately teaching himself the rudiments of accounting. But when he left Goyllarisquisga after five years in 1930, he had learned an occupation that would stand him in good stead for the rest of his life. Without his initial advantages, none of it would have been possible.[28]

Mauricio Huamán's migratory experience was also simplified by the fact he came from a relatively well-off family. A native of Acolla, Huamán did not migrate until 1920, when he was twenty-two years old. He began as a *tubero*'s assistant, wearing boots as he sloshed around in the water inside the mine, learning to connect tubes for the drainage system. Once he learned the work, he quickly became a master *tubero*, earning four soles per day. But he did not stay in the mines at this early date. Instead, Huamán returned to Acolla after his twenty-third birthday and was married a few months later. Only the next year did he go back to Morococha, this time with his wife, and settle down.

As a stable worker in Morococha through the latter half of the 1920s,

[28] All the information on Artica comes from Interviews with Felipe Artica, I and II, Huancayo, June 1977.

Mauricio Huamán benefited greatly from the changes taking place in the mining industry. First as a machinist and then as a drill operator, he earned five soles a day between 1926 and 1930, a hefty sum for mine labor in those days. Though the room the corporation gave him was small, he and his wife lived there permanently, returning to Acolla for only two or three days during harvest to supervise the work on their fields. And while it is clear that they brought their crops to the mine at least partially to supplement their income and help them save, they also returned to Morococha with their barley, wheat, and peas because, Huamán insisted, "the food you grow yourself has a different taste."

After the strikes and the depression closed down the mines in 1930, Mauricio Huamán returned to Acolla and never went back. He dedicated himself to commercial agriculture, cultivating the lands he had inherited from his father in addition to some that he bought with the money he had saved. In 1935 he went to Jauja and studied to become a court clerk. After getting his diploma in 1936, he returned to Acolla to serve as mayor. Once his term was up he settled down in Jauja and worked as a clerk, returning to Acolla only to see to his lands and supervise the laborers he had hired.[29]

Overall, then, the comparison of migrant life histories yields as many differences as it does similarities. Among the latter, perhaps the most striking is the effect that the 1920s had on migration patterns. The transformation of the industry with the construction of the Oroya smelter created a demand for a more permanent and skilled labor force, and most mineworkers felt the pressure in some way. Huamán and Solís, for example, made the transition from temporary or seasonal wage labor to becoming resident workers for periods of at least several years. Colca was apparently forced to transfer from Morococha, where he had worked off and on for over twenty years, to the smelter at Tamboraque. And the Oroya smelter's smoke damage, by cutting into the productivity of the livestock and agricultural sectors, also affected migration. Felipe Artica, for instance, was among those who migrated for the first time due to the smoke, and then never went back to live permanently in their villages. But in this regard it is also interesting that none of the other men we have analyzed mentions having received an *enganche* during the 1920s. Indeed, as another migrant told me, *enganche* was no longer necessary: "people just arrived."[30]

[29] All the information on Huamán comes from Interview with Maurico Huamán, Jauja, February 9, 1978.
[30] Interview with Germán Maita, Acolla, February 7, 1978.

But the differences, especially those between the experiences of rich and poor peasants, are equally dramatic. As had always been the case with important changes in the regional economy, the development of industrial mining in the central highlands had very different implications for the various sectors of the peasantry. While Huamán was able to live with his wife permanently in the mining town and still accumulate enough money for land, housing, and education, Solís only built his house on the sweat of his entire family's labor. Huamán retired from the mines after only four years of permanent work, becoming a prosperous farmer and a court clerk. Solís, on the other hand, worked in the mines at the same salary until he was fired during a reduction of the labor force. He never received a pension, nor did he receive compensation for his second-degree case of lung disease.[31]

Such a diversity of experience was bound to generate divergent attitudes toward mining and the U.S. company. The lower strata of the peasantry, as symbolized by Solís, were paid miserable wages by the Cerro de Pasco Corporation and treated very poorly. The North American bosses, they felt, insulted them. Only with the development of the union did things start to change, and then only to some extent.[32] Many migrants from the middle to wealthy peasantry, on the other hand, saw the North American corporation, as did Felipe Artica, as "a great school." Whether they learned new skills directly in the mining centers, or paid to learn them later with money accumulated in the mines, they took advantage of their migratory experience to move up the social scale. When they returned to their villages in the 1930s and 1940s, they became the community's new generation of mayors and representatives, anxious to make their villages progress as they had. Some left the village for good, becoming white-collar employees in Jauja, Huancayo, or Lima. Others stayed to cultivate the land they had bought, becoming middle-level agrarian entrepreneurs.[33] But no matter what they did after they left, most felt that the mines had given them the opportunity to advance. "People took a chance," Germán Maita, a successful *Acollino*, told me. "That is why there are so many professionals in Junín today."[34]

Yet in the final analysis, though migratory experience might vary by individual or socioeconomic group, migration as a process had had,

[31] Interview with Fortunato Solís.
[32] Ibid.
[33] For a more detailed analysis of the migrants' political and agricultural activities, see below, Chapter IX.
[34] Interview with Germán Maita.

by the end of the 1920s, a fairly dramatic effect on the peasant household and the village in general. Within the household, though the
possibility of an extra income might avert total proletarianization, the
increasing permanence of mine work contributed to the commodification of labor by cutting down on the viability of reciprocal labor
exchange and increasing the use of wage labor. In the village, even if
migrants' associations contributed money for public works, the long
absences of *comuneros* shrank the available pool of community labor
and made even the simplest maintenance tasks more complicated. On
the whole, as migration tied the village more closely to the regional
and national economies, it set the scene for a major transformation of
community relationships.

Migration and Proletarianization: The Overall Balance in the Village

In September 1929, four years after it was initially formed, the
Association of Sons from the District of Marco residing in Casapalca
donated to their village of origin all the necessary materials for a system of running water. As the organization's president Santos Romero
explained to the *comuneros* at a reception the town gave him in October, all the pipes and other materials had been imported from the
United States. With the help of the Backus and Johnston Company,
Marco's sons had not only brought the pipes into Peru without import
duties, but had also managed to get the freight costs waived on the
Central Railway. Even with these savings, Romero explained, the association had spent over 10,000 soles; but there was no problem because the organization's fund included contributions of over 15,000.
The surplus was already being used to make a fountain for the central
plaza, and the main bowl would soon be finished and brought to Marco
from the Acho foundry in Lima.

Warming to his subject, Romero declared that the association had
great plans for the progress of Marco. To prolonged applause, he informed the gathering that future contributions would go to constructing a grain mill, using hydraulic power, at the spring of Pichjapuquio.
But there was something the village could do in return: in order to
assure the successful completion of these projects, the contributors
should be given special status within the community with regard to
labor obligations. Thus, Romero argued, all members of the association should receive complete exoneration from communal work during the months they were contributing to the fund. Upon presentation

of a receipt, they should be immune from all penalties for noncompliance that might be exacted by the municipal agents.[35]

Given how easily they manipulated money and influence, the *Marqueños* working in Casapalca can hardly be considered representative of the migrant population as a whole. Yet precisely because they were exceptional, they brought into sharper relief a contradiction that all migrants shared in relation to their communities of origin. On the one hand, by providing their villages with revenue for public works, they maintained communal responsibility and solidarity and helped the community in ways that nonmigrants could not. Indeed, as the desire for public works and the demand for revenue expanded in the 1920s, the migrants' associations played a vital role. But on the other hand, the increasing permanence of migration meant that migrants could not participate in communal work obligations, and thus did not form a part of their villages in the traditional ways. And the shortage of communal labor generated by this situation could become a difficult problem for village officials.

At the level of the community, then, the positive role of the associations or committees for the various districts was to help migrants keep up an allegiance to their villages when the physical realities of migration were eroding traditional forms of unity. The associations were formed in mining centers or other places with the purpose of collecting money for public works. They usually required that each member contribute a *tarea*, or day's wages, per month to the committee's coffers. The money collected was sent back to the villages of origin to be used for specific purposes, such as a fountain in the plaza, a library, or even in some cases to install running water or electric generators. Though some associations disbanded as quickly as they were formed once their goal had been met, others continued to operate over several decades, providing migrants with a vital tie to their villages, helping to reinforce community responsibility, and playing an important financial role in community construction.[36]

Despite these prominent contributions, however, committees also played a negative role from the point of view of the community. When migrants contributed money to the village, they felt it was their legitimate right to be exonerated from communal labor obligations. The

---

[35] AMM, Libro de Actas, II:212–13, 230, 231, 232–33, 284–85; and III:3–4, 4–6, 8, and especially 15–16 (reception of Romero).

[36] Interviews with Mauricio Huamán, Germán Maita, and Fortunato Solís; AMM, Libros de Actas, passim; AMA, Libros de Sesiones, passim; and Hutchinson, "Sociocultural Change," pp. 56–57.

Marqueños in Casapalca demanded this exoneration in 1929 in exchange for a continued active role in financing the district's construction projects. The *Acollinos* in Morococha asked for the same thing in 1936.[37] And this tension between migration and labor obligations created problems in many villages. In 1930, when the village of Chocón signed a communal obligation pact, the part of the agreement specifically addressing migration would have struck a responsive chord throughout the region:

> The *comuneros* who leave for the mining centers with the purpose of working [there] will let the authorities know, but without exemption from their corresponding quotas. . . . all those ungrateful traitors to the communal interest, will lose the right to use [communal] pastureland, being considered alien to the village: they must also pay for the damages they cause the community. . . . when the authorities decide to carry out a communal or private project, all the *comuneros* must appear for work without any excuse . . . those absent will be fined between one and two soles, depending on the nature of the particular job.[38]

Ultimately, once migration could no longer remain a purely seasonal phenomenon, it began to raise crucial questions about the nature of community and community membership. Was it necessary to fulfill a certain quota of work to be considered a member of the village? Could one simply pay for membership by donating money to a migrants' association? Was it in fact possible to find a monetary equivalent for communal obligations or communal rights? Charging a fine for noncompliance seemed to imply that some equivalent could be found. It was also tempting, particularly in the case of rich migrant committees like the *Marqueños* in Casapalca, to accept donations of money in exchange for work exemptions. Yet no matter how one interpreted it, the fact remained that migration, by commodifying relationships and separating them out from the intricately woven fabric of local life, was changing the very context within which community could be defined.

In addition to raising the question of community for the village as a whole, migration also brought up issues of community solidarity for the migrants themselves. Here again, the migrants' committees provide a good illustration of the contradictions involved. On the one

---

[37] AMA, Libros de Sesiones, 1934–1939, "Sesión de Junta," July 10, 1936, p. 156.
[38] ANF, Protocolos Notariales, Luis Salazar, Book 66: December 30, 1930, 1916v–20.

hand, an association could often unite migrants from a village across social and economic lines. In 1923, for example, when the first Comité Hijos de Acolla (Committee of the Sons of Acolla) was formed in Morococha, workers in a variety of jobs attended the initial ceremony.[39] By defining the progress of the community as a common goal, all *comuneros* from that district, whether rich or poor, skilled or unskilled, could work together for the common good. Migrants who stayed in the mines often worked on a series of projects or committees, gaining important organizational experience and earning respect from coworkers and fellow villagers.[40] But on the other hand, it is easy to overemphasize the success of the associations as mechanisms for social integration.

As was true for the rest of the migration experience, the committees could mean very different things for rich and poor peasants. In Casapalca, the experience of the Comité Pro-Campana, the committee set up to procure a bell for Acolla's church, showed that it was often the poorer villagers in the less prestigious jobs who did all the footwork and unsuccessful petitioning, while the employees and managerial staff from the same community could simply sit back and use their influence. "How we suffered for that bell," Fortunato Solís, a delegate on the association's organizing board, told me. Because the corporation refused to automatically discount a day's pay from each month's wage, the delegates were forced to walk many miles each month, collecting from room to room, in Casapalca and nearby Bellavista. Only a year later did the company accept the *descuento por caja* (automatic discount), and only because, according to Solís, "there were some fellow villagers who worked as managers, and the superintendent knew them."[41]

In contrast to what happened in Casapalca, Acolla's village committee in Morococha was, from the very beginning, dominated by well-off peasants with high-paying jobs. From the time it was founded in August 1923, the monthly contribution was set at five soles, a day's wage only for the better-paid employees. The committee received the *descuento por caja* immediately, evidencing good connections with the administration. And over the next fifteen years, the Morococha committees contributed not only a clock, but also a library and an electric generator to their community.[42]

[39] "Acta de Fundación del Comité Pro-Acolla," and Interview with Germán Maita.
[40] Interviews with Mauricio Huamán, Germán Maita, and Fortunato Solís.
[41] Interview with Fortunato Solís.
[42] "Acta de Fundación del Comité Pro-Acolla," 1; Interviews with Mauricio Huamán and Germán Maita.

Whether in the village or the work centers, therefore, the increasing permanence of migration in the 1920s added a degree of class tension to the relations among *comuneros* that had not been there in the past. Wealthier migrants, by bandying about impressive accumulations of money and showing off their influence with the mining companies, could continue to be considered "good sons" of the district even if they stopped fulfilling their traditional obligations to the village. Because they could afford to pay the fines, they did not have to work for the community and had more control over their labor time. Poorer migrants, on the other hand, could neither forsake their jobs and appear for the work parties, nor forsake the work parties to keep their jobs. They were forced to pay fines to the communal authorities in lieu of their village obligations, and wages to agricultural day laborers taking their place on their private plots. They could afford neither, much less both; and because they had little to offer in prestige or connections, they bore the brunt of the communal backlash against noncompliance.[43]

In the end, perhaps the most important effect of the 1920s on the central highland peasantry was the advancement of class differentiation within the village. Migration, though it could not by itself create a proletariat, certainly contributed to this change. It generated within the community both a wealthy sector eager to transform its money into capital, and a pauperized sector increasingly dependent on a wage and on the market. It helped commodify labor and communal relationships. Overall, migration made it increasingly difficult for the peasant community to revert to subsistence, and when the crisis of the 1930s broke in village society, it was impossible to turn back. Instead of retiring into the safety of communal institutions, the central highland peasantry faced poverty and an ever more complete and painful process of proletarianization.

[43] That there was a communal backlash is clear from ANF, Protocolos Notariales, Luis Salazar, Book 66: December 30, 1930, 1916v–20; and AMA, Libros de Sesiones, 1934–1939, p. 156 and passim.

CHAPTER EIGHT

Crisis in the Villages

It used to be that / all the hills and plateaus / belonged

to the community.

"They say that the community / is a thing that matters only

to Indians," / murmured the elders, chewing their coca.[1]

In Peru, as in other parts of Latin America, the world crisis of the 1930s raised painful questions about the nature of dependency and development. In August 1930, Lieutenant Colonel Luis M. Sánchez Cerro organized a victorious revolution in Arequipa that finally brought down the eleven-year-old dictatorship of Augusto B. Leguía, a government increasingly corrupt and compromised by foreign capital. Because it tended to throw the economy back on its own resources, the precipitous and generalized decline in export demand and direct foreign investment only emphasized how important foreign involvement had become to Peruvian prosperity. As the state and the economy began to recover from the shock of the period from 1929 to 1932, then, it seemed necessary to rethink a series of issues connected with national development. As was happening in other countries in Latin America, Peruvian policymakers and entrepreneurs began to confront the implications of *desarrollo hacia adentro* (inward-directed development).[2]

Yet in contrast to other areas, the repercussions of the world crisis in Peru did not inspire a concerted, government-directed program of industrialization. While new investments of national capital were substantial in this period, the majority were concentrated in the extrac-

---

[1] The first quote is from José María Arguedas, *Yawar fiesta* (Lima: Populibros Peruanos, n.d.), p. 15. The second quote is from Augusto Mateu Cueva, *Trabajadores del Campo*, 2d ed. (Lima, 1955), p. 90.

[2] *Desarrollo hacia adentro*, or inward-directed development, is a general term coined to refer to the type of development undergone by many Latin American societies during their relative independence from the international market (1930–1945). For general histories of the period for Peru, see especially Frederick B. Pike, *The Modern History of Peru* (New York: Frederick A. Praeger, 1967), and Rosemary Thorp and Geoffrey Bertram, *Peru 1890–1977: Growth and Policy in an Open Economy* (New York: Columbia University Press, 1978).

tive and export sectors, particularly cotton, mining, and petroleum.[3] Efforts to expand industry remained localized or regional, and generally in the hands of individual entrepreneurs.[4] The government's role in development tended to be indirect, and took two main forms. First, the state encouraged national integration and the expansion of the internal market through programs of roadbuilding and education. And second, it provided a support network for the sectors and classes who, though suffering unemployment or dislocation because of the depression, were still important to the overall reproduction of the society.[5]

There was a potential contradiction, however, between the government's commitment to continued economic expansion and its social welfare aims. Insofar as expansion did not ensure an end to unemployment, the state still needed to facilitate subsistence and a minimal level of consumption to urban workers unable to find jobs. Some of the programs set up to deal with this problem held possible benefits for entrepreneurs. The *restaurantes populares*, established in major cities to provide the unemployed with inexpensive meals, helped support a labor supply until it was needed again in the industrial sector, while at the same time keeping down the level of popular discontent. The roadbuilding and public works programs organized by the Junta Pro-Desocupados (Committee to Help the Unemployed) expanded infrastructure and could provide members of the elite with access to cheap labor for private projects if they had the right connections.[6] Yet in other cases, the government's goal of providing subsistence for the urban lower classes could come into conflict with its overall aim of supporting economic expansion, especially with regard to the agrarian sector.

[3] Thorp and Bertram, *Peru*, pp. 147–48, 182–83.
[4] For an interesting analysis of some of these efforts, see Baltazar Caravedo Molinari, *Burguesía e industria en el Perú, 1933–1945* (Lima: Instituto de Estudios Peruanos, 1976).
[5] Pike, *Modern History*, pp. 268–72.
[6] The general law on the creation of the popular restaurants was given on June 7, 1932. See Agustín Barcelli S., *Historia del sindicalismo Peruano*, 2 Vols. (Lima: Editorial Hatunruna, 1971), I:301. For the popular restaurant in Oroya, see APJ, "Oficio del Subprefecto de Yauli al Prefecto del Departamento," Oroya, September 1, 1937. For the activities of the Junta Pro-Desocupados, see APJ, "Oficio de Pedro de Osma, Presidente de la Comisión Distribuidora de Fondos Pro-Desocupados, a Eduardo Risco, Presidente de la Junta Departmental Pro-Desocupados de Junín," Lima, October 15, 1931; "Oficio de Cipriano Proaño, Ex-Presidente de la Junta Pro-Desocupados de Junín, al Director de Obras Públicas y Vías de Comunicación, Ministerio de Fomento," Cerro de Pasco, October 15, 1931; and "Oficio de A. E. Risco G., Junta Pro-Desocupados de Junín, al Prefecto del Departamento," Huancayo, January 30, 1932.

A good example of this was the growing problem with the food supply in Lima. Since the depression kept food prices low, agrarian investors preferred to place their money in crops providing a higher return to capital, such as cotton exports. The supply of basic staples thus tended to fall throughout the decade, forcing the state to intervene in an attempt to guarantee adequate provisions to the major urban markets. Beginning in 1930, for example, the state encouraged wheat production through government purchase, preferential freight rates on railroads and highways, and other measures. Despite these efforts, however, large-scale or commercial wheat production did not expand significantly.[7] The government then made some attempts to extend credit and other advantages to small peasant producers in the hope of expanding the wheat supply, but to little avail. And at no point was the state successful in convincing the larger agricultural concerns to invest in food staple production. The result was that, by March 1940, scarcity and the threat of major price rises forced the government to place controls on some key food staples. By the end of the year shortages began to develop, and the situation improved little if at all in the 1940s.[8] At least in the case of the urban food supply, then, the interests of the state and those of the agrarian fraction of the elite operated at cross-purposes.

Differences between the state and agrarian elites also existed with regard to the peasantry. The depression, by throwing peasant migrants out of work, exacerbated an already difficult situation in many villages. Because it cut off an important source of income for a household economy already strapped by differentiation and population pressure on the land, the world crisis raised the issue of subsistence in a particularly dramatic way. In this context, it is perhaps no accident that increasing numbers of peasant villages began to apply for

[7] For the general situation regarding food production, see Thorp and Bertram, *Peru*, pp. 197–99. On the case of wheat, see Thorp and Bertram, *Peru*, pp. 393–94, footnotes 61 and 62.

[8] On shortages and the 1940s, see ibid., pp. 199–200. On government wheat policies and the small producer in the central highlands, see APJ, "Oficio de la Dirección de Agricultura y Ganadería, Ministerio de Fomento, al Prefecto del Departamento de Junín, sobre la instalación de un campo demostrativo del cultivo del trigo," Lima, September 12, 1925; "Oficio de la Dirección de Agricultura y Ganadería, Ministerio de Fomento, al Prefecto del Departamento de Junín, sobre la instalación de un campo demostrativo del cultivo del trigo," Lima, October 5, 1925; and especially "Solicitud del Alcalde del Concejo Distrital de San Gerónimo de Tunán al Prefecto del Departamento de Junín y Huánuco [sic]," San Jerónimo, December 20, 1934, and attached copies of: "Contrato de Préstamo de Semillas para los Campos Demostrativos," San Gerónimo, November 5, 1933, and "Resolución Suprema del Presidente de la República sobre el cultivo del trigo," Lima, September 15, 1933.

official recognition as Indian communities in the 1930s, utilizing an article of the 1920 constitution which provided them with services and with state support in maintaining intact their communal landholdings. The state actively encouraged official recognition, since it provided an avenue for more direct government control over village affairs and aided in the reproduction of the peasant sector.[9] Even if it was necessary to the overall economic and political stability of the country, however, government support for the Indian communities often went against the interests of the dominant classes in the countryside. For one thing, the peasants were quick to use the new bureaucracy to resurrect age-old boundary conflicts with surrounding haciendas. But equally important, the support structure and legitimation that the newly revamped Dirección de Asuntos Indígenas (Bureau of Indian Affairs) provided to communal entities could become a weapon turned against expansionist agrarian entrepreneurs.[10]

In general, therefore, while the overall purpose of state action was to support economic development and the entrepreneurial initiative of dominant groups, in practice the type of investment or production most beneficial to society as a whole was not always the most profitable for individual capitalists.[11] In the case of Lima's food supply, the need to reproduce an urban working class ran counter to the short-run interest of the agrarian bourgeoisie. While favoring national integration and securing the production of food staples, the legal recognition of Indian communities could also challenge the legitimacy of land claims by *hacendados*, the Catholic church, or commercially oriented farmers. Thus under specific circumstances, the government could be forced to intervene against the most immediate interests of a particular fraction of the dominant classes. And while these conflicts were neither deep nor long-lasting, on occasion they enabled peasants

[9] Most sources concerned with the period are in agreement on this point. See, for example, Pike, *Modern History*, pp. 254–55, 271–72; and Norman Long and Bryan R. Roberts, "Peasant Cooperation and Underdevelopment in Central Peru," in Long and Roberts (eds.), *Peasant Cooperation and Capitalist Expansion in Central Peru* (Austin: University of Texas Press, 1978), pp. 297–328, especially 314–15.

[10] Examples of the way communities used the Dirección de Asuntos Indígenas have filled many books of *expedientes*. A precious source for historians and social scientists, these books were located at the regional offices of SINAMOS, throughout Peru, when I used them in 1978. For a more specific analysis of this strategy, see the examples presented later in this chapter.

[11] Several theorists have applied this rationale to explain why the state sometimes finds it necessary to help in the reproduction of a peasant sector that grows essential food crops. For a good summary of recent literature on Latin America, see especially Richard L. Harris, "Marxism and the Agrarian Question in Latin America," *Latin American Perspectives*, V:4 (Fall 1978), 2–26.

and other members of the lower classes to use one side against the other in their own battles for subsistence.

In many ways, the central sierra was a microcosm of the social and economic tendencies described for Peru as a whole. There was, first of all, a marked trend toward nationally oriented development in the 1930s. After the initial crash, local investment and entrepreneurial efforts in mining and livestock-related industries, particularly textiles, increased. The national government, by pushing forward the construction of the central highway with labor from the unemployed local population, contributed to this revival.[12] Expanding demand on the mining market then gave new impulse to commercial agriculture, pushing forward the commodification of land. The overall tendency was toward innovation, diversification, and expansion and, in the absence of foreign investment, it was national investors who took the lead.

The first sector to experience renewed investment was mining. Though the world depression continued to limit the profitability of copper, in the 1930s conditions on the international market favored increased production of gold, silver, lead, and zinc. Mineowners from the central sierra, many with a long history of local entrepreneurial involvement, were among the most active in these new ventures. Of the twenty gold-mining companies initiated in this decade with significant national capital, ten had the participation of entrepreneurial families active in the central highlands. The same was true of silver, lead, and zinc production, in which Lizandro Proaño, member of an old and prestigious mining family in Cerro de Pasco, by converting the family's smelter at Tamboraque, led the boom in concentration and export.[13]

The combination of local initiative and depressed foreign investment substantially increased national capital's share of the mining industry. In gold, the share of production attributed to national miners went up from 42 to 71 percent between 1933 and 1940. National capital's share of lead production went from 41 percent in 1935 to 67 percent in 1946, while in zinc the increase was from 0 to 64 percent in the same years. And a similar trend was visible in the export sector as a whole. Between 1930 and the end of the 1940s, foreign capital's share of exports fell from around 60 percent to 30 percent or less.[14]

[12] Pike, *Modern History*, p. 271; and APJ, "Oficio de Cipriano Proaño, Ex-Presidente de la Junta Pro-Desocupados de Junín, al Director de Obras Públicas y Vías de Comunicación, Ministerio de Fomento," Cerro de Pasco, October 15, 1931.

[13] Thorp and Bertram, *Peru*, pp. 156–60.

[14] Ibid., pp. 159, 160, and 153.

In keeping with this national and regional trend toward the revival of local capital investment, the central sierra city of Huancayo became the site of a budding textile industry. The first factory was founded in 1928, but the thirties saw the initial expansion of the industry as a whole. By the forties, there were four large factories, three owned by the Prado family and one by the Pardo family, and approximately twelve medium-sized establishments in Huancayo. Producing for the regional mining market, the industry obtained its raw materials from surrounding haciendas, particularly those from the area's *sociedades ganaderas*. Indeed, the expanding textile industry in the region provided a much-needed alternative for the *sociedades'* production at a time of international crisis.[15]

Also in response to the mining market, commercial agriculture gained new dynamism at the regional level. Some local merchants and landowners accumulated additional land and intensified production for the market. Pedro Aizcorbe, for example, ex-*enganchador* and agrarian entrepreneur, bought a piece of well-watered valley land from the parish of Jauja in 1931.[16] Two years later, he started a livestock business there. Isaías Grandes, who had been renting the hacienda Yanamarca since the death of his brother Wenceslao in 1928, also extended his agricultural interests in this period. Not only did he buy the hacienda San Juan de Yanamuclo, an extremely valuable commercial property on the Mantaro Valley floor previously owned by the Valladares family, but he expanded its limits through purchase of peasant lands in the area and intimidation of surrounding smallholders. In addition, Grandes apparently attempted to increase commercial production on the hacienda Yanamarca during the thirties. Starting in 1931, the *colonos* on that hacienda instituted court proceedings against him, claiming that he was trying to reduce the size of their subsistence plots while augmenting and speeding up the labor obligations they owed him.[17]

[15] Bryan R. Roberts, "The Bases of Industrial Cooperation in Huancayo," in Long and Roberts (eds.), *Peasant Cooperation and Capitalist Expansion*, pp. 129–62, especially 129, 143, and 161n. With regard to the *sociedades ganaderas* rerouting their production to the internal market, that is, the local textile industry, this would seem to make sense not only because of the international crisis, but also because efforts to improve the flocks had not managed to keep pace with foreign demand for longer and finer woolen fibers.

[16] ANF, Protocolos Notariales, Luis Salazar, Book 68: November 9, 1931, 888v–96v.

[17] On Aizcorbe's efforts to start a livestock business, see RPI, Tomo 59, Inscripción No. 30, Asiento No. 6, p. 118. On Grandes and the hacienda San Juan, see APJ, "Oficio del Secretario General de la Federación Departmental de Junín al Prefecto del Departamento," Lima, July 25, 1938; and ANF, Protocolos Notariales, Anselmo Flores Espinoza, Book 12: April 6, 1938, 1055v–56v. On Grandes and the hacienda Yanamarca, see APJ, "Oficio del Director General de Fomento al Director de Gobierno," Lima,

Agrarian expansion tended to encourage commodification of land, pushing up the price on commercially exploitable properties and generating high profits on many transactions. The hacienda Pancán, which Aizcorbe bought from Jauja parish's Obra Pía del Carmen, was a good example of these tendencies. The ownership of this hacienda, which was located in the *paraje* of Putaj, in the village of Pancán, had been contested between the parish and several other claimants, including the Ibarra family from Jauja and the community of Pancán itself, for many years. The Supreme Court had ruled in favor of the parish in the proceedings with Pancán's *comuneros* only two months before the sale. In 1927, moreover, the parish had paid the Ibarras 3,000 soles to desist from any further claims to the same land. Yet all these expenditures, whether in money or in court costs, proved justifiable; Aizcorbe bought the property four years later for 20,000 soles. And the Obra Pía was not the only one to make a handsome profit off this transaction. Two years after buying the hacienda, Aizcorbe mortgaged it to the Banco Agrícola del Perú for 30,400 soles in order to start a livestock business.[18]

As the experiences of both Aizcorbe and Grandes clearly show, attempts to expand agrarian production could easily generate peasant resistance. The main reason for this was that efforts at commercialization often presented a direct challenge to the village economy. Since the peasants of Pancán saw the property in the *paraje* of Putaj as belonging to the community, its sale by the Obra Pía del Carmen to Aizcorbe was, in their view, an attack on their communal rights and collective subsistence. Grandes' purchase and expansion of San Juan de Yanamuclo, on the other hand, constituted a more individualized form of pressure on specific household economies. Yet in both cases, the ultimate result was an additional claim on a rapidly shrinking resource base in the villages.[19]

July 8, 1931, and attached documents; RPI, Tomo 60, Inscripción No. 74, Asiento No. 2, pp. 265–69; and Giorgio Alberti and Rodrigo Sánchez, *Poder y conflicto social en el Valle del Mantaro* (Lima: Instituto de Estudios Peruanos, 1974), pp. 135, 137–38.

[18] Data on Pancán have been drawn from the following sources: ANF, Protocolos Notariales, Luis Salazar, Book 68: November 9, 1931, 888v–96v; ANF, Expedientes y Libros Judiciales, "Luis I. Ibarra contra la Obra Pía del Carmen, sobre propiedad de los terrenos 'Putaj,'" began June 23, 1906; and RPI, Tomo 59, Inscripción No. 30, Asientos No. 4–6, p. 118.

[19] That peasants resisted these attempts at expansion, defining them as attacks on their subsistence, is clearly seen in the following documents: APJ, "Oficio del Secretario General de la Federación Departamental de Junín al Prefecto del Departamento," Lima, July 25, 1938; "Oficio de la Confederación Regional del Centro al Prefecto de Junín," Lima, December 2, 1929; "Oficio de varios comuneros de Pancán al Prefecto

At the regional level, then, the essential contradiction between elite and lower classes was similar to that at the national level. The former wished to expand their investments and increase their profits, careless of what this could mean in social welfare terms. The peasantry was interested in assuring subsistence and some modest level of consumption in the face of an income and employment crisis. It was in this context that short-term differences in goals or policy between the state and the agrarian elite showed themselves most clearly. Whether through the Dirección de Asuntos Indígenas, the courts, or the political authorities, the state mediated numerous elite-peasant disputes during the 1930s in an effort to limit elite incursions on the reproduction of the peasant sector. Even though the various state agencies usually decided in favor of the elite, there were instances in which government representatives were willing to uphold the side of the peasantry. The central sierra villages, their inhabitants united behind a common ideology of subsistence and a shared desire for community survival, proved extremely adept once again at exploiting disagreements between government officials and members of the regional elite.

It would be a mistake, however, to assume that the village population was united across the board. Since the beginning of the twentieth century, the increasing pace of social and economic differentiation had sharpened contradictions inside the community, and the crisis of the thirties did nothing to alleviate them. Already in the 1920s, but with more force in the 1930s, a stratum of peasant entrepreneurs had begun to take part in agricultural production for the regional and Lima markets.[20] Particularly after numerous unemployed migrants returned to their villages, the growing desire of *comuneros* for education, urbanization, and public works ran up against a shrinking revenue base. Since the district capital tended to monopolize revenues, villages with *anexo* status found themselves losing out in the competition for services. Struggles developed over land, revenue, and labor both within and between communities, as emerging peasant elites battled with each other and their fellow villagers for control. Against a backdrop of limited resources, village elites pressed for the privatization of communal property and the commodification of communal relationships.[21]

---

del Departamento," December 1927; and "Solicitud de los miembros de la comunidad de Pancán al Prefecto del Departamento," Jauja, November 25, 1931. Of course, the resource base in the villages was shrinking proportionally rather than absolutely, as the population expanded and the accumulation of property increased.

[20] See Chapter IX.

[21] By commodification of communal relationships, I mean the process by which traditional village relations, such as reciprocal exchanges of labor between households,

Facing an ever-present threat of pauperization, poorer *comuneros* invoked communal ideology and collective survival as their best form of insurance. How these confrontations worked themselves out depended not only on the balance of power in the villages, but also on how successfully each faction courted allies at the regional and national levels.

Seen as a whole in the 1930s, the lines of conflict and alliance among and between sectors of the central highland population were complex indeed. The village, divided between an innovative and individualistic group of accumulating peasants and the poorer peasants who continued to call on traditional reciprocity in an effort to survive, could unite only if a common threat to all demanded immediate and collective action. The regional elite, actively profiting from and participating in the national investment boom of the period, encountered tenacious resistance in its efforts to expand from a peasantry still able to close ranks in the face of such a clear and present danger. In the midst of this the state, interested both in development and in the control over and reproduction of the peasant sector, was caught squarely in the middle. And once again, as in the past, the key battles in this larger confrontation were fought at the grass roots level: from case to case, year to year, and village to village.

The Commodification of Land

One of the most important, violent, and ubiquitous struggles that went on in the villages during the 1930s was over the issue of land: whether or not it was or should be privately owned; who had the best right to any given piece; and how to define the boundaries between properties. Although it was not an even or easy process, the general tendency through the decade was toward privatization and the more careful, scientific demarcation of frontiers between holdings. It is in this sense, then, that we can speak of the commodification of land. For in this period, land in the central highlands came increasingly to be regarded as a commodity, a good to be measured, bought, and sold just like any other.

---

labor contributions to the community, or various ceremonies or fiestas, are progressively separated from their collective village context, becoming commodities in the sense that they are increasingly defined in monetary or market terms. For a more concrete definition of the process, see the examples given in the second half of this chapter.

Clearly, the decade of the 1930s was not the first time that commercialization of land had occurred in the central sierra, nor for that matter elsewhere in Peru. As we have already seen, since the Spanish conquest land privatization and speculation had formed a part of most periods of commercial penetration and economic boom. At least in the central region, moreover, conflicts arising in the 1930s were often intimately connected to previous battles.[22] What made the thirties different was not the fact that commodification occurred, but its purpose and context. For the first time, the process was not part of the ebb and flow of commercial versus subsistence production characteristic of noncapitalist agriculture. Instead, entrepreneurs struggling to privatize land were now interested in producing commodities for an internal market of national dimensions, a market on which an ever-widening proportion of the Peruvian population relied.[23] Although ups and downs could still occur, the essential character of this transition could not be reversed. And this irreversibility gave the struggle over commodification and privatization an immediacy and finality it had not possessed in the past.

The village participated in the battle over land at three distinct levels. Regionally, while traditional disagreements resurfaced between haciendas and communities, the primary confrontation was with the Catholic church over rights to commercial property claimed by the *cofradías*. Between villages, disagreements arose over how to define traditional rights of communal land use in private terms, and how to fix a permanent line of demarcation over pasturelands where livestock had always randomly and collectively grazed. Within the village, political authorities led a drive to break up communal holdings, selling or renting them to obtain revenue for public works, and giving

[22] This was especially true of the conflicts between haciendas and communities, in which the longer the conflict went on, the older the documents each side produced. See, for example, Archivo SINAMOS, cc 205a (Marco), Expediente 7842, "Relativo a la controversia que sostienen las comunidades de Marco, Janjaillo, Tragadero y Poma-cancha con don José F. Cajigao sobre propiedad de Oxabamba y otros," May 1946–August 1948; and APJ, "Oficio del Director de Fomento al Prefecto de Junín, sobre el acta de conciliación entre Todos los Santos y la Sociedad Ganadera del Centro," Lima, September 4, 1934.

[23] It is important to emphasize the national dimension of this internal market, since that is precisely what distinguishes it from the regionalized, fragmented, partial internal markets that can develop in commercialized, noncapitalist social formations. This developing national market was both the result of capitalism's increasing dominance in the Peruvian social formation as a whole, and a precondition for the continued expansion and penetration of capitalist relations of production into other parts of that social formation.

plots as compensation to those whose properties had been affected by
new construction. But at all levels, the question of landed property—
its definition and use—was paramount for the peasantry in the thirties.

Of the many conflicts involving communities and the church, perhaps the most famous was that between the Obra Pía del Carmen and
the community of Pancán. The battle was brought to national attention in the late 1920s through articles published in national and regional newspapers, and was intensely debated by some of Peru's *indigenista* and leftist organizations. The *comuneros*, in addition to taking
the matter through the courts, repeatedly petitioned departmental
and national authorities and appealed for help to various associations
dedicated to the protection of the Indian peasantry, such as the Patronato de la Raza Indígena and the Confederación Regional del Centro. But the case of Pancán was especially interesting because it so
clearly demonstrated the complex and multifaceted nature of land
conflicts of this type.[24]

As was true of much property controlled by the church, the land in
Pancán had been used to provide for the expenses of a *cofradía*, specifically the one dedicated to the cult of the Virgen del Carmen. The
name of the organization had been changed to Obra Pía after the state
began its own battle with the church over who should control *cofradía*
lands in 1889,[25] but this did not change the use to which *cofradía*
properties were put. From the point of view of the peasants in Pancán, the fact that the *cofradía* received the benefits from renting out
the property in Putaj did not give the church permanent title to the
land. It simply meant that the village was willing to grant possession
of the plot to the *cofradía* to finance the cult of the Virgin. When the
parish decided to sell the property outright, therefore, the villagers
protested. While they were willing to pay a certain sum of money to
the parish to assure that they could keep the land,[26] they could not
accept the permanent alienation of Putaj to someone else. The parish
in Jauja, on the other hand, saw all *cofradía* or *obra pía* properties as
belonging legitimately and exclusively to the church. According to the

[24] In addition to the documents cited in footnotes 18 and 19, see *Labor* (Lima), No.
9 (August 18, 1929), pp. 6–7, and No. 10 (September 7, 1929), p. 7; *Los Principios,
Periódico Mensual de Propaganda* (Jauja), No. 13 (November 1, 1929), pp. 5–6; and
APJ, "Informe del Subprefecto de Jauja sobre Pancán," Jauja, December 12, 1929,
attached to "Oficio de la Confederación Regional del Centro."

[25] *Los Principios*, No. 33 (July 1, 1931), p. 6. Interestingly enough, this simple name
change sufficed to allow the church to retain control of most *cofradía* properties.

[26] *Labor*, No. 9 (August 18, 1929), p. 7.

press, the archbishop of the diocese had decided to alienate the majority of church holdings in the 1920s, a move considered nothing more than an exercise of the church's legal rights as a property holder.[27] And in the interpretation of Jauja's ecclesiastical authorities, this decision included Putaj.

Thus Putaj was simply one of the earliest, most publicized, and longest-lasting examples of an intensifying and generalized community-parish confrontation over property. At stake was not only the issue of who had the best legal right to any given asset, but also the more fundamental questions of subsistence, community survival, and the definition of property itself. Similar conflicts occurred throughout the central highlands. In the Yanamarca Valley, for instance, battles developed over many holdings of the Jauja and Marco *cofradías* during the 1930s, as church authorities attempted to privatize and sell them, while villagers tried to retain them as community property.[28] Of these many clashes, the case involving the village of Marco and the grain mill of Jatun Ulay that continued from 1939 to 1942 is perhaps the best documented. This battle, begun when it was rumored that the parish wanted to sell the mill to a third party, bore a startling resemblance to the Pancán case.

According to Marco's representatives, in a 1918 transaction legalized by private document, the village had granted usufruct of the community mill of Jatun Ulay to the parish in order to finance the yearly festivities for Mary Magdalene, patron saint of Marco. Since that time, various individuals had rented the mill from the parish, but this did not mean that the church owned it—at least not in the eyes of the community. By the 1930s, the purpose for which the property had been granted to the parish was no longer valid, since the annual celebration in the village was organized and paid for by the *alférez*, or "lieutenant" in charge of the fiesta. "In addition," concluded the village's *personero* (legal representative) in his initial complaint to the Dirección de Asuntos Indígenas,

[27] Ibid. Though the pace of sales increased in the 1920s, the actual decision to begin alienating church lands was made around 1915. See ANF, Protocolos Notariales, Luis Salazar, Book 28: July 6, 1915, 443–46v.

[28] Archivo SINAMOS, cc 205 (Marco), Expediente 25425, "Levantamiento de plano del conjunto de tierras de la comunidad de indígenas de Marco," began December 15, 1936, 132–36v; and "Expediente sobre la reivindicación del molino de propiedad comunal," 1938; Archivo SINAMOS, cc 239 (Tragadero), Expediente 10530, "Sobre el levantamiento del plano de la comunidad de Tragadero, 'Litigio entre la parroquia de Jauja y la comunidad de Tragadero,'" December 1937–August 1938, 103–110; and conversations with Moisés Ortega, Acolla, 1977–1978.

we know that the administrator of church property is trying to sell the mill, going against the articles . . . in the Constitution that guarantee the integrity of communal property.[29]

Interestingly enough, in his answer to the *personero*'s presentation the administrator of church property did not even offer to present clear title to the mill. Instead, he supported his counterclaim on the fact that the parish had been in possession of Jatun Ulay for over twenty years, pointing out that in Peruvian civil law possession was the main criterion for judging ownership. While he did not deny the existence of legal guarantees for communal property, the priest continued, he thought the authorities should consider each case individually, according to the definitions of property laid down in the Civil Code. And he concluded his petition on a mildly threatening note:

> Aware of the fact that the mill located in the *paraje* Jatun Ulay belongs to an *obra pía* of Marco parish, your office will please declare groundless the revindication proceedings initiated by the *personero* of the community of Marco, thus avoiding conflicts which could have deep implications for the life of the church, as a measure to cut the community's intentions in the bud, since they constitute aggression against the Catholic religion, which is helped and protected by the state.[30]

As in the case of Putaj, therefore, the parish could not provide definitive proof of title to Jatun Ulay, since usufruct and possession had depended on custom and tradition. Nor could the village present adequate proof of ownership for, as the *personero* of Marco pointed out, most communities did not possess perfect titles to their land.[31] Once again, the underlying issue had to do with the changing definition, use, and value of landed property. As the commercialization of agriculture proceeded apace, the church wished to profit from the boom by selling its *cofradía* holdings. With declining resources in the villages, peasants wanted to use the same properties for subsistence and added revenue that would stay in the community. Ultimately, the inability of the parish and community to reach any kind of compromise on Jatun Ulay proved that their interests on the question were completely irreconcilable. The fact that the Dirección decided in favor of the church, despite the lack of documentation, simply proved

---

[29] Archivo SINAMOS, cc 205 (Marco), "Expediente sobre la reivindicación del molino," 4.
[30] Ibid.
[31] Archivo SINAMOS, cc 205 (Marco), Expediente 25425, 132.

that church prestige and an appeal to the protection of religion were still powerful weapons in these conflicts.

With the sale of Putaj and Jatun Ulay, as well as many other *cofradía* holdings, the church played an important role in facilitating agricultural commercialization. In most cases, the buyers were innovative merchants and agriculturalists, often on the forefront of efforts toward economic expansion and investment. Because *cofradía* land was usually among the best and most fertile in any given village, its privatization and alienation proved a huge boon to local agrarian entrepreneurs. Yet, as the example of Jatun Ulay again shows, the commodification and sale of church lands did not always unite the community as a whole against an outside usurper.

When Marco lost its rights over the mill to the *cofradía* in mid-1939, the parish priest of Jauja, Francisco Carlé, sold it to Víctor Colca Gerónimo, sacristan of Marco parish in the early 1930s, peasant entrepreneur, and himself a *comunero* from Marco.[32] Members of the village immediately began another action before the Dirección de Asuntos Indígenas, this time against Carlé and Colca. While they did not contest the parish's usufruct rights to Jatun Ulay, the peasants continued to protest the sale of the mill. They also claimed that, in the sale contract, Carlé had included a sizable quantity of communal grazing land within the boundaries he gave the property. But for the peasants, the worst affront of all was the complicity of Víctor Colca. A villager himself, Colca knew the boundaries on the contract were false. Not only did he keep quiet, however, but he took advantage of the situation to prohibit community livestock from entering the pastures, and had even planted some of the fields with commercial crops. Thus, concluded the *personero* of Marco, Víctor Colca might be "our fellow *comunero*," but it was also true that he had "been converted into a *gamonal* [local political boss]."[33]

In addition to touching on major questions such as the definition of property or the right to subsistence, village battles with the *cofradías* also uncovered and encouraged class conflict within the community. If a local entrepreneur was willing to ally with the church against his

[32] For the sale contract, ANF, Protocolos Notariales, Anselmo Flores Espinoza, Book 15: July 11, 1939, 427v–29. On Víctor Colca's background, conversations with Moisés Ortega, Acolla, 1977–1978.

[33] Archivo SINAMOS, cc 205 (Marco), Expediente 4366, "Relativo a las reclamaciones por el personero de la comunidad de Marco, contra don Francisco Carlé vicario foráneo de la provincia de Jauja y don Víctor Colca, por compraventa y apropiación de las tierras de propiedad de la mencionada comunidad, 'Recurso presentado por el personero de Marco, Segundino Rafael Hidalgo,' " February 26, 1942, 1–2.

or her fellow villagers, the potential advantages were substantial. Colca, for example, was able to use the profits he made from the mill to become well established in the Yanamarca Valley as a major producer of commercial onion for the Lima market.[34] And he was not the only inhabitant of the area to benefit from transactions with the church. Of the eight sales of *cofradía* property in the valley recorded by Jauja notary Anselmo Flores Espinoza between 1938 and 1940, seven were to individuals residing in the area's villages.[35]

Ultimately, the battle over *cofradía* assets provides a good example of how commodification affected village life. On the one hand, customary forms of property rights became unviable, forcing a redefinition of private property. On the other hand, the increasing integration of villages into the national economy, with the accompanying commercialization of production, property, and social relationships, called into question basic communal traditions, especially the provision of subsistence to all.[36] Finally, as entrepreneurs from the communities began actively to take part in the process of integration and commercialization, communal solidarity against incursions broke down even further. Thus it is hardly surprising that struggles over land were not limited to *cofradías*. Occurring both within and between villages, they uncovered deep tensions in the peasant society and economy.

In March 1936, twenty-four *comuneros* from Tragadero and Muquillanqui sent a letter to the judge of the primary claims court in Jauja, requesting a survey of the communal property "Apay" or "Licuy." They explained that the land, which measured approximately 300 *yugadas* (100 hectares), had belonged to their communities "since time immemorial," and that at present forty-four people from their villages were considered the actual "owners." In the absence of fertilizer and in order to let the land rest, Licuy had not been formally

---

[34] See Chapter IX.

[35] ANF, Protocolos Notariales, Anselmo Flores Espinoza, Book 12: August 22, 1938, 1381–82v; Book 14: January 4, 1939, 10v–12; Book 15: May 2, 1939, 291v–93, July 3, 1939, 417–18v, July 11, 1939, 427v–29, August 8, 1939, 482v–84; Book 16: September 4, 1939, 559–60; Book 20: December 27, 1940, 1730–32. The eighth contract, incidentally, was not celebrated with an outsider either, but with the community of Marco.

[36] The analysis of subsistence in this chapter, in terms of its changing meaning in the context of commodification, as well as its use as an ideological concept in class struggle, owes much to those scholars who have developed the concept of "moral economy": E. P. Thompson, *The Making of the English Working Class* (London: Victor Gollancz Ltd., 1964); E. P. Thompson, "The Moral Economy of the English Crowd in the Eighteenth Century," *Past and Present*, No. 50 (February 1971), pp. 76–136; James C. Scott, *The Moral Economy of the Peasant* (New Haven and London: Yale University Press, 1976); and Eric R. Wolf, *Peasant Wars of the Twentieth Century* (New York: Harper and Row, 1969).

planted during the 1935/36 agricultural year, though some individuals had sown small amounts of vegetables for household use. Now it was necessary to prepare the land by April or May, so that it might be planted in October for the coming season. But Muquillanqui and Tragadero had heard that the neighboring community of Marco intended to deprive them of Licuy. Thus, the petitioners concluded, they wished to carry out a judicial inspection of the area, so that their possession of the property could become a matter of legal record.[37]

After notifying Marco's political authorities and distinguished citizens, a representative of the court carried out an official survey of Apay on March 18, 1936. Starting at the property's southernmost boundary and moving north, the official found thirty-two separate plantings of one-eighth to one *yugada* each, most of them vegetables. Aside from two plantings that no one could identify, peasants from Muquillanqui presented uncontested claims to eleven of the plots, Tragadero claimed three, and four *Marqueños* identified theirs. Every one of the remaining twelve was claimed by two individuals, one from each side of the dispute. Finally, on the part of the land lying fallow, the court representative found herds of grazing sheep that belonged to peasants from Muquillanqui and Tragadero.[38]

While not denying the existence of disagreements over Licuy, the official who carried out the inspection was forced to conclude in his final report that all three villages had legitimate rights to the property. These were fixed and defined from year to year by a customary pattern of rotation. Every other growing season, the heads of household who had been granted an "apay" could each plant up to two *yugadas* of wheat. In the intervening years, any person who wished to do so could plant small areas with subsistence crops, or graze their animals in the natural pasture growing on the unused areas. Since 1936 had been an off year, the official concluded, it was not surprising that the majority of the planted area belonged to Muquillanqui, for this was the closest village to Licuy.[39]

The dispute might have ended there except for the fact that Marco, in an effort to raise money for public works, rented the entire area of Licuy to the brothers Jorge and Antonio Richter Silva, mechanics

[37] ANF, Expedientes y Libros Judiciales, "Tragadero y Muquillanqui contra Marco, sobre nulidad de un contrato de arrendamiento," began April 6, 1936, "Primer recurso de los vecinos de Tragadero y Muquillanqui," 1–2.

[38] Ibid., "Diligencia de Inspección Ocular," March 18, 1936, 11–14v.

[39] Ibid., 14–14v.

residing in Jauja.[40] Once Tragadero and Muquillanqui confirmed the existence of this contract, their *apoderado*, Juan Estanislao Solís, brought a suit against Marco to have it declared null and void. In the ensuing battle, which lasted a year and a half, each side did its best to obscure the other's claim in Apay. And to ensure that they would also be protected by networks of patronage and clientele, Muquillanqui and Tragadero entered their own rent contract on two-thirds of Apay with Carlos Hildebrando Madrid, a member of the Jauja elite.[41]

In the absence of a clear and overriding claim on either side, the parties reached a compromise agreement in Jauja on December 27, 1937. The community of Marco, as "mother community," granted to Tragadero one-fourth of Licuy's surface area on the northern side. It also recognized sixteen *yugadas* (given the way the *yugada* was defined in the contract this grant amounted to only four hectares rather than five), adjacent to those of Tragadero, to the community of Muquillanqui. In exchange, the two daughter communities agreed to respect Marco's possession over the rest of Apay, and annul their rent contract with Madrid. Furthermore, in keeping with the overlapping quality of community claims, Tragadero also agreed to cede to Muquillanqui seven *yugadas* (one and three-fourths hectares) of the area they had received from Marco.[42]

In the final analysis, the struggle over Licuy involved some of the same issues as the *cofradía* battles. Much of Tragadero and Muquillanqui's claim to Apay centered around the question of communal subsistence and solidarity. Both villages had historically been a part of the community of Marco, and they argued that this membership gave them the right to certain amounts of property and sustenance. Since Tragadero and Muquillanqui had initially broken off from Marco as one unit, Tragadero also owed Muquillanqui a certain access to resources.[43] Interestingly, the ruling in the case took all these com-

[40] ANF, Protocolos Notariales, Anselmo Flores Espinoza, Book 4: March 9, 1936, 974–77v.

[41] For the general tenor of arguments on both sides, see ANF, Expedientes y Libros Judiciales, "Tragadero y Muquillanqui contra Marco," passim. For Muquillanqui and Tragadero's own rent contract, see ANF, Protocolos Notariales, Anselmo Flores Espinoza, Book 6: July 8, 1936, 1294–97.

[42] ANF, Expedientes y Libros Judiciales, "Tragadero y Muquillanqui contra Marco . . . , 'Transacción,' " 132–32v.

[43] On the process through which Tragadero and Muquillanqui sought their independence as separate communities, see Archivo SINAMOS, cc 205 (Marco), Expediente 13382: "Relativo a las diferencias suscitadas entre las comunidades de Marco y Tragadero, sobre establecimiento de servidumbre por el paso de ganado," 46–50; and Archivo SINAMOS, cc 239 (Tragadero), Expediente 10530: "Levantamiento de plano de la comunidad de indígenas de Tragadero," 9–10. On the use of subsistence as a

plex and overlapping rights into consideration. Marco, while granting part of Apay to each village, gave a much larger section to Tragadero, "daughter" of Marco but "mother" to Muquillanqui. Tragadero, in turn, also gave part of its share in Apay to Muquillanqui, fulfilling its separate communal responsibility.

In addition to raising the problem of subsistence, therefore, the case of Licuy also evidenced the complexity of any effort to define traditional community property in private terms. In various parts of the central highlands, the acceleration of population growth in the twentieth century had resulted in the formation of new villages within the territorial limits of the old. As these new population centers began to break off from their "mother *ayllu*" or community of origin, they wished to exert their own domain in plots which had previously remained undivided. But given the intricacy of overlapping community claims, the result was, in many cases, an extremely frustrating and inconclusive legal process that demonstrated the impossibility of faithfully translating communal property rights into their privatized equivalent.[44]

The interweaving of customary and collective tenures also caused problems when it came to setting firm lines of demarcation between villages. When increasing numbers of villages applied for official recognition as Indian communities in the 1930s, engineers began to draw up maps of the lands claimed by each one. They soon found, however, that much land on the borders between communities was used in common, and each had a different opinion about the proper placement of a *lindero*. In addition, most villages owned lands within the frontiers of their neighbors. Thus many became worried that, once a firm line had been drawn, they would lose their properties on the other side.[45]

---

justification for Muquillanqui and Tragadero's claim to Apay, see ANF, Expedientes y Libros Judiciales, "Tragadero y Muquillanqui contra Marco," passim.

[44] For some other examples of attempts to define private rights in communal property, as well as the difficulties involved, see, ANF, Protocolos Notariales, Luis Salazar, Book 66: December 30, 1930, 1916v–20; Archivo SINAMOS, cc 205 (Marco), Expediente 25425, "Levantamiento de plano del conjunto de tierras de la comunidad de indígenas de Marco," began December 15, 1936, especially Marco vs. Concho, over pastures of Azapampa, Mesapata, and Umpajasha, 98–99, 104.

[45] For examples of the process of official recognition and the drawing up of maps, see Archivo SINAMOS, cc 170 (Comunidad de Acolla), "Expediente relativo al reconocimiento e inscripción oficial de la comunidad de indígenas de Acolla," and "Levantamiento del plano de conjunto de las tierras de la comunidad"; Archivo SINAMOS, cc 205 (Marco), Expediente 25425, "Levantamiento del plano del conjunto de tierras de la comunidad de indígenas de Marco"; and Archivo SINAMOS, cc 239 (Tragadero), Expediente 10530, "Levantamiento del plano del conjunto de tierras de la comunidad

Conflicts multiplied as a result of these fears. When Tragadero applied for official recognition in 1936, for example, it battled four out of five neighbors over where the lines of demarcation ought to be. Even though all four disputes ended in conciliation, the agreements recognized the legitimacy of continued collective usufruct to common pasturelands. As events of the following years were to show, this meant that conflict could reemerge at any moment. And the same was true of many villages. Indeed, the bid for official recognition in the thirties set into motion confrontations that remained unsolved for decades; some even to this day.[46]

On one level, clashes between communities over property definition were nothing new. Villages had always quarreled over what land belonged to whom, where cattle or sheep could graze, and which was the proper path for one community's livestock to take through the other's fields. These squabbles usually took on a greater immediacy during periods of commercialization. But on another level, the fights of the 1930s were not the same. As communities became more integrated into the national market and political system, their wish to modernize intermingled with the desire of a new generation of peasant entrepreneurs to transform village agriculture. The end result was a process of commodification and privatization of resources within the village that could never be reversed.

Starting in the 1920s and continuing into the 1930s, communities in the central sierra were gripped by a desire for modernization and urbanization. Inspired by returning migrants, who wished to bring their villages into the twentieth century, as well as by national cam-

---

de indígenas de Tragadero." In this last *expediente*, the agricultural engineer drawing up the maps mentions specifically that the communities of Marco and Muquillanqui, which border on Tragadero, are fearful of losing their rights to the lands they possess within Tragadero's borders (see 9–10).

[46] For the examples of conflict pertaining to Tragadero, see Archivo SINAMOS, cc 239 (Tragadero), Expediente 10530, 11, 12, 22, 23, 26, 29; and Expediente 16753, "Relativo a las divergencias suscitadas entre la comunidad de indígenas de Tragadero, contra la comunidad de Acolla." With regard to the long-lasting nature of some of the border conflicts, perhaps the best proof lies in the fact that, when I asked for copies of the maps of various communities in 1978, the archivist at SINAMOS warned me that they had no legal value, since many of the lands were still in dispute. While living in the Yanamarca Valley, I was also told that several of the bordering areas between the villages of Concho and Marco were still under litigation. The struggle over the pastures of Oxapampa, between these same communities, lasted until 1963 (see Archivo SINAMOS, cc 205 [Marco], Expediente 25425). And in the case of Acolla and its neighbor, Paca, the conflict over bordering pasturelands was still going strong in 1961 (see Archivo SINAMOS, cc 170 [Comunidad de Acolla], "Levantamiento del plano").

paigns to integrate and educate the rural population, peasants became involved in an intensifying competition to advance public works at the local level. Whether this meant opening or widening village streets, establishing electrical generators and reliable supplies of running water, paving the plaza, or opening up new schools for village children, one thing was always certain: it would cost money. During the 1920s, much of the financial burden was taken up by migrants' associations at the mining centers or in Lima. Even then, however, community officials were sometimes forced to resort to more extreme measures and sell community lands.[47] And when the crisis of the 1930s limited employment opportunities for village migrants both regionally and nationally, communities wishing to keep up the pace of public works expansion found themselves turning, with growing frequency, to the extreme measures.

In a general meeting on May 6, 1937, Acolla's district council resolved to take some energetic steps to insure the completion of the necessary public works in the community. First of all, the district officials decided "[t]o sell vacant lands belonging to the community, especially those located near the borders with neighboring communities . . . keeping in mind the location or quality of the plots which a duly named commission will determine in order to set a just price." In addition, the resolution called on the council to charge rent to the owners of sheep and pigs found grazing on communal pasturelands. Since this was an emergency measure, it would only apply for one year; that is, unless the owner of the livestock had not been keeping up with her or his labor contributions to the village. Those in violation of their community obligations would have to keep paying from year to year, and would also have to pay twice as much as the others. "These rents," the resolution concluded,

as well as the profits from the lands [we sell] . . . , will go to the fund we have established to buy materials for the Boys' School No. 511 which is presently under construction; for materials needed for the reconstruction of the church and [for] all other public works that need to be finished so that they can be inaugurated during the celebration of the fiftieth anniversary of the creation of the district which will occur the next 26th of October; [all of] this, because of

[47] See, for example, ANF, Protocolos Notariales, Luis Salazar, Book 56: April 27, 1926, 1516–17v and 1517v–19; Book 62: October 26, 1928, 2293v–98, and December 18, 1928, 2468v–72v.

the shortage of funds and money, which the village and *cuarteles* just do not have for the public works already in progress.[48]

The decisions by Acolla's municipal council were only one example of the kind of steps villages took in the 1930s to expand their access to revenue. Increasingly, local authorities sold, rented, or mortgaged community lands; raised the quotas of labor and materials each *comunero* had to contribute; and charged for pasture and water rights. Some of these plans had a tendency to backfire, especially since district representatives encountered growing opposition to the higher communal obligations.[49] Besides, the more money a community raised, the more it seemed to need. For in addition to paying for public works, it had to finance litigation with *cofradías* and neighbors over lands, pay for the expensive process of official recognition, and confront its own members on the issue of property affected by urbanization schemes.

Throughout the thirties, village officials came face-to-face with *damnificados*—those members of the community whose lands lay in the path of new streets, schools, or other projects. One possible solution to the controversy was monetary compensation, but this merely increased the amount of money the village needed. In many instances, moreover, it was impossible for the owner and the council to agree on a just compensatory sum, with the result that the community was forced to institute expropriation proceedings. And as Acolla discovered in the cases of Gregorio Bravo and Martín Huatuco, this sequence of events led directly to great frustration and expense.[50]

A much more viable solution to the problem was the *permuta* or *canje*, whereby the village exchanged the affected plot for one of equal value from communal holdings. In the Yanamarca Valley, both Acolla and Marco frequently used this strategy. The municipal council of Marco, for example, decided in 1930 to widen the avenue leading from Pachascucho to Marco, since this was the main route from the district to Jauja. The council's members also decided to plant eucalyptus along all the streets connecting Marco's central plaza to the surrounding villages of Acolla, Concho, Pachascucho, and Tragadero, and calculated they would need three meters on each side to allow

[48] AMA, Libro de Sesiones, 1934–1939, Asamblea de Junta General, May 6, 1937, pp. 224–28.

[49] Ibid., pp. 24, 43–45, 156, 194–96, 224–26, 239, and passim.

[50] On the struggle with Bravo over a piece of land affected on the street known as the Girón Grau, see ibid., pp. 6, 12, 179, 188 and 227–28. On the struggle with Huatuco, see ibid., pp. 27, 29–30.

for the trees. To compensate the many owners whose land would be affected, the district officials decided to grant each one an equivalent piece in the Hechadero-la Pampa "because," they explained, "that land is the exclusive property of this community."[51]

Hechadero-la Pampa was the name given to the expanse of pasturelands located in the middle of the valley, near the Yanamarca River. Acolla also exchanged or sold communal land there in order to compensate villagers affected by the opening of new streets or the construction of schools.[52] As a result, throughout the thirties an intense process of privatization went on in Hechadero-la Pampa. By the beginning of the 1940s, in fact, a small land boom was occurring in the area as the rumor spread that pampa land was particularly well suited for commercial agriculture.[53] And because of the particularly dramatic quality of commodification in that locality, Hechadero-la Pampa provides a good example of how privatization affected the village economy as a whole.

Traditionally, the Hechadero had been reserved as a communal grazing area because it tended to flood during rainy season. Between October and April, and sometimes as late as June, it served as pasture for the animals of village households. When the district councils initially proposed exchanging Hechadero land for plots affected by construction, therefore, people protested on two counts. First of all, the *damnificados* disliked the idea of getting wet, swampy pasture, where their crops were bound to rot, in exchange for good agricultural land. But even more important, those who depended on income from their animals also objected, since privatization constituted a direct threat to the balance of their household economies.[54]

Indeed, by closing off yet another alternative to the peasant household, the commodification of land in the Hechadero facilitated social and economic differentiation within the village. As opportunities expanded in commercial agriculture, those with resources hastened to carve out new properties in the fertile pampa. Those without resources found it necessary to limit, or even eliminate, the flocks that

[51] AMM, Libro de Actas, 1929–1943, Sesión Ordinaria, November 3, 1930, pp. 54–57.

[52] William B. Hutchinson, "Sociocultural Change in the Mantaro Valley Region of Peru: Acolla, A Case Study," Ph.D. Dissertation, Indiana University, 1973, p. 59; and AMA, Libro de Sesiones, 1934–1939, p. 6.

[53] Hutchinson, "Sociocultural Change," pp. 59–60; and Chapter IX.

[54] Hutchinson, "Sociocultural Change," pp. 59–60. For a more detailed analysis of the role of the pampa in the valley's ecology and agropecuarian balance, see Chapter II.

helped them get by. Clearly, then, the privatization of community land provided a strong impulse toward proletarianization. But this was also true of the commodification process as a whole.

Whether the battle over privatization took place between the village and an outsider, among villages, or within one village, it was part of a larger transformation shaking the very roots of the peasant economy and society. When a *cofradía* gained the right to sell a piece of property, when one village obtained exclusive rights to an area previously shared by several, or when a community alienated land to pay for paving a plaza, the resulting shrinkage of subsistence was felt far beyond the limits of the specific case. Of course, the connection between privatization and a household's resource base was not always as direct or obvious as in the case of the Hechadero. But even if a piece of communal land did not play a central role in subsistence, once lost it could no longer be used or rented out to obtain revenue. Since the only alternative way to finance public works or litigation was to tax the villagers in some way, this usually meant that the *comuneros* had to pay more, whether in money, goods, or labor, for their community membership. And very often, there simply was no more room in the family budget for such outlays.

In the final analysis, though access to land and its fruits was the cornerstone of the peasant economy, it could not be easily separated from other aspects of peasant society. Nowhere was this interdependence more obvious than in the changes going on in the 1930s. After all, it was during this decade that villagers discovered the secret of turning land into schools, roads, electrical plants, pavement, and many other things. It was also during this decade that land became more fully a commodity, just another factor in the production of agricultural goods for the market. But perhaps most essential, the alchemist's formula for these transformations was found by converting into commodities still other elements of peasant life: community revenue and communal labor.

Labor, Revenue, and Politics

Questions of labor, revenue, and local politics had always been intimately connected in peasant society. By calling on traditions of reciprocal labor exchange, for example, political authorities in the villages organized communal work parties to build, repair, and maintain public buildings, roads, irrigation canals, and the like. Community membership itself, and access to village resources, was defined in terms of a quota of labor time that households owed to the community as a whole. At the district level, political officials disposed of the revenue raised through taxes, fees, and *remates de ramos* administered by the municipal councils, and controlled the labor for public works that each *anexo* owed the district capital. And since most communities were *anexos* of a district, communal and district control over labor and revenue tended to intermingle and overlap.[55]

Given the broad resource base manipulated by municipal councils, it is hardly surprising that much conflict in the late nineteenth and early twentieth centuries centered around the issues of district creation and district politics. As village populations grew, communities struggled to obtain independent district status, and thereby control their own revenue and labor drafts. The old district councils, for their part, attempted to block these bids and cement their dominance over *anexo* populations. The crucial question here was the way in which available revenue and labor were used, for *anexos* often felt they were merely contributing to the progress and advancement of the district capital and getting nothing in return.

Even though these quarrels over district status were phrased in broadly communal language, however, political independence did not benefit the entire village population. While obtaining independence increased the revenue available to a community for public services, it also consolidated the local elite's dominance over village affairs. Wealthy peasants then attempted to privatize their access to labor, using it in the expansion of commercial enterprises and the construction of patron-client ties with the regional elite. Ultimately, therefore, the attainment of district status did not insure political or economic independence for the majority of village peasants. As was clear from experience in the Yanamarca Valley, an *anexo* could escape from the frying pan of dependence and exploitation, only to fall into the fire of manipulation by local notables.[56]

In many ways, local politics in the 1930s was just a continuation of these tendencies. A further rise in population, and the expansion of public works construction in the context of a shrinking revenue base, intensified competition between district capitals and dependent villages over who should control *anexo* labor and the proceeds from *anexo* taxes. As in previous battles over political independence,

[55] Richard N. Adams, *A Community in the Andes: Problems and Progress in Muquiyauyo* (Seattle: University of Washington Press, 1959), pp. 27–49; and Chapter II.

[56] Examples of this for the Yanamarca Valley can be found above, Chapters III and IV.

emerging elites at the community level were eager to move the process in the direction most beneficial to their own private interests. And ironically, the generation of wealthy peasant innovators who had handled the previous confrontation over district status, now converted into the established members of their own municipal councils, were just as eager to prevent further fragmentation as their foes had been earlier in the century.[57]

But there were also important differences. First of all, municipal authorities had always been able to enlist the aid of other political allies, such as prefects, subprefects, and provincial councils, in their quarrels with recalcitrant *anexos*. The latter, on the other hand, had never possessed an alternate set of institutions upon which they could call.[58] This changed in the 1930s, with the strengthening of the Dirección de Asuntos Indígenas. Once villages were recognized officially as Indian communities, they could use this part of the state apparatus as an alternative to the district and provincial hierarchy. Of course, the Dirección was careful to separate its own area of competence from what concerned the municipality.[59] But *anexos* achieving official recognition could at least force their district capitals to confront them as equals through the Asuntos Indígenas bureaucracy, something that had not been possible before.

An even more crucial difference, however, was the context in which the new battles occurred. In the 1930s, the world crisis sharpened the contradictions of the search for revenue at the local level. Though the regional and national economies recovered rapidly from the initial crash, enterprises used the opportunity provided by the depression to rationalize production. Many cut down on the number of workers they needed or, to take the example of the central sierra mining industry, rehired only those with no record of political activity.[60] This

[57] Archivo SINAMOS, cc 205 (Marco), Expediente 25425, "Solicitud de Florencio A. Barzola, Alcalde de Marco," March 7, 1937; APJ, "Solicitud de las autoridades de Acolla al Alcalde del Concejo Provincial de Jauja," Acolla, March 15, 1932; and Archivo SINAMOS, cc 239 (Tragadero), Expediente 10530, 160.

[58] As Acolla and Marco's bids for district status both show, the only way to seek political and economic independence was through the same bureaucracy whose basic interests lay in denying that independence. As a result, the only way to guarantee success was through personal, patron-client networks. See above, Chapters III and IV. Of course, the strengthening of the Dirección de Asuntos Indígenas did not eliminate personal relationships, but it provided a separate institutional framework through which peasant villages could work.

[59] The Dirección's care in separating out the various spheres of competence is clear from Archivo SINAMOS, cc 239 (Tragadero), Expediente 10530, 154–66.

[60] Hutchinson, "Sociocultural Change," pp. 61–62. Heraclio Bonilla points out that,

limited employment opportunities for villagers in the larger economy, and migration no longer served as the automatic safety valve and source of village revenue that it had in the past.

Indeed, the partial closing of employment possibilities on the outside helped speed up the process of differentiation and proletarianization within the villages. Innovative and wealthier peasants who had previously migrated now stayed in the community, accumulating land and engaging in agrarian production for the Lima market. Some of the poorer peasants who had used seasonal migration to supplement a meager income, or who had become permanent residents in the mining centers, now found that agricultural wage labor was one of their few remaining alternatives. The new generation of peasant entrepreneurs was, of course, happy to hire proletarianized villagers. And the emergence of these incipient new class relations was bound to transform both the purpose and meaning of community politics and struggles over revenue.[61]

In January 1930, various authorities from the district of Acolla complained to the prefect of Junín about the conduct of Justo Quillatupa, governor of their municipality. "[I]n the . . . more than two years he had held the office," they wrote,

> he has not tried to second the efforts of the other authorities; and quite the contrary he has systematically placed obstacles in the way of our village's progress, advising the inhabitants not to work gratuitously [for the community], thus taking from us the labor that we need for the completion of many public works, such as finishing the façade of our school, repairing the church, and the building of doors for the school; for all of which it is indispensable [to have access to] a determined number of workers to help the carpenters, whether in the transportation of wood over considerable distances, or to lift the finished doors and place them correctly, etc., etc.

Besides, the petitioners concluded, Quillatupa was a drunken, corrupt, and nearly illiterate man, and the rest of the village agreed that he did not deserve to hold office. Representing the district of Acolla,

---

after 1930, workers for the mines were required to have a higher level of skills (*El Minero de los Andes*, Lima: Instituto de Estudios Peruanos, 1974, p. 57). Alberto Flores Galindo states that, after 1930, all workers who entered the mining labor force were carefully checked out as to their background, and made to promise they would not take part in union activities (*Los mineros de la Cerro de Pasco, 1900–1930*, Lima: Pontifica Universidad Católica del Perú, 1974, p. 107).

[61] See Chapter IX, below, for a more complete analysis of this point.

therefore, they requested his removal from the post and his substitution by a more deserving candidate.[62]

Whether or not all the charges against the governor were true, what made him most objectionable to the other officials was that some of the villagers were probably willing to listen to him. As only one of many quarrels, conflicts, and problems that Acolla faced in the 1930s on the question of public works, the ousting of Quillatupa pointed to the increasing tension in Acolla over communal obligations. In a mad scramble to inaugurate all the new construction for the celebration of Acolla's fiftieth anniversary as an independent district (1936), the municipal councils of the decade stopped at nothing to raise more funds or levy new labor drafts. These additional contributions in money, labor, and kind were then used to open new streets, build several schools, open a new cemetery, pave the central plaza and build a fountain, reconstruct the parish church, and collaborate with the Junta Pro-Desocupados in repairing the Jauja-Tarma highway.[63] Clearly, the burden of these extra obligations was quite onerous for the *comuneros*, since in addition to the usual labor and materials that households provided for the repair of roads, bridges, and other public facilities, they now had to contribute labor, cement, adobe bricks, money, and tools on a much more regular basis. Worst of all, the projects encountered so many obstacles that not only were they not ready for inauguration in 1936, but they also ate up so much revenue that it was necessary to postpone the anniversary celebration itself.[64]

Despite the particularities of Acolla's situation, however, it was not alone in facing an income and labor pinch during the 1930s. In many other communities, especially the *anexos* of a district, people chafed under the heavy labor and tax burdens placed on them to advance public works construction. In Marco, for example, the 1930s witnessed the widening of many streets, the construction of several schools, the paving of the central plaza, and the initiation of a large irrigation project. Members of the district were asked to contribute to each plan. And though the projects were for the exclusive benefit of Marco, the communities of Concho and Tragadero complained that all the

[62] APJ, "Solicitud de las autoridades municipales de Acolla al Prefecto del Departamento," Acolla, January 23, 1930.

[63] AMA, Libro de Sesiones, 1934–1939, pp. 6, 7, 11, 14, 40, 43–47, 116–17, 119–22, and passim.

[64] AMA, Libro de Sesiones, 1934–1939, Sesión de Junta, August 11, 1936, pp. 159–63; Sesión Extraordinaria, September 1936, pp. 163–66.

anexos had to labor on them without pay and finance them through various taxes.[65]

Even the inhabitants of the district capitals, who stood to gain most from the projects, could take only so much in labor exactions. Throughout the 1930s, Acolla's municipal council was forced to fine, threaten, and charge extra for the use of communal resources, all in an attempt to force *comuneros* to show up at communal work parties. The architects, carpenters, and other specialists directing construction complained that people were not keeping their promises.[66] And in 1936, when the members of Acolla's Comité in Morococha requested an exoneration from their communal labor quota for having contributed money to the village, the mayor refused, explaining that "if they were exonerated from community work there would [soon] be no one to work for the progress of the town."[67]

Ultimately, therefore, the public works projects of the thirties did not turn out to be the cheerful and progressive collective enterprises that district officials wished them to be. A partial explanation is simply that the household's relationship to the community had always been double-edged: peasants usually weighed the cost of furnishing free labor time to the village against the benefits accruing from community membership.[68] While the pressure to participate was extremely strong, compliance was not necessarily a foregone conclusion, especially once commercialization and the need for money increased the incidence of seasonal migration from the villages. In this context, it would seem that the labor exactions of the 1930s, coming as they did at a time of increasing proletarianization, simply pushed households beyond their limit of endurance. But it is also true that the projects did not benefit the community as evenly as it may have seemed at first glance.

Public works fever was caused not only by a wish for modernization in the general or abstract sense, but also by the desire to integrate the village more fully into the national economy and political system. At the local level, those with the highest stake in the process were clearly the wealthier villagers, the ones accumulating and investing in

[65] On Marco's various public works projects, see AMM, Libro de Actas, 1929–1943, pp. 54–57, 65–66, 215, 258. On protests by *anexos* because they were forced to contribute labor and revenue to those public works, see Archivo SINAMOS, cc 205 (Marco), Expediente 25425, 99 and 104; and Archivo SINAMOS, cc 239 (Tragadero), Expediente 10530, 154–59.

[66] For complaints from specialists, see AMA, Libro de Sesiones, 1934–1939, pp. 194–96, 239. For the need to use fines and other measures to force compliance, see AMA, Libro de Sesiones, 1934–1939, pp. 43–47, 194–96, 223–31, and 239.

[67] AMA, Libro de Sesiones, 1934–1939, Sesión de Junta, July 10, 1936, p. 156.

[68] See Chapter II.

commercial agriculture. For them, community schools were beneficial not because education was inherently good, but because schools could teach the new generation the rudimentary skills they needed to be successful in the larger society. Paving the plaza, urbanizing the village, and building new roads were not only symbolic of the town's "coming of age," but could also make it more attractive to merchants, truckers, transportation companies, and others interested in tapping local markets. And finally, by actively advancing various construction projects as district officials, wealthy and innovative peasants hoped to develop a reputation as dynamic and progressive, improving their connections with provincial and national politicians and obtaining more patronage for themselves and their villages.[69]

At least for the wealthier members of the community, therefore, the desire for integration came from a combination of community solidarity and personal interest. Acolla's municipal authorities, for example, petitioned the central government for aid with five different projects between 1937 and 1938: the elevation of Acolla to the status of city; the creation of a rural school to be added to the Boys' School No. 511; the regulation of water use in the district; the completion of two primary schools; and the donation of 30,000 soles for the construction of an electrical plant. A community representative, who was also a member of the village elite, received two soles per day to go to Lima and present Acolla's case before the relevant sections of the state bureaucracy.[70] Given the inevitable frustrations, delays, and problems that arose from dealing with the national government, the officials doubtlessly needed a fairly high degree of communal responsibility and dedication in order to persevere. Equally important, however, in the case of a successful petition it would be the very same officials, because of their comparative wealth, position, and connections, who would be in the best position to benefit from it.

The same tendencies existed on the western side of the Yanamarca Valley. In August 1935, when the provincial council sent a letter to the various districts asking for public works contributions to help celebrate the four hundredth anniversary of the founding of Jauja, Mar-

[69] For a similar analysis of the wealthy peasant's motivation in advancing village "development," see Carlos Samaniego, "Peasant Movements at the Turn of the Century and the Rise of the Independent Farmer," in Long and Roberts (eds.), *Peasant Cooperation*, pp. 45–71; and Marcelo Grondin, "Peasant Cooperation and Dependency: The Case of the Electricity Enterprise of Muquiyauyo," in ibid., pp. 99–127.

[70] AMA, Libro de Sesiones, 1934–1939, pp. 208, 214–21, 274–82, 379–85, 399–400, and 402–406. On the specific information regarding the community's representative, pp. 399–400.

co's district council wrote back suggesting a road from Jauja to Oroya, passing through Cachicachi. After noting the benefits the road would bring Jauja and the Yanamarca Valley, the municipal authorities offered to donate district labor until the project was completed, as long as the government contributed the money necessary for expenses.[71] In effect, what the district officials wished to do was to obtain outside financing to build their own road to the mining centers, a scheme with great potential for developing market production in their area. But unfortunately for the local notables, though the villages of the district finished work on the Yanamarca Valley portion, the road was never a commercial success.[72]

In addition to offering opportunities to the innovative and well-connected sectors of the village population, national integration also required that villagers learn to use the basic styles of modern politics. Eighteen months after Marco suggested building the road to Oroya, for example, Francisco Limaylla, then mayor of the district, announced the arrival of Francisco F. Baldeón, attorney for the Superior Court in Huancayo. According to Limaylla, Baldeón's purpose in visiting the district was "to deliver, with his own hands, a gold medal to the hardworking and progressive communities of this district, for having worked with enthusiasm and care on the road from Jauja to Oroya, via Marco-Concho-Tambo-Zavala." Thus, Limaylla continued, it was the council's obligation to provide Baldeón a good reception, including a lunch prepared by the community. When Baldeón presented the medal, the presidents of the three cuarteles should reciprocate by toasting him with champagne, while the mayor of Jauja's provincial council would present a special diploma to the community of Marco.[73] And Acolla was not far behind in the competition for fanfare. When the minister of education and other high officials of the central government traveled through Jauja in late November 1937, village authorities decided to present the ministers personally with petitions regarding the various public works projects being carried out in the district. The municipal council accordingly voted nearly one hundred soles, to be raised by contributions from the comuneros, for a recep-

[71] AMM, Libro de Actas, 1929–1943, Sesión Extraordinaria, August 12, 1935, pp. 134–35.

[72] It is clear, from ibid., p. 154, that the work on the Yanamarca Valley portion was completed. It is also clear from observation and conversation in the valley that the road was never a commercial success, probably because other routes—particularly the Tarma-Oroya road, or the Tarma-Jauja-Oroya road passing through Acolla—were preferred.

[73] AMM, Libro de Actas, 1929–1943, Sesión Ordinaria, March 7, 1937, p. 154.

tion that included gifts, firecrackers, a band of musicians, and several cases of beer.[74]

As the experiences of Acolla and Marco both show, even if the projects and petitions did not always turn out exactly according to plan, they certainly fulfilled the purpose of integrating the districts more completely into the national bureaucracy, society, and culture. By the end of the 1930s the larger villages in the Yanamarca Valley, while they might not have electricity, looked modern enough not to be embarrassed in front of an urban visitor. The *comuneros* were sophisticated enough to receive important guests with gifts, speeches, music, and champagne. District children, now able to prepare themselves more adequately in local schools, were beginning to gain admission to national universities. And the process continued to accelerate in subsequent decades.[75]

Yet the cultural, political, and economic benefits were not spread evenly across the various strata of the village population. To take the example of Acolla, though the poorer *comuneros* helped pay the expenses of village representatives in Lima and contributed to the music, beer, and gifts for the education minister's visit, they could not hope to share equally in the increased educational opportunities that resulted. Their children, especially the girls, were needed for household tasks and could not always attend school with regularity. Even if they managed to finish the education available in the community, it was doubtful that they could be spared and financed long enough to enter the university.[76] And the same rule applied in other villages and projects. In the case of road construction, while poorer villagers had to keep up with their quotas of labor, materials, and money, they did not enjoy the fruits of the work to the same extent as those with good commercial connections.[77]

Inevitably, this differential access to the rewards of political and economic integration caused friction within the district capitals in this period; but the main lines of battle were drawn between the district seat and its *anexos*. In December 1932, for example, the notables of

[74] AMA, Libro de Sesiones, Asamblea General del Pueblo, November 22, 1937, p. 277; Asamblea de Junta General, November 24, 1937, pp. 286–87.

[75] For the first case of an *Acollina* entering the University of Trujillo, see ibid., p. 345. By the 1970s, many more families had managed to send at least one child (usually a boy) to the university, though many students from the villages lived a hand-to-mouth existence and employment was not easily attainable once they graduated.

[76] See, for example, Interview with Lydia Solís de Maita, I, Acolla, 1977. While this tendency started to change for families with moderate incomes by the 1960s and 1970s, female children continued to be the most expendable when it came to education.

[77] See Chapter IX for a more thorough treatment of this question.

Concho, an *anexo* of Marco, petitioned the provincial council in Jauja, requesting economic independence for their village. They argued that the revenue from their *remates* and licenses went directly to municipal coffers, and that they never received any of it back. "Our petition is founded on the following reasons," they continued:

1. That all the villages of Peru, especially those in the province of Jauja, are trying to achieve economic independence from the districts to which they belong, in order to collect and administer their small rents, so that they may work for their material and intellectual betterment; 2. That with no help from the state, we are building a school, according to a design sent to us by the Dirección General de Enseñanza [General Office of Education], Model No. 5, which is presently only half-finished; and that in order to complete it, we need materials, such as wood, roof tiles, cement, etc., and we have no resources. 3. After finishing this work, we will go on to repair our plaza, municipal and judicial buildings, etc. For all these projects we need revenue and if our rents are allowed to remain with us, we will be able to advance the works already mentioned superficially [*sic*].[78]

They were convinced their petition would succeed, the notables concluded, because the provincial council, despite the grave crisis through which the region was passing, seemed committed to freeing all the villages under its jurisdiction from the burden of economic dependence. And at least initially, they seemed to be right; within three weeks, the provincial mayor granted the petition, with the only condition that Concho's municipal agent keep careful books and pass them on to the district council in Marco.[79]

Concho was not the only village in the Yanamarca Valley to make a move for financial independence. Earlier in the same year Pachascucho, *anexo* of Acolla, had sent a similar request to the inspector general of education and the provincial mayor of Jauja. Pachascucho's representatives also justified their petitions by pointing out that they were in the process of building a school, and that Acolla did not return to them any part of the taxes and revenue collected in their village. As in the case of Concho, the provincial mayor decided the issue in favor of Pachascucho, though the local officials were again obliged to present an annual accounting of rents and expenditures to the council

[78] APJ, "Solicitud de los agentes municipales de Concho al Alcalde del Concejo Provincial de Jauja," December 7, 1932.

[79] Ibid., "Resolución adjunta," December 26–27, 1932.

of their district.[80] But in contrast to the other case, Acolla's district authorities immediately presented a counterprotest to the mayor of the provincial council, arguing that economic independence for Pachascucho was against the law, and that it would interfere with the municipal budget for the present fiscal year.[81] This prompted a revision of the case before the prefect of the department.

In his covering letter to the prefect, the provincial mayor reiterated his perception that Pachascucho's request was justified. "The [Provincial] Council decided to approve the said petition," he wrote,

> inspired by the desire to protect and support a village as progressive as Pachascucho, which is about to finish its school, [that has been] duly constructed by the Dirección de Enseñanza, and which has planned a series of local public works necessary for the progress of the village.
>
> The District Council of Acolla, in a similar way to many other districts, has not lived up to its obligations to protect [its *anexos*] . . . , practicing an absurd centralism, [and] disposing of the few funds gathered from Pachascucho's taxes.[82]

The proof of Acolla's unjust behavior, he added, was to be found in their counterpetition. After all, how could Pachascucho's economic independence disrupt the district's budget, unless the *anexo* was simply not receiving the rents collected in their village? Then the mayor ended his letter with a call for moderation, emphasizing the partial character of any *anexo*'s economic freedom, and making clear that final control over the administration of rents must remain with the municipality.[83]

Though the prefect confirmed the decision of the provincial council,[84] the matter of *independencias económicas* did not end there. By 1937, the favorable decisions handed down in previous years had resulted in such a multiplication of requests and counterprotests that the inspector of district councils decided to put the controversy to rest once and for all. In a memorandum dated April 8, 1937, he re-

[80] APJ, "Solicitudes de los representantes de Pachascucho al Inspector de Enseñanza y al Alcalde del Concejo Provincial de Jauja," Jauja, January 2–3, 1932, and "Resolución adjunta," March 5, 1932.

[81] APJ, "Protesta de las autoridades municipales de Acolla al Alcalde del Concejo Provincial," Acolla, March 15, 1932.

[82] APJ, "Oficio del Alcalde Provincial de Jauja, elevando en grado de revisión el expediente de los comuneros de Pachascucho," Jauja, March 23, 1932.

[83] Ibid.

[84] APJ, "Resolución del Prefecto del Departamento de Junín sobre la independencia económica de Pachascucho," Huancayo, April 7, 1932.

versed all the decisions taken by his predecessor, arguing that *anexo* independence was completely illegal. This was particularly true, he said, because *anexos* granted economic independence had taken it to absurd lengths, to the point that "municipal agents have decided that they are authorized to name various municipal inspectors and other officials, hold meetings, record minutes, and designate secretaries and treasurers, constituting in this way, at the margin of municipal law, small [district] councils." In the opinion of the inspector, therefore, the only way to stop these abuses was to abolish the *independencias económicas* altogether.[85] And Jauja's provincial council, in a meeting held on April 29, resolved to approve the inspector's decision.

Aside from terminating the controversy at the administrative level, the memo showed that, in the last instance, the district and provincial hierarchy could not afford to open the Pandora's box of *anexo* independence. In a decade when national, provincial, and local authorities were all encouraging modernization, urbanization, and public works, scarcity of revenue made the actual attainment of these goals patently impossible for many villages. School construction provided an excellent example of the ironies involved. While an agency of the central government made available standardized plans for school construction, a kind of "paint-by-numbers" guide in models one through five, the state itself did not insure sufficient or equitable access to the funds necessary to follow the plans. Whether for schools or other projects, communities were reduced to fighting among themselves over scarce resources. In such a situation, the generalization of *independencias económicas* could easily result in the substantial decline of resources for the district capitals and severely limit their control over dependent villages. Thus the district and provincial bureaucracy, with its own interests to defend, could not afford to remain sympathetic to the plight of *anexos* for very long.[86]

But in addition to the important political, financial, and bureaucratic problems they raised, *anexo* rebellions were important because they were the tip of a much larger iceberg. Under cover of a village battle for public works, peasants were also asking questions about subsistence, proletarianization, and communal responsibility. If the villages of Acolla and Marco manipulated the revenues from all the

---

[85] APJ, "Oficio del Alcalde distrital de Acolla al Prefecto del Departamento, informándole sobre la resolución del Inspector de Concejos Distritales y la aprobación del Concejo Provincial de Jauja," Acolla, May 11, 1937.

[86] These various contradictions are obvious from a careful examination of the documents listed in footnotes 78–85.

communities in their districts, what they were in effect doing was stripping neighbors of their resources in order to advance the interests of a single, wealthy, and innovative segment of the valley population. The rest of the valley's inhabitants could not let such a move go uncontested. It is hardly surprising, therefore, that when the path for protest through the provincial council closed in 1937, villages sought new channels for airing their grievances. Increasingly, the most obvious alternate route went straight through the Dirección de Asuntos Indígenas.

On October 2, 1940, the communal and municipal authorities of Tragadero sent a letter to the Dirección, charging that Marco's municipal council was illegally pocketing revenue that belonged to their community. According to the petitioners, the rents obtained from cemetery taxes, licenses for public entertainment, and several other sources were the property of the community rather than the district. Because Marco was charging these rents, Tragadero had been unable to complete work on their boys' and girls' schools, and the village had no municipal or judicial buildings. "Our village finds itself . . . in a lamentable state of underdevelopment," the authorities complained, "neglected by the district to which we belong." The only way to correct the situation, they concluded, was to give Tragadero control over its own communal revenues.[87]

As the subprefect of Jauja and the mayor of Marco were quick to point out, Tragadero's petition was yet another instance of *independencias económicas*, only this time couched in the "communal" language proper for Asuntos Indígenas. In the reports they sent to the Dirección, both officials declared the request to be unfounded, basing themselves on the April 1937 memorandum written by the mayor of Jauja's provincial council.[88] But the mayor of Marco, Ezequiel Hurtado, went even further. It was necessary to differentiate more carefully between municipal and communal revenues, he explained. The former, defined in the law governing municipalities, included rents, cemetery rights, market taxes, public entertainment, fees for the alignment of new buildings, and so on. The latter included all proceeds from communal work parties, the collective hiring out of communal labor, and the renting of pasturelands and other communal properties.[89]

[87] Archivo SINAMOS, cc 239 (Tragadero), Expediente 10530, "Sobre cobro de las rentas municipales de Tragadero," 154–58.

[88] Ibid., 159 and 160.

[89] Ibid., 160.

Given Hurtado's position as mayor of the district, he clearly had a sizable ax to grind in the matter of Tragadero's financial status. Thus he understandably forgot to mention that the distinction between communal and municipal revenues was a great deal easier to make in theory than it was in practice. In previous decades, the municipal government had taken on many of the functions technically belonging to the community. By the 1930s, it was the district council that controlled most levies of communal labor and rented out, sold, or otherwise disposed of communal property.[90] Indeed, when the community of Tragadero attempted to control its "legal" sources of revenue, such as communal lands, it encountered the same problems and resistance as with the attempt to administer "illegal" sources.[91] And that was precisely the point. At the district level, control over land, labor, and revenue became so intermingled that it was practically impossible to separate out one from the others. Besides, the district capital claimed to have the best right to all of them.[92]

Hurtado finished his reports to Asuntos Indígenas by making one final attempt to discredit Tragadero's request in the eyes of the authorities. The real motivation behind the petition, he charged, was not the advancement of the village as a whole, but the desire on the part of a few manipulators or "smart alecks" (vivos) to control the rents for their own purposes.[93] In a sense, Hurtado was among those most qualified to make such a judgment, since he had been at the forefront of a similar effort by Marco's notables when they led a drive for independent district status in 1907, separating themselves from Acolla.[94] The fact that all the municipal and communal authorities from Tragadero had signed the request, however, would seem to disprove his allegation.[95] Still, Hurtado's statement contained deeper implications.

[90] AMA, Libros de Sesiones, 1923–1928, passim; and 1934–1939, passim; and AMM, Libros de Actas, 1907–1918, passim; 1922–1929, passim; and 1929–1943, passim.

[91] This was certainly the case in the struggle with Marco over "Licuy" or "Apay." See above, this chapter.

[92] A particularly striking example of this intermingling is provided by the struggle between the communities of Concho and Marco over communal pasturelands that took place in 1931. In the final resolution, in exchange for formalizing their claim in the communal pastures, Concho agreed to contribute a quota of free labor time to the construction of Marco's rural school. Clearly, therefore, control over labor and control over land were sufficiently intermingled so that a district could exchange one for the other with a dependent village.

[93] Archivo SINAMOS, cc 239 (Tragadero), Expediente 10530, "Sobre cobro de las rentas," 160.

[94] See above, Chapter V.

[95] Archivo SINAMOS, cc 239 (Tragadero), Expediente 10530, "Sobre cobro de las rentas," 154.

In essence, he was claiming that anyone who looked below the surface of Tragadero's apparent communal solidarity would find hidden conflicts, divisions, and self-interested motives. And especially if we examine this petition in a broader context, there seems to be a great deal of truth to his claim.

As was the case with most *anexo*-district battles, Tragadero's conflicts with Marco contained both a village and a class dynamic. As a village, Tragadero wanted its fair share of the lands, labor, and revenue belonging to the district as a whole. On this the entire population could agree, at least in principle. If it came time to divide and privatize communal property, Tragadero should receive a just portion. If the district was building schools, roads, plazas, or irrigation canals, their village should not be shortchanged. Clearly, the battle over revenue fell in this general "united-front" category; so did the 1936 battle over communal lands. But on other, more complicated issues, there could be important disagreements within the village.

Though they were willing to make judicious and selective use of the Dirección de Asuntos Indígenas, Tragadero's more established notables did not wish to turn the Dirección into an alternate source of power that challenged the municipal hierarchy. After all, many of them had a long history of service in the district and lower echelons of the provincial bureaucracy. Some were tied to the Marco elite through patronage or marriage.[96] Thus it is hardly surprising that the less prestigious, often more radical, *comuneros* served as the village's *personeros* (representatives) before the Dirección de Asuntos Indígenas.[97] In at least one instance, moreover, these *personeros* used the Dirección to bring charges against a group of prestigious villagers for "obstructing" the progress of Tragadero. And in that case also, the *personeros* were accused by the notables of wanting to manipulate village revenues for their own personal profit.[98]

In the final analysis, the Dirección de Asuntos Indígenas presented an alternate forum in which communities could raise issues of subsistence, expropriation, and abuse that could not be adequately handled by the regional political system. From the state's point of view, the purpose of this forum was to halt the destruction of the Indian

[96] See above, Chapters II, IV and V; and Archivo SINAMOS, cc 239 (Tragadero), Expediente 2278, 4–4v.

[97] ANF, Protocolos Notariales, Anselmo Flores Espinoza, Book 8: January 27, 1937, 68–70; Archivo SINAMOS, cc 239 (Tragadero), Expediente 2278, "Relativo a la queja formulada por la comunidad de Tragadero . . . contra Víctor Camarena y otros," Jauja and Lima, July–October 1937, 4–4v.

[98] Archivo SINAMOS, cc 239 (Tragadero), Expediente 2278, 4–8.

community, thus guaranteeing the survival of a small producer sector that seemed increasingly essential in the provision of basic food crops for the urban market. For the peasants, however, the establishment of the Dirección came at a time of radical social, economic, and political transformation in the central highlands. Under the circumstances, it is hardly surprising that they used Asuntos Indígenas, and the municipal structure, as weapons in the changing struggle between rich and poor. In some cases, emerging elites were able to manipulate both sets of institutions for their own purposes. In other cases, opposing groups entrenched themselves in separate bureaucracies, using them to define and resolve the new class issues that were emerging in the period. Whatever specific form the battle took, however, it was generally true that, once the 1930s were over, the meaning of "community" in the central sierra had been forever changed.

Community and Class Conflict

For many reasons, the decade of the thirties marked an important watershed in the development of capitalism in Peru's central highlands. By forcing communities to turn inward on their own resources, the world depression intensified the process of internal social and economic differentiation that had been going on for many decades. Unable to satisfy their expanding needs by depending on a shrinking revenue base, villages sought additional help by opening outwards, integrating themselves ever more completely into the national economy and political system. In the context of this integration, the commodification of land and communal relationships took on a new meaning, as capitalist relations began to develop at the very heart of peasant society. The proletarianizing sector of the village population, wishing to stem the tide of pauperization, called on traditional reciprocity and subsistence ideology as their only weapons in a changing class struggle. The emerging entrepreneurial sector, wishing to take advantage of new production and market opportunities, attempted to push forward the commodification of all property and village relationships. No matter what form a conflict took—*cofradía* vs. community, village against village, one community's population divided against itself, or some combination thereof—the central question behind it all was the emergence of capitalist relations at the village level. Thus, even if the outward form of communal relationships continued to look the same, their content was being profoundly altered.

An important aspect of these changes was the spread of commodification into all corners of community life. Clearly, the transformation of communal lands into private property was a key part of the process; but so was the privatization of other spheres and relationships within village existence. One such sphere was communal labor, to which each household theoretically owed a certain quota. As long as the village economy had remained geared toward subsistence and a local agricultural cycle, this obligation presented no problem, since most public works construction or maintenance was also seasonal and could be handled by occasional levies of household labor. By the 1930s, however, the combination of increased mobility, heavier public works construction, and the competition between district capitals and *anexos* had brought the traditional system of labor exaction into crisis. As fewer and fewer people met their labor obligations, the community was forced to fine *comuneros*, or charge them extra for communal services such as access to water or pasture. Village migrants, particularly mineworkers, attempted to substitute money payments for their labor contributions.[99] From the point of view of both the village and the individual *comunero*, therefore, the tendency was toward calculating communal labor time in monetary terms; that is, toward the commodification of communal labor.

In the sphere of private labor exchanges the same trend, already present in the 1920s, spread further in the thirties. Because families bore heavy burdens of taxation and labor exaction, it was increasingly difficult to guarantee a reciprocal labor exchange within a given period of time. As we have already seen, this problem was exacerbated by migration.[100] The overall result was a growing reliance on wage labor to meet the additional needs of the individual household.

The combination of these various tendencies—the privatization of communal land, the commodification of private and communal labor, continuing social and economic differentiation, and the ever more complete integration of the peasant community into the national economy and political system—created the conditions under which an agrarian bourgeoisie could begin to emerge at the village level. Building on previous accumulations of land and wealth, profiting from the economic and political changes of the 1930s, taking control of village politics, and relying on labor from the proletarianized *comuneros*, this incipient agrarian bourgeoisie began to take shape in the late thirties and into the forties. Its emergence marked the most important change

[99] See above, Chapter VII.
[100] See above, Chapter VII.

to take place in the peasant community during the fourth and fifth decades of the twentieth century. With this change came an entirely different set of class relations and conflicts that transformed the meanings not only of the word "community," but also of the words "progress," "development," and perhaps most importantly, "poverty."

CHAPTER NINE

Peasants Become Farmers: Capitalist Agriculture and the Peasant Entrepreneur

I used to like money, no? And the truth is that I am still very fond of money, even today.

—Agustín Ortiz, capitalist farmer.

In the late 1930s Eleuterio Gerónimo, former miner, part-time photographer, and native of Acolla, posed for a historic photograph with his wife and children. Smiling broadly, the Gerónimo family stood with their hoes and shovels, surrounded by piles of the money they had made planting onion for sale on the Lima market. Even though Gerónimo was the first to record his success in black and white, he was not the pioneer of commercial onion production in the Yanamarca Valley. That honor belonged to Víctor Colca, a distant cousin from Marco, who stood behind Gerónimo's camera and snapped the picture.[1]

Until Víctor Colca planted the Bermuda onion in Marco between 1937 and 1938, no one in the Yanamarca Valley had ever planted anything but scallions, and then only enough for family consumption with perhaps a small surplus. It was therefore not surprising that, especially at first, people tended to laugh. They would look at Colca's fields, then poke each other's ribs and ask: why so much onion? But the reason for onion, and particularly Bermuda onion, soon became very clear. Because this larger, slightly purple-tinged variety stored well, it could be shipped to Lima without much damage. At first this was done on the railroad but, by the early 1940s, an increasingly active fleet of trucks began to travel the newly completed road between Acolla and Jauja. And with the new decade, a growing number of local peasant entrepreneurs discovered, as Gerónimo had, that there was a great deal of money to be made in onion.[2]

[1] Conversations with Moisés Ortega in Acolla, at various times during 1977 and early 1978; ANF, Protocolos Notariales, Anselmo Flores Espinoza, Book 5: April 17, 1936, 1093v–94v; and "Acta de Fundación del Comité Pro-Acolla en Morococha, 1923," Archivo Personal de Germán Maita, Acolla.

[2] Conversations with Moisés Ortega; Interview with Agustín Ortiz, Acolla, February 12, 1978; and William B. Hutchinson, "Sociocultural Change in the Mantaro Valley

This apparently sudden bonanza in commercial agriculture was the product of a series of parallel trends in the late 1930s. Nationally, the recovery from the depression combined with the beginning of the second World War to generate a modest industrial boom. Along with this came a major migration to the towns, and the subsequent expansion of urban markets. At the regional level, the reopening of numerous mining centers also expanded demand for foodstuffs. But because the government began to control prices in an effort to guarantee minimal consumption in the cities, large landowners were not interested in growing staples for internal consumption, preferring the more profitable export products. Thus it was up to the small producers to supply urban markets, especially Lima, with cash crops.[3]

In many parts of the central highlands, social and economic developments in earlier decades had created a generation of wealthy and entrepreneurial peasants both willing and able to take advantage of these new opportunities, and the Yanamarca Valley was no exception. Among the wealthier families who had accumulated in the mines, the second generation was ready to carry an innovative spirit into agriculture. Several other entrepreneurs, following a more directly agrarian path, were also ready to use their land, wealth, and influence in experimental ventures. With regard to infrastructure, the participation of this same generation in municipal politics during the 1930s had already cleared the way, through the privatization of community lands and the construction of roads and public works, for the expansion of agrarian capitalist activity.[4]

But in addition to making some enterprising peasants rich, the com-

---

Region of Peru: Acolla, A Case Study," Ph.D. Dissertation, Indiana University, 1973, pp. 59–60.

[3] On industrial expansion, rural-urban migration, and the reopening of mines, see Hutchinson, "Sociocultural Change," p. 60; and Frederick B. Pike, *The Modern History of Peru* (New York: Frederick A. Praeger, 1967), pp. 250–81. On the problem of urban food supplies and government policy, see Chapter VIII of this book and Rosemary Thorp and Geoffrey Bertram, *Peru 1890–1977: Growth and Policy in an Open Economy* (New York: Columbia University Press, 1978), pp. 196–200.

[4] For the creation of a generation of wealthy and entrepreneurial peasants see, in addition to the case studies presented later in this chapter, Richard N. Adams, *A Community in the Andes: Problems and Progress in Muquiyauyo* (Seattle: University of Washington Press, 1959); Giorgio Alberti and Rodrigo Sánchez, *Poder y conflicto social en el Valle del Mantaro* (Lima: Instituto de Estudios Peruanos, 1974); Marcelo Grondin, "Peasant Cooperation and Dependency: The Case of the Electricity Enterprise of Muquiyauyo," in Norman Long and Bryan R. Roberts (eds.), *Peasant Cooperation and Capitalist Expansion in Central Peru* (Austin: University of Texas Press, 1978), pp. 99–127; and Carlos Samaniego, "Peasant Movements at the Turn of the Century and the Rise of the Independent Farmer," in Long and Roberts, *Peasant Cooperation*, pp. 45–71. For the role of municipal government in preparing the way for agrarian capitalist activity, see Chapter VIII of this book.

bination of favorable markets and Bermuda onions was destined to transform the very nature of agriculture in the Yanamarca Valley. For the first time, an entire crop was planted, cultivated, and harvested exclusively for sale. Despite the inevitable reverses, some of the pioneers in onion production were to make lasting fortunes in the 1940s and 1950s. As accumulations became more secure, the characteristic accoutrements of capitalist agriculture began to appear: tractors, trucks, fertilizers, insecticides, and—most importantly—the growing use of wage labor. When the unpredictability of onion prices became troublesome, some of the onion magnates transferred a portion of their fortunes to potatoes, a much more dependable and capital intensive crop. Thus profit and innovation, rather than consumption, prestige, or subsistence, began to dictate decisions in agriculture. In a phrase, what happened in the Yanamarca Valley was that a generation of wealthy peasants became capitalist farmers.

Commercial Agriculture and Initial Accumulations

In and of itself, accumulation of land and commercialization of agriculture was nothing new in the Yanamarca Valley. But in the 1920s, with the development of an industrial mining economy, commercial agriculture became a more viable and dependable investment. Not only did an industrial mining sector generate more extensive and permanent markets for labor and goods in the region, but it also provided new alternatives for accumulation and education to those willing and able to take advantage of them. Miners who developed managerial skills, for example, found themselves able to take on new roles in municipal administration, or much better able to manage commercial and agrarian ventures, when they returned to their communities. Those who had accumulated money while working in the mines invested it in land, education, and innovation upon returning home. Even those wealthier peasants who had never migrated could take advantage of the dependable market for food or manufactures that the mining economy provided.[5]

By the 1930s, the growth of an internal market of national proportions further stimulated entrepreneurial activity. Since the 1920s, rural-urban migration, urbanization, industrialization, and foreign investment had combined to create new demand for agricultural products throughout the country, and especially in Lima. The road-building

[5] For the role of the mining industry in transforming village life, see Chapters V, VI, VII and VIII.

activity of the thirties, coming on the heels of Leguía's program of *conscripción vial*, had established a relatively efficient network of highways tying various regions to each other.[6] As labor migrations between and among regions became more common, the dispersed and incipient fragments of a labor market that already existed in Peru began to come together. And with the integration of markets for labor and goods at the national level, entrepreneurs who considered engaging in commercial production for a wider market found they had both the broader opportunities and the security that had been missing in the past.

By the mid-1930s in the Yanamarca Valley, a group of entrepreneurs stood ready to take advantage of this new situation. Some, such as Eleuterio Gerónimo, Mauricio Huamán, and Germán and Laureano Maita, had increased their ability to accumulate by migrating to the mines.[7] Others, like Bacilio Alvarez, Víctor Colca, and Teodoro Ortiz, seem to have taken a more strictly agrarian, community-oriented route.[8] In all cases, these innovative, ambitious peasants increased their influence in the villages by serving on the municipal councils. And they were usually the first to present themselves when prize pieces of communal land went up for sale.

Bacilio Alvarez was a case in point. Born in Muqui, Alvarez married Paula Alvaro, a native of Acolla, and settled down in his wife's village. Having inherited less than a third of one hectare of land from his parents, Alvarez went on to buy, by the time he was thirty-eight years old, over two additional hectares—divided into fourteen *chacras*—in various parts of Acolla, some of it from the community. Although the actual amount of land this represented was not overly impressive, a majority of the plots were located in the better *parajes*. Then in 1931 Alvarez paid one thousand soles for a *cerco* (fenced or walled-in property) of eucalyptus trees. This was quite a valuable addition to his holdings, especially if we remember that wood was in great demand locally and regionally, both in village construction and in the mining centers. And to round off his situation, Alvarez served as mayor of Acolla district in the mid-1930s, just when the major impulse for public works construction, the urbanization of the village, and the privatization of community lands was getting off the ground.[9]

[6] See Chapters VI and VIII.

[7] "Acta de Fundación del Comité Pro-Acolla"; Interview with Germán Maita, Acolla, February 7, 1978; Interview with Mauricio Huamán, Jauja, February 9, 1978.

[8] While I have not found any evidence disproving a connection with the mines, I have not found any evidence proving that these men migrated, either.

[9] ANF, Protocolos Notariales, Luis Salazar, Book 55: January 29, 1926, 1216v–18;

The Maita brothers were also successful at integrating their economic and political interests. After migrating to work in Morococha in the early 1920s, both Germán and Laureano settled down in Acolla. While Laureano served as mayor in the late 1920s, making an initial push for public works, urbanization, and increased commerce, Germán immediately began to accumulate land. In addition to buying land privately, he took advantage of community privatization to accumulate some valuable plots. In 1928, while Laureano was mayor, the community decided to sell some property to finance the construction of the village church. It was Germán Maita who came forward and offered 900 soles for a *chacra* belonging to three *cuarteles* of the community. Located in Ticanapampa, a choice and humid *paraje*, the property measured one and one-third hectares and bordered on other lands belonging to Germán. And because it was directly on the road to Jauja, the commercialization of its products was particularly convenient.[10]

Teodoro Ortiz represented yet another path toward accumulation. In part, Ortiz followed the same general strategy as his fellow villagers. By combining influence in community government with some intelligent purchases, he and his wife, Lucía Navarro, were able to put together several modest yet fertile pieces of land in the late 1920s and early 1930s.[11] But Ortiz had an additional advantage. His father-in-law, José Navarro Flores, also owned some fertile and valuable agrarian properties and, in the late 1930s, decided to divide them up among his children.[12] Thus by the early 1940s the Ortiz-Navarro family, although certainly not accumulating large amounts of property, had managed to put together a minimum of two or three hectares of land in the more desirable areas. And as they and some of their neighbors would find out, it was not the size but the value of the plots that ultimately counted.

Book 67: February 15, 1931, 119–20v; and Anselmo Flores Espinoza, Book 2: March 12, 1935, 125v–27. AMA, Libro de Sesiones, 1934–1939, Sesión Extraordinaria, April 13, 1934, pp. 9–12; and Sesión de Junta General Extraordinaria, August 29, 1934, pp. 49–52.

[10] "Acta de Fundación del Comité Pro-Acolla"; AMA, Libro de Actas, 1923–1928, especially pp. 37–38, 47–48; Interview with Germán Maita; and ANF, Protocolos Notariales, Luis Salazar, Book 60: December 6, 1927, 1165v–67; Book 62: October 18, 1928, 2260–64.

[11] ANF, Protocolos Notariales, Luis Salazar, Book 62: December 4, 1928, 2428v–32v; Book 69: December 31, 1931, 1091–93; and AMA, Libro de Actas, 1934–1939, Sesión Extraordinaria de Junta General, November 28, 1935, pp. 123–27, especially p. 125.

[12] ANF, Protocolos Notariales, Luis Salazar, Book 72: February 6, 1934, 947–49; Anselmo Flores Espinoza, Book 4: February 7, 1936, 905v–906v; Book 5: April 13, 1936, 1084v–85v.

Despite the widespread commercial activity and land accumulation that was going on in Acolla, however, the initial step toward capitalist agriculture was not taken there. Instead, a former sexton of Marco's church, with extremely good connections to the local church hierarchy, planted the first crop of Bermuda onion.[13] Unfortunately, it is somewhat difficult to know what was going on in Víctor Colca's mind when he planted onion. One thing we do know is that his move toward capitalist agriculture was not his only commercial or entrepreneurial venture. Since the mid-1930s, Colca had been renting the grain mill in Marco that belonged to a local *cofradía* and, in 1939, bought it from Marco parish. Though the community contested the boundaries included in that sale, as well as the actual ownership of the mill, Colca apparently planted one of his first onion crops on the disputed land.[14] But even if it is impossible to reconstruct the process by which Colca first planted a totally commercial crop, the same is not true of what happened afterward.

Once the results of Colca's decision became apparent, there was a boom in onion production in the Yanamarca Valley. Eleuterio Gerónimo and Teodoro Ortiz were among the pioneers of onion cultivation in Acolla, and they were followed by many others. Because onion was so labor intensive, it could be grown profitably on a plot of any size. The only necessity was a high level of humidity. Thus it was an attractive commercial crop for anyone who had access to family labor, even if they did not have a great deal of land. And by the 1940s in the Yanamarca Valley, many families were precisely in that situation.[15]

In addition to furnishing a commercial crop that was adaptable to many different households, onion production also contributed to changing the ecological and land tenure systems in the valley. Because onions need a great deal of moisture, for the first time in history the humid lowlands near the Yanamarca River began to appear attractive as agricultural plots. As urbanization and public works construction advanced in the valley's towns, more and more people demanded that their expropriated plots be compensated with lands from

[13] Conversations with Moisés Ortega; Interview with Agustín Ortiz; Archivo SINAMOS, cc 205 (Marco), Expediente 4366: "Marco vs. Francisco Carlé y Víctor Colca," 1942.

[14] Archivo SINAMOS, cc 205 (Marco), Expediente 4366; and "Expediente sobre la reivindicación del molino de propiedad comunal," 1939.

[15] Conversations with Moisés Ortega; Interview with Agustín Ortiz; Hutchinson, "Sociocultural Change," pp. 59–60. For the progress of social and economic differentiation in the Yanamarca Valley, see Chapters VI, VII and VIII of this book.

the communal pampas near the river. This led to an imbalance between animals and available pasturelands, and the intensification of inter- and intracommunity disputes about the ownership and utilization of the common pampa lands.[16]

Finally, however, the inevitable happened. As more and more people grew onion, the market became glutted and prices plummeted. Many entrepreneurs, ruined as quickly as they had become rich, decided to bide their time with future commercial enterprises. Others, able to weather the crash more successfully, decided to diversify their production.[17] In either case, entrepreneurs in the valley had reached a critical threshold in the development of agriculture, for profit and market considerations were now at the forefront of production decisions. Still, it would take a second generation, building on the experience and accumulation of the first, to consolidate their gains and build a truly capitalist agricultural business.

The Capitalist Agrarian Enterprise

When Teodoro Ortiz first planted onion in a small lot by his house, he used to talk to his son about the plans he had to make money and expand his agrarian enterprise. But Agustín Ortiz Navarro, a restless young man in his early twenties, did not want to listen.[18] Having been the first in his family to receive a secondary education at the Colegio San José in Jauja, Agustín was interested in finding new vistas and trying out new professions. By the time he was thirty, he had worked as a miner, merchant, shopkeeper, and teacher. His family, friends, and neighbors all thought he was crazy. "The crazy one is back again," they would say, because he had worked at so many different jobs without making economic progress. Yet as he remembered thirty years later, Agustín Ortiz soon made them all eat their words.

Thinking back on his personal history, don Agustín felt that the differences between him and his friends began to show while he was still in secondary school. The Colegio San José, being the only sec-

---

[16] Hutchinson, "Sociocultural Change," pp. 60–62; AMA, Libro de Actas, 1934–1939; AMM, Libro de Actas, 1929–1943; Archivo SINAMOS, cc 205 (Marco), Expediente 13382, "Relativo a las diferencias suscitadas entre las comunidades de Marco y Tragadero sobre establecimiento de servidumbre por el paso de ganado"; cc 239 (Tragadero), Expediente 16753; and the *expedientes* for official recognition submitted by the communities of Acolla, Concho, Tragadero, and Marco.

[17] Hutchinson, "Sociocultural Change," pp. 60–61.

[18] Unless otherwise noted, the data used in the case study of Agustín Ortiz are from my interview with him in Acolla on February 12, 1978.

ondary school in the northern Mantaro Valley at that time, attracted the sons of most wealthy or forward-looking villagers as well as the sons of the provincial elite. And yet it was quite deficient, for it did not prepare the students for choosing a career or deciding what to do once they finished. Many of don Agustín's classmates, in fact, did not continue their education. Others decided to take up more traditional professional careers: teaching, law, perhaps even medicine. But the young Agustín, impatient with what he considered the useless aspects of traditional education, decided to follow a more practical route. He went to a school for mining foremen and, after three years, emerged with a diploma proving him knowledgeable at middle-level administration and intermediate mining technology.

Even so, the mining industry did not provide sufficient opportunities and, only a few years later, don Agustín moved into commerce. Working side by side with his wife, he plied the market routes between Jauja and Lima, stopping in Oroya, carrying a wide variety of products from one weekly fair to the next. Whether it was chicken, fruit, or motor oil, the couple sold their wares in the marketplace, often becoming the laughingstock of don Agustín's neighbors. Under these circumstances, it did not take long for the embarrassment and trouble of petty trading to outweigh the slim profits, especially since don Agustín began to agree with the main criticism leveled against him, that he had not finished high school and additional special training in order to end up a butcher and small-time merchant on the village plaza. Shortly thereafter, Agustín Ortiz decided to try his hand at teaching.

But the teaching career, predictably enough for don Agustín's perennial critics, went the way of all previous attempts. It is difficult to know exactly why—even don Agustín himself is not sure. It probably had a great deal to do with the nature and limitations of most highland schools, the lack of funds, and especially the frustrations of an impatient, dynamic man trying to teach what he considered to be outdated, outmoded, or even irrelevant subject matter. But whatever the reasons, the result was that Agustín Ortiz found himself once again without an occupation, being laughed at in Acolla. It was at this point that he decided to try his hand at agriculture.

As don Agustín never tires of explaining, when he started to work the land he began with nothing. Aside from a mule, which he bought with borrowed money, he accepted everything on loan from his parents—even the agricultural tools he used. And once again, his neighbors and friends laughed. Several of his old schoolmates offered to take him on as a subordinate in their work. Others, apparently in good faith, reminded him that he had studied primary and secondary school, in addition to special training, and that it was a tragic waste for him to end up working the land. But, according to don Agustín, the many comments and criticisms only served to strengthen his resolve to succeed.

The rockiness of don Agustín's initial path into agriculture should not blind us to the fact that, despite his lack of tools and funds, he already belonged to the second generation of agrarian entrepreneurs. Even though he had not been interested in previous years, by the time he settled down to work the land he was both willing and able to build on the knowledge that his father, along with other innovators, had accumulated. From the very beginning, for example, he diversified his commercial crops, planting both onion and potato. He also put great stock on the fertile and humid lowlands near the Yanamarca River. And his reliance on previous experience seemed to bring him early success. The potatoes he planted on the pampa grew "as big as trees," and within a few years he was well on his way to buying his first piece of machinery.

Besides the many similarities between don Agustín and his father's generation, however, there were also important differences. For one thing, even if Teodoro Ortiz could offer his son experience and funding, don Agustín also used bank credit to expand his business. The fact that he was willing to seek larger, more impersonal loans was already a major break with previous attempts at small-scale commercial agriculture. In addition, don Agustín was interested in mechanization and improved agricultural technology to a much greater extent than his predecessors. But perhaps the most important difference between don Agustín and previous peasant innovators was his continuous, restless need to know, to change, to grow, and to learn from his mistakes. As future events would show, it was this impatient and inquisitive streak that allowed him to transform a major reversal into a major breakthrough.

Just as don Agustín was beginning to expand his business—he had recently bought his first tractor—there was a particularly rainy season. All the predictions of the agricultural traditionalists came true as the natural drainage tunnel in Tragadero, where the Yanamarca River usually went underground, backed up due to the unusually large amount of water. The entire pampa was flooded, and don Agustín's lowland potato and onion fields were completely ruined. Forced to start over, weighed down by outstanding bank debts, he lived the recurring nightmare of the peasant entrepreneur. "I owed the bank money for a long, long time," don Agustín remembered. "For several years I just dragged myself along. But with some effort, some willpower, I managed to regain some of the positive spirit, the moral backbone I had lost. And I kept on working." Not only did he keep on working; he also forced himself to learn from such a disastrous mistake.

The first lesson he acknowledged was that the traditional system of land utilization had existed for a reason. It was precisely because of the dangers associated with flooding that the pampa had been reserved for pasture. Don Agustín decided to learn from traditional technology on this point—never again did he rely on the humid lowlands for agricultural purposes. He also realized that, over the years, the agricultural lands in the Yanamarca Valley had been distributed according to clear and rational criteria. Much of the commercially desirable land had been privatized early, and belonged to families from the Jauja and Marco elites. The remaining choice properties had gone to the *cofradías*, or maintained their status as communal plots In order to make optimal use of existing resources, therefore, the key was not to plant on newly opened or privatized lands, but rather to exploit those properties that had already proven their profitability. The best way to accomplish this, it turned out, was not through costly or sticky purchase attempts, but simply by renting the land from its current owners.

The second lesson don Agustín learned from the pampa disaster was, in some ways, the exact opposite of the first. In order to keep progressing, or even to stay in the same place, an entrepreneur had to keep innovating. Innovation, moreover, was not exclusively an independent process, but was intimately connected with the observation and imitation of other entrepreneurs. Precisely due to the flooding, and the moral crisis it caused him, don Agustín began to travel to neighboring villages to see what other entrepreneurs were doing. In Chocón and Huancas, to the southwest of Acolla, he found that several farmers were doing quite well with more technologically sophisticated methods of potato cultivation. He decided to imitate them and learn from them. "Over there in Chocón," he explained, "the Espinoza family taught us, well they opened our eyes since they saw we were interested in their lands. And it was precisely on their lands, no? . . . They rented to us, taught us what we had to learn. . . ."

Learning from failure, then, proved to be don Agustín's secret weapon. Starting out as an impatient and somewhat arrogant entrepreneur, he learned from the flooding of his fields to understand and incorporate the best of traditional agriculture. His travels in the years after the pampa disaster taught him to observe the techniques of others, to keep informed as to the advances being made in technology, to ask questions and imitate other farmers. Yet in the final analysis, what would prove most successful was his combination of innovation and caution, his method of selective imitation. This mix of the traditional with the modern, combined in such a way as to yield the highest possible profits while minimizing risk and expenditure, would become the unique stamp of the Agustín Ortiz enterprise.

In comparison with the decade between the mid-1940s and the mid-1950s, the fifteen years up to 1970 were not a period of major transformations for the Ortiz business. Instead, don Agustín slowly consolidated his gains, expanding the amount of land he rented, slowly and selectively buying some additional pieces, experimenting cautiously with fertilizers, insecticides, and various forms of labor relations. In the years when prices were high, he took advantage of increased profits to buy land and machinery. When prices were lower, he could ride out the storm with minimal damage. While he certainly learned a great deal over these years, what is most salient about the process of expansion was that it vindicated what he had already gleaned from his earlier experiences: it paid to innovate cautiously, incorporating tradition along the way. Thus, when the next possibility for major innovation came along, don Agustín was able to take advantage of it smoothly and easily.

Sometime around 1970, Agustín Ortiz decided to act on the realization that some of the people to whom he was selling potatoes were reselling them as seed. "In 1970 several already asked me for potato seed," he remembers.

> I would sell a little bit, I would sell for consumption, and people would exploit me. Because the commercialization of seed was not yet controlled by law, they would buy as if for consumption purposes and then sell it as seed. So I realized what they were doing, and we began to sow potatoes specifically for seed.

It was with this transformation from consumption potatoes to seed potatoes that don Agustín's business took on its truly mature form. By the middle to late seventies, he was considered one of the most important producers of potato seed, not only in the central highlands, but in the entire country. Renting lands along the entire Mantaro Valley, as well as in the Yanamarca Valley and Tarma, he marketed his crop both nationally and internationally.[19] His weekly salary expenditures on permanent personnel, which did not take into account seasonal wage laborers or other labor arrangements, amounted to well over $1,000. He owned a fleet of fifteen large diesel trucks, many tractors, and other assorted agricultural machines. Aside from investing in numerous urban properties around Lima, he and his wife took yearly trips to different areas of the world. But most important, his agrarian enterprise was organized so that every part of it was there for one reason: it was the most rational way to achieve the highest profit possible.

Perhaps the best example of this careful rationalization can be found in don Agustín's use of various systems of labor relations and organization of production, depending on the crop and region where he is working. In the case of onion, for example, he uses the traditional and time-tested method of *al partir*.[20] Renting community property in Muquillanqui, on the humid lower slopes of the western side of the valley, he distributes it among various people with whom he has worked for over twenty years:

> I divide it [in strips of] about 300 meters by 12 meters. They plant with me, like a partnership. I give them land, money, and use of a vehicle. They give nothing but labor, no? And everyone goes to plant what they want. They put themselves on a long list of family members, godchildren, and relatives who plant with me. . . . My wife goes out to distribute the lands. . . . Afterward I prepare the land for them, I give them fertilizer, I give them money, well, until the harvest. When I get the money from the sale of the harvest, I give a check to each one, I distribute the earnings. But I give them money and all they need until I can cancel what they owe.

Clearly, this system of relationships is not contractual wage labor in its classic form. Rather, don Agustín takes advantage of a number of personalistic and paternalistic ties, including ritual kinship, family connections, and debt, to cement a series of ongoing, year-to-year exchanges between himself and a number of households in the area. Yet he does not use this system for tradition's sake, but simply because it is the most rational and effective way to plant onion.

---

[19] I am grateful to the people from the Centro Internacional de la Papa (C.I.P.) working in the central highlands, especially Alan Benjamin and Ludy Ugarte, for their help in placing Agustín Ortiz in a larger context.

[20] For an explanation of how *al partir* was used in the nineteenth century, see Chapter II.

Because onion is extremely labor intensive and fluctuates wildly in price, it does not benefit from economies of scale. Rather than invest large amounts of capital in wage labor and machinery, therefore, don Agustín prefers to give over the exploitation of the land to others, distributing the risk more evenly while at the same time saving himself the trouble of actual cultivation. As he explained,

> in onion the work is more complicated, it becomes more difficult. First one must sprout seedlings, and during two months there is constant irrigating and replanting. Then you must take out the seedlings, and replant them once again. Then those small seedlings require constant care and it is a bit difficult for me, no? One cannot do this. I have tried in small plots, but I can't.

For the heavy day-to-day demands of onion cultivation, then, don Agustín is able to exploit the household economy of local families. At times of planting and harvest, however, when labor demands are particularly high, it is necessary to supplement family labor. Here, don Agustín again evidences an innovative and unorthodox mixture of labor relations. While using some wage laborers, to whom he pays the minimum wage and nothing more, he also supplements his labor needs with unpaid labor from various community institutions. As he pointed out, this mixture cuts down on labor costs:

> This [part of the cycle] demands constant work. Oof! How many workers this would mean, and how much money! Thus we use, so to speak, the communities, the institutions, even the schools, no?— to go plant onion . . . high school, from the eleventh and twelfth grades, we use these students. If we stick to the plan—one day, two days they give us, and then they save us [a great deal], and then we give them their football, and they are happy. Because in part. . . . This does not reach the records of the government in this form, but rather in another form. . . . Because the truth is that we should fill out a form for everyone, all workers should be paid, no? But with regard to payment we pay everybody, no?—because one has to be very good [to them] to get them to work, to select personnel. We do not try to get quantity, but rather quality. The young men work with quite a bit of enthusiasm. . . . We take good care of them, etc., and with that we do quite well. The rest of the people, we hire anyone we see in the street and they all work together.

But clearly, in addition to lowering labor costs, don Agustín's use of unpaid community labor forms a part of a much larger relationship of reciprocity, generosity, and redistribution which he consciously maintains with the various community organizations in the Yanamarca Valley. It is only in the context of a much broader exchange that his ability to use communal labor can truly make sense. Since 1955, for example, he has served as *personero*, or official representative, of Acolla in its dealings with the national government.[21] And he is completely conscious of the ways in which his generosity toward community institutions can aid in his success as a capitalist farmer:

> I subscribe myself, so to speak, to the cause of humanity, to the people, the institutions, I unite myself to them. I say this because it depends on . . . Marco, for example, gives me all its lands in the *puna* [high plateau], it gives me Muquillanqui . . . Marco gives me these lands through a private arrangement, here I have the map, the sketch we made, all the lands, so to speak are . . . all are rented, no? Pieces, pieces, pieces . . . and so they give me the advantage. And I serve them in all that I can. But one must sow in order to reap, do good works if one wants to profit. So I give them gifts, for example, for the institutions in Acolla . . . the other day I saw a man, who said, no?—Acolla will not be able to repay don Agustín, I think, for all the favors that not even to a son are usually given. Perhaps because of this I have the advantage, the communities give me their land, they deny me nothing! One must learn to sow correctly!

In the case of onion, then, don Agustín exploits the advantages of community reciprocity, as well as those of the household economy, at the level of production. But he also reaps the benefits of the larger business at the market level. Because he handles the marketing himself he can, in times of low prices, manipulate the marketplace by keeping his substantial crop in storage until the price goes up—an alternative which is totally closed to the small producer. Yet despite the surface similarities in labor relations, use of asymmetrical reciprocity, and monopoly of commercialization, it would be a mistake to equate don Agustín's production system with that of previous, noncapitalist peasant entrepreneurs. Rather than using this system because it is the only one available, don Agustín uses it because it is the most rational and profitable way to grow onion. Perhaps a comparison with his system for potato production will best illustrate the point.

The case of the potato is completely different. Not only can planting

[21] Archivo SINAMOS, "Expediente del Reconocimiento e inscripción oficial de la comunidad de Indígenas de Acolla," Constancia, November 12, 1955.

be mechanized, but it can be done early and the potatoes stored, so to speak, in the ground until the beginning of the growing season. Further, given the spacing and pattern of the rows, weeding is minimal and can also be done mechanically. In the long run, moreover, the potato is a much more predictable, profitable, and productive crop. "The secret of those who grow potatoes," don Agustín explained,

> is that the potato always yields a lot of money. Let's say a plant gives, say, two kilos, no? Two kilos with a high level of technology. And even if one cultivates it with middle-level techniques, one can still expect it to produce, no? On one hectare you can sow, depending on the density, between thirty and forty thousand plants. Then it gives a great deal because it is a highly productive crop. It justifies the expense, no? You spend a lot of money, but the potato compensates you for it.

Given the nature of the potato, then, both in production and marketing, it can be grown in a more purely capitalist fashion. Don Agustín uses only wage labor, and exploits only those lands where the fertility and available surface make the marginal utility of potato production very high. Because the relatively high level of mechanization increases the productivity of labor, it is possible to rely on a comparatively small permanent labor force. Thus he can reserve the majority of the profits for himself, in a situation where risk is low. And yet even in potato cultivation, he knows how to utilize the debts of generosity he has built up with the Yanamarca Valley communities in order to gain access to the best and most productive lands.

In Mesapata, along the high plateau that frames Marco to the west, don Agustín has about 100 hectares of community land planted with potato. In a sense, therefore, he is able to translate communal reciprocity and prestige into profitable means of production. He is also careful to invest in the reproduction of this prestige over the longer run. In 1978, in the same general area, he rented 15 hectares of land from Concho. "I am paying them without having planted the land," he explained,

> which is another great advantage. Without planting I will pay, in order to have the land rest. And with that money they are building their . . . their—how do you call it—their school, I think. I have given them, I think, 400,000, I don't remember if it's 380,000 or 400,000 [soles][22] in advance for that.

[22] The equivalent of between $4,000 and $5,000 in 1977/78 soles.

Overall, then, it seems clear that Agustín Ortiz's business is a quintessentially capitalist enterprise, not only in terms of size, but also with regard to how decisions are made. Over the past thirty years, its driving force has been profit, in order to reinvest, in order to grow and innovate. When don Agustín uses apparently more "traditional" labor relations, such as *al partir* or unpaid communal labor, he chooses to do so consciously, even though wage laborers are available, because it is the cheapest, most profitable way to perform those particular tasks. The dramatically different context and purpose of these relations, moreover, makes it difficult to equate them with their precapitalist counterparts. When production and market conditions allow a heavier capital investment, he is the first to mechanize and use wage labor. And since he wants to be ready to reallocate resources when new market or productive conditions emerge, he puts great stock on keeping his capital relatively mobile, quickly deployable to take advantage of new opportunities. It is in this context that his reliance on land rentals, rather than landownership, can most easily be explained.

At the level of large property, landownership was not traditionally organized according to market criteria. Instead, landowners defined the territorial boundaries of their haciendas in such a way as to include lands for subsistence, for market production, for grazing, and for distribution to *colonos* in order to retain a labor force. The key, in this sense, was adaptability: the possibility of combining various kinds of production in different proportions, depending on changes in the economic cycle. In addition, local power—especially in terms of developing networks of patron-client relations—depended, among other things, on the kind of prestige that landownership provided. Because the original hacienda units were defined according to these various criteria, therefore, they are not ideal units for exploitation by capitalist agricultural businesses.[23] This is true especially because the opportunity cost of the capital invested in buying such properties is

[23] I use the term "agricultural" very specifically here, for in the case of livestock the various *sociedades ganaderas* have managed to exploit preexisting territorial units fairly efficiently. Useful studies on the "traditional" hacienda, its adaptability, and the complexity of its internal logic, include: Enrique Florescano (ed.), *Haciendas, latifundios y plantaciones en América Latina*, Simposio de Roma organizado por CLACSO (Mexico City: Siglo XXI Editores, 1975); Henri Favre, "Evolución y situación de la hacienda tradicional en la región de Huancavelica," in José Matos Mar (ed.), *Hacienda, comunidad y campesino en el Perú* (Lima: Instituto de Estudios Peruanos, 1976), pp. 105–138; Pablo Macera, "Feudalismo colonial Americano: el caso de las haciendas peruanas," in Pablo Macera (ed.), *Trabajos de historia* (Lima: Instituto Nacional de Cultura, 1977), III:139–227; Murdo Macleod, *Spanish Central America: A Socioeconomic History, 1520–1720* (Berkeley and Los Angeles: University of California Press, 1973); and the classic article by Eric Wolf and Sidney Mintz, "Haciendas and Plantations in Middle America and the Antilles," *Social and Economic Studies*, 6:3 (1957), 380–412.

much too high—something that was not true in the past. Thus, rather than sink his capital into the purchase of such a large property, don Agustín prefers to rent only those portions of the haciendas that are highly productive and fertile. In this way, he can utilize the good sections without also having to invest in the bad.[24]

But there is yet another reason for preferring land rental to land-ownership. Since don Agustín's business is very carefully and intricately organized to yield the highest profits possible, he is extremely vigilant in his selection of which land is best for which crop. There are certain very fertile lands, for example, which may be good for growing crops for local consumption, such as broad beans, barley, quinoa, or corn, but which will not do for potatoes or onion. Given the high humidity needs of onion, moreover, its exploitation on a medium to large scale also necessitates very specific and easy access to water. In the case of potatoes, high levels of mechanization and capital investment mean that only extensive, flat, and carefully selected lands can be exploited profitably. Yet given changing market conditions, don Agustín must be prepared to move fairly rapidly from one kind of land to another, depending on the relative profitability of different crops. It is easier to do this if he rents, rather than owns, the land he has in production. Of course, not all rental contracts can be broken quickly or easily, nor is it always possible to change production decisions to follow prices. But overall and in the long run, land rental is both a smaller and more short-term investment of capital than landownership.

Don Agustín's experiences with building a capitalist agrarian enterprise have generated in him the typically capitalist ideology of the self-made man. Again and again during our Sunday morning conversation, he would return to the fact that he began with nothing, building his business bit by bit, on the basis of hard work, failure, and painful experience. "As you know," he told me, "all men who are great have suffered on the basis of hard work. They are not born great." He also differentiated himself openly and consciously from others who did not belong to that class of great men, both among his predecessors and his contemporaries. When speaking of other, less fortunate villagers in Acolla, for example, he bemoaned the effects of intense land fragmentation, low levels of technology, and scarcity of

[24] The one exception to the rule is don Agustín's hacienda Bellavista, in Tarma; but it tends to prove the rule, since don Agustín rented it for quite a while before deciding to buy it.

credit on the production possibilities of the family economy. But he also blamed the people for their fate:

> They are people who are somewhat lazy, who can't dedicate themselves to constant, serious, formal work. Thus they aren't motivated. The majority of them live, well, a bit low in terms of their economic level, no?

And he was equally scathing in his criticisms of previous generations of wealthy peasants who had not made the transition to capitalist agriculture. Referring to the Hurtado family, for example, don Agustín remarked:

> I had the hacienda of the Hurtados in Quishuarcancha for a period of twelve years. . . . And, so to speak, they lacked a technical sense, a sense, shall we say, of the present, of the fact we are in the twentieth century and need to take advantage of things more quickly, no? Man's life is not measured, shall we say, in terms of the years he has lived, but by how much he has worked, how well he has taken advantage of the opportunities presented to him. We must justify, so to speak, how each minute has been lived, and more than anything how each opportunity has been utilized. So it seems that they did not know how to take advantage, how to use time efficiently.

So this is the story of Agustín Ortiz, who in the space of a generation went from wealthy, restless peasant entrepreneur to self-conscious capitalist farmer. Even if he were the only one of his kind in the central highlands, his story would be important because it embodies, in so many ways, the essential meaning of the transition from one mode of production to another. But what is perhaps most interesting about Agustín Ortiz's story is precisely the fact that he is not an isolated case.

The Agrarian Enterprise in a Larger Context

In the twenty years between the late 1930s and the 1950s, don Agustín's story was being repeated, with numerous variations, in many parts of the Mantaro Valley and its environs. Building on a previous process of social and economic differentiation within the villages, a group of peasant entrepreneurs, some of them with migration experience, began to invest in new commercial enterprises. Though there was much diversity, several important similarities stand out. First of all, in the great majority of the cases, those entrepreneurs who succeeded were building on previous accumulations, whether these came from agriculture, commerce, or migration. Secondly, although the actual activities in which these entrepreneurs engaged could vary from truck farming to manufacturing to artisanry, they all had one thing in common: they were geared to take advantage of a much broader and more secure internal market. And thirdly, despite the fact that most new entrepreneurs knew how to use community and family relationships to further their economic goals, the growth of their enterprises signified a major transformation, both in terms of class structure and relations of production, within the villages.

One important nucleus of small- to medium-scale capitalist activity was the area around Jauja, including the Yanamarca Valley. In the latter, several farmers accompanied don Agustín in his rise to wealth. The Espinoza family of Chocón, for example, has already been mentioned as having predated, and aided, Ortiz in his transition toward commercial potato production. But others stand out also, including the Romero clan of Chocón; the Bueno family of Huancas, whose members rent land in the Yanamarca Valley; and the Yaringaño brothers, natives of Acolla. Interestingly, don Agustín sees the Yaringaños as having followed in his footsteps, to the point where they now compete in everything at the valley level. And to a large extent, don Agustín is right. The only major difference between his path and that of the Yaringaño family is that, in their first generation of accumulation, they made their money in the mines rather than in commercial agriculture.[25]

Looking outside the Yanamarca area, we find other notable entrepreneurial efforts in the Jauja region. Perhaps most dramatic at the individual level is the case of Gregorio Hilario, now a large-scale producer of potato seed. In addition to running an extremely efficient business, Hilario seems to take great pleasure in buying small pieces of fertile land, most of them located on the Mantaro Valley floor, from members of the old Jauja elite. One weekday in early 1978, I had occasion to observe such a sale in the office of one of Jauja's notaries. As Hilario sat back in his chair, a broad smile on his face, two elderly ladies with well-known last names proceeded, through clenched teeth,

[25] My information on other entrepreneurs in the Yanamarca Valley comes from a combination of sources: direct observation; conversations with Moisés Ortega; and my interview with Agustín Ortiz. On the initial accumulation of the Yaringaños, the Agustín Ortiz interview and "Acta de Fundación del Comité Pro-Acolla."

to call him "don Goyo" and sell him one of their few remaining commercial properties.[26]

For "Goyo" Hilario, then, the transition is complete. Similar things have also occurred, at a more general level, in several villages. The village of Huertas, directly south of Jauja, is a case in point. A community where many of Jauja's elite families used to own garden plots, Huertas has now become a center of commercial truck farming as a result of labor migration, accumulation, and transference of land titles. Its neighbor, the village of Julcán, has become a center of medium-scale shoe manufacturing for the Mantaro Valley urban market and the regional mining market.[27]

Moving much further south to the area around Huancayo, we find that a similar pattern has emerged, though in this case it responds to the stimulus of Huancayo's burgeoning urban market. In the community of Pucará, a group of wealthy peasants took some capital they had accumulated in agriculture and, around 1930, founded a transportation business to connect various villages to Huancayo. This company, the Empresa de Transportes Mariscal Cáceres, owned eleven buses by 1955. And in the same period, yet another group of Pucará natives developed vegetable truck farming to serve Huancayo, especially the restaurants.[28]

The community of San Agustín de Cajas, located on the eastern bank of the Mantaro River, provides yet another interesting instance. In the 1920s and 1930s, San Agustín's traditional hat-making industry went into decline due to competition from other products that were found with greater regularity on the regional market. Starting in the 1930s, a group of villagers who had migrated to the mines and to Lima used their accumulated wealth to begin a brick industry to serve Huancayo's construction trades. By the 1940s and 1950s, San Agustín had become a center of brickmaking, and had generated both a class of medium-sized capitalist entrepreneurs and a class of proletarianized brickworkers.[29]

Closer to Jauja along the Mantaro's eastern bank is the village of Matahuasi, where recent studies have also unearthed a strikingly sim-

[26] My information on Gregorio Hilario's business comes from the C.I.P. researchers, especially Ludy Ugarte, and from the Agustín Ortiz interview. I observed the incident of land purchase at the Archivo Notarial Flores.

[27] Information on Huertas and Julcán comes from direct observation in Jauja; ANF, Protocolos Notariales, especially Manuel Víctor Morales; and conversations with Rodrigo Sánchez, Huancayo, August–September 1975.

[28] Alberti and Sánchez, Poder y conflicto social, pp. 75–90.

[29] Ibid., pp. 91–97.

ilar pattern. When outside employment opportunities dried up in the 1930s, the wealthy migrants returning to the community established a series of commercial enterprises, including timber businesses, trucking and transport, dairy farming, and milk trading. Especially telling, in terms of the transformation of class relations, was the conflict emerging in the second half of the decade over the alienation of *cofradía* lands. As in other parts of the region, the Catholic church decided to sell the *cofradía* lands in Matahuasi during the 1930s and members of the community, in an effort to prevent what they considered a privatization of communal resources, sent a delegation of *personeros* to Lima to present their case to the Dirección de Asuntos Indígenas. Several of the *personeros*, however, turned out to be wealthy individuals interested in buying the land for themselves, and they proceeded to do so despite their avowed commitment to represent the village as a whole. As a result, the poorer *comuneros* organized their own committee to push for the legal recognition of Matahuasi, using the Asuntos Indígenas bureaucracy to contest the private deal with the church. Though they were unsuccessful in their bid to restore communal control over ex-*cofradía* lands, the poorer villagers apparently did establish the legally recognized community structure as a political beachhead from which they have continued to struggle against the larger landowners. These, in turn, have used their choice *cofradía* plots as the basis for successful dairy farming enterprises serving the urban and mining markets. In the 1970s several of the original purchasers of those lands became leaders of a milk-marketing cooperative organized in the 1960s during the Belaúnde administration. Employing the proletarianized villagers on their lands and in their firms, these capitalist farmers have utilized the cooperative structure and ideology to further their personal interests, taking advantage of the access to government credit and technical assistance that the cooperative provides. The poorer villagers, for their part, are not members of the cooperative, are hostile toward it, and have continued to confront the dairy farmers politically through the use of community institutions.[30]

[30] The summary of events in Matahuasi is a composite of the following sources: Julian Laite, *Industrial Development and Migrant Labour in Latin America* (Austin: University of Texas Press, 1981), pp. 104–18; Norman Long and Rodrigo Sánchez, "Peasant and Entrepreneurial Coalitions: The Case of the Matahuasi Cooperative," in Long and Roberts, *Peasant Cooperation*, pp. 265–95; and David Winder, "The Impact of the *Comunidad* on Local Development in the Mantaro Valley," in Long and Roberts, *Peasant Cooperation*, pp. 209–40. The analysis of the process in Matahuasi presented in these three sources, however, is fundamentally at odds with mine, since without the benefit of historical hindsight these authors have misunderstood the significance of their data and do not believe that a major transformation in class relations has taken place.

And finally, no overview of the central sierra's small- to medium-sized enterprises would be complete without mentioning the artisans. Whether it is the textiles from San Pedro de Cajas, the carved gourds from Cochas, or the silver from San Gerónimo de Tunán (to mention but a few examples), artisan production in the central highlands has entered the manufacturing stage. Often organized in large "sweat-shops" or family enterprises, artisanry serves a national and international market. In addition to supplying tourists with their souvenirs and foreign handicraft stores with their merchandise, artisan products from the central region have taken over, in a somewhat imperialist fashion, the markets in other parts of the highlands. The central sierra style has also become a favorite among urbanites in Lima who are interested in their country's "traditional" past. Yet we only have to look at these newly rich businesspeople, with their private electric generators, stereo systems, gold watches and sunglasses, to realize that we are no longer dealing with traditional peasant artisans.[31]

It is evident, therefore, that in the last two generations the central highland region has witnessed a major transformation: the development of a local, middle-level bourgeoisie from peasant origins. The actual process, timing, and extent of this transition has varied greatly from community to community, depending on the nature of the local resource base, the type of articulation with other villages and with markets, the history of commercial penetration in agriculture, and the actual form the struggle between classes has taken at the village level. In many distant *puna* villages or smaller, poorer communities, transformations have been slow and uneven.[32] In others, the poorer *comuneros* have been more successful in their use of collective pressure and have forced greater concessions from the nascent entrepreneurial class.[33] Yet strikingly, in most cases where the transition has been

[31] Information on artisanry comes from direct observation in the Mantaro Valley, 1977–1978, and from conversations with María Angélica Salas, Huancayo, 1977, and Susana Lastarria, Madison, Wisconsin, 1979. For some interesting analyses of artisan production in the development of capitalism, see Mirko Lauer, "Artesanía y capitalismo en el Perú," *Análisis*, No. 5 (May–August 1978), pp. 26–48; and María Angélica Salas, "Artesanías y campesinado en el Valle del Mantaro: agonía de una tradición," *Perú Agrario*, No. 4, 1978.

[32] This is evident in the Yanamarca Valley, where differences in the development of capitalist relations between larger, richer villages (Marco and Acolla) and smaller, poorer ones (Muquillanqui, Tragadero), as well as between the valley floor and the surrounding *puna* communities (Curicaca, Huashua, Pomacancha) are still great. Though we disagree on the ultimate conclusions to be reached, see also the comparison of Ataura and Matahuasi made by Laite, *Industrial Development*, pp. 104–18.

[33] This seems to be the case in Sicaya, where *cofradía* lands under dispute between

complete, it has involved a combination of similar elements: the return of migrants during the 1930s and the establishment of commercial enterprises to take advantage of new regional and national markets; the privatization of communal and *cofradía* lands and their
purchase by wealthy local entrepreneurs; the channeling of new
struggles over subsistence through community structures, particularly
the Asuntos Indígenas bureaucracy; and the partial masking of emerging wage labor relations through the continuing use of communal institutions, language, and reciprocal and kinship ties.

As is usually the case with such major transformations, the emergence of an agrarian bourgeoisie from peasant origins has encountered
important obstacles within the peasant sector. These have taken three
main forms. First, the community's use of local reciprocity and redistribution traditions in an attempt to place limits on individual accumulations. Secondly, the values of the pioneering capitalists themselves, who are not free of ambivalence and doubt when engaging in
new forms of profit-maximizing behavior. And finally, the inherent
weakness of the family enterprise, which historically seems to encounter great difficulty in maintaining continuity from one generation
to the next.

Though most central highland villages had long ago lost their self-
sufficient peasant economies, many of the social and cultural values
associated with traditional peasant society continued to play an important role in local relationships and consciousness. Certainly this
was the case with the community's use of moral economy and reciprocity, in alliance with state institutions, to limit differentiation. In
1938, for example, when agrarian entrepreneur Víctor Colca bought
some *cofradía* property from Marco's parish priest, the community
used the Dirección de Asuntos Indígenas as a forum to contest the
legality of the church's claim to that property. While the confrontation
was certainly part of a larger struggle between communities and the
church over the alienability of *cofradía* lands, it also served to place
a kind of moral sanction on Colca's innovative, individualized behavior.[34] And Colca was not the only individual to experience such a
sanction. As we have seen, in fact, the widespread occurrence of similar confrontations would seem to indicate that, despite the communal

1927 and 1931 remained community property rather than being sold to individuals (see
Winder, "The Impact of the *Comunidad*," p. 216).

[34] For the specific case of Colca, see Archivo SINAMOS, cc 205 (Marco), Expediente
4366; and "Expediente sobre la reivindicación del molino." For other battles over *cofradía* property, see Chapter VIII of this book, as well as the sources in footnote 4 of
this chapter.

and "developmentalist" language in which they were couched, they prefigured a new and incipient form of class struggle within the villages: that between a rural bourgeoisie and a rural proletariat.[35]

Indeed, perhaps one of the most interesting aspects of this new struggle is the fact that it is both universally recognizable, and historically unique. As a result of the transition to capitalism, it is familiar to all who have studied similar processes in other parts of the world. But as the culmination of events involving a specific culture, a previous set of social and economic relations, and a particular history of class conflict, the form taken by the new classes and their confrontation is unique to the central highlands. Just as the wage laborer is still embedded in a household unit, even if overall an unviable one, so capitalist forms of labor exploitation and resistance are often enmeshed in communal language and reciprocal ties, despite the radical transformation of their meaning and function. And this should come as no surprise. After all, these new relationships are developing in a dependent capitalist social formation and in a village society; effective strategies of surplus extraction and of survival will incorporate those cultural, social, and economic legacies from the past that can be useful in the present.

In addition to the objective, material impediments that community resistance and class struggle have placed in the way of the innovative local capitalist, the use of moral economy and community reciprocity has had less tangible, but equally important, effects on the entrepreneur's consciousness. Through the combined use of community pressure, ostracism, and ridicule, businesspeople could easily be made to feel that their behavior was crazy, selfish, and wrong. Even Agustín Ortiz, who was never taken to court by his fellow villagers, felt the brunt of his neighbors' ridicule. Indeed, still today he remembers the jokes and veiled criticism he received throughout his early years as an agrarian entrepreneur, and takes great pride in the fact that he "showed them." Equally striking, he is the first to emphasize that he fulfills his responsibility to the community, whether it is through monetary contributions, sponsoring fiestas, or representing the village in its political affairs.

When a generation of entrepreneurs makes the economic transition from one mode of production to another, they carry with them an ideological and cultural burden that is difficult to shake. It is in this context, perhaps, that the high rate of conversion to Protestant fun-

[35] See Chapter VIII.

damentalism among central highland entrepreneurs makes the most sense.[36] Of course, conversion to Protestantism has a strictly economic rationale, since it allows people to escape the expenses and redistributive functions of the village fiesta complex. But ideologically, it provides legitimacy for a new, more individualistic world view. It also substitutes a new definition of "community," which includes only other Protestants and is thus much more to the entrepreneur's liking, for the old, which included all villagers. And since most communal activities tend to be accompanied by some degree of drinking, dancing or coca chewing, conversion also facilitates the dismissal of village pressures as "the work of the devil."[37] Ultimately, however, conversion to Protestant fundamentalism is only the extreme solution to a more general problem: how the new bourgeois deal culturally, morally, and ideologically with their pattern of social and economic behavior.

If the emerging agrarian bourgeoisie manages to deal successfully with problems of community pressure, class struggle, and moral ambivalence, they must still face the lack of continuity in their family enterprises. Agustín Ortiz, for example, has been unable to interest his children or their spouses in taking over the business, and his experience seems a common one. Because the new bourgeoisie sends its children to Lima and educates them as professionals, few of them wish to return to their villages and inherit the family enterprise. Only those children who become apprentices to their parents from an early age seem to take an enduring interest in the business. Yet even here, it seems reasonable to assume that the same problem will confront the next generation.[38]

Both in economic and cultural terms, then, what seems most important to emphasize about the development of capitalism in the central highlands is how new and transitional it still is. Like England in

[36] The fact that most carvers in Cochas are Protestant came up in conversation with Seymour Dubrow, a Canadian anthropologist doing a study of Cochas in 1977–1978. Direct observation would seem to confirm this tendency for other entrepreneural groups. Furthermore, some comparative literature for other parts of Latin America would seem to suggest that conversion to Protestantism is a fairly generalized alternative in times of great change or upheaval. See, for example, Sidney W. Mintz, *Worker in the Cane: A Puerto Rican Life History* (New York: W. W. Norton and Co., 1974); and Wesley Craig, "The Peasant Movement of La Convención," in H. A. Landsberger (ed.), *Latin American Peasant Movements* (Ithaca: Cornell University Press, 1969), pp. 374–98.

[37] I am grateful to Lydia Solís de Maita for the analysis of her uncle's conversion that helped me develop this point. Interview with Lydia Solís de Maita, 11, Acolla, 1977.

[38] Here it seems especially appropriate to point out that a similar crisis of succession hit the first and second generations of capitalist family business in Europe. See E. J. Hobsbawn, *The Age of Revolution, 1778–1848* (New York: New American Library, 1962) and *The Age of Capital, 1848–1875* (New York: Charles Scribner's Sons, 1975).

the initial years of the Industrial Revolution, the new order has established somewhat shaky foundations in the old. The first generation of agrarian bourgeois has accumulated slowly, confronting the vestiges of traditional peasant culture. They must still face the critical problem of succession, as the enterprises move from one generation to the next. As was true of the first capitalists during the "manufacturing period" of European industry, therefore, the central highland entrepreneurs remain vulnerable. With the benefit of historical hindsight, it seems reasonable to assume that, at some point in the relatively near future, the proletarianized sector of village society will be able to use the crisis of continuity to bring the issues of moral economy, subsistence, and class struggle back into the forefront of village politics.[39] The outcome of such a renewed confrontation, however, remains in doubt.

[39] In some villages, at least, the new Estatuto de Comunidades put into effect by Velasco's government in 1970 provided just the kind of conjuncture that other factions needed to challenge the political control of the new entrepreneurs. See Alberti and Sánchez, *Poder y conflicto social*, pp. 179–93, and Long and Sánchez, "Peasant and Entrepreneurial Coalitions," pp. 290–91.

Proletarians in a Village Society: The

Peasant Community Revisited

Entering Acolla's plaza very early on a December or January morning, just as the sun begins to climb over the brilliantly green hills, the village seems to have that timeless quality associated with agricultural communities all over the world. The recent arrival of the rains has washed down the dusty storefronts, and encouraged the cactus to grow ever taller on the adobe walls. A small group of men has gathered near the municipal building to discuss the most recent or pressing district issues. A peasant woman, her clothes mud-spattered and threadbare, picks her way through the puddles as she coaxes a bull and some sheep down the road toward the newly green pampa. Several groups of women and men, carrying picks and shovels, hurry past on their way to plant their *chacras*. Little by little, as the population awakes, smoke starts to rise from the kitchen chimneys in many of the houses. As Acolla prepares to face the new day, the casual traveler in the plaza can easily feel nostalgia for an unhurried and picturesque village past.

But that impression is soon shattered. Slowly at first, almost imperceptibly, women, men, and children holding various types of agricultural implements form groups in the plaza. Dressed in old, tattered clothes, the women and girls wearing the traditional Yanamarca hat made of rough, homespun wool, they wrap their *mantas* and ponchos tighter to ward off the early morning chill. Suddenly, the noise of diesel engines can be heard approaching, and a group of trucks, some yellow and some red, enter the square. Already carrying other people who look much the same as those standing around, the trucks pick up those waiting in the plaza before heading out toward the fields. The red trucks belong to Agustín Ortiz, and will take people to cultivate his potatoes or perhaps to help with the early stages of onion planting. The yellow trucks will carry laborers to the Yaringaño brothers' properties, or to those they have rented from other owners. In a matter of minutes, the square is back to its original state. The only difference is that we have just witnessed Acolla's version of a

classic social encounter: employer and worker have met in the marketplace, and the latter has nothing to sell but his or her labor power.

One purpose of this book has been to explain how those people got
there—how an already commercialized, yet still relatively self-sufficient and autonomous peasant economy was tied into and transformed
by capitalism. That, in turn, is a story shaped by class struggle, a
conflict that moves history, defining the limits within which change
and "development" can occur. As the accumulated experience of past
and present generations in Acolla shows us, people make their own
history, though not always within conditions they themselves create,
and not always with the results that they themselves may want. Perhaps a periodization of recent Peruvian history, as seen from the side
of the village, will help to illustrate this point.

Our story began in the last decades of the eighteenth century, when
Latin America in general and Peru in particular were integrated into
the circulation networks of the new world system that took shape with
the Industrial Revolution. This process generated a new "intermediate" elite anxious to break the colonial monopolies, and the first bourgeois rumblings in many parts of the Iberian colonies. But the willingness of this new group to take action depended not only on their
own position, but also on their relationship to the lower classes. From
Mexico to the Río de la Plata, the combined effect of Túpac Amaru
and Toussaint L'Ouverture made elites wary of the possible conse-
quences of rebellion. Everywhere, the timing and nature of elite action was conditioned by their perception of the balance of class forces.
In this context, Peru was but a microcosm of a larger problem; and
only in the central highlands did the new elite feel confident enough
to participate in the move for independence.

After independence was achieved, the new elite's success in establishing control over the economy and society also depended on the
form and outcome of class conflict. Because the continued viability of
the subsistence economy and the peasantry's continued access to means
of production made labor scarce and expensive, elite efforts to revitalize production were only partially effective. Even in those sectors
where revitalization was most impressive, peasant resistance to proletarianization put significant limits on the possibilities for accumulation and transformation of the economy. Finally, after a concerted
attempt by the elite and the state to modernize the economy under
Piérola (1895–1900) was frustrated by peasant resistance, it seemed
necessary to seek development through an unequal alliance with foreign capital.

During the first three decades of the twentieth century, capitalism gained dominance in the Peruvian social formation as a whole. At the center of this process was an alliance between the emerging national bourgeoisie and foreign capital, as mediated through a developing state. The Oncenio (1919–1930), under the direction of Augusto B. Leguía, represented this alliance in its classic form. During the Oncenio, foreign investment in production, the financing of infrastructure, and the integration of a national internal market, set the tone for the dominance of capitalism. In the central highlands, these trends were represented by the growth of the Cerro de Pasco Corporation and the installation of an industrial mining system.

As in the earlier period, however, transformation was constrained and slowed down by difficulties with the proletarianization of labor. Through the use of *enganche* and *contrata*, foreign capital initially allied with merchants and networks of commercial capital already established in the central sierra. But in the long run, this alliance stunted further change because it did not transform relations of production. Since *enganche* and *contrata* simply intensified existing forms of exploitation, they did not proletarianize labor nor adapt well to a more technologically sophisticated industry. Ultimately, therefore, foreign capital was forced to break off its alliance with local commercial capital, construct the Oroya smelter, alter the system of labor relations and labor acquisition, and reorganize production.

In addition to imparting a new rhythm to production and extraction and encouraging the greater permanence of the labor force, the smelter caused extensive smoke damage that destroyed important productive resources in a number of the area's villages. This damage, when added to changes internal to the peasant community—social and economic differentiation, migration, population growth, and the depression of the 1930s—contributed to the proletarianization of a socially significant sector of the village population. In a sense, it was foreign capital, with its greater strength and resilience, that succeeded where local entrepreneurs had not. Because it could import both capital and forces of production, the foreign company was able to hold out longer than local entrepreneurs in the war of attrition that was necessary to wear down village self-sufficiency, and ultimately forced the issue through the technological transformation of the industry. But it is also important to emphasize that, even as they were losing the battle against proletarianization, the peasants' struggle set the contours for how the transition to capitalism was to take place.

With the 1930s, the scene was set for capitalist relations to begin to dominate at the village level. In the past, the peasant household had followed a noncapitalist cycle of activity, in which periods of intense commercialization and participation in the larger economy were interspersed with periods of depression and retreat into subsistence. Because of its adaptability, and the constant availability of self-sufficiency as an alternative in times of slump, this cycle had allowed peasants to take part in the commercial economy for centuries without the permanent separation of a socially significant portion of the village population from the means of production. Intense commercialization, however, could challenge village or household self-sufficiency by advancing internal differentiation, and over the long run this could erode the noncapitalist cycle of the peasant family economy. In the central highlands this erosion had begun before independence, particularly in the commercial boom of the 1780s, and intensified again from the 1860s on; but the crucial decades turned out to be the 1920s and 1930s. By the beginning of the thirties, the erosion of the household and village economies meant that subsistence was no longer an assured refuge for the peasantry. Instead, households entered a new cycle in which depression meant increasing differentiation—accumulation for some and poverty for others—rather than renewed self-sufficiency.

During the depression and the years that followed, the subsistence alternative was closed off for good by the intensifying political, economic, and cultural integration of the village into the nation. An emerging class of peasant entrepreneurs at the local level played an important role in speeding up this integration. They encouraged the spread of a modernizing ideology and the desire for progress, and benefited most from the progress that did take place. In an effort not to be "left behind," the village population as a whole participated in their own expropriation, for the commodification of communal lands, labor, and relationships that accompanied modernization cut down on the resources collectively available to the community.

The events of the 1930s, then, helped to generate a new class contradiction within the peasant community, as the political and economic conditions were created for an agrarian bourgeoisie of peasant origins to confront a rural proletariat. Of course, this process of class formation was not uniform throughout the central highlands, and probably progressed more rapidly in the Yanamarca and Mantaro Valleys than in the more marginal *puna* areas. Still, its importance lies in the fact that it occurred in the most dynamic parts of the region. And again, as in the past, the path taken by the agrarian bourgeoisie was conditioned and defined by class conflict within the village, a struggle channeled through community institutions and informed by subsistence ideology.

But, one might ask, if this historical process of transition and class formation has reached its culmination at the local level, why is the rural proletariat so hard to find? After all, numerous social scientists have visited the central sierra communities, lived in them, and written about them, and yet no one has emphasized or even identified the existence of a rural proletariat. Indeed, if we think back to Acolla's plaza on that early December or January morning, it is easy enough to identify Ortiz and Yaringaño and to be impressed by their trucks. The other side of the class equation, by contrast, is more hidden and faceless, more easily camouflaged by the outwardly picturesque and traditional veneer of village life. Why is this the case?

A partial answer to this question is that the conclusions of studies on the central highlands have been defined as much by the assumptions from which they began, and the questions they chose to address, as by the empirical data available. When the central sierra communities first became the object of scholarly attention in the 1920s, *indigenista* intellectuals were seeking the roots of Peruvian nationality, and in some cases the possible raw material for a transition to socialism, in the country's Indian past. Wishing to incorporate the marginalized native populations into the mainstream of national life, they also hoped to find in Andean tradition the answer to questions concerning their own national identity and purpose. In the vital and dynamic communities of the central region, which contrasted dramatically with the classic image of the Indian as brutalized and downtrodden by centuries of exploitation at the hands of *hacendados* and *gamonales*, these intellectuals found proof that the Indian community was potentially progressive. In their eyes, the example of the central highlands showed that communal institutions could form a basis for future rural development and integration in Peru as a whole.[1]

Subsequent generations of scholars have pursued these themes in various ways. For some, influenced by cultural anthropology and modernization theory, the "progressive" *mestizo* culture of central highland villages implied that the diffusion of modernism was not to-

---

[1] See especially the work of Hildebrando Castro Pozo, "Del ayllu al cooperativismo socialista," *Biblioteca de la Revista de Economía y Finanzas* (Lima: P. Barrantes Castro, 1936), II, *Nuestra comunidad indígena* (Lima: Editorial Lucero, 1924), and "Social and Economic-Political Evolution of the Communities of Central Peru," in Julian H. Steward (ed.), *Handbook of South American Indians*, Smithsonian Institution, Bureau of American Ethnology Bulletin No. 143 (Washington, D.C., 1946), II: 483–99.

tally destructive. The weapons of modern society, they argued, were being used to preserve Andean traditions in a new form.[2] Others, concerned with political models of "internal colonialism," saw the same Mantaro Valley culture as the result of the region's strong integration into national life. The arrival of the railroad, the development of industrial mining, and the intensification of commerce spawned a process of social mobilization—migration, the diffusion of new ideologies, the creation of new alliances—which broke down the "traditional-oligarchical" system of rural domination.[3] Whatever their specific emphases, however, most scholars shared an important assumption: to understand why the Mantaro Valley was "different" from other highland regions, they analyzed the "community" as an undifferentiated whole, which then became the recipient of cultural and economic change. Without denying the importance of the cultural and communal dimensions of village life and ideology, it is nonetheless necessary to dig deeper, to look inside the village and see the internal class dynamic of integration and change.[4]

Only in the last few years has there been a shift toward a class analysis of the historical development of central highland villages. Recent research has begun to reexamine peasant mobilization, communal solidarity, and village "progress," pointing to how an emerging "rich farmer" or "wealthy peasant" sector has manipulated these events for its own benefit. Starting in the second half of the nineteenth century, according to this interpretation, the wealthy sector has sought to profit from the integration of the village into the nation, transforming the meaning and purpose of communal institutions. But even though the new research has followed the process up to the present, it has

[2] See Richard N. Adams, *A Community in the Andes: Problems and Progress in Muquiyauyo* (Seattle: University of Washington Press, 1959); José María Arguedas, *Dos estudios sobre Huancayo* ("Evolución de las comunidades indígenas," "Estudio etnográfico de la feria de Huancayo"), Cuadernos Universitarios (Huancayo: Universidad Nacional del Centro del Perú, n.d.); Gabriel Escobar, *Sicaya: Cambios culturales en una comunidad mestiza andina* (Lima: Instituto de Estudios Peruanos, 1973); and Harry Tschopik, *Highland Communities of Central Peru*, Smithsonian Institution, Institute of Social Anthropology (Washington, D.C., 1947).

[3] Giorgio Alberti and Rodrigo Sánchez, *Poder y conflicto social en el valle del Mantaro* (Lima: Instituto de Estudios Peruanos, 1974); Howard Handelman, *Struggle in the Andes: Peasant Political Mobilization in Peru* (Austin: University of Texas Press, 1975); and F. Lamond Tullis, *Lord and Peasant in Peru: A Paradigm of Political and Social Change* (Cambridge, Mass.: Harvard University Press, 1970).

[4] I do not mean to imply that none of the previous studies have recognized the existence of internal class relations of some kind. Adams, Escobar, and Alberti and Sánchez have all mentioned socioeconomic differences within the villages. But the class dynamic of community life, and of the integration of the village into the nation, has not formed an important part of their analyses.

stopped short of affirming the existence of a new class contradiction in the village. Instead, scholars have argued, there is neither a "pure" peasantry nor a "pure" proletariat in the central sierra.[5]

It is relatively easy to explain the failure of earlier studies to analyze the internal class relations in the central sierra villages by pointing to their assumptions and methodology. This is not the case with the more recent research, however. After all, if scholars using a class analysis have agreed that a "pure" peasantry no longer exists in the region, yet have also hesitated to proclaim the existence of a rural proletariat, the empirical reality of the situation must be complex enough to make difficult any assessment of underlying class relationships. I would argue that this is due to the particular form that capitalist transformation has taken in the region—a form that has itself depended on the historical development of social relations in the central highlands.

One way in which the central region is unusual is that the transition process in the Mantaro Valley has been spearheaded by a bourgeoisie of peasant origins. In areas where the hacienda has been politically and economically predominant, such as the northern coast and northern highlands, capitalism has developed as the result of transformations in the large property sector, with *hacendados* becoming agrarian bourgeois through investment, displacement of small and medium landholders, and the transformation of *colonos* and others into a rural proletariat. In the central sierra, on the other hand, despite foreign investment in mining and the large livestock sector's attempt to transform relations of production through the development of the *sociedades ganaderas*, the historic strength and dynamism of the Mantaro peasant economy and its strategic control of valley resources meant that it was in the villages that the major transition in agriculture had to take place. In contrast to the "Junker model" of capitalist development common in other areas of the country, therefore, the Mantaro

[5] For this approach, see Norman Long and Bryan R. Roberts (eds.), *Peasant Cooperation and Capitalist Expansion in Central Peru* (Austin: University of Texas Press, 1978), especially the following essays: Long and Roberts, "Introduction," pp. 3–44; Carlos Samaniego, "Peasant Movements at the Turn of the Century and the Rise of the Independent Farmer," pp. 45–71; Marcelo Grondin, "Peasant Cooperation and Dependency: The Case of the Electricity Enterprise of Muquiyauyo," pp. 99–128; and, for the argument that neither a "pure" proletariat nor a "pure" peasantry exists in the central highlands, Long and Roberts, "Peasant Cooperation and Capitalist Expansion in Peru," pp. 297–328. For another variation on a similar theme that focuses on the migrant worker and the continuing tie to the village, see Julian Laite, *Industrial Development and Migrant Labour in Latin America* (Austin: University of Texas Press, 1981).

has followed a "peasant model." Yet because the "peasant model" is so unusual in Latin America, and because capitalism in agriculture is usually associated with large farms and heavy mechanization, it has been easy to dismiss class differences at the local level and see them merely as differences between rich, middle, and poor peasant households.[6]

A second and even more important aspect is the question of community: that set of relationships and concepts that has so clearly fascinated previous generations of social scientists. In other regions of Peru where capitalism has developed in agriculture, communal institutions have often been relatively weak or nonexistent.[7] The tendency has been to see the survival of community institutions as a sign of resistance to capitalism. Yet in the central region, "community" has served as a weapon both of class struggle and class transformation. Indeed, as in other parts of Peru with a communal tradition, communal ideology and relations of reciprocity have been a double-edged sword since the colonial period. On the one hand, the rich have used them to get access to labor and political power, which they could then manipulate for private profit. On the other hand, the poor have called on communal ideology and reciprocity to guarantee subsistence and remind the rich of their redistributive responsibility to the village as a whole. As the work of several scholars has shown for other parts of the Andean region, this implicit tension, which worsened in times of heavy commercialization, helped to generate several crises in village

[6] For an analysis of capitalist development on the northern coast, see Peter F. Klarén, *Formación de las haciendas azucareras y los orígenes del APRA*, 2d ed. (Lima: Instituto de Estudios Peruanos, 1976). For the northern highlands, see Carmen Diana Deere, "Changing Relations of Production and Peruvian Peasant Women's Work," *Latin American Perspectives*, IV: 1 and 2 (Winter and Spring 1977), 48–69, and "The Development of Capitalism in Agriculture and the Division of Labor by Sex: A Study of the Northern Peruvian Sierra," Ph.D. Dissertation, University of California, Berkeley, 1978; and Lewis Taylor, "Main Trends in Agrarian Capitalist Development: Cajamarca, Peru 1880–1976," Ph.D. Thesis, University of Liverpool, 1979. The "Junker model" and the "peasant model" of capitalist transition represent, in agriculture, the "two ways" for the development of capitalism discussed by Marx and subsequent authors: the first involving large proprietors or merchants, and thus conservative; the second involving petty producers, and thus progressive. See Karl Marx, *Capital* (New York: International Publishers, 1967), III:334–35; Maurice Dobb, *Studies in the Development of Capitalism*, rev. ed. (New York: International Publishers, 1963), especially pp. 123–61; and Kohachiro Takahashi, "A Contribution to the Discussion," in Rodney Hilton (ed.), *The Transition from Feudalism to Capitalism* (London: Verso Edition, 1978), pp. 68–97, especially 87–97.

[7] This is certainly true on the coast, where the precipitous decline of native populations during the colonial period left little in terms of a communal tradition. In the northern highlands as well, the dominance of the hacienda and the tendency toward atomization in the Indian villages are commented upon in the literature cited.

society during the colonial period.[8] In an area as commercialized as the central sierra, these problems were particularly prevalent. Yet the viability of community and communal ideology was maintained into the twentieth century.

In the nineteenth and early twentieth centuries, the institutions of community and household reciprocity continued to mediate conflict and channel cooperation in ways that were beneficial to the village as a whole. These institutions were successful not because local society was a paradise of solidarity, but because they enforced the primacy of collective peasant interests and survival over specific squabbles at the individual, group, or even village level. Yet such success was predicated on the continued existence of a collective peasant interest, of a common goal that all villagers, whether rich or poor, could see as their own. This meant that community institutions were viable only as long as the peasantry continued to face the outside world primarily as a block, rather than as individuals. Under these conditions, the wealthy peasants had an interest in preserving community solidarity because, as intermediaries between the village and the larger society, they were dependent on traditional relations of reciprocity for their access to labor and political power. The poorer peasants, for their part, were also eager to maintain community solidarity because only through patron-client and reciprocity relations could they hope to enforce their claims to subsistence and protection, both within the village and in the regional economy at large. Once both groups began to develop stronger, more direct ties with the world outside the village, however, the situation could start to change rapidly. As we have seen, that was precisely what was happening by the 1930s. With the growing importance of national alliances along class lines, communal solidarity within the village began to decline.

Ironically enough, this occurred at the precise moment that the state, interested for its own reasons in reproducing the peasant sector, was encouraging the reinvigoration of community institutions and had officially recognized the existence of communal entities. In the context of a revitalized community structure, the emerging peasant bourgeoisie was able to use communal language and "progress" as

[8] See, for example, Karen Spalding, *De indio a campesino: cambios en la estructura social del Perú colonial* (Lima: Instituto de Estudios Peruanos, 1974), pp. 31–60, 147–93; Steve J. Stern, *Peru's Indian Peoples and the Challenge of Spanish Conquest: Huamanga to 1640* (Madison: University of Wisconsin Press, 1982), pp. 158–83; Nicolás Sánchez-Albornoz, *Indios y tributos en el Alto Perú* (Lima: Instituto de Estudios Peruanos, 1978), especially pp. 99–110; and Brooke Larson, "Caciques, Class Structure and the Colonial State in Bolivia," *Nova Americana* (Turin), No. 2 (1979).

weapons for accumulation and class transformation. At the same time, however, the proletarianized sector of the village population struggled to use the same community ideology and institutions to halt class transformation and insure subsistence. Out of this confrontation emerged an uneasy compromise, in which the peasant bourgeoisie either converted to Protestantism as a way out of their economic or moral bind, or else found a way to adapt or use communal ideology for its own ends. As our analysis of Agustín Ortiz has shown, a recognition of "community" could sometimes become the most efficient and profitable way to run an agrarian capitalist enterprise.

Ultimately, the point to emphasize is that, even if community language and ideology are still used to articulate and define local struggles, the class content of those struggles has changed completely. In the sense that a substantial portion of the village population continues to have some tie to the land, no matter how tenuous it may be, fragments of a peasantry remain. But whether in terms of structure or consciousness, it is no longer possible to speak of the peasantry as a class in the central highlands. It is the continuing use of ritual kinship, family ties, and "communal" or "peasant" language, both by the rural bourgeoisie and the rural proletariat, that obscures this in a village setting. As Sidney Mintz points out in the case of the Caribbean, this type of "village camouflage" is prevalent even in areas where the agricultural proletariat is more easily identifiable.[9]

Aside from the survival of communal language and institutions, the existence of a proletariat is further obscured by the fact that wage laborers still inhabit households with some access to means of production. From the point of view of the agrarian capitalist, this is convenient for several reasons. First of all, given the eminently seasonal labor needs of agriculture, the need to reproduce labor power during the parts of the year when it is not employed has always been a problem for the capitalist enterprise.[10] Secondly, because the cultivation

[9] Sidney W. Mintz, "The Rural Proletariat and the Problem of Rural Proletarian Class Consciousness," *Journal of Peasant Studies*, I:1 (April 1973), 291–325.

[10] In the Caribbean sugar industry, this resulted in the dreaded *tiempo muerto* (dead time), when workers lived on credit that was payable during the months they were employed. See, for example, Sidney W. Mintz, *Worker in the Cane: A Puerto Rican Life History* (New Haven: Yale University Press, 1960), and Maurice Zeitlin, *Revolutionary Politics and the Cuban Working Class* (Princeton, N.J.: Princeton University Press, 1967). In other areas of Latin America, capitalist enterprises have relied on various forms of household economy to partially reproduce a wage labor force. See, for example, Manoel Correia de Andrade, *A terra e o homem do Nordeste* (São Paulo: Editôra Brasiliense, 1963); and Catherine Le Grand, "Colombian Transformations: Peasants and Wage Laborers in the Santa Marta Banana Zone, 1900–1935," Paper

of certain crops is unavoidably labor intensive and cannot benefit from the increased labor productivity brought on by mechanization, it is important to have available a supply of cheap labor. On both counts, then, the household—while unable to reproduce itself independently—can cheapen the cost of labor power to capital by enabling capitalists to keep wages below subsistence and sometimes to utilize family labor, and by sustaining workers in the slack periods of the agricultural cycle. And from the point of view of the rural proletarian, the survival of the household is also convenient, for it provides a hedge against unemployment and the vagaries of the market in a dependent capitalist economy where subsistence exclusively through wage work is not always assured.

In the central highlands, then, the household serves as an ideal material base for the rural proletarian. This is true not only because of the nature of dependent capitalism and of agriculture more generally, but also because the household economy has historically been so strong in the region. Thus the transition to capitalism has built upon preexisting social and economic relations. It is in this sense that the survival of the household is best understood. The family economy, rather than constituting a separate mode of production, is intimately intertwined with capitalism both at the level of production and of reproduction.[11]

Yet another circumstance that tends to hide class divisions in the central sierra communities is the unequal, dependent nature of capitalist development in Peru. The need to petition and struggle with the state for even the most basic public services can unite the village population across class lines, at times masking and postponing internal conflicts. Further, the unequal exchange between village and city makes difficult the reproduction, from generation to generation, of the capitalist class in the villages. As we have seen, the sons and daughters of agrarian bourgeois, rather than taking over the family enterprise, have tended to integrate themselves into the urban middle and professional classes at the national level. Though it is still too early to tell what will happen, one result of this tendency might be the trans-

---

presented at the Tenth National Meetings of the Latin American Studies Association, Washington, D.C., March 4–6, 1982.

[11] It is difficult to imagine the household economy as a separate mode of production at any point in history. While household production has existed within a wide variety of modes of production, it has not reproduced itself independently of those modes. To consider the household economy to be more than a subordinate *form* of production, therefore, gives the concept mode of production such a wide applicability as to greatly lessen its theoretical value.

formation of many central sierra communities into "villages of proletarians"—conglomerations of households helping to reproduce wage
labor for agrarian (and urban) capital. Certainly the phrase "orphan of
its illustrious children," coined to describe the Mantaro Valley town
of Mito, is an apt description of this trend.[12] Ultimately, therefore,
just as dependency has affected the nature of the national bourgeoisie
in Peru, so it has affected the form of class struggle in the countryside.
In neither case, however, should this blind us to the underlying character of class relations.

Dependent capitalism and unequal exchange between city and
countryside have also affected the nature of class conflict by encouraging the formation of networks. Defined as forms of association that
cut across class lines and broaden people's access to resources by
uniting them along gender, kinship, or ethnic lines, networks have
recently been the object of intensive interest on the part of social
scientists studying the Peruvian highlands. Because networks tie people into relationships that can protect subsistence and make available
new job or educational opportunities in both city and countryside,
they are often the soundest strategy for survival in a society with a
shaky economic base and extremely limited resources. Often, therefore, villagers will give priority to the protection of network interests
over class interests. As a result, "[n]etworks cross-cut multiple dimensions of social inequality, tend to undermine collective action in
rural communities, and to inhibit a class-based analysis of social inequality."[13] And yet the existence of networks does not invalidate the
existence of classes. Not only are networks used for survival, but they
are also used for accumulation. Indeed, because of the edge they
provide in competition with other firms, local businesspeople actively
extend and nurture rural-urban networks. Since they mediate access
to crucial commercial and business connections as well as to cheaper

[12] Long and Roberts, *Peasant Cooperation*, p. 22.
[13] The quote is from Susan C. Bourque and Kay B. Warren, "Denial and Reaffir-
mation of Ethnic Identities: A Comparative Examination of Guatemalan and Peruvian
Communities," Program in Latin American Studies, Occasional Papers Series No. 8,
University of Massachusetts at Amherst, 1978, p. 33. Other studies dealing with networks include: Bourque and Warren, "Multiple arenas for state expansion: class, eth-
nicity and sex in rural Peru," *Ethnic and Racial Studies*, III:3 (July 1980), 264–80, and
Women of the Andes: Patriarchy and Social Change in Two Peruvian Towns (Ann
Arbor: The University of Michigan Press, 1981); and Bryan R. Roberts, "The Interrelationships of City and Provinces in Peru and Guatemala," in Wayne A. Cornelius and
Felicity M. Trueblood (eds.), *Anthropological Perspectives on Latin American Urbanization*, Latin American Urban Research, Vol. 4 (Berkeley, CA: Sage Publications,
1974), pp. 207–35.

sources of labor power through the exploitation of kinship and gender relations, networks in fact serve as a strong basis for the reproduction of local capitalist enterprises.[14]

Finally, the attempt to define the nature of class relations in the central highlands involves methodological problems present in the analysis of any complex historical process. Again and again, periods of heavy commercialization have generated processes that look vaguely capitalist, yet without "completing" the transformation. Conflicts over the same piece of land, for example, have come up repeatedly over centuries in times of intensified commodification. Battles about district status have always involved the emergence of a new elite at the village level that attempts to establish an independent power base by controlling revenue, labor, and politics. Periods of intensified labor migration have raised tensions between outside and village activities, and helped to increase the distance between rich and poor. How is it, then, that one decides which period of change is the crucial one? When does commodification of land become "complete"? When is the new elite emerging in the village an agrarian bourgeoisie rather than just another group of precapitalist entrepreneurs? When does migration permanently upset village equilibrium and irrevocably commodify labor? And, perhaps most importantly, when does the preexisting difference between rich and poor become the base for a new process of class formation?

These questions can only be answered historically, looking at the context of each particular event, and trying to understand the dynamic of change hidden within each process. No change, no matter how dramatic, is without links to what has gone before; it is both nourished and impeded by preexisting structures. Thus the Cerro de Pasco Corporation relied, in its first years, on existing networks of commercial capital and on local technology to consolidate its hold on the central sierra mining industry. But it was also this preexisting base that then blocked further expansion until foreign capital set into motion a dramatic transformation of the entire regional economy. And the same was true of previous differentiation, accumulation, and migration at the village level. Without those inroads, the dominance of capitalist relations would not have occurred as rapidly or as com-

---

[14] In addition to the case of Agustín Ortiz, instances of this can be found in Roberts, "The Interrelationships of City and Provinces," pp. 226–27, and Laite, *Industrial Development*, pp. 115–16. For an analysis of the role of women as a "female underclass" in agriculture and gender-differentiated wage structures, see Bourque and Warren, *Women of the Andes*, especially pp. 139–44.

pletely; yet at a certain point, migration and accumulation could also serve as a brake on the process of proletarianization.

Thus no major transformation, no matter how earthshaking, is unilinear, uncomplicated, or textbook-perfect. Even on the other side of transition, as Agustín Ortiz has shown us, the most successful adaptations mix continuity with change, tradition with innovation. All change contains within itself the remnants of the past, and is conditioned by those remnants. All reality generates from inside itself the seeds of the future, and is threatened by them.

In the case of the central highlands, a past history of commercialization made the region particularly vulnerable to the penetration of capitalist relations. At the same time, the peasant community and its institutions provided the framework within which transformation and class struggle took place. Those who would wait to find a "pure" proletariat before announcing the area transformed may have to wait a long time. Perhaps they have also accepted somewhat uncritically the conventional version of how "classic" the capitalist transition was in Europe itself. For even in Europe it is clear that change, as the result of human confrontation and struggle, has never taken a perfectly predetermined path.[15]

But to return once more to Acolla's town square, it is difficult not to wonder, as we stand there in the present and look back at two hundred years of Yanamarca's history, what some of the principal characters in our story might think if they could stand beside us. What would Mariano Castillo, one hundred and twenty years old in 1914, think of his valley in 1980? How would Narcizo Hurtado, *subenganchador* and small-time *gamonal*, react to Agustín Ortiz's trucks and his comment that the Hurtados did not belong in the twentieth century? Most importantly, how would the peons on the hacienda Yanamarca, the Comas guerrillas, and all other veterans of previous class struggles view the new encounter between employer and worker in Acolla's marketplace?

These are not idle questions. On one level, the present is nothing more than the culmination of all previous actions, conflicts and confrontations, and these somewhat dusty historical characters belong in it as much as we do. Perhaps this is why history can never remain

[15] For a recent example of the ongoing debates on European transition, see Robert Brenner, "Agrarian Class Structure and Economic Development in Pre-Industrial Europe," *Past and Present*, No. 70 (February 1976), pp. 30–75, and the debate in subsequent issues of the journal; and Robert Brenner, "The Origins of Capitalist Development: A Critique of Neo-Smithian Marxism," *New Left Review*, No. 104 (July–August 1977), pp. 25–92.

merely a study of the past. Written by human beings, it is informed by and intermingles with the changing realities of the present. Made and experienced by human beings, it can provide us with the tools to change the future. In the central highlands, the past struggles of peasants and their use of communal language and institutions survive into the present, shaping the form in which proletarianized villagers continue to challenge the beneficiaries of capitalist transformation. And as has always been true in the past, this challenge will define the alternatives open for future change in the central sierra of Peru.

Appendixes

I. Description of the 1899 Yanamarca Valley Census

The 1899 Yanamarca Valley Census, in manuscript form, was found in the Archivo Prefectural de Junín. It was apparently part of a larger effort to record statistics about the central sierra communities, since manuscript censuses for other villages, following the same general pattern, were also found. In the case of the Yanamarca Valley, only the censuses for Acolla and Tragadero have survived in complete form. There were efforts to collect data in neighboring villages, particularly Chocón and Marco, that were never completed. The census provides no clues as to why that might have been the case.

The population is divided by household, marital status, and sex. All the married couples, husband and wife, are listed first, followed by widowed males, single males, widowed females, and single females. Information is provided for each household (including married couples and widowed females and males) on age, landholding (useless), number of sheep, *arrieraje* activity and number of animals, commercial activity (whether or not the person is a merchant), migration to the mines, handicraft work of various kinds, number of children (male and female), literacy, language, and place of birth. For single women, data are recorded on age, landholding (again useless), number of children, literacy, language, and place of birth. For single men, information is given on age, landholding (useless), additional occupations outside agriculture, literacy, language, and place of birth.

I discussed the reliability of the census materials with don Moisés Ortega, himself an amateur historian of the valley and well versed in local tradition. The data on land tenure (in which everyone appeared as owning no land) were obviously incorrect, and probably the result of suspicion that the information might be used for tax purposes. As far as it was possible to verify, the information on family structure, livestock, additional occupations, and migration was accurate, and the census itself relatively complete. In all, the use of oral history techniques to verify manuscript census materials proved extremely valuable.

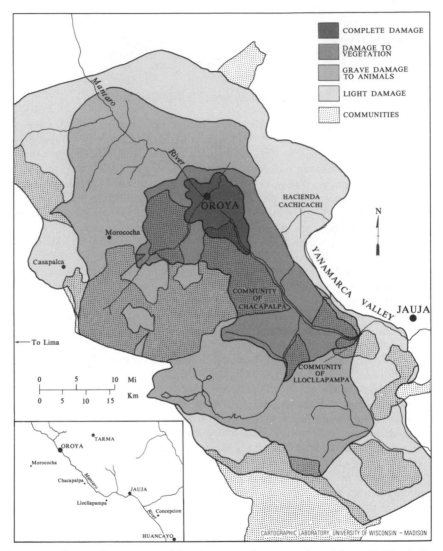

Map 6. The Smoke Damage of the Oroya Smelter. Based on Adrian DeWind, Jr., "Peasants Become Miners: The Evolution of Industrial Mining Systems in Peru," Ph.D. Dissertation, Columbia University, 1977, Ch. 5, p. 3.

II. Communities Claiming Smoke Damage from the Oroya Smelter

Community	Granted Indemnification	Amount (soles)	Remarks
1. Acaya	No	—	—
2. Acolla	No	—	See note.
3. Canchayllo	No	—	See note.
4. Chacapalpa	Yes	7,319.25/yr	See note.
5. Collao	No	—	—
6. Curicaca	No	—	—
7. Esperanza	No	—	—
8. Huamacancha	No	—	—
9. Huaripampa	No	—	—
10. Huari	Yes	4,500/yr	See note.
11. Huayhuash	No	—	—
12. Huayhuay	Yes	4,500/yr	See note.
13. Huaynacancha	Yes	7,506.47/yr	3,310 hectares received. See note
14. Humi	No	—	—
15. Huricolca	No	—	—
16. Limacpuquio	No	—	—
17. Lluellapampa	No		See note
18. Marcapomacocha	No	—	See note.
19. Mata Chico	No	—	See note.
20. Mata Grande	No	—	See note.
21. Oroya Antigua	Yes	10,188.44/yr	675 hectares received. See note
22. Paccha	Yes	2,690/yr	See note. The corporation also gave a one-time subsidy of 30,000 soles as an emergency contribution.
23. Pachachaca	Yes	3,500/yr	See note.
24. Pacte	No	—	—
25. Parco	No	—	—
26. Pomacancha	No	—	—
27. Pomacocha	Yes	1,628.55/yr	Indemnification was raised to 3,257.10/yr in 1969. See note.
28. Sacco	Yes	6,130.68/yr	See note.
29. Santa Ana	No	—	—
30. Suitucancha	Yes	2,500/yr	See note.
31. Tarmatambo	No	—	See note.
32. Yauli	Yes	695.40/yr	See note.

Granted indemnification:		19%	
Granted lands under the Agrarian Reform:		56%	

Sources: Adrian DeWind, Jr., "Peasants Become Miners: The Evolution of Industrial Mining Systems in Peru," Ph.D. Dissertation, Columbia University, 1977, Ch. 5, p. 14. Alberto Flores Galindo, *Los mineros de la Cerro de Pasco* (Lima: Pontífica Universidad Católica del Perú, 1974), pp. 46 and 49.
Note: Received land expropriated from the corporation during the Agrarian Reform.

III. Description of the "Census of Acolla's First Cuartel" (1934)

Handwritten in several small notebooks, the "Census of Acolla's First *Cuartel*" (1934) was found in the municipal archive in Acolla. Given the minute detail of some of its information, it was clearly an internal community product, done by people familiar with local life. Unfortunately, it proved impossible to confirm who had actually carried it out.

Although there are no subdivisions to make this obvious, the internal organization of the census listing is by household. The census takers apparently went from door to door, recording all the inhabitants (present or absent) in each dwelling. In this way, it was possible to ascertain who was migrating or had migrated to the mines, and to confirm the cases in which several members of the same household migrated together. Despite the lack of clear categories and divisions, it was possible to confirm hypotheses on the internal organization of the census through oral history techniques, using interviews to check the census for disparities.

The main problem with the census is that, because it only includes the first *cuartel*, it is difficult to know how representative it is for the village as a whole. The first *cuartel* is at the center of the village near the plaza, and judging from a history of local settlement patterns, this tends to be a wealthier and older part of town. The area near the hacienda Yanamarca, where much of the ex-*colono* population tended to gather, is not represented. Nor is the zone further to the south near Pachascucho, where some newly wealthy families seem to have settled. By looking at the first *cuartel*, therefore, one tends to see Acolla in terms of its more notable and prestigious families, and less in terms of its poorer or "upstart" inhabitants. Still, the richness of the data, particularly in terms of household occupational structure, more than makes up for this deficiency, especially if one keeps the census' shortcomings in mind and does not generalize too widely from its results.

The following information is provided for each individual in each household: sex, occupation, age, marital status, literacy, and race. In addition to household migration patterns, the most interesting data to emerge show how few people define their occupation as agriculture. While this might have something to do with the uniqueness of the *cuartel's* population, only 29 percent of the men define their occupation as agriculture. The same trend holds true for women, most of whom prefer to define themselves as *hiladoras* (spinners) even though this is only one of their many household and agrarian activities. In addition to the fact that more and more people were clearly working outside the rural sector in this period, part of the trend seems to be related to the declining prestige associated with agrarian activity. Thus, those people with several activities to choose from would be less and less inclined to give agriculture as their main occupation.

Glossary

acomodanas. Advances of clothing, food, alcohol, or coca given by the mine-owner or *hacendado* to his or her labor force.

aguardiente. A rough liquor made from sugar cane, and used extensively in various types of peasant community rituals.

al partir. An agreement between the owner of a plot of land and another person, in which the former provides the land, the latter the seed and labor, and the product is divided two ways. Also used to refer to a similar agreement with regard to livestock.

alcalde. A mayor, a local municipal official usually appointed by the national bureaucracy (in the colonial period, the Spanish state), and owing primary loyalty to it.

alférez. Literally, lieutenant. In village custom, the person in charge of organizing and financing a yearly fiesta.

anexo. A town or village attached to a political district whose capital is elsewhere; literally, an annex to a political district.

apiri. A mine laborer in the late nineteenth and early twentieth centuries (as well as earlier) who was responsible for carrying the bags of ore out of the mine on his back.

apoderado. The recipient of a power of attorney, in charge of handling litigation or any other type of legal proceeding.

arrendatario. In the central highlands, the lessee of a large property, usually an hacienda.

arrieraje. Mule driving, transportation of commercial goods on muleback.

arriero. Muleteer, the person in charge of mule trains.

arroba. Unit of measure with an approximate weight of 25 pounds.

aviador. A merchant providing credit for production, especially in mining.

barretero. A mineworker in the late nineteenth and early twentieth centuries, in charge of digging the ore out of the mine wall.

cacique. Originally a Caribbean term, it refers to a local Indian chieftain.

cajón. A large box or chest that in the mining industry served as a standard measurement for ore.

carrero. By the early twentieth century, a mineworker who loaded chunks of ore onto railway cars underground, in preparation for the ore to be transported out of the mine.

caudillo. Regional boss, patron, or chieftain.

ceja de selva. Literally, "eyebrow of the jungle"; it refers to the area of transition between the highlands and the Amazonian jungle, where the warm, subtropical climate permits the cultivation of sugar, coffee, fruit, and other products unadapted to the higher altitudes.

cerco. Fenced or walled-in agricultural property, usually for the cultivation of commercial crops.

chacra. A small or medium-sized agricultural plot.

cofradía. A religious lay brotherhood in charge of organizing worship for a particular image or saint. While most were male, there were some female *cofradías.* There were also "Spanish" and "Indian" *cofradías.*

colono. One of the names given to the resident laborer on a large estate, who in exchange for labor obligations got access to certain subsistence rights such as land and pasture.

comisario. Sheriff or local chief of police.

compadre. Or *comadre,* in the female; a co-godparent.

compadrazgo. An institution of ritual kinship, co-godparenthood.

comunero. A member of a peasant or Indian community, whose status was defined by his or her (usually his) position as head of household, and who in exchange for labor obligations received certain rights within the communal structure.

conscripción vial. Labor conscription for highway construction. During the Leguía regime (1919–1930), all male residents of Peru between the ages of eighteen and sixty years were supposed to work on road construction and maintenance for six to twelve days a year. In practice, however, the draft only affected peasant communities.

contrata. In the nineteenth century, the name given to *enganche.* In the twentieth century, the custom of contracting out the extraction of minerals to a specific individual, who then had the responsibility for organizing the production process and acquiring the necessary laborers.

contribución de indígenas. Indian head tax.

contribución personal. Indian (or community peasant) head tax.

corregidor. A local Spanish official in the colonial period, in charge of administrative and judicial functions and often associated with the *repartimiento de mercancías.*

cuartel. From the end of the nineteenth century, an administrative subdivision of a peasant village.

damnificado. At the district or village level, a property owner whose land lay in the path of a new street, school, or other public works project.

denuncio. A claim made to the government declaring the intent to exploit a particular mine or piece of land.

descuento por caja. In the mining centers, the practice of automatically discounting dues for an organization from each month's wage, which of course greatly simplified collection.

Dirección de Asuntos Indígenas. Office of Indian Affairs, in charge of handling official recognition of Indian communities under the 1920 constitution and any complaints brought forward by a community's representatives.

Dirección General de Enseñanza. General Office of Education.

encomendero. Owner of an *encomienda*, or early colonial grant of rights to labor and tribute. The word designates relatively "old stock" within the colonial elite, and usually high prestige.

enganche. The process through which a merchant "hooks" a peasant, advancing money or goods and requiring him to work the debt off at a mine or hacienda.

fiador. A guarantor of a loan or contract, liable financially for the fulfillment of the agreement if the principal party did not comply. The guarantee provided, usually in the form of property, was called a *fianza*.

fuero de domicilio. Under Peruvian law, a provision that guarantees citizens immunity from arrest and prosecution while they are within their private residences.

galga. A boulder, used as a primitive weapon by rolling it down a hill onto the enemy's forces.

galguero. A soldier in charge of pushing *galgas* down on the enemy from the tops of the surrounding hills.

gamonal. Local political boss or patron who usually fulfills a function of mediation with the larger society or political system. The word also carries the connotation of oppressive, tyrannical behavior.

granadero. A member of a crack or elite corps in the army.

guarache. In mine labor, a work shift lasting thirty-six hours, which is then repeated after only twelve hours of rest. Common in the late nineteenth and early twentieth centuries.

hacendado. Owner of an hacienda, or large agricultural and livestock estate that combined production for subsistence with production for the market.

huacchas. Livestock, usually sheep, belonging to the peasant shepherds who worked for an estate; generally of poor quality.

Huancas. Inhabitants of the ethnic kingdom that existed in the Mantaro Valley before the Spanish conquest.

indigenista. Subscribing to the intellectual and political tendency emerging in Peru at the end of the nineteenth and the beginning of the twentieth century that gave the Indian a central and respected place in the past and future development of Peru, and protested against the exploitation suffered by the Indian race.

independencias económicas. Name given to the attempt by dependent villages, or *anexos*, to wrest control of local revenue and labor drafts from the district capitals in the 1930s.

ishapa. A reciprocal exchange between the owner of a herd of sheep and the owner of an agricultural plot, usually lasting three years. The former uses his or her flock to fertilize the land, in exchange for receiving access to half the plot.

kuraka. The Andean term for local chief or authority, whose legitimacy was based on Andean tradition and the maintenance of certain reciprocal obligations with the rest of the community.

jaula. Literally, cage; word referring to the elevators in the mines used to connect the various underground levels.

Junta Vial. The council at the provincial level, made up of the justice of the peace, mayor, and subprefect, that set policy for the *conscripción vial* program and supervised the construction itself.

lampero. Mineworker who used a *lampa*, or shovel, to break up the mineral loosened by a dynamite explosion.

Libra peruana. Literally, Peruvian pound. Initially at parity with the British pound sterling, the *Libra peruana* was equivalent to ten soles.

lindero. A boundary between two agricultural properties.

manta. A shawl or carrying cloth used by people, usually women, for warmth and to carry loads or small children on their backs.

maquipurero. In the late nineteenth and early twentieth centuries, a mineworker hired directly, independent of *enganche*, and on a more permanent basis.

marco. A weight measure for silver, equivalent to approximately eight ounces.

mayordomo. An elected officer of a lay brotherhood, in charge of organizing the annual celebration of the brotherhood's saint, and financing expenses. Another possible meaning is an administrator on an hacienda.

mejorero. A peasant who resided, with his or her family, on an estate for a limited number of years. In exchange for a plot of land on which the family could grow the commercial crop of the area (in addition to subsistence goods), *mejoreros* were expected to provide additional labor for the owner and, at the end of their contract, to give up rights to the improvements they had made on "their" plots. This labor arrangement was common in subtropical areas where it was necessary to bring new land into cultivation.

mestizo. A person with mixed Indian and white heritage, racially, culturally, or both.

mita. A state-sponsored forced labor draft, originating during the Toledan reforms of the 1570s.

montonera. Irregular guerrilla force or armed band, organized informally in the countryside to support a particular political cause. *Montoneras* were used in an auxiliary capacity by the regular army in the Wars of Independence as well as the War of the Pacific. A member of one of these forces was called a *montonero.*

obra pía. Literally, a pious foundation. The name was given to some *cofradías* in an attempt to circumvent the late nineteenth-century law making their properties liable for government intervention.

obraje. A textile workshop during the colonial period, whose main market was the mines.

olluco. A type of root crop, similar to certain varieties of the potato.

Oncenio. The name given in Peruvian politics to the eleven-year dictatorship (1919–1930) of Augusto B. Leguía.

paraje. A localized area within the territory of a village, corresponding roughly to a microenvironment with specific agricultural characteristics, and given a particular name.

patria. Homeland, nation.

patriota. Literally, a patriot; a term used to designate those who supported independence in the early nineteenth century.

perforador. Mineworkers who opened holes in the walls of the mine in order to plant a dynamite charge.

perito. In a land conflict, an "expert" or educated person from the area who was familiar with the local *parajes* and could help to interpret the boundaries listed in the relevant documentation.

permuta. An exchange of properties of equivalent value, used either for the purpose of land consolidation or because a plot had been affected by public works plans or urbanization. Synonymous with *canje.*

personero. The legally constituted, elected representative of a legally recognized Indian community, who was in charge of presenting the community's case before the Dirección de Asuntos Indígenas.

pongaje. Personal service in the house of the landowner, usually performed by members of peasant households resident on the estate.

protesto de letra vencida. The serving of legal and formal notice that a promissory note on a debt has fallen due.

puna. High Andean grasslands located above the timber line, adaptable mainly to the raising of sheep and llamas and the cultivation of a few hardy Andean crops.

quinoa. A hardy Andean cereal crop, whose seeds are rich in protein; adaptable to high elevations.

quintal. A measure of weight, equivalent to one hundred pounds.

ramo. A particular branch of municipal service, such as lighting the streets or collecting market taxes. The municipal governments auctioned off the exclusive right to carry out these services, and to the revenue collected in relation to them, to individuals on a yearly basis.

real. A unit of currency used in the colonial period and nineteenth century; eight were equal to one peso.

repartimiento de mercancías. A forced distribution of goods in the Indian communities during the colonial period, in which local officials compelled Indians to buy commodities which often the Indians did not need.

Socavón de Yanacancha. A drainage tunnel built in the mining region of the central highlands during the late eighteenth century that permitted a renewed boom in silver production.

sociedad ganadera. A joint stock company including several livestock haciendas, whose purpose was to capitalize and improve cattle or sheep production.

sol. Peruvian currency adopted in the nineteenth century. At different points, the sol was either on a silver or a gold standard.

solar. A small urban property or lot.

suplicar. Literally, to beg. A ritual custom in which one peasant household would "beg" aid, almost always in labor, from another in order to complete a specific project. The aid would then be reciprocated on a similar project sometime in the future.

tinterillo. Related to the word *tinta* (ink), this term refers to someone versed in the legal process, sometimes but not necessarily always a lawyer, who profits from—and therefore tends to instigate or encourage—litigation.

Tribunal de Minería. A mining association created in the Peruvian viceroyalty during the Bourbon Reforms (1786). Its purpose was to provide mineowners with credit and up-to-date technological information.

tubero. A mineworker in charge of connecting tubes for the drainage system inside the mines.

vales. Receipts or scrip given out by *enganchadores* or the mining company itself, in lieu of cash, as payment for wages. Workers were then forced to redeem these at a designated store, usually at much higher prices.

vecino. Citizen of a village or municipality.

yugada. Traditional unit of measurement for land, said to be the amount a yoke of oxen could plow in one day. In the central highlands, the equivalent of approximately one-third hectare.

zafacasa. The roofing and inauguration of a new house, involving ritual and elaborate festivities.

Bibliographical Essay

The sources upon which this study has drawn include a wide variety of manuscript materials, some published documents, and a broad range of secondary works. It would be impossible, in the space of a few pages, to list all the materials consulted in the course of research and writing. Instead, the purpose of this essay is to list, and comment on, those materials that have had some bearing, whether empirical or theoretical, on the analysis presented here. I have divided these up into five subcategories: unpublished documents; published documents; secondary materials, Peru; secondary materials, central highlands; and theoretical and comparative materials. Rather than being exhaustive, this listing provides a guide for those who wish to check the empirical base of the study, or who wish to pursue some of the issues raised in greater depth.

UNPUBLISHED DOCUMENTS

Since each document cited in the footnotes is identified completely, I will not present here a list of individual documents found in each archive. Instead, I will comment more generally on the archives used, the type of information generally found in each collection, and what was of specific interest for my study.

AFA—Archivo del Fuero Agrario (Lima)

This archive, organized after the Agrarian Reform, contains documents from some of the haciendas and *sociedades ganaderas* that were expropriated. It has proved to be invaluable in the study of agrarian and livestock activities in the highlands, as well as in the study of labor relations between *hacendados* and their *colonos*. A number of excellent and pioneering studies, some cited later in the essay, have been based on this collection. Of particular importance to my study were the earlier documents of the Sociedad Ganadera del Centro and the Sociedad Ganadera Junín that dealt with *enganche* and labor relations, particularly the correspondence of the administrators. In addition, the archive contains a set of books about the mines of Eulogio E. Fernandini, including *enganche, arrieraje*, and mining records.

AGN—Archivo General de la Nación (Lima)

This archive contains a large collection of nineteenth-century notarial documents compiled under various notaries. In addition to the usual catalogues, there are two indexes of special value to researchers. One is the "Indice

Terán," which lists notarial documents by region as well as name. While it is a complex system to use, necessitating several rather intricate steps in cataloguing before reaching the actual document, it is extremely useful given the size of the collection. There is also a separate, and excellent, catalogue of wills and testaments.

I found the sale contracts, wills, and hacienda inventories particularly valuable. Since a certain degree of wealth or prestige was necessary before people from the central highlands would travel down to Lima to sign contracts, these documents dealt with the regional elite. By looking at the books from about 1820 to 1890, it was possible to trace the development of the new elite families in the period immediately after independence.

AHM—Archivo Histórico Militar (Lima)

A small archive specializing in military documents, the AHM proved useful on the period of the War of the Pacific. In addition to the memoirs of Ambrosio Salazar y Márquez, the collection contains various types of army records and political documents. In the former category one finds the correspondence of the heads of special military expeditions sent to pacify different parts of the country, while in the latter are reports by prefects and subprefects. Both are valuable for understanding events at the local level.

AMA—Archivo Municipal de Acolla (Yanamarca Valley)

AMM—Archivo Municipal de Marco (Yanamarca Valley)

These two archives contain records of municipal government activity, especially the minutes of the various municipal council meetings. On occasion, as in the case of Acolla, it is possible to find some local census data. There are also some books of correspondence. The main problem here is that no effort is made to keep a systematic record of earlier materials. A book that is there one day may have been removed the next. Also, since the main purpose of the office is administrative rather than archival, it can be difficult to get long-term access to the documents.

District council documents proved to be valuable in shedding light on the workings of local government and power relations: who held the power, and what they did with it. Most Libros de Actas or Libros de Sesiones were also informative on the questions of public works projects. They were most complete, and also most useful, for the period of the 1930s.

ANF—Archivo Notarial Flores (Jauja)

The largest notary public office in Jauja, the Notaría Flores also has an archive in which the records of three previous notaries are stored, going back to the mid-nineteenth century. The same archive has kept, though in a somewhat haphazard manner, a series of judicial documents. The material consulted can be divided into two subcategories: Protocolos Notariales, or notarial books; and the Expedientes y Libros Judiciales, or judicial and court documents.

The Protocolos, which include the books of Manuel Víctor Morales (1860–1895), Luis Salazar (1880–1930), and Anselmo Flores Espinoza (starting in 1930), contain an extremely diverse set of contracts. On the one hand, there is information on the regional elite—land and labor conflicts, commercial and debt relations, and political connections (through rentals, *remates de ramo*, and *fianzas*). One also finds data on the "intermediate" merchant groups: commerce, landholdings, patron-client networks. For the village, there is information on the village elite: its ties to the Jauja elite as well as its commercial dealings and landholdings. Sale contracts and wills also provide clues to local patterns of land tenure, though again it is important to remember that usually it is the well-off peasants who have the money and time to make the trip to Jauja. And finally, the Protocolos have data on indebtedness, *enganche*, and differentiation.

In the judicial and court documents, one finds hacienda-community land conflicts, *enganche* cases, and some criminal cases, particularly violent crimes such as assault or murder. These documents are often most interesting for the information that emerges as a sideline to the main subject, especially data on patron-client networks, commerce, employment, land tenure, and labor relations. But they also help to determine which time periods had the highest incidence of land conflict or debt problems. Also among the judicial documents at the Notaría are local records from the offices of the justice of the peace in the various villages. These are especially helpful for getting under the skin of village life—small debts between peasants, conflicts between neighbors, family disputes of various kinds. They thus provide a much more colorful and accurate picture of land conflict, land tenure, debt relationships, and internal village conflicts than do the regional documents.

APJ—Archivo Prefectural de Junín (Huancayo)

Among the documents at the Archivo Prefectural are *solicitudes y expedientes*, letters and requests by various individuals addressed to the prefect and other political authorities. These provide data on the relationship of the village to the state, village conditions and relations, local and regional labor problems, and peasant mobilization and class conflict. There is also correspondence between government officials, both regional and national. This correspondence contains information on local and departmental politics, conflict and repression, the relationship of the state to the regional elite, and issues of labor and infrastructure. Finally, census materials give a sense of employment and migration patterns and broaden the understanding of social and economic differentiation within the village.

BNP—Biblioteca Nacional del Perú, Sala de Investigaciones (Lima)

The collection here is somewhat more diffuse. Within the sizable manuscript holdings, I found mainly political and government documents, such as prefects' reports and material on the creation of political districts. There are also a few extremely important documents on mobilizations at the time of the War of the Pacific and the subsequent pacification efforts. The most valuable part of the collection, in addition to these manuscript sources, is the collection of old pamphlets and published sources, which will be discussed in greater length further on in the essay.

RPI—Registro de la Propiedad Inmueble de Junín (Huancayo)

A register of property and transactions which began in the 1890s, this archive provides good data on regional investment and entrepreneurship. It also bears witness to the development and change of legal definitions of property. Finally, the RPI gives a good historical profile of the regional elite's economic activities, and allows the researcher to trace the overall changes as foreign capital begins to take over the mining industry. Two *registros* are especially valuable: the Registro de Sociedades, which records commercial, agricultural, and mining societies that were formed throughout the central region; and the Registro de Propiedades, which records transactions, loans, sales, and other contracts as they apply to particular pieces of landed property.

SINAMOS—Archivo de Comunidades, Oficina Regional de SINAMOS (Huancayo)

In 1978, this collection housed the *expedientes* from the old Dirección de Asuntos Indígenas. Since the formation of a new civilian government and the subsequent demise of SINAMOS, however, the *expedientes* may have been moved again. As is often true with other documents, despite the fact that most of the material from these *expedientes* is dated 1930 or later, many cases call on proof dating back many decades, if not centuries. It is not uncommon, for example, to find the colonial titles of an hacienda presented as evidence in a 1940s conflict. This is also a good place to look for documents on the church's role in the villages.

In the case of the Yanamarca Valley, the *expedientes* provide excellent information on village conflicts over revenue, land, and labor. They also allow a detailed analysis of village-*cofradía* struggles, and give much insight into land, labor, and class issues within the community during the 1930s.

UNI—Universidad Nacional de Ingeniería, Archivo (Lima)

Here the Tesis de Minería, descriptive essays written by the first class of graduates from the school in the 1880s, provide an extremely valuable inside view of mining production and labor relations in the central highlands at that time. Each graduate was required to travel to a mining center, spend some time there observing the system of production and labor relations, and write a report that served as part of his thesis. These reports usually included a description of the technology, labor system, and investment rationale of the enterprise. Some also provided details on the profitability of individual mines.

YC—Latin American Collection, Manuscripts, Yale University
The correspondence of the United States consul at Callao, both received and sent, is on microfilm for the nineteenth century. It gives a great deal of information on the development of the commercial economy. The letters from the consular agents in various parts of the country, including Cerro de Pasco, have data on regional events and patterns of investment.

PRINTED AND PUBLISHED DOCUMENTS

Several published memoirs provide important information on the central highlands. Andrés A. Cáceres, *La guerra del 79. Sus campañas (Memorias)* (Lima: Carlos Milla Batres, 1973), and Antonia Moreno de Cáceres, *Recuerdos de la campaña de la Breña (Memorias)* (Lima: Editorial Milla Batres, S.A., 1974), are both excellent on the strategic and patron-client aspects of the War of the Pacific. Pedro Dávalos y Lissón gives, in his autobiography *Cómo hice fortuna*, 2 Vols. (Lima: Librería e Imprenta Gil, 1941–42), valuable information on investment and the central sierra mining industry for the last years of the nineteenth century. Nemesio A. Ráez, *Monografía de la Provincia de Huancayo (1898)* (Huancayo: Universidad Nacional del Centro del Perú, n.d.), gives some important details on the War of the Pacific and the nature of local economic activity.

Pamphlets located at the BNP give data on the central sierra mining industry and other sectors of the regional economy. Estevan Delsol, *Informe sobre las minas de Salpo, Quiruvilca y Huamachuco en el Departamento de La Libertad* (Lima, 1880), is good on mining technology. Dora Mayer, *La conducta de la Compañía Minera del Cerro de Pasco* (Callao: Imprenta del Concejo Provincial, 1914), is the basic *indigenista* treatment of labor relations in the first period of U.S. investment in the mining sector. Manuel Pardo, *Estudios sobre la provincia de Jauja* (Lima: Imprenta de la Epoca, 1862), is an interesting overview of the local economy and its problems. Carlos Renardo Pflücker, *Exposición que presenta Carlos Renardo Pflücker al Supremo Gobierno con motivo de las últimas ocurrencias acaecidas en la hacienda mineral de Morococha* (Lima: Imprenta del Correo Peruano, 1846), and "Antenor Rizo Patrón al Congreso pidiendo protección para la industria minera" (Lima, 1870), both give important data on the problems of the nineteenth-century mining industry.

In addition to the memoirs and pamphlets, some miscellaneous published sources deal with various aspects of central sierra history. The Comisión Nacional del Sesquicentenario de la Independencia del Perú has published the

Colección documental de la independencia del Perú (Lima, 1971–73), in which Tomo V, in several volumes, is on guerrillas and *montoneras* in the central region. The Concejo Municipal de La Merced put out, in 1969, a collection of documents for the one hundredth anniversary of the district's founding. Called *Los pioneros de Chanchamayo*, it contains information on the first *hacendados* who settled in the area in the latter part of the nineteenth century. Great Britain and the United States both have interesting information, especially on coffee production and mining, in their *Consular Reports* series. The British reports, which are ultimately the most complete, have been compiled by Heraclio Bonilla, *Gran Bretaña y el Perú, 1826–1919: Informes de los cónsules británicos* (Lima: Instituto de Estudios Peruanos, 1975), in several volumes. Ricardo Martínez de la Torre, in his *Apuntes para una interpretación marxista de la historia social del Perú*, 4 Vols. (Lima: Compañía Impresora Peruana, S.A., 1949), Vol. 4, dedicates an entire section to the mining strikes of 1929 and 1930, reproducing documents and eyewitness accounts of various events. The Boletines del Cuerpo de Ingenieros de Minas, various numbers and dates, put out by the Ministerio de Fomento, is a crucial source for studying the progress of the mining industry in all its aspects during the first decades of the twentieth century.

SECONDARY MATERIALS: PERU

Although much research still remains to be done on the nineteenth and twentieth centuries, there is already a body of rich historical literature dealing with a series of important issues. On independence, the pioneering work was Heraclio Bonilla and Karen Spalding (eds.), *La independencia en el Perú* (Lima: Instituto de Estudios Peruanos, 1972). John Lynch, *The Spanish-American Revolutions, 1808–1826* (New York: W. W. Norton and Co., Inc., 1973), provides a much-needed comparative perspective and good information on the role of the lower classes. On the Andean rebellions of the period, see Oscar Cornblit's pathbreaking article "Society and Mass Rebellion in Eighteenth-Century Peru and Bolivia," in Raymond Carr (ed.), *Latin American Affairs*, St. Anthony's Papers, No. 22 (London: Oxford University Press, 1970), and Alberto Flores Galindo (ed.), *Túpac Amaru II: 1780* (Lima: Ediciones Retablo de Papel, 1976).

There are several good general histories of the nineteenth and twentieth centuries. The classic remains Jorge Basadre, *Historia de la República del Perú*, 6th ed., 17 Vols. (Lima: Editorial Universitaria, 1968–69). Frederick B. Pike, *The Modern History of Peru* (New York: Frederick A. Praeger, 1967), is particularly good on intellectual and political history. More recent attempts at theoretical innovation include Rosemary Thorp and Geoffrey Bertram, *Peru 1890–1977: Growth and Policy in an Open Economy* (New York: Columbia University Press, 1978), and Ernesto Yepes del Castillo, *Perú 1820–1920: Un siglo de desarrollo capitalista* (Lima: Instituto de Estudios Peruanos-Campodónico Ediciones, 1972).

For their importance in defining the contours of historical debate, no historian can afford to ignore Heraclio Bonilla, *Guano y burguesía en el Perú* (Lima: Instituto de Estudios Peruanos, 1974); Julio Cotler, *Clases, Estado y Nación en el Perú* (Lima: Instituto de Estudios Peruanos, 1978); Pablo Macera, *Trabajos de historia*, 4 Vols. (Lima: Instituto Nacional de Cultura, 1977); and José Matos Mar (ed.), *Hacienda, comunidad y campesino en el Perú* (Lima: Instituto de Estudios Peruanos, 1976). Pioneering theoretical work on issues relevant to this study has been done by William Bollinger, "The Bourgeois Revolution in Peru: A Conception of Peruvian History," *Latin American Perspectives*, IV:3 (Summer 1977), 18–54; José María Caballero, *Economía agraria de la sierra peruana antes de la reforma agraria de 1969* (Lima: Instituto de Estudios Peruanos, 1981); Rodrigo Montoya Rojas, *A propósito del carácter predominantemente capitalista de la economía peruana actual* (Lima: Ediciones Teoría y Realidad, 1970), and *Capitalismo y no capitalismo en el Perú: Un estudio histórico de su articulación en un eje regional* (Lima: Mosca Azul Editores, 1981); Guillermo Rochabrún, "Apuntes para la comprensión del capitalismo en el Perú," *Análisis*, No. 1 (January–March 1977), pp. 3–24; and Karen Spalding, "Estructura de clases en la sierra peruana: 1750–1920," *Análisis*, No. 1 (January–March 1977), pp. 25–35. Analogous regional studies on time periods and issues similar to those treated in this book include: Manuel Burga, *De la encomienda a la hacienda capitalista: El valle del Jequetepeque del siglo XVI al XX* (Lima: Instituto de Estudios Peruanos, 1976); Carmen Diana Deere, "The Development of Capitalism in Agriculture and the Division of Labor By Sex: A Study of the Northern Peruvian Sierra," Ph.D. Dissertation, University of California, Berkeley, 1978; Peter F. Klarén, *Formación de las haciendas azucareras y los orígenes del APRA*, 2d ed. (Lima: Instituto de Estudios Peruanos, 1976); the work of Nils Jacobson on the southern highland department of Azángaro, still in progress; and Lewis Taylor, "Main Trends in Agrarian Capitalist Development: Cajamarca, Peru, 1880–1976," Ph.D. Thesis, University of Liverpool, 1979.

SECONDARY MATERIALS: CENTRAL HIGHLANDS

Among the many anthropological community studies on the central sierra, the most notable are: Richard N. Adams, *A Community in the Andes: Problems and Progress in Muquiyauyo* (Seattle: University of Washington Press, 1959); Gabriel Escobar, *Sicaya: Cambios culturales en una comunidad mestiza andina* (Lima: Instituto de Estudios Peruanos, 1973); and William B. Hutchinson, "Sociocultural Change in the Mantaro Valley Region of Peru: Acolla, A Case Study," Ph.D. Dissertation, Indiana University, 1973. José María Arguedas, *Dos estudios sobre Huancayo* ("Evolución de las comunidades indígenas," "Estudio etnográfico de la feria de Huancayo"), Cuadernos

Universitarios (Huancayo: Universidad Nacional del Centro del Perú, n.d.), provides a summary of previous anthropological work, and sets the scene for much of the work that was done on the central sierra during the 1960s and early 1970s. Finally, a number of "mobilization" studies of the central sierra were done in the early 1970s, of which the most interesting are Giorgio Alberti and Rodrigo Sánchez, *Poder y conflicto social en el valle del Mantaro* (Lima: Instituto de Estudios Peruanos, 1974), and Howard Handelman, *Struggle in the Andes: Peasant Political Mobilization in Peru* (Austin: University of Texas Press, 1975).

Starting with the pioneering work of Juan Martínez Alier, *Los huacchilleros del Perú* (Lima-Paris: Ruedo Ibérico-Instituto de Estudios Peruanos, 1973), an important body of literature has developed on the livestock sector in the central highlands, particularly the *sociedades ganaderas*, and the shepherds' resistance to proletarianization. See also Víctor Caballero, *Hacienda Conocancha: Desarrollo capitalista y proletarización*, Taller de Estudios Andinos, Serie: Andes Centrales, No. 1 (La Molina: Universidad Nacional Agraria, 1975), and his more recent work on the Sociedad Ganadera Junín; Florencia Mallon, Gerardo Rénique, et al., *Lanas y Capitalismo en los Andes Centrales*, Taller de Estudios Andinos, Serie: Andes Centrales, No. 2 (La Molina: Universidad Nacional Agraria, 1977); Gerardo Rénique, *Sociedad Ganadera del Centro: Pastores y Sindicalización en una Hacienda Alto Andina. Documentos 1945–1948*, Taller de Estudios Andinos, Serie: Andes Centrales, No. 3 (La Molina: Universidad Nacional Agraria, 1977), and *Comunidades Campesinas y "Recuperaciones" de Tierras. Valle del Mantaro*, Taller de Estudios Andinos, Serie: Andes Centrales, No. 4 (La Molina: Universidad Nacional Agraria, 1977–1978).

Some recent work has begun to apply the concept of class struggle to the study of the peasant community. See Norman Long and Bryan R. Roberts (eds.), *Peasant Cooperation and Capitalist Expansion in Central Peru* (Austin: University of Texas Press, 1978), especially Long and Roberts, "Introduction," pp. 3–44; Carlos Samaniego, "Peasant Movements at the Turn of the Century and the Rise of the Independent Farmer," pp. 45–71; Marcelo Grondin, "Peasant Cooperation and Dependency: The Case of the Electricity Enterprise of Muquiyauyo," pp. 99–128; and Long and Roberts, "Peasant Cooperation and Underdevelopment in Peru," pp. 297–328. See also Gavin A. Smith, "Socio-economic Differentiation and Relations of Production among Rural-Based Petty Producers in Central Peru, 1880 to 1970," *Journal of Peasant Studies*, 6:3 (April 1979), 286–310.

Work on the mining sector has also expanded noticeably in recent years. For a history of the Cerro de Pasco mines, see John Fisher, "Silver Production in the Viceroyalty of Peru, 1776–1824," *Hispanic American Historical Review* 55:1 (February 1975), 25–44, the first article to argue that silver production in the area expanded in the years immediately preceding independence, and *Minas y mineros en el Perú colonial, 1776–1824* (Lima: Instituto de

Estudios Peruanos, 1977). For recent treatments of the development of a mining labor force, see Heraclio Bonilla, *El Minero de los Andes: Una aproximación a su estudio* (Lima: Instituto de Estudios Peruanos, 1974); Adrian DeWind, Jr., "From Peasants to Miners: The Background to Strikes in the Mines of Peru," *Science and Society*, 29:1 (Spring 1975), 44–72, and "Peasants Become Miners: The Evolution of Industrial Mining Systems in Peru," Ph.D. Dissertation, Columbia University, 1977; Alberto Flores Galindo, *Los mineros de la Cerro de Pasco, 1900–1930* (Lima: Pontífica Universidad Católica del Perú, 1974); and Julian Laite, *Industrial Development and Migrant Labour in Latin America* (Austin: University of Texas Press, 1981). On the question of the Oroya smelter, see especially the work of Julian Laite, "Industrialisation and Land Tenure in the Peruvian Andes," Paper presented at the Symposium on Landlord and Peasant in Peru, Cambridge, England, 1972, and "Processes of Industrial and Social Change in Highland Peru," in Norman Long and Bryan R. Roberts (eds.), *Peasant Cooperation and Capitalist Expansion in Central Peru* (Austin: University of Texas Press, 1978), pp. 72–98.

Finally, some studies with broader implications for the region include, for the Wars of Independence, Raúl Rivera Serna, *Los guerrilleros del centro en la emancipación peruana* (Lima: Edición Talleres Gráficos Villanueva, S.A., 1958). For the rebellion of Juan Santos Atahualpa and the cultural history of the Campa Indians in the *ceja* region, see Stéfano Varese, *La sal de los cerros*, 2d ed. (Lima: Ediciones Retablo de Papel, 1973). Recent work on the War of the Pacific includes Heraclio Bonilla, "The War of the Pacific and the National and Colonial Problem in Peru," *Past and Present*, No. 81 (November 1978), pp. 92–118; Henri Favre, "Remarques sur la lutte des classes au Pérou pendant la guerre du Pacifique," in Association Française pour l'Etude et la Récherche sur les Pays Andins, *Littérature et Société au Pérou du XIXème siècle à nos Jours* (Grenoble: Université de Langues et Lettres, 1975), pp. 54–81; and Nelson Manrique, *Campesinado y nación: Las guerrillas indígenas en la Guerra con Chile* (Lima: Centro de Investigación y Capacitación and Ital Peru, S.A., 1981), "Los movimientos campesinos en la Guerra del Pacífico," *Allpanchis*, No. 11–12 (1978), pp. 71–101, and "La Guerra del Pacífico y los conflictos de clase: Los terratenientes de la sierra del Perú," *Análisis*, No. 6 (September–December 1978), pp. 56–71. Adolfo Bravo Guzmán, *La segunda enseñanza en Jauja*, 2d ed. (Jauja, 1971), and Ricardo Tello Devotto, *Historia de la provincia de Huancayo* (Huancayo: Casa del la Cultura de Junín, 1971), both regional histories of parts of the Mantaro Valley, present extremely rare data and reproduce documents that are difficult to find elsewhere. And on rural-urban networks and the relationship among class, ethnic, and gender factors in defining social inequality in highland Peru, especially the central area, see Susan C. Bourque and Kay B. Warren, *Women of the Andes: Patriarchy and Social Change in Two Peruvian Towns* (Ann Arbor: The University of Michigan Press, 1981); and Bryan R. Roberts, "The Interrelationships of City and Provinces in Peru and Guatemala," in Wayne A.

Cornelius and Felicity M. Trueblood (eds.), *Anthropological Perspectives on Latin American Urbanization*, Latin American Urban Research, Vol. 4 (Berkeley, CA: Sage Publications, 1974), pp. 207–35.

THEORETICAL AND COMPARATIVE MATERIALS

This study owes a great deal to Marxist theoretical treatments of the peasantry and the development of capitalism, particularly the following classic studies: Karl Marx, *Capital*, 3 Vols. (New York: International Publishers, 1967), I; V. I. Lenin, *The Development of Capitalism in Russia* (Moscow: Progress Publishers, 1974); Karl Kautsky, *La cuestión agraria* (Lima: Universidad Nacional Mayor de San Marcos, 1972); Witold Kula, *Teoría económica del sistema feudal* (Mexico City: Siglo XXI Editores, 1974); and Rodney Hilton (ed.), *The Transition from Feudalism to Capitalism* (London: Verso Edition, 1978). Also very important is A. V. Chayanov, *The Theory of Peasant Economy*, ed. Daniel Thorner, Basile Verblay, and R.E.F. Smith. Published for the American Economic Association (Homewood, Ill.: R. D. Irwin, 1966).

Recent Marxist work on the peasantry has broken new ground in many ways. See, for example, Barbara Bradby, "The Destruction of Natural Economy," *Economy and Society*, IV:2 (1975), 127–61; Chantal de Crisenoy, "Capitalism and Agriculture," *Economy and Society*, VIII:1 (February 1979), 9–25; Michael Duggett, "Marx on Peasants," *Journal of Peasant Studies*, II:2 (January 1975), 159–82; William Roseberry, "Peasants as Proletarians," *Critique of Anthropology*, III:11 (1978), 3–18; and Keith Tribe, "Introduction to de Crisenoy," *Economy and Society*, VIII:1 (February 1979), 1–8. Also important in this regard are the comparative materials available on the transition to capitalism in Indian agriculture, particularly the debate between Utsa Patnaik and others on the nature of agriculture in India: Utsa Patnaik, "Development of Capitalism in Agriculture," *Social Scientist*, II:1 (August 1973), 15–31; N. Ram, "Development of Capitalism in Agriculture," *Social Scientist*, II:5 (December 1973), 3–19; and Doug McEachern, "The Mode of Production in India," *Journal of Contemporary Asia*, VI:4 (1976), 444–57.

The following works on Latin America have important comparative value for agrarian history: Manoel Correia de Andrade, *A terra e o homem do Nordeste* (São Paulo: Editôra Brasiliense, 1963); Roger Bartra, *Estructura agraria y clases sociales en México* (Mexico City: Era, 1974); Arnold J. Bauer, *Chilean Rural Society from the Spanish Conquest to 1930* (Cambridge: Cambridge University Press, 1975), and "Rural Workers in Spanish America: Problems of Peonage and Oppression," *Hispanic American Historical Review*, 59:1 (1979), 34–63; Kenneth Duncan and Ian Rutledge (eds.), *Land and Labour in Latin America: Essays on the Development of Agrarian Capitalism in the Nineteenth and Twentieth Centuries* (Cambridge: Cambridge University Press, 1977); Enrique Florescano (ed.), *Haciendas, latifundios y plantaciones en América Latina*, Simposio de Roma organizado por CLACSO (Mexico City:

Siglo XXI Editores, 1975); and Tulio Halperín Donghi, *Historia contemporánea de América Latina*, 5th ed. (Madrid: Alianza Editorial, 1975).

Finally, I have also benefited from the insights of theoretical literature on specific problems and phenomena that I encountered during the course of my research. On the role of women in the transition to capitalism: Annette Kuhn and AnnMarie Wolpe (eds.), *Feminism and Materialism: Women and Modes of Production* (London: Routledge and Kegan Paul, 1978); and Rayna R. Reiter (ed.), *Toward an Anthropology of Women* (New York: Monthly Review Press, 1975). On patronage and clientele: Frances Rothstein, "The Class Basis of Patron-Client Relations," *Latin American Perspectives*, VI:2 (Spring 1979), 25–35; Steffen W. Schmidt, James C. Scott, Carl Landé, and Laura Guasti (eds.), *Friends, Followers and Factions: A Reader in Political Clientelism* (Berkeley and Los Angeles: University of California Press, 1979); and Eric R. Wolf and Edward Hansen, "*Caudillo* Politics: A Structural Analysis," *Contemporary Studies in Society and History*, IX (1967), 168–79. On "moral economy" and subsistence ideology: Eric J. Hobsbawn, *Primitive Rebels* (New York: W. W. Norton and Co., Inc., 1959); James C. Scott, *The Moral Economy of the Peasant* (New Haven: Yale University Press, 1976); the pioneering article by E. P. Thompson, "The Moral Economy of the English Crowd," *Past and Present*, No. 50 (February 1971), pp. 76–136; and Eric R. Wolf, *Peasant Wars of the Twentieth Century* (New York: Harper and Row, 1969). Finally, Richard L. Harris, "Marxism and the Agrarian Question in Latin America," *Latin American Perspectives*, V:4 (Fall 1978), 2–26, presents an excellent summary of recent Marxist debates on the Latin American peasantry and the development of capitalism.

Index

Abeleyra, Petronila, 45
Acaya, 196; *anexo* of Marco district, 201
Acobamba: *montonera* writes letter to Jacinto Cevallos, 89–92; outrage against *hacendados*, 92; *montonera* particularly militant, 93, 110; member of Comas Alliance, 111–12; contracts with Cevallos on hacienda Punto, 113–14
Acolla: household economy in, 24–25; communal lands, 25, 27, 287–89; property of *cofradías* in, 34; incident with hacienda Yanamarca, 1790, 38n; social and economic differentiation, 68n, 148; migration, 68n, 153, 254–63; penetration of commercial capital, 70–71; patterns of social and cultural interaction, 71, 154; *arrieraje* in, 72, 72n, 145; commercial landholdings in, 146–47; livestock holdings, 153; pampa of, 168; protests against abuses of Onofres, 216–18; petition on smoke damage, 227; associations of mineworkers from, 255, 265–66; public works construction, 287–89, 293–96; difficulties with communal labor, 294–95; entrepreneurial activity, 1930s and 1940s, 311–12, 313; picturesque veneer hides proletarian relations, 334–35
————politics: changes in institutions, eighteenth century, 37n; political styles, 71, 154–55; creation of new district, 71n–72n, 105–107, 132, 151; conflict with surrounding villages, 106–107, 132, 200–201, 299–300; position in Cáceres-Piérola conflict, 132, 133n, 155
Acomodanas, 73
Acopalca, hacienda, 175, 175n
Acostambo: role of *montonera* in War of the Pacific, 88, 93
Agriculture: traditional system in central highlands, 17, 19–20, 21, 22; Andean, 19, 24, 25, 28; commercial, 19, 69–70, 176–78, 273–74, 308–14

Aguardiente, 57, 60, 179
Aizcorbe, Pedro A., 177–78, 185, 225, 273–74
Al partir, 30
Alcalde, Indian, 37–38
Alvarez, Bacilio, 311
Alvarez, Custodio, 49, 52–53
Alvarez Calderón family, 174
Alvariño, Francisco L.: represents peasants against government *enganche*, 162–63; acquires labor by force, 163; role in subtropical agriculture, 179–80
Alvaro, Paula, 311
Amalgamation. *See* Mining, central highlands: patio process
American Vanadium Company, 182
Ampuero, José T., 198
Ancón, Treaty of, 99–100
Andamarca: followers of Juan Santos Atahualpa attempt to take, 48; member of Comas Alliance, 111–12; negotiations with Ramón Valle Riestra, 116–17; guerrillas resume incursions into nearby towns, 117
Andía, José G.: commercial activities, 131n, 148, 185; role in *enganche*, 139, 139n
Anexo. *See* District politics, central highlands
Anlacalla: *paraje* of, 69; pass at, 69
Apata, 159
Apay, communal property of. *See* Licuy
Apiri, 73
APRA (Alianza Popular Revolucionaria Americana), 238
Aquino, Doroteo, 76
Arenales, Juan Antonio Alvarez de, General, 49, 50
Arequipa, 49, 185, 255
Argote, Domingo, 115
Arias, Jacoba, 24
Arrieraje: Mantaro Valley as major center, 17; substantial profits available in, 20; participation of peasants in, 37, 72;

Florencia E. Mallon is Assistant Professor of Modern Spanish
American History at the University of Wisconsin, Madison.

Library of Congress Cataloging in Publication Data

Mallon, Florencia E., 1951–
The defense of community in Peru's central highlands.

Bibliography: p.
Includes index.
1. Peasantry—Peru—Cordillera Central Region—History.
2. Cordillera Central Region (Peru)—Rural conditions.
3. Economic development. 4. Capitalism. I. Title.

HD559.C67M34   1984   330.985′206′0880625   83–42565
ISBN 0–691–07647–2
ISBN 0–691–10140–X (lim. pbk. ed.)